KU-280-402

A MEASURE OF DIVERSION ?

CASE STUDIES IN INTERMEDIATE TREATMENT
Edited by Robert Adams, Simon Allard, John Baldwin and Jim Thomas

Cover design by Dominic Mackintosh
Typeset by James Preston
Printed by AB Printers Limited,
71 Cannock Street, Leicester LE4 7HR
Published by the National Youth Bureau,
17-23 Albion Street, Leicester LE1 6GD
ISBN 0 86155 040 4   April 1981
Price £6.95 including postage and packing

CONTENTS

PREFACE

The idea for this book was originally conceived by Robert Adams and John Baldwin, who approached the National Youth Bureau's Youth Social Work Unit, which is funded by the DHSS to provide a national information service on intermediate treatment. In view of the paucity of substantial literature on the subject, the Unit readily agreed to join the undertaking and Jim Thomas, a member of its staff, became a co-editor. Later, to complement the editorial team and expedite the completion of the book, Simon Allard was asked to join as a fourth co-editor.

The editors share responsibility for this publication, and have worked together throughout, both in the collaboration with the case study contributors and in preparing the other chapters. The task of drafting the editors' chapters was shared among us. Robert Adams took primary responsibility for Chapters 1 and 15; Simon Allard for Chapters 3, 11 and 14; John Baldwin for 2, 10 and 12; and Jim Thomas for Chapter 13. However, this does not fairly reflect the division of labour, since all the drafts were subjected to criticism by the other editors, who frequently contributed original material and even redrafted the chapters. It was only by this collective and time consuming approach that the book finally emerged in a form which the editors from our different perspectives were happy to take joint responsibility. In addition to these roles, Simon Allard, together with Christine Allard, was responsible for editing the case studies, and Jim Thomas for general co-ordination.

We are extremely grateful to our case study contributors, who have had to tolerate repeated requests from the editors for additions and changes, and at the last may have found that for lack of space the final version of their studies omitted material that they had produced at our request.

For any writer, this is a painful process, but doubly so for those who are writing about work to which they have been personally committed for a number of years. Our hope, nevertheless, is that this book provides them with the means of communicating what they consider important about these projects. The contributors also had an opportunity to comment on the editors' comparative analysis of the case studies, though here the final word was with the editors.

We also want to record our gratitude to colleagues who have read and commented on various draft chapters; and in particular to Geoff Aplin, Nora Dixon, Jim Hodder, Ray Jones and John Paley, who reviewed some of the case studies in draft, and to Dave Ward, who looked at some of the other chapters. Their comments proved invaluable and frequently led to modifications, but needless to say, they bear no responsibility for the contents of this book, which lies entirely with the editors.

We are also greatly indebted to Christine Allard, who did the major part of a difficult and heavy task, editing the case studies into their final form: this meant finding ways to get all that the contributors wanted to say within the space available for them and winning the authors' approval for this.

INTRODUCTION

Under the name of 'intermediate treatment', the 1970s have seen substantial growth in community based projects for children and young people who are seen as problematic or 'in trouble'. The concept of intermediate treatment, originally intended as a resource for the juvenile courts, has proved flexible to the point where it slips between the fingers of definition. Consequently, much of the limited literature on the subject has been concerned with identifying aims and structure, and with securing an accepted place in social policy and in the network of social services for young people. There is also a literature of practice, as social workers have tried to record their experiences in what, for many, was a new kind of work. However, most of this literature is of limited scope, narrative rather than analytic, and without any framework for comparing or extending its implications.

Intermediate treatment is now moving out of the experimental phase. On the one hand there are many projects which have accumulated some years of experience, and on the other, there is a growing readiness by local authorities to invest in this field of work. It seemed to the editors that the time was ripe for a collection of case studies which would provide more substantial accounts of the development of intermediate treatment in practice, through narrative, analysis and evaluation of six distinctive and diverse projects.

The basic purpose of this book, therefore, is to stimulate, to teach and to share experience. By focusing on the concrete realities of specific projects, it hopes to provide learnings for a range of readers: for practitioners and students, insights into methods of working with difficult young people, their families and communities; for those concerned with management, planning and development, insights into some of the organisational issues and hurdles that stand between the conception and the actual provision of services; and for policy makers, insights into some of the unexpected results of attempts to develop creative community based programmes for young offenders in the context of the existing legal framework and climate of public opinion. In addition there were two further aims. The first was to explore the usefulness of case studies in the field of intermediate treatment through the development and application of a standard framework for description, analysis and comparison. The second was to make some tentative prescriptions for the future development of intermediate treatment, and to indicate the need for some fundamental changes in the whole area of social policy for problem youth.

Because of the approach adopted, we have given only limited attention to certain areas which require much more thorough consideration. We recognise that there is often a theoretical vacuum underlying the activities of practitioners as well as a number of value assumptions which remain unstated. For our part, we have encouraged the case study writers to be as explicit as possible about the rationales for their projects, and have attempted to locate the theoretical perspectives adopted by each. However, we would emphasise that this book does not claim to develop a substantial theoretical position of its own. On the other hand we do think that we have tried to look theoretically at some ways of broadening the whole debate concerning intermediate treatment.

3

The subject under consideration continues to generate a good deal of argument. Between the nine contributors to this book, there is considerable variance of individual positions. Although the editors themselves represent a range of liberal and radical standpoints, we have explored our differences, often through lengthy debate, in the hope of reaching an agreed position. For instance we started out with the important assumption that, whatever else intermediate treatment may be, it is about dealing with delinquent and other children who pose a problem for society. On some other issues, it has not proved possible to reach a consensus. We have obviously tried to minimise any gross inconsistencies, but any which remain must stand as evidence of the difficulty of reconciling different approaches to work with problem youth.

The six case studies are the core and raison d'être of this book. However we felt that these must be set in context. Thus Chapter 1 examines some of the political and social policy changes which have affected society's response to problem youth, especially in post-war Britain. Chapter 2 attempts to identify the philosophical and theoretical roots from which intermediate treatment has emerged. As part of national and local policy, intermediate treatment has developed, or failed to do so, within the framework and constraints of central and local government organisation. Chapter 3 examines this organisational framework, and offers a classification of existing models of intermediate treatment. It should be noted that these chapters are not intended to provide a systematic introduction to intermediate treatment, and they do assume some knowledge by any reader of the way in which it was conceived and developed. A more general, albeit superficial, account of this and the place of intermediate treatment in the network of services for young people is provided in Appendix I.

As has already been mentioned, the case study contributors were given a framework to guide them and make comparison more possible. Further details of this, the reasons for choosing the case study approach and the process by which the book developed are contained in Appendix II. From the start it was our intention to provide some comparative analysis, primarily to draw out issues of wider interest, and to examine whether, in spite of diversities between individual projects, any common features and guidelines for future practice emerged. The four comparative chapters focus on objectives (Chapter 10), organisation (Chapter 11), practice (Chapter 12) and evaluation (Chapter 13) of the projects. Issues raised in these chapters have been selected by the editors, and our handling of them will no doubt imply certain conclusions. However it was decided not to give full rein to our convictions until we came to Chapter 14, where we have identified certain key issues and reached our conclusions on them. In doing so, we were constrained, as the projects are, by the existing political and legal framework. In Chapter 15, we have examined some of the options that would be open for responding to problem youth, given the possibility of radical alterations to the existing juvenile justice system.

CONTEXT

CHAPTER 1
THE SOCIAL AND POLITICAL CONTEXT OF INTERMEDIATE TREATMENT

INTRODUCTION

This introductory chapter attempts to locate those forms of social work intervention which have come to be known as intermediate treatment within their social and political context. The legal nature of intermediate treatment is predominantly defined in Section 12 of the 1969 Children and Young Persons Act, as a condition which can be attached to a supervision order requiring a young person's participation for up to 90 days or 'sessions'. (Appendix I provides a brief historical outline of legislation and social policy for juvenile offenders, including the main provisions of the 1969 Act.) The intention of the legislators was to fill a yawning gap between individual casework with children and their families on the one hand, and long term residential care on the other. Consequently, it has been taken to mean everything from an individual volunteer working with a young person on motorcycle maintenance, to a large therapeutic community offering a continuous, residential programme over a three month period. In general terms, the Act was intended to facilitate new forms of supervision in the community by social workers and probation officers, which were designed to bring children 'in trouble' or 'at risk' (euphemisms for delinquents and truants) *'into contact with a different environment, interests and experiences which may be beneficial'* to them [1].

This bland description is deceptive. In practice, the implementation of the 1969 Act in general, and of intermediate treatment in particular, has been fraught with difficulties. A change of government just after its passage through Parliament meant that some of its more important provisions were never put into effect. Since that time other provisions have been amended, and throughout the period intermediate treatment has been near to the centre of general debates about law and order and particular ones about the goodness, necessity for, or effectiveness of, community based social work with delinquents and those at risk of becoming involved in crime.

Different Political Perspectives

The story of changing approaches to community child care or youth control can be told from a variety of perspectives. Depending on the stance adopted, it is possible to describe concepts like intermediate treatment either as imaginative and potentially radical developments, or as rather dangerous extensions of social control in the community, or perhaps even as a mixture of the two. A reading of the literature generated from within social work practice might indicate that certain assumptions about the positive aspects of community care can be taken for granted. However, it needs to be borne in mind that the liberal assumptions about community child care embodied in the 1969 Act do not now, if they ever did, rule unchallenged. The liberal position has probably always been

7

hemmed in by conservative and radical stances. These labels do not correspond to the three main British political parties; but it is suggested that the perspectives held by people about the way in which problem youth should be handled cannot be divorced from their political beliefs and moral values.

The liberal position reflects the influence of positivist theories over the past century concerning personality in general and juvenile delinquency in particular, and emphasisés the need to match the treatment of problem youth to their individual needs [2]. Admittedly these treatment oriented assumptions increasingly acknowledge sub-cultural or sociological theories; but this does not alter the fact that the focus remains on the individual and his adaptation to what society sees as normal, acceptable behaviour. This school has been so dominant that it is not uncommon for liberal accounts of social policy development to give the impression that it is an inexorable process of *discernible trends . . . uneven progress*[3], rather than an unceasing battle between competing ideologies, with accident and compromise playing a large part in what actually happens. It is the very dominance of the liberal position which makes it so important to look critically at its assumptions. For instance, the liberal advocacy of community care has been influenced or reinforced by the increasing recognition of the harmfulness or ineffectiveness of institutions [4]. However, the danger remains that this support for community care may amount to little more than vague but persistent claims that community based programmes are innovative and imaginative. More insidicus still, the implicit assumption is often that just as residential institutions are by their very nature bad, so anything which passes for community activity must be better, and key words like 'community' and 'participation' remain with their meanings untranslated into practical implications.

The conservative position, while not entirely rejecting a 'welfare' element, leans more closely to a classical approach to crime and the juvenile justice system. It attracts support from those who believe that the primary function of the justice system is the protection of the community, and that consequently the criterion for judicial processing should be the nature of the offence rather than the personality or social circumstances of the offender. Since the late 1960s, the preoccupation of those who share this view has increasingly become known as a concern for 'law and order', and their criticisms of the 1969 Act have concentrated on its inability to control problem youth in general, and what is often described as a 'hard core' of dangerous and persistent offenders, in particular. They resist any attempt to transfer power from magistrates to social workers, and blame the emphasis on compassion for creating more sympathy for the criminal than the victim. The substance and flavour of this position is well illustrated by extracts from speeches made by Sir Keith Joseph:

'Socialism has taught that it is deprivation, not delinquency, that lies behind crime and violence. Many socialists have tended to believe that children grow up with a natural sense of right and wrong and need neither to be taught moral values nor to be encouraged in self-restraint and self-discipline.' [5]

Equally, declining moral standards and increasing crime and violence were *'not to be excused by the fashionable alibis of our time — that the offender has no job, or a boring job, or a low paid job, or a less than ideal home. There were more unemployed, less money and worse homes in the 1930s, but much less crime and violence. Besides, most crime today is committed by people who are not poor or unemployed or badly housed.'* [6]

8

While it would be quite wrong to suggest that there is only one liberal or conservative position, there are at least two quite distinct radical perspectives. One of these takes the view that the 1969 Act should be repealed and replaced by legislation which restores the concept of due process and makes the principles of justice paramount for all those passing through the courts. The position is forcefully represented among the proposals of a new pressure group called Justice for Children, which was established in 1977 [7]. On the other hand, the radical left adopts socialist or even Marxist theories and argues that the seeming benevolence of the liberal treatment philosophy overlays a more sinister and unchanging conflict of class interest and the maintenance of the caste system, with its differential between powerless clients and powerful ruling interests, as represented by social workers, who are consciously or unconsciously agents of social control [8]. It also considers that the 1969 Act, notwithstanding the rhetoric which surrounds it, actually continues to focus on containing or modifying the behaviour of the child, and, by implication, legitimises the existing social order rather than challenges it. The radicals may be divided, but they are agreed on one thing and that is that the things done to children in the name of treatment can actually be worse than the punishment they were intended to replace. Moreover, as Stanley Cohen has pointed out [9], the call to decarcerate young offenders by placing them in community programmes may be very laudable in theory, but by blurring the boundary where the apparatus of social control ends, widening the net to include new client groups, and using benevolence to mask the intrusiveness of community care, this strategy could easily be counter-productive. In other words it might replace incarceration within a residential institution by containment within a 'ghetto' community.

The purpose of this chapter is not so much to choose between these political perspectives, as to provide a context for examining a number of case studies of intermediate treatment practice. Nonetheless this context can best be provided by a critical account which attempts to grapple with the confused and often conflicting ideologies which have influenced both policy and practice. It certainly seems necessary to penetrate the surface of the liberal advocacy of intermediate treatment, and at least entertain the possibility that its development owes more to economic than humanitarian factors, and represents merely a change rather than a progressive development in the arrangements made to control problem youth in Britain in the 1970s. This critical account will be concerned with the development of the child care industry over the last 150 years, as a prelude to considering how the interaction between criminological theories and more or less informed public responses to problem youth led to the 1969 Act. The final section will indicate how subsequent developments, like the Act itself, reflected unresolved tensions between different ideological stances.

Growth of the Child Care Industry

The Industrial Revolution created a need for more systematic ways of socialising the younger generation to prepare them for roles in the industrial economy, and specifically of dealing with the threats to public order that were seen to be posed by working class youth in the great urban centres. One feature of this process has been the creation of 'childhood' as an inferior and immature status, and more recently the addition of 'adolescence' as an inherently problematic and transitional one [10]. As society moved from the protection of the young to the positive promotion of their welfare, it made them still more dependent by using more segregated and institutionalised means to socialise them, from play in the nursery to recreation in the youth clubs and to education in the schools for ever longer years [11].

This trend can be seen clearly in child care and delinquency control. The efforts by Mary Carpenter and her allies in the 1850s to segregate children from adults in reformatories of their own have their sequel in the establishment of special courts for juveniles in 1908, and even in efforts to raise the age of criminal responsibility in the 1969 Act. From the industrial schools of the same period a direct line leads to today's provisions, whereby a 16 year old can be removed from home until the age of 19 because he or she is deemed beyond parental control.

The growing intervention by the state into the lives of children and young people presupposed two requirements: first, the organisational, financial and manpower resources; and secondly, the rationales to justify it. Of major significance over the last century and a half has been the development of increasingly large scale, centrally administered organisations for the purpose of mediating between problem youth and the laws of the land [12]. The social upheaval and urban squalor of the Industrial Revolution produced waves of legislation designed to tackle the insanitary and badly housed state of the urban working class. This is not to suggest that such measures were inevitable or economically determined; they should be seen, rather, as the outcome of struggles between the requirements of capitalism, enlightened self-interest, and an element of genuine altruism [13]. They led to the establishment of novel welfare and administrative bureaucracies, and the raising of large sums of money through taxation and local rates to support them. While these efforts were largely directed towards changing the environment, provision was expanded to deal with the casualties. For the Victorians, the solution to problem youth, as to other problem categories, was large warehouse-like institutions, whose management often mirrored the arrangements of life and labour made by mill owners or steel masters. These institutions have declined in recent decades as their costs have risen, but the more fundamental change of that period is still with us in growing measure: the expansion of local government and the rise of the welfare bureaucracies.

Such bureaucracies require their own personnel, and this development was furthered by educated women of the late 19th century seeking emancipated yet socially acceptable roles as teachers and social workers [14]. From a small number of philanthropists and reformers have proliferated today's clusters of professions and semi-professions concerned with the education, welfare, treatment and control of problem people.

For these philanthropists, the children of the slums were not only to be protected from exploitation by employers, but also to be saved from the neglect and corruption of family and neighbourhood, preferably by removal to the cleansing atmosphere of the countryside [15]. Their rationale for intervention is exemplified in the caring but carbolic didacticism of Mary Carpenter, who advocated the remoulding of problem children to correct deficient early socialisation:

' . . . When we reflect that the early moulding of the young child's mind depends almost entirely on the mother, and that these neglected children, who are in great danger of joining the criminal class, if they have not done so, are to become parents of the next generation, surely express provision should be made for their training and reformation.' [16]

Her words are almost prophetic of John Bowlby's concept of maternal deprivation, which was to influence social workers so profoundly almost exactly one hundred years later [17]. Indeed, such views were powerfully fuelled by the positivist revolution in thinking, and more particularly by the expanding influence of psychological theories of child development, which had some impact towards the end of the 19th century, but did not reach their apotheosis in social work until well into the present century. The crucial, and some would say disastrous, contribution of such theories was the rationale they afforded to the well meaning in the child rescue or treatment business from Dr Barnardo up to the present day. Their influence is so pervasive that echoes of Mary Carpenter can be heard in the words that Mr Callaghan used as Home Secretary when introducing the 1969 Children and Young Persons Bill in the House of Commons: he spoke of the need to *prevent the deprived and delinquent children of today from becoming the deprived, inadequate, unstable or criminal citizens of tomorrow.* [18] . . . *'We want to get hold of these children at a sufficiently early stage to ensure . . . that the young sapling is not twisted or bent in ways that make the child grow up stunted.'* [19] Thus the need to deal with known offenders became merged with the desire to intervene in the lives of many other children. The 'deprived and delinquent', or what the 1968 White Paper, *Children in Trouble* [20], called *'those at risk and in trouble'*, have their germ in Mary Carpenter's children of *'the perishing and dangerous classes'*. The thinking is deeply rooted, though its influence has ebbed and flowed across the century.

The apparatus of intervention has meanwhile continued to grow, and most markedly in the period since the Second World War, for the welfare bureaucracies generally and specifically for community child care [21]. The welfare state had several roots, but it owed its development most immediately and directly to a groundswell of popular radicalism in the early war years, and the way this was articulated in the Beveridge Report of 1942 [22]. The major legislative programme of the Attlee Government brought about important social advances, but it soon became apparent that the impulse which gave it birth was insufficient to achieve the promised nirvana [23]. However the failure of Beveridge's universalistic provisions to reach the clients at the bottom of the social pile, especially the poor and the deviant, was certainly no disadvantage to the aspiring, nascent profession of social work. Indeed it became obvious that social problems and the social work profession were far from withering away as an anachronism in a new affluent society: with the 'rediscovery' of poverty and an increase in reported crime, attention was diverted towards dealing with those who slipped through the welfare net. The local authority structures responsible for the delivery of social work services were subjected to a succession of reforms and reorganisations, during which the child care service grew greatly.

The Seebohm Report on the personal social services [24] was published in 1968, and in 1971 the various local government welfare services were reorganised and combined, as the report had recommended. It was an idealistic document designed to provide a more powerful 'social services' department, which could command more finance, and as a consequence be able to provide a more comprehensive, less stigmatising and more accessible service to the whole community. Yet it reflected contemporary preoccupations with corporate efficiency as a basis for family focused social work [25]. Momentum was created and the number of social workers climbed: it was as though the new social services departments were self-generating, self-elaborating and mutually competitive. The reorganisation of local government in 1974 coincided with further expansion in social services staffing, stimulated, it could be argued, by the increasing demand for better publicised and more accessible welfare services. Social work with the young more than maintained its share, not least because—as the child care lobby had rightly predicted—the 1969 Act was to *'bring more children and young people within its* (the child care service's) *direct influence and responsibility.'*[26]

THE RESPONSE TO PROBLEM YOUTH

Focus on Youth

Traditionally the younger generation has always represented both the hope of and the threat to the older generation. History may not repeat itself exactly, but there are great cyclical themes which keep surfacing, and the preoccupation with youth is certainly one of them. Thus, in this century, war and impending war have twice focused attention on the loyalty of youth and control of youthful unrest[27]. However, the concern about youth in the last two decades or so has other causes. One general factor may be that in a rapidly changing world, what young people do comes to represent wider aspects of social change[28]. Indeed, where change is concerned, the young initially excite envy for their capacity to cope with it, then they attract resentment for the enthusiasm with which they embrace it, and finally are blamed for creating it. A more specific factor was the new prosperity of the 1950s, which enabled young people at work to keep more of their earnings for personal consumption, and so create a market for clothes, records and other distinctive products of the 'teenage pop culture'[29].

The disproportionate emphasis on examining the world of youth may be understandable, but since the war it has resulted in a number of popular stereotypes: that this was an age of privilege for youth, enjoying freedoms and economic independence unknown to their parents when they were young; or that the new affluence percolated down throughout society to create an undifferentiated mass culture of consuming youth.

A critique of this position has been provided by studies demonstrating that youth cultures are class based, and that throughout this period there have been pockets of alienated and troubled youth, sometimes displaced from established working class neighbourhoods by extensive redevelopment schemes[30]. However, given these popular fictions, many adults found the successive manifestations—in teddy boys, mods and rockers, skinheads, punks and Rastas—bewildering, and indeed threatening, particularly when in the 1960s more middle class youth joined in the rejection of society's values through the hippie culture and student militancy.

Public response to the youth question has been ambivalent. One way of resolving the ambivalence is illustrated in the local press, which distinguishes sharply between the 'fine young people' on schemes to help the elderly and 'youths' who appear in magistrates' courts. With adolescents in trouble, reactions may depend on whether they are perceived as 'children', whose parents are to blame, or 'young people', beyond an age that calls for under-standing and compassion—terms, incidentally, reflected in the 1969 Act.

These generalisations aside, the 1960s were marked by increasing public concern about violence in schools, gang outbreaks and vandalism. In this critics were backed by the crime statistics, though it is perhaps significant that while the statistics showed similar rises in juvenile delinquency and adult crime, it was the former that aroused more public concern. The mass media fanned the reactions of an already anxious public with a succession of moral panics, which presented the more extreme manifestations of youth as a major challenge to public respectability and the country's existing way of life [31]. Not surprisingly, calls were heard for the return of National Service and the birch.

Nevertheless, this spirit did not become dominant in the formulation of public policy until the 1970s, under the label of 'law and order'. The architects of the 1969 Act appear to have remained impervious to this kind of thinking, and we must look elsewhere for the more benign influences that informed the Act [32].

Social Work and the Psychiatric Deluge

These more benign responses were largely those of workers in the child and youth field, expressing what can be called liberal ideas in the professional language of the day. They can be broadly categorised into two approaches: those based on psychological theories, and those based on more sociological ones.

Social work, in its casework heyday, was largely swamped by a tidal wave of psycho-analytic or psychiatric literature. This deluge may have swept across America and thence to Britain half a century earlier [33], but its consequences were still very evident in the 1950s in terms of the psychiatric world view in both social work training and practice. The ideas proved powerful because they offered an explanation for the failure of the welfare state to eradicate poverty within the context of general affluence. They suggested that the cause of the difficulties which overwhelmed some people could be attributed to a weakness in the individual personality, the culture of poverty or some kind of cycle of deprivation.

In this atmosphere the work of Bowlby, arguing the causal link between maternal deprivation and problem behaviour [34], both reflected and reinforced the thinking of aspiring professionals and the further development of casework. Psychological theories that stressed the importance of early socialisation and of the mother-child relationship within the family also underpinned the movement in child care away from institutions and towards a more home or community based version of social work.

The child care profession was not a unified or cohesive group, but among its ranks a powerful lobby, with strong democratic or Fabian leanings, emerged in the 1960s. This period eventually saw Fabian ideas about the value of incremental social reform in general and family based child care in particular winning out over other ideas and becoming embodied in the 1969 Act. It is therefore important to understand the assumptions on which these ideas were based, which attributed delinquency largely to personality failure or to family circumstances, or to an interaction between the two. The pedigree is a long one, but the flavour can be captured through some work published by Stott in 1952: he saw delinquency as *just one sort of personality failure, which can mask as great a variety of dys-function as can a high temperature ... Furthermore one discovers the same individual varying his pattern of breakdown to induce delinquent symptoms at one time and "maladjusted" symptoms at another, or both at once.* [35] Here he anticipated the merging of the distinction between the deprived and the depraved, which also marked the 1962 Report of the Advisory Council on the Treatment of Offenders [36], and the Labour Party's Longford Report in 1964 [37]. Stott's emphasis, moreover, was on social as well as psycho-

13

logical pathology, since *'if delinquency is seen as part of the wider evil of unhappy childhood* (and) *if we prevent the latter, delinquency will also be prevented, as with the removal of the cause of a disease the symptoms disappear.'* [38]

In the 1960s it was the 'problem family' that emerged as a central concern of social work advocates. This notion was elaborated by the Ingleby Committee in 1960 [39], and further developed by Peggy Jay and Margaret Stewart, whose 1962 Fabian essays [40] gave them influence with the Longford Committee. The latter proposed a new family service designed for problem families, the apathetic and the ignorant, and concluded that social work was the answer for the maladjusted who had slipped through the net of universalistic welfare. Their report also maintained that it was often a matter of chance whether a child was treated as deprived or depraved, and suggested that delinquency was, in fact, a special form of deprivation. Finally, it expressed the hope that the new family service would be able to ensure an all embracing treatment and care for children who suffered *'any kind of handicap—physical or mental disability, emotional disturbance or maladjustment'.* [41] This train of thought is reflected in the 1965 White Paper, *The Child, the Family and the Young Offender* [42], and above all in the Kilbrandon Report for Scotland [43]. As legislative proposals, the former was abortive, while the latter resulted in the 1968 Scottish Social Work Act, but through both these channels, and others, the influence of social work thinking fed into the 1969 Act for England and Wales.

Delinquency Theories and Labelling

Another source for more benign or understanding responses to problem youth was the influence of sociological theories designed to explain delinquent subcultures. Thus, following the pre-war work of the Chicago school in attempting to understand youthful gangs, Cohen, writing in 1955, saw the gang as a subculture, in the sense of a collective effort by young people to resolve adjustment problems produced by dislocations in the larger society [44]. More simply, Miller came to the conclusion that delinquency was a natural product of lower class values, since these were in conflict with the middle class values enshrined in the law [45]. Cloward and Ohlin, combining Merton's concept of anomie with Cohen's delinquent subculture, developed the theory, divided gangs into 'conflict', 'criminal' and 'retreatist', and suggested that the nature of the gang depended on the opportunities available [46]. They also concluded that there were more criminals among the working classes because the latter were denied equal access to legitimate means of advancement.

There is an appreciable time lag between the development of any new theory and its assimilation by policymakers or practitioners, and it is not possible to trace the precise pathways by which delinquency theories influenced those who framed the 1969 Act. There are suggestions that by the early 1960s these ideas were known to policymakers, and they did have some influence on practice in the youth service, even if less than one per cent of its budget at that time was spent on special projects aimed at delinquents [47]. Moreover, as child care became more oriented towards the community, social workers did look more closely at youth work to see what they could usefully borrow.

There is also evidence that labelling theory has had a more pervasive influence, although the same caution needs to be expressed about the causal links between theory and policy making. Becker, in his seminal work [48], suggests that no action is intrinsically good or bad, but rather that each act depends upon how it is defined by those with the power to make such definitions. He warns against focusing on a person's early childhood experiences, and claims that labelling somebody as criminal is both unjust and counterproductive. In a very general sense, these kinds of ideas were already in the aid in Britain. The 1964 Longford Report wanted to abolish the juvenile courts, so that children could be treated without what it considered to be the 'stigma' of criminal proceedings. In 1962, treating delinquents in isolation from their law abiding peers was a matter of concern to the Advisory Council on the Treatment of Offenders: in considering the Boston Citizenship Training Scheme, it accepted the project's focus on individual treatment, remedial literacy and physical education, but rejected the exclusive focus on offenders, on the grounds that it risked the contamination of the less experienced by the more experienced. So the report rejected specialised facilities in favour of making greater use of existing youth and further education provision [49].

One of the ironies is that this reliance on existing facilities failed to take into account the extent to which alienated and labelled youth perceived itself as excluded from that system. The upsurge in compensatory social and educational programmes during the 1960s, such as educational priority areas and community development projects, was an attempt to provide non-stigmatising positive discrimination. It gave working in the community, and particularly youth work and community work [50], an unprecedented vogue, and it is probably not too fanciful to suggest that this larger and more broadly based move towards social intervention in the community tended to influence the thinking about community care in social work in the 1970s. Indeed as the 1970s progressed, intermediate treatment took on—in the eyes of some people, at least— much of the glamour, novelty, innovativeness and the apparent opportunities for effecting radical change, that were previously associated with community work.

Drawing Together the Strands

These various strands of thought can only lead to legislation when they are accepted by those who propose and enact it, so the views of the Home Office and its Child Care Inspectorate were very important. Derek Morrell, the Assistant Under Secretary, and Joan Cooper, the Chief Inspector, can together be regarded as prominent architects of both the 1969 Children and Young Persons Act and the Community Development Projects, which reflected so many consonant ideas.

Derek Morrell was determined to put the treatment of young offenders in a broadly educational context. In 1968 he had pleaded for a more eclectic approach to child care in the community as well as the residential setting, and advocated *'ending those distinctions between therapy, child care training and a formal education which are false, and relating to form a coherent whole those which are valid'* [51].

The child care professionals in the Inspectorate were well placed to trawl the country for ideas, take the temperature of practice, and, by drawing on the findings of the Home Office Research Unit, could formulate possible policies and advance them for translation into legislation. Joan Cooper herself [52] had visited the USA in the early 1960s and had been impressed by the Californian community programmes and others concerned with youth enrichment; she had there come into contact with the ideas of Albert Kahn, whose book foreshadowed much of the thinking and terminology of the liberal advocacy of the 1969 Act. He spoke of children 'in trouble' comprising the delinquent and the neglected in naturally blurred groups, extending to the 'potential' and the 'vulnerable' who needed 'preventive intervention' [53].

Pressure accumulated from diverse professional sources, not purely social and youth work, to facilitate a more benign response by central government to problem youth, in the form of additional community based disposals. The Inspectorate, coincidentally responsible for overseeing attendance centres, found frustration among many policemen running them that they could not use the legal framework to engage young people in positive activities outside the centres. The magistracy was asking for additional choices to be provided between what it saw as loose or ineffective means like fines or supervision and custodial sentences or residential care. The costs of existing institutional facilities were concerning both the Treasury and local government officials and pressure was increasing to find cheaper alternatives. Policymakers were becoming aware that in other parts of Europe as well as America, questions were being asked about institutional effectiveness and alternatives were being tried out. All these influences, too, went into the writing of the 1968 White Paper, *Children in Trouble* [54], and the 1969 Bill that followed.

THE 1969 ACT AND ITS SEQUEL
Confusion and Compromise

It was suggested above that the story of the official control of problem youth can most usefully be seen as a continuing fight for supremacy by competing ideologies, with each generation having to strike a balance between creating measures sufficiently harsh to discourage imitation and sufficiently humane to avoid attracting sympathy for the criminal. It is often forgotten that the 1965 White Paper, *The Child, the Family and the Young Offender* [55], strongly advocated a welfare approach, and the political storm following this far-reaching proposal necessitated a strategic withdrawal from this exposed position. So it is not surprising that its successor, *Children in Trouble,* and the subsequent legislation should be a compromise, or that they should enshrine a number of internal contradictions reflecting, but not resolving, these conflicting ideologies.

The proposal, for instance, that the minimum age of criminal responsibility should be raised to 14 indicates that the writers were influenced by both maturation and labelling theory. The notion that the vast majority of young people grow out of crime as they emerge from adolescence and assume responsibilities associated with work, marriage and parenthood was given added weight by a number of self report studies. These indicated that almost all young people were engaged in one or more acts of delinquency during their childhood and adolescence [56]. Combined with the dangers of labelling, these theories argued persuasively for raising the age of criminal responsibility and towards a policy of radical non-intervention. However, although *Children in Trouble* recommended the raising of the age of criminal responsibility, it was as if the writers were aware that radical non-intervention was too much for the public to stomach, and in its own way even posed a threat to the social work profession. Then, having accepted the normality of juvenile delinquency and the need to decriminalise it, the writers distinguished a small minority of more persistent and serious offenders, whose behaviour was due to various factors such as *'unsatisfactory family or social circumstances, a result of boredom in and out of school, an*

16

indication of maladjustment, immaturity or a symptom of a deviant, damaged or abnormal personality' [57].

Although structure and conflict theories were supported by a considerable body of literature, and although *Children in Trouble* recognised that many children were driven along a predetermined course by inexorable forces largely outside their control, the above quotation reveals the extent to which the writers were still strongly influenced by psychological causation theories. It did look to some as if a deal had been struck in which it was agreed, consciously or unconsciously, to accept the offender as deprived rather than depraved and to treat him as a patient rather than punish him as a criminal — all in return for being allowed to concentrate on the individual and ignore the criminogenic factors within the structure of society, for which the solutions are so very much more expensive. The curious logic of the White Paper, as if spawned by an unholy alliance between labelling and psychological causation theories, reflects the need to satisfy, at least partially, both the criminal justice and the welfare lobbies.

Symbolic Nature of the Act

As it turned out, the tide of events was flowing against the move to decriminalise juvenile delinquency, and the election of the Heath government in 1970 led directly both to the emasculation of the 1969 Act and the increased likelihood of a backlash before it was implemented. Admittedly Mr Callaghan as Home Secretary was still claiming, in his speech on the second reading of the Children and Young Persons Bill in 1969, that the purpose of intermediate treatment *'. . . is to bring youngsters in trouble into contact with others taking part in the normal constructive activities of young people of their own age — social, educational, recreational, helping others.'* [58] At the same time it is probably fair to conclude that many informed members of the general public had been convinced that traditional methods for dealing with juvenile delinquency had been tried and found wanting. Consequently they were prepared to acknowledge that it was worth exploring new methods, which focused on the needs of the individual rather than the seriousness of the offence, provided that these new methods not only proved to be more humane but also more effective in reducing delinquency.

In fact, although the legislation contained a number of fairly radical proposals, the new Tory administration soon made it clear that it had no intention of raising the age of criminal responsibility from 10 to 14, of phasing out attendance and detention centres, or even of compelling the police to consult with the social services to determine whether care or criminal proceedings were required [59].

Following the passing of the Act, the interesting phenomenon is that the social work profession and the Department of Health and Social Security were so caught up in the propaganda war which they had been waging that they failed, or could not bear, to recognise for a very long time the symbolic nature of their victory. Listening to their public pronouncements, an outsider could be forgiven for thinking that juvenile delinquency had been abolished. Confusion was created by the fact that the legislation and the philosophical assumptions underlying it appeared to give a mandate both for treating individuals 'in trouble' and also for broadly compensatory, non-stigmatising programmes in which 'deprived' and 'normal' children could be integrated together. Much energy was spent in trying to determine where the balance should lie between treatment and prevention. The DHSS *Guide to Intermediate Treatment* [60], published in 1972, never mentions delinquency and even in 1974, Joan Cooper, by then Director of the DHSS Social Work Service, was still lending her authority to a very generalised, if not amorphous, interpretation of the concept:

> *'Intermediate treatment is intended for the whole age range from 0-18 years. Within it can be encompassed an informal play group for an 'at risk' 3 year old under supervision or an opportunity for motor repair work in a group for a 16 year old traffic offender.'* [61]

As late as 1977, a DHSS circular made clear that local authority treasurers should be more flexible and allow money allocated to intermediate treatment to be used for children who were not the subject of a specific court order [62]. Here was official blessing for using intermediate treatment to provide a preventive service for children at risk.

The position was summed up by a joint working party, representing virtually all the professional organisations concerned with child care, which reported in 1978 that one of the most fundamental things to recognise about the Children and Young Persons Act, 1969, was that it was always more of a banner than a piece of legislation. As an Act, particularly in its truncated form, it was always weak, giving effect to a few relatively unimportant changes.

> *'As a symbol of a battle between competing ideologies, however, where its very existence is percieved as a victory by one group and a defeat by the other, it remains very powerful.'* [63]

The 1969 Act under Attack

The 1969 Act was born at a pivotal period. The climate in the country was flowing against the liberal values which were given legislative effect. Indeed the law and order lobby was able to ensure that crucial sections of the Act were never brought into effect. Although the number of children committed to care by the courts actually dropped during 1971 and 1972 (the first two years after the Act was brought into effect), the conservative lobby, consisting largely of magistrates and police, mounted a vigorous and sustained campaign to have the 1969 Act changed. This attack was made explicit in a pamphlet, published by the Society of Conservative Lawyers in 1974, entitled *Apprentices in Crime.* This argued that the Act had mistakenly taken away the power of magistrates to punish and that local authorities often failed to act upon care orders which they now had the discretionary power to implement. Further it pointed out that the depraved child was not always deprived, and that the assumption, embodied in the 1968 White Paper *Children in Trouble,* that *'an offender is always in need of care and protection from an environment deprived of physical and emotional support'* was sometimes wrong [64]. The ideological basis of this attack on the 1969 Act was apparent in the way the Society blamed a reported increase in juvenile crime on the failure of the Act, in 1973, before provisions like intermediate treatment were even operational [65].

The anger of magistrates was often focused on the discretionary power of local authorities to implement both care orders and intermediate treatment requirements as and when they considered it appropriate. Plainly a small proportion of children, committed to the care of local authorities, was sent home either because there were no vacancies or because social workers considered that course of action to be in the interests of both the child and the community. However, as the previously mentioned joint working party pointed out, the real cause for alarm lay not so much in the small number of cases where magistrates and social workers were in disagreement, but much more in the high level of agreement and the apparent enthusiasm with which social workers recommended residential or even custodial measures [66]. Nevertheless, there was a widespread sense of mourning among magistrates for what they perceived as their lost powers, compounded by their fear that the courts were consequently being brought into disrepute. It soon became apparent that the strategy, adopted by the more sophisticated members of the 'law and order' lobby, was to distinguish between the majority, for whom the Act was adequate and possibly even beneficial, and the minority of serious and persistent offenders. In 1974, a Scotland Yard statement argued this point:

> 'Perhaps from misguided conception, present legislation and its application is leading us towards an ever increasing hard core of criminals of the future, instead of successfully separating those juveniles who genuinely require help from those who require strong punitive measures or restricted environment.' [67]

As conflict and controversy over the delivery of services to problem youth continued to mount, a parliamentary committee under the chairmanship of Renée Short was set up late in 1973 to consider the whole question [68]. The Magistrates' Association recommended the introduction of residential and secure care orders, which would have dramatically decreased the local authorities' room for manoeuvre, and Mr Stanger, considered one of the more sympathetic magistrates and committed to the potential usefulness of intermediate treatment, criticised 'the lustreless schemes which had been approved' and the programmes which he had heard described as '60 days of continuous ping-pong' [69]. Even the National Association of Probation Officers, which had welcomed intermediate treatment in 1970, felt obliged to describe the passing of the 1969 Act without either the resources or adequately trained or experienced staff to implement it as a mistake [70].

The radical response

Criminologists tended to focus on what were seen as the somewhat invidious assumptions of the treatment approach inherent in the Act. David May suggests what these assumptions were:

> '1 that explanations for delinquency are to be found in the behavioural and motivational systems of delinquents, and not in the law or its administration...
>
> 2 that in some identifiable way delinquents are different from non-delinquents.' These differences are usually located 'in systems of norms and values, socialisation experiences or psychological disorders...
>
> 3 that the delinquent is constrained and cannot ultimately be held responsible for his actions. The constraints might be physiological, psychological or sociological' and .. 'lead, almost inevitably, to delinquent conduct...
>
> 4 that delinquent behaviour per se is not the real problem. It possesses significance only as a pointer to the need for intervention. It is the presenting symptom that draws attention to the more intractable disease.' [71]

There was a convergence between this view and that of the previously mentioned pressure group, Justice for Children, which criticised the social welfare approach of the juvenile courts, arguing that:

'This leads to the logical assumption that, like a patient with a disease, delinquents need a course of 'treatment'. But there is mounting controversy as to whether involuntary treatment, prescribed by the court and social services, can be anything but punishment . . . judicial impartiality and fairness, especially in sentencing, have been severely hindered by the welfare approach. This has resulted, on occasion, in grave injustice to children. To make matters worse, the present juvenile court system is manifestly unsuccessful, as shown by the reconviction rates. There is also an increasing body of opinion which believes that 'treatment' can have a negative effect on a child and his family.' [72]

The banner of radical evidence to the Short Committee was carried mainly by the National Council for Civil Liberties, which pointed to the infringement of liberties in the treatment approach, derided its ineffectiveness *'if the roots of crime lie in the structure of society and in the physical environment'*, and suggested that *'the best 'cure' for young offenders is the passage of time.'* [73]

Liberal defence

In the face of this formidable onslaught from both conservative and radical directions, the liberals defended the Act on the basis that the admittedly unsatisfactory state of affairs could not be attributed to it, since it had never been fully implemented either through lack of political will or resources. They also pointed out that the expertise in the children's departments, upon which the Act depended, was absorbed within months into the larger social services departments. The Seebohm changes took place in 1971, and the social work profession was subjected three years later to local government reorganisation, which certainly took its toll in terms of the motivation of both managers and practitioners towards setting up new schemes in what many saw as the nebulous and ill-defined field of intermediate treatment.

Furthermore, the financial crisis, which struck in 1974 and brought to an end a period of rapid expansion in the social services, had a disastrous impact on the development of intermediate treatment. Many local authorities, preoccupied with setting up a new department, had only allocated intermediate treatment a token few hundred pounds to service programmes over a population of several hundred thousand people. So when the cold winds of financial restraint began to blow, intermediate treatment had a weak budgetary platform from which to develop, and no 'fat' which it could afford to shed. The British Association of Social Workers, in its evidence to the Short Committee, highlighted the trend away from community care in direct opposition to the spirit of the Act. It referred to the reduction in supervision orders (formerly probation orders) between 1969 and 1973, and showed that this had been counterbalanced by a corresponding increase in Borstal, detention and attendance centre orders during the same period [74].

Developments Since the Act

In spite of all its potential advantages, intermediate treatment has remained a peripheral activity as far as the helping professions are concerned. The explanation for this strange outcome lies as much in organisational factors as in the value assumptions on which the legislation was based and the historical context, which have already received consideration. The setting up of social services departments, followed by local government reorganisation, did have a considerable impact. Management was often too preoccupied to give a coherent lead and social workers were often too inexperienced to grasp the opportunities inherent in intermediate treatment. The decision to ask children's regional planning committees to spend the period up to 1973 producing a plan on community homes led quite directly both to the channelling of resources into residential care and also to delay in the development of intermediate treatment and community care.

When the schemes of intermediate treatment were finally produced in 1973 and 1974, they were criticised for amounting to little more than long lists of existing community facilities, even though this was in line with the guidance offered by the DHSS. This approach depended to a large extent on the co-operation of the youth service, and its enthusiasm was quickly replaced by caution when it became apparent that any additional resources were unlikely to be diverted in its direction. Similarly the probation service, with the uncertainty about its role and its continued involvement with juveniles, did not make its expected contribution. Consequently, by the time the Short Committee was sitting, a DHSS witness found herself saying:

> 'We now see that it is not really a matter of linking children up necessarily with just what is established in the way of youth or children's groups in a locality; but that it does call for the development of imaginative schemes which will not just attract the interest of these children but will involve them in activities in the community in which they are . . .' [75]

An interaction between the economic situation, the growing power of the 'law and order' lobby, and the practice of social workers was responsible for a gradual shift in thinking away from a largely preventive approach and towards social intervention with a smaller, clearly identified, group of young offenders. The emphasis began to change from innovative work in the community with relatively large numbers of children 'in trouble' and 'at risk' towards decarceration and reducing the numbers of delinquents in residential care. This change can be attributed to either professional conversion or economic imperatives. Wherever professional conviction coincides with the direction dictated by financial constraints, it always proves a powerful combination. The government response to the Short Committee was given in a White Paper published in 1976 [76]. While it resisted the most controversial recommendations — limiting the discretionary power of the local authorities and introducing new short sentences of two to 21 days in detention centres — the government conceded a number of points, including more explicit sanctions for breach of supervision or failure to pay a fine, which were embodied in the Criminal Law Act, 1977. In addition, the DHSS expended considerable energy on persuading both local authorities and regional health authorities to build more secure accommodation for young people.

At the same time, it strongly endorsed the Short Committee's view that 'urgent attention should be given to non-residential forms of care: intermediate treatment, day care, supervision and fostering' [77], and its efforts to promote intermediate treatment were continued by the Conservative Government which took office in 1979. The latter held a traditional Tory stance in distinguishing 'the hard core, a tiny minority of habitually law breaking juveniles for whom a *firmer sentencing policy is the only answer'* from *'the very much larger number of youngsters actually or potentially in trouble . . . in need of treatment, advice and education'* [78]. However, its delinquency control perspective was clear, and intermediate treatment was grouped with the courts, police and probation service as 'law and order' services that should be protected from expenditure cuts [79].

Focus on delinquency

Meanwhile, the liberals had gradually become aware of their exposed position and the extent to which they had lost ground since the passing of the Act, and this recognition was encapsulated in the Personal Social Services Council's 1977 report by its study group on intermediate treatment [80]. Although the PSSC report was concerned to locate the preventive functions of inter- mediate treatment within the context of much broader programmes to alleviate structural deprivation, it made it quite clear that:

> *'the primary aims of intermediate treatment should be to reduce delinquent behaviour and prevent new involvement in anti-social behaviour; to reduce the need for institutional care; and to prevent the inappropriate placement of a child or young person in a residential establishment.'* [81]

The liberals were not alone in their concern at the increasing number of juveniles sent to detention centres and Borstal: the 1978 total was almost triple the 1969 figure. [82] The PSSC report urged that intermediate treatment should be seen as not just an addition, but sometimes an alternative, to residential care. However, it was left to a report from NACRO [83] to suggest that systematic decarceration was one of the three optional strategies available. The argument for decarceration was made by radical criminologists and reinforced by research indicating that the creation of community programmes without an accompany- ing commitment to a corresponding reduction in residential provision tends to have the effect of identifying new client groups rather than dealing with existing clients in an alternative way. In other words new children, who have not been formally identified as delinquent, are drawn into the expanding network of community based programmes that are widely seen to be for delinquents [84].

In some local authorities, the need to find cheap alternatives to residential provision for problem youth produced a modest transfer of resources from institutional to intermediate treatment budgets; and in a few cases this was accompanied by an attempt to give close attention to police cautioning pro- cedures and social workers' practice, to try and minimise the extent to which juveniles penetrated the juvenile justice system [85]. The priority was seen as intensive work with a small number of juveniles, mainly as an alternative to residential care.

Such efforts were radical, in that they focused attention on the system for processing problem youth, rather than on individuals, groups or neighbourhoods as clients for treatment. Their radicalism lay in prescribing where the boundaries of social intervention should be rather than in what should go on within them. But the decision to concentrate upon work with a few delinquents highlighted ways in which such proposals were not as radical as they seemed. Within some intensive units for work with delinquents as an alternative to care or custody, the methods of intervention displayed a strong orientation to individualised behaviour control [86].

CONCLUSION

The new rhetoric of decarceration had the merit of meeting the fundamental complaint from radical criminologists that community care threatened to extend central control into the community. At the same time it excused or allowed the reassertion of the old familiar treatment ideologies, which encouraged a focus on the individual at the expense of wider social factors. So, the irony of the allegedly radical response by liberal advocates of the 1969 Act, intent on restricting the focus of intermediate treatment to a smaller number of identified offenders, was that this was entirely consistent with the positivist philosophy of control and treatment underlying all welfarist legislation. The consequence is that even in those authorities prepared to make a significant reallocation of resources to intermediate treatment, the liberal, therapeutic, individually focused ideology remained paramount, and this form of intervention still constituted a peripheral aspect of the total strategy for dealing with problem youth.

Furthermore, the possibility of developing more broadly based community programmes looked increasingly remote as it became clear that efforts to blur the line between delinquent and non-delinquent through preventive social work might actually have the effect of labelling more rather than fewer children. The rhetoric of community social work, with consciousness raising, local participation and the stimulation of community effort, seemed to have collapsed in the cost-conscious mid 1970s. Meanwhile, the debate about the most effective way of handling problem youth continued throughout the decade—a debate, moreover, that owed more to the increasing preoccupation with problem youth than to any increase in the 'problemness' of youth itself.

References

1   Department of Health and Social Security (1972), *Intermediate treatment: A guide for the regional planning of new forms of treatment for children in trouble*, London: HMSO, p.6.
2   For a critique of positivist theories about criminality, see Taylor I., Walton P. and Young J. (1973), *The new criminology*, London: Routledge and Kegan Paul.
3   Younghusband E. (1978), *Social work in Britain, 1950-1975: A follow up study*, London: Allen and Unwin, Vol. 1. In an account of the child care service since the war, she says: *'The following account shows not only the ups and downs, the task that grew more rewarding and more daunting with fresh knowledge, . . . the extremes within discernible trends, the uneven progress revealed by research studies, but also the steady commitment that created the children's service and made it responsive to individual needs.'*
4   Cornish D.B. and Clarke R.V.G. (1975), *Residential treatment and its effects on delinquency* (Home Office Research Study No. 32), London: HMSO.
5   *The Guardian*, March 20 1978.
6   *Ibid.*
7   Geach H. and Szwed E. (undated), *Justice for Children: Aims and objectives*, Justice for Children.
8   Radical Alternatives to Prison, Young Offenders Group (undated), *Children out of trouble*, Radical Alternatives to Prison. See also, Fitzgerald M. (1975), 'The power of the definers and the powerlessness of the defined: Developments in Massachusetts', *New Era*, Vol. 56, No. 6, pp. 126-131.
9   Cohen S. (1979), 'Community control: A new utopia', *New Society*, March 15 1979, Vol. 47, No. 858, pp. 609-611. Also, Thorpe D., Paley J. and Green C. (1979), 'Ensuring the right result', *Community Care*, May 10 1979, No. 263, pp. 25-26.
10 Gillis J. (1974), Youth and history, New York: Academic Press. Aries P. (1973), *Centuries of childhood*, Harmondsworth: Penguin.
11 Plumb J.H. (1973), 'Children: The victims of time', in Plumb J.H., *In the light of history*, London: Allen Lane, Part II, Essay 5, pp. 153-165.

12 Scull A. (1977), *Decarceration,* Englewood Cliffs, NJ: Prentice Hall, Ch.2.
13 For a critique of Scull's tendency towards reductionism and economic determinism, see Matthews R. (1979), ' 'Decarceration' and the fiscal crisis', in Fine B. *et al,* (eds.), *Capitalism and the rule of law: From deviancy theory to Marxism,* London: Hutchinson, pp. 100-117.
14 Platt A.M. (1969), *The child savers: The invention of delinquency,* Chicago and London: University of Chicago Press.
15 See e.g: Carlebach J. (1970), *Caring for children in trouble,* London: Routledge and Kegan Paul, pp.24, 60-63.
16 Carpenter M. (1851), *Reformatory schools for the children of the perishing and dangerous classes and for juvenile offenders,* London; reprinted, London: Woburn Press, 1968, p.317.
17 Bowlby J. (1953), *Child care and the growth of love,* Harmondsworth: Pelican. The fact that this has since received rigorous criticism (See eg Rutter M. (1972), *Maternal deprivation re-assessed,* Harmondsworth: Penguin.) suggests that its appeal then lay partly in the rationale it offered for social work.
18 *Hansard's Parliamentary Debates* (Commons), Vol. 779, March 11 1969, Col. 1176. (Second Reading of the 1969 Children and Young Persons Bill.)
19 *Ibid.,* Col. 1190. On the persistent faith in the reforming powers of the countryside, see his statement that intermediate treatment activities *'may involve going away, for instance, for adventure training or to a harvest camp'. (Ibid.,* Col. 1180.)
20 Home Office (1968), *Children in trouble,* Government White Paper, Cmnd. 3601, London: HMSO.
21 The child care service was established by the 1948 Children Act, following the Curtis Report (*Report of the Care of Children Committee* | 1946|, Cmd. 6922, London: HMSO.)
22 *Social insurance and allied services* (Beveridge report), (1942), Cmd. 6404, London: HMSO.
23 Miliband R. (1973), *Parliamentary Socialism: A study in the politics of labour,* London: Merlin Press. Also, George V. and Wilding P. (1976), *Ideology and social welfare,* London: Routledge and Kegan Paul.
24 *Report of the Committee on Local Authority and Allied Personal Social Services* (Seebohm Report), (1968), Cmnd. 3703, London: HMSO.
25 Hall P. (1976), *Reforming the welfare: The politics of change in the personal social services,* London: Heinemann.
26 Kahan B. (1970), 'The child care service', in Townsend P. *et al., The fifth social service: A critical analysis of the Seebohm proposals,* London: Fabian Society, p.63.
27 Thus, the 1939 Government Circular which created the present Youth Service argued that the *'strain of war and the disorganisation of family life have created conditions which constitute a serious menace to youth'* (Board of Education (1939), *In the service of youth,* Circular No. 1486, HMSO). See also Pearson G. (1978), 'Social work and law-and-order', *Social Work Today,* April 14 1978, Vol. 9, No. 30, pp.19-24.
28 Hall S. and Jefferson T. (eds.) (1976), *Resistance through rituals,* London: Hutchinson.
29 Abrams M. (1959), *Teenage consumer spending,* London: Press Exchange.
30 Hall S. and Jefferson T., *op. cit.*
31 A case study of media amplification and societal response to the mods and rockers is provided in Cohen S. (1980), *Folk devils and moral panics,* Oxford: Martin Robertson, 2nd edition.
32 For an account of how the 1969 Act reached the statute book, see Bottoms A.E. (1974), 'On the decriminalization of English juvenile courts', in Hood R. (ed.), *Crime, criminology and public policy: Essays in honour of Sir Leon Radzinowicz,* London: Heinemann, pp.319-345.
33 Woodroofe K. (1962), *From charity to social work in England and the United States,* London: Routledge and Kegan Paul, p.119.
34 Bowlby J., *op. cit.*
35 Stott D.H. (1952), *Saving children from delinquency,* London: London University Press, p.152.
36 Advisory Council on the Treatment of Offenders (1962), *Non-residential treatment of offenders under 21,* London: HMSO.
37 Labour Party Study Group (1964), *Crime — a challenge to us all* (Longford Report), London: Labour Party.
38 Stott D.H., *op. cit.,* p.204.
39 *Report of the Committee on Children and Young Persons* (Ingleby Report), (1960), Cmnd. 1191, London: HMSO.
40 Donnison D., Jay P. and Stewart M. (1962), *The Ingleby Report: Three critical essays* (Fabian Research Series, No. 231), London: Fabian Society.
41 Labour Party Study Group, *op. cit.,* p.17.
42 Home Office (1965), *The child, the family and the young offender,* Government White Paper, Cmnd. 2742, London: HMSO.

43 *Children and young persons: Scotland* (Kilbrandon Report), (1964), Cmnd. 2306, Edinburgh: HMSO.

44 **Cohen A. (1955), *Delinquent boys: The culture of the gang,* Glencoe, Illinois: Free Press.**

45 Miller W.B. (1958), 'Lower class culture as a generating milieu of gang delinquency', *Journal of Social Issues,* Vol. 14, No.1, pp.5-19.

46 Cloward R. and Ohlin L. (1961), *Delinquency and opportunity: A theory of delinquent gangs,* London: Routledge and Kegan Paul (first published New York: Free Press, 1960).

47 Smith C.S. (1966), 'The youth service and delinquency prevention', *Howard Journal,* Vol. XII, No. 1, pp.42-51.

48 Becker H. (1963), *Outsiders: Studies in the sociology of deviance,* New York: Free Press.

49 Advisory Council on the Treatment of Offenders, *op. cit.*

50 The link between these two, and the participation of young people in their community, are the themes of the major youth service report of the period: *Youth and community work in the 70s: Proposals by the Youth Service Development Council* (Milson-Fairbairn Report), (1969), London: HMSO.

51 Morrell D. (1968), 'The educational role of the approved schools', in Sparks R.F. and Hood R.G. (eds.), *The residential treatment of disturbed and delinquent boys* (Papers presented to the Cropwood Round-table Conference), Cambridge: Institute of Criminology, p.50.

52 Interview with Joan Cooper by one of the editors.

53 Kahn A.J. (1963), *Planning community services for children in trouble,* New York: Columbia University Press, pp.25-28.

54 Home Office (1968), *op. cit.*

55 Home Office (1965), *op. cit.*

56 See eg Belson W. (1975), *Juvenile theft: The casual factors,* London: Harper and Row.

57 Home Office (1968), *op. cit.,* para.6, p.4.

58 *Hansard's Parliamentary Debates* (Commons), Vol.779, March 11 1969, Col.1180.

59 Home Office (1970), *Government policy on children in trouble* (Press notice), London: Home Office, October 1 1970.

60 Department of Health and Social Security, *op. cit.*

61 Cooper J. (1976), 'Intermediate treatment as a concept and a reality', in DHSS Social Work Service Development Group, *Intermediate treatment: Report of a residential conference held at Birmingham, 2-5 December 1974,* London: HMSO, p.6.

62 **Department of Health and Social Security (1977), *Children and Young Persons Act, 1969: Intermediate treatment* (Local authority circular 77(1)), London: DHSS.**

63 Joint Working Party of Child Care Organisations (1978), *The Children and Young Persons Act 1969: An interim evaluation,* Birmingham: British Association of Social Workers, p.2.

64 Committee of the Society of Conservative Lawyers (1974), *Apprentices in crime: The failure of the Children and Young Persons Act 1969,* London: Society of Conservative Lawyers, p.7.

65 *Ibid.*

66 Joint Working Party of Child Care Organisations, *op. cit.*

67 *The Guardian,* July 2 1974.

68 *Eleventh report from the Expenditure Committee: Children and Young Persons Act, 1969* (Social Services Sub-Committee, Chairman: **Renée** Short), (1975), 2 Vols, HC 534-I, 534-II, London: HMSO.

69 *Ibid.,* Vol. II, *Minutes of evidence and appendices,* para. 542, p.132.

70 *Ibid.,* para. 801, p.196.

71 May D. (1971), 'Delinquency control and the treatment model: Some implications of recent legislation', *British Journal of Criminology,* Vol. 11, No. 4, pp.359-370.

72 Geach H. (1978), 'Justice or Welfare?', *Youth in Society,* No.31, p.11.

73 Expenditure Committee, *op. cit.,* Vol.II, p.269.

74 *Ibid.,* p.215.

75 *Ibid.,* para.1865, p.396.

76 Home Office (1976), *Children and Young Persons Act 1969: Observations on the Eleventh Report from the Expenditure Committee,* Government White Paper, Cmnd. 6494, London: HMSO.

77 Expenditure Committee, *op. cit.,* Vol. I, *Report,* para.129, p.xxxix.

78 From the speech by Patrick Jenkin, Secretary of State for Health and Social Security, to the DHSS conference on intermediate treatment, Sheffield, July 9 1979, in *Getting on with IT* (conference report), London: DHSS, p.1.

79 *Ibid.,* p.2: also *Hansard Parliamentary Debates* (Commons), Vol. 970, July 17 1979, Col.1437.

80 **Personal Social Services Council (1977), *A future for intermediate treatment: Report of the Intermediate Treatment Study Group* (Chairman: Mia Kellmer Pringle), London: PSSC.**

81 *Ibid.,* p.39.

82 Between 1969 and 1978, in the sentencing of juveniles for indictable offences only, Borstal committals rose from 818 to 1,860, and detention centre orders from 1,827 to 5,528; supervision (formerly probation) orders declined from 19,759 to 15,433, and care (formerly fit person or approved school orders) from 5,865 to 5,345. (Source: *Criminal Statistics, 1978,* Tables 6.10, 6.12).

83 *Children and young persons in custody: Report of a NACRO working party* (Jay Report) (1977), Chichester: Barry Rose (for the National Association for the Care and Rehabilitation of Offenders).

84 Such arguments were fuelled by American research: Lerman P. (1975), *Community treatment and social control: A critical analysis of juvenile correctional policy,* Chicago and London: University of Chicago Press. Klein M. and Teilmann K.S. (1976), *Pivotal ingredients of police juvenile diversion programs,* Washington, D.C.: US Department of Justice, National Institute of Juvenile Justice and Delinquency.

85 Thorpe D. (1979) 'The Wakefield IT Project: A radical approach to management of delinquency', *Social Work Service,* No.20, pp.45-48. Vincent J. (1979), *New initiatives in intermediate treatment,* London: Social Policy Research.

86 Sussex J. (1979), *Medway Centre, Day Training Centre and Close Support Unit: Treatment within the community,* Kent Probation and After-Care Service, Gillingham Community Service Centre.

CHAPTER 2
VALUES, THEORIES AND
PRACTICE OF
INTERMEDIATE TREATMENT

INTRODUCTION

The previous chapter has identified three different ideological positions in relation to the handling of juvenile delinquency: the conservative, liberal and radical positions. The first two, and to a lesser degree the third, have all influenced recent legislation and the current debate about juvenile justice. Intermediate treatment shares with other measures introduced by the 1969 Children and Young Persons Act the confusing and often conflicting expectations of legislators and society in relation to the handling of problem youth.

This chapter will examine the values on which the practice of intermediate treatment is based, and some of the theories which have guided it. Insofar as values are related to ideologies, one might expect to find a neat, consistent classification which would link ideology and practice. This chapter will indicate that such a link is not evident, and that at times there is a clear conflict between them.

For the sake of clarity, we have adopted a four-fold classification, within which the theories which have influenced the practice of intermediate treatment may be grouped [1]. These are:

- the justice approach
- the treatment approach
- educational approaches
- the social change approach

The justice approach seems most closely related to the conservative ideology referred to in Chapter 1, in that it emphasises the authority of legal institutions and the need to punish or control deviant youth. However, those who are concerned about the protection of the rights of children and are alarmed at the extension of secondary sentencing by social welfare agencies, would join with conservatives in espousing the justice approach to dealing with young offenders, though for quite different reasons and usually with different intentions as to the outcome.

Both the treatment and educational approach fit most readily the liberal ideology, and were given prominence in the policy developments of the 1960s. The treatment approach, which has strongly influenced the development of the social work profession, is based primarily on the concept of individual or social pathology. On the other hand, education emphasises the normal processes of maturation, which need to be nurtured and stimulated.

Each of these approaches is based on the assumption that existing social, political and economic institutions are either inherently sound, or unlikely to be radically changed. To a greater or lesser extent, they are concerned with individual adaptation to society's norms, and may therefore be seen, in the radical's view, as instruments of social control. The radical ideology, as applied to problem youth, seems to point in two, rather different, directions. The logical outcome for labelling theorists would be to make no official intervention, a process which has been termed 'radical non-intervention' [2]. Any contact, not only with the police and the courts, but also with 'treatment' agencies, compounds the deviant label and makes further deviance more likely. The other direction is that of political awareness and social change. Although many practitioners would accept these as valid targets for their work with problem youth, they usually have to operate within a system which is at best suspicious and often directly resistant to the practical application of such objectives.

The following sections will examine each of these approaches in more detail, and identify the major influences, in terms of values and theories, which have affected the practice of intermediate treatment.

THE JUSTICE APPROACH

The justice approach is based on the following assumptions:

- that crime is a moral act committed against the rules laid down by the society in which the offender lives;
- that a person is responsible for his own actions and knows right from wrong;
- that unless the converse can be proved (for example, that at the relevant time he was not responsible for his actions), the offender should be punished for his crime;
- and finally, that the degree of punishment required should be determined by the courts in accordance with the seriousness of the offence.

The legal system is established not only to determine whether a person is guilty or innocent of a particular offence, and to pass sentence if the case is proved, but also to protect the defendant from arbitrary or unnecessarily long periods of incarceration. Thus the increase of indeterminate sentences within the English legal system is viewed by those who adopt a justice approach with some alarm, as the protection of the individual defendant against 'secondary sentencing' by the Executive is gradually eroded.

The juvenile court has retained the power to make certain fixed term sentences, such as the detention and attendance centre orders, and also to impose fines. The court may also fix the length of a supervision order and set certain conditions or requirements on it. Thus, under the 1969 CYP Act, Section 12, an intermediate treatment requirement can be attached to a supervision order. As such it may be regarded as part of the tariff system, between a supervision order with no requirement and a care order. The White Paper, *Children in Trouble,* expresses this clearly when it states: *'Existing forms of treatment available to the juvenile courts distinguish sharply between those which involve complete removal from home and those which do not. The juvenile courts have very difficult decisions to make in judging whether circumstances require the drastic step of taking a child away from his parents and his home.'* [3] Intermediate treatment was intended in part to resolve this dilemma.

An intermediate treatment requirement has a maximum length of 90 days, within a supervision order whose length is fixed by the court. Within the time limit of the requirement, however, the supervisor has considerable discretion as to the timing and selection of facilities or even whether to invoke the requirement. Under the terms of the 1977 Criminal Law Act amendments, breaches of requirement of supervision orders can now be dealt with by the courts, which are empowered to impose sanctions.

Control of Delinquency

Thus although intermediate treatment was introduced in an Act designed to decriminalise the juvenile court in dealing with children under 14 and to limit prosecutions of young persons, it has become and is likely to remain part of the sentencing structure of the court. This feature, and the fact that statutory agencies provide the resources as part of their responsibilities for dealing with offenders, have major effects on the aims and implementation of intermediate treatment. First, it means that however effective it is in creating self-confident and socially skilled young people, a basic aim, in the eyes certainly of magistrates and statutory agencies, must be to stop or at least decelerate the process of delinquent activities of those who are involved in it. The Personal Social Services Council report on intermediate treatment underlines the importance of this in its statement of aims: *'We consider the primary aims of intermediate treatment should be to reduce delinquent behaviour and prevent new involvement in anti-social behaviour; to reduce the need for institutional care; and to prevent the inappropriate placement of a child or young person in a residential establishment.'* [4]

Secondly, if the courts regard intermediate treatment as part of the tariff available to them, as a step between a supervision order with no condition and a care order, then many young offenders made subject to such requirements will have already failed to respond to other sentences and may be appearing in court for a fourth or fifth time. The more comprehensive a diversionary system through juvenile liaison schemes or informal social work intervention, the later in a child's delinquent career will he or she tend to receive an intermediate treatment requirement. Although this seems to run counter to the official emphasis on non-segregation between offenders and other young people, it is natural that agencies will tend to direct resources towards those for whom they have a statutory responsibility.

A third important difference created by the placement of intermediate treatment within the justice system is the effect on the young person. What happens when he is arrested for an offence? A series of people become interested in him; most of them are likely to respond negatively. If he is charged and brought to court, then police, school teachers, parents, social workers and magistrates will question him about the offence and criticise his behaviour with varying degrees of harshness. The delinquent act is highlighted to the exclusion of other aspects of his life. The status he may have achieved in the eyes of his peers is countered by the disapproval of adults. Matza [5] has described the mechanism by which delinquents justify their own behaviour by attacking the inconsistent and unfair treatment they attribute to the courts, police and social workers. It is argued by those who stress the need for preventive work that the young person is less likely to welcome and embrace the aims and methods of the project when introduced to it through the criminal justice process than through some other channel.

On the other hand, it can be argued that intermediate treatment should concentrate its attention on those young offenders who are at risk of incarceration. The PSSC report, in making a recommendation for a more intensive form of intermediate treatment, highlighted the failure to develop types of intervention for the more difficult and persistently delinquent [6]. It drew attention to the rapid increase in the number of juveniles committed to Borstal, matched by a similar rise in the number sent to junior detention centres. Considering the very high failure rate of Borstals in dealing with juveniles, and the fact that many of those reconvicted are sentenced to further periods in institutions, the implications of sending juveniles to Borstal are very serious.

About the age of 17 or 18, there seems to be a trend towards natural remission, so that the occasional offender of early adolescence is more likely to have found other preoccupations, such as work, a girlfriend and other responsibilities. Institutional experience prior to this age will have inhibited this natural process by removing opportunities and blocking job prospects. For these and other reasons attributable to the criminalising process of institutions, it will also have made the young person discharged from such an institution more susceptible to further convictions. It is therefore fundamental to any policy of community based intervention that resources be directed towards keeping out of such institutions the 15 or 16 year old with four or five previous offences and ripe for a custodial sentence.

In proposing a form of intensive intermediate treatment the PSSC report stresses the need both for control, in ensuring that young offenders participate in the scheme, and for sanctions if the young person does not comply with the conditions explained to him and his family at the outset. This emphasis on control is considered justified, if it leads the courts to divert young offenders from an institutional sentence into a community based provision. It has, however, caused some conflict between those who see intermediate treatment as a last step before incarceration and those who are more concerned about preventing children from penetrating the juvenile justice system so deeply.

There are also other elements of intermediate treatment practice which appear to be more closely related to the justice than to the treatment model, and three of these will now be examined, alongside the view of delinquent behaviour to which they seem related.

'Delinquency is a Response to Boredom'

Many social workers preparing social enquiry reports are familiar with the argument, from both young defendants and their parents, that delinquency is a response to boredom. It is not necessarily related to the presence or absence of leisure facilities, but more to the social distance which prevents young offenders from using them. Davies and Gibson [7] point out that delinquents and near-delinquents are usually too hot to handle in youth clubs, and that the skills required for work with delinquent adolescents are not readily available within the youth service. This would appear to be in direct conflict with the desire expressed in the 1968 White Paper and subsequent official statements that wherever possible delinquents should be dealt with alongside their non-delinquent peers and preferably within existing facilities. Social workers who try to place young offenders in existing facilities might share Davies' and Gibson's view, finding

30

either that the youth clubs could not contain potentially disruptive members, or that those who had been so labelled and excluded previously from youth clubs would be unwilling to return.

Social workers have tended to respond by setting up activity groups primarily for young offenders on supervision orders. There seem to be two major aims of such groups: firstly to create the opportunity for individual relationships and counselling, but secondly to occupy members with a range of activities which will not only increase their interests and skills but will also remove them from the arena in which they might be committing offences. Although the length of contact involved in many projects still provides plenty of opportunity for offending, the extension of interest in a child's leisure activities has been identified by Harriet Wilson [8] as one factor in making a child less likely to offend in a delinquent neighbourhood.

The supervision of leisure time is made explicit in measures such as attendance centre orders, which are deliberately designed to remove known or potential trouble makers from the football terraces. In the United States, surveillance appears to be an important factor in developing a range of community based alternatives for young offenders. For instance, the Youth Advocates programme [9], based in Pennsylvania, requires contact between offenders referred by the courts and their volunteer advocates for a period of 15 or 30 hours per week. If intermediate treatment projects are to satisfy the courts that young offenders who would otherwise have been incarcerated can be maintained in the community, they will be expected to provide a more extensive surveillance of the leisure time activities of their members, especially at the peak periods for committing offences. To the extent that this removes the freedom to determine their own leisure activities, intermediate treatment will be meeting the demands of the justice approach to control the activities of young offenders, in such a way as to reduce their likelihood of offending.

'Delinquents Lack Moral Fibre'

The notion that delinquency is associated with a weak character has been influential in the development of earlier measures within the penal system. The march of Borstal boys in 1930 from Feltham in Middlesex to build the new, open Borstal at Lowdham, near Nottingham, was underpinned by the belief that physical challenge and endurance are essential to character building [10]. Intermediate treatment has been closely associated from the start with the Outward Bound movement, which not only provides physical challenge, but also the opportunity for teamwork and interdependence. The aims of this movement, as analysed by Roberts, fall into two main categories. The first is concerned with personal development in areas such as self-confidence and self-discipline and *to stretch trainees so that previously latent qualities of character will emerge'*. The second category aims to *'heighten trainees' awareness, sensitivity and responsiveness to the needs of others, thereby increasing their willingness to help'.* [11]

There seem to be a number of elements in the Outward Bound philosophy and method which appeal to those who adopt a justice approach. First, they involve strenuous physical activity, which even when enjoyed by the participants, is likely to be painful at times. Secondly, there has been a tendency to associate fresh air with moral reawakening. Thirdly, the courses are usually short and any changes wrought in attitude or behaviour are likely to be rapid. The difficulty seems to be in sustaining the benefits of this short, invigorating experience when the young people come down from the mountain and return to lowland, often inner city, areas of Britain. The opportunities for continuing either the experience or the activities in their own community are often rather remote. Moreover, the values which may be temporarily transmitted are usually middle class ones, and may not survive the transition to the indigenous culture, where other more powerful and immediate forces operate to re-emphasise the old values.

'Delinquents Ought to Repay Society'

The notion of reparation is a key element in our penal system, and for a long time courts have been able to order compensation to be paid by the offender to the victim. However, this concept was cast in a new light by the introduction of community service orders under the 1972 Criminal Justice Act. One reason why this measure has gained wide public support is that it combines an element of punishment, in terms of loss of free time and hard, unpaid labour, with the notion of repaying a debt to society. From the offender's view point, it avoids a prison sentence, which the offence may have warranted. It also has definite time limits set by the court, and offers the chance to provide a positive service which might enable the offender to shake off his criminal label.

It has been suggested that community service orders should be extended to include juveniles. In this case, a further step would be placed in the tariff to block the persistent offender's progression towards a residential institution. Within the framework of intermediate treatment, there is scope for developing community service that can be matched to the potential of those offering it. Motivation, which is crucial to its success, can be developed and sustained, so that there is a greater chance of providing a service of some quality and consistency. The advocates of community service emphasise the opportunities for the offender to adopt new, non-deviant roles; however, the primary aim, as seen by society and the courts, is that of reparation through enforced and unpaid labour.

Each of the approaches described above is directed at either controlling or changing the delinquent's behaviour. They are not necessarily punitive in intent, but insofar as they restrict individual freedom or make other demands on his time and behaviour, they require the sanction of the courts, which also have a responsibility to protect the individual from unjustified intervention by social control agencies.

It is at this point that the conservative ideology and the more radical supporters of children's rights meet. For some time in the United States and more recently in Britain, there has been increasing concern that the rights of children, including young offenders, are being infringed by the discretion and power, granted to social welfare agencies, to make decisions affecting the incarceration of children placed in their care by the courts. Decisions made under care orders relating to the type of establishment and the length of stay are not subject to review by the courts, except where the child or his parents or the local authority apply for a revocation of the order. It is argued that such decisions, made on an assessment of the child's needs and his response to the treatment prescribed, do not necessarily take account of the seriousness of his offence, nor the child's best interests as perceived by himself. Although this concern with children's rights might lead to a different conclusion from those who wish to punish or control young offenders, both parties would prefer a system of juvenile justice, based on clearly established procedures and the protection of individual rights, to the treatment approach which places the crucial decision making power in the hands of professionals.

THE TREATMENT APPROACH

The treatment approach is based on the assumption that the young offender is not fully responsible for his actions under a certain age. This has long been recognised by the English legal system, in that it must be proved that a child is capable of forming an intent to commit an offence. Below the age of ten, it is assumed that a child is not capable of such intent. For those over the minimum age of criminal responsibility, it has been possible to argue, although in relatively rare cases, that a person is unfit to plead, usually on the grounds of mental disorder. Toby[12] has argued that society needs to punish those who deviate from its norms in order to reward the majority who conform. Crime is seen as a deliberate flouting of social norms. However, if a person can be shown not to be capable of such a deliberate act, punishment can be waived, and instead he may receive treatment. The primary objective of this is also to produce conformity to society's norms, but by more humane means.

The difficulty posed in relation to young offenders is that of determining at what age and to what degree the individual is responsible for his actions. Those who support a 'treatment' approach argue that delinquency is often directly related either to an unstable home environment or to a disadvantaged community, and that the individual offender is not responsible for either. Thus, he should be dealt with in a similar manner to those who may display other forms of social deprivation. The argument may go further in that society has a responsibility to protect its young members at times from their own parents, and that if the home or family relationships are deemed to be counter-productive to the development of the child, he might be removed from home, less for the actual offence, and more because of the circumstances which enquiries related to the offence have uncovered. Such a child may be kept away from his home for a longer period than the offence itself would warrant, if this can be shown to be 'in the child's best interests'.

A fundamental tenet of the treatment approach is that the causes of an individual's behaviour can be identified by systematic assessment of individual and family pathology. The White Paper, *Children in Trouble,* indicated some of the causes of more serious or persistent offending: *'Sometimes it is a response to unsatisfactory family or social circumstances...., an indication of maladjustment or immaturity, or a symptom of a deviant, damaged personality'.* [13]

Rather than advocating a more punitive response to the more serious young offender, the architects of the White Paper encouraged the development of a treatment approach through the replacement of the approved school order by the new care order, which placed the responsibility for individualised treatment programmes in the hands of the professional staff involved. While the former approved school order was indeterminate, minimum and maximum periods were set, and the review of the individual's progress was subject to some external monitoring. The care order is more firmly based on the treatment model in that it continues until the eighteenth birthday unless revoked earlier, and the child's placement and the length of stay is entirely dependent on the evaluation by residential and field social workers of the child's progress, and their assessment of the readiness of his home for the child's return.

Intermediate treatment is presumed to fall largely within the orbit of the treatment model. Its philosophy and many of its aims, like the name itself, would suggest such a fit, and the discretion of the supervisor in placing the young person in an appropriate facility at the 'right time' strengthens the link. In addition, intermediate treatment is primarily the responsibility of social service departments and carried out to a considerable extent by social workers. The development of social work theory and methods and the training of social workers have been strongly associated with the treatment model. Thus there is a professional frame of reference which tends to perceive delinquency in pathological terms and treatment as the appropriate response to handling young offenders.

Individual Counselling

Given the discouraging evidence of research studies on the effectiveness of individual counselling with young offenders, intermediate treatment was seen as an opportunity for creative relationship therapy with adolescents in a more informal, relaxed environment, where some of the barriers created by court orders could begin to be dismantled. The emphasis, however, was still very much on the individual relationship between young person and adult. The activities, sometimes the whole programme, were seen as a vehicle to the achievement of a better relationship.

But to what end? Firstly, it is argued that certain types of behaviour can be learnt by direct modelling. This process would operate through imitation of certain adult behaviour which was clearly specified. Other less explicit forms of modelling occur as children adopt some of the attitudes of those adults whom they respect. Secondly, intermediate treatment offers scope for individual counselling, especially where the worker is also involved in work with the child's family. The child will often use the relaxed atmosphere of residential living or an informal activity, to share his thoughts with an adult and to seek guidance. Many practitioners emphasise the value of the relationship itself in providing support, control and stimulus to supplement the parental role, which is often inadequately fulfilled in the child's own home.

Recent trends in social work thinking have moved away from long term supportive casework to shorter periods of intervention, based on a mutually agreed plan of work with the client[14]. This approach involves the client more fully in a joint effort to resolve the problems presented. Similar principles have been applied to work with young offenders through intermediate treatment: at the point of entry a plan would be worked out between the supervisor, the child and parents, and the project worker, as to what should be achieved by involvement in the project; and this can then be used as a basis for evaluation of the child's progress. While this method places the client in a stronger position, and allows him to participate in the choice of objectives, it is based on the assumption that worker and client together will move towards the kind of behaviour change or self-control which will match the requirements of courts and social work agencies which sanction the project.

One type of individual work which is not based on the treatment approach is that where the supervisor places the young person in contact with a volunteer who will share some interest or leisure activity or teach him some particular skill.

Although recommended by central government in its guidelines [15] as a valuable form of intermediate treatment, this method is still under-used, perhaps because it does not fit the treatment model. It would, however, help in broadening the horizons and enriching the life of the young person—two aims of the social education approach, which will be developed in a later section.

Family Intervention

Social work has moved steadily over the last 20 years towards a family based service. This was given official backing by the Ingleby report [16], which emphasised the need to maintain the family unit intact, and recommended that the local authority should be able to spend money to that end. The Seebohm report had at its core the need to provide services to support the family in times of stress [17]. This was matched by the increasing involvement of social workers with the whole family, rather than individual members, and the extension of family casework methods beyond the specialised agencies which had pioneered them.

In some ways, intermediate treatment could be seen as a reversal of the trend towards family based work. It provides a direct meeting ground between social workers and their young clients, away from the confines of home and office, and even in its less intensive forms it provides much more such contact than the average supervision order. Although a number of schemes have stressed the need for the same worker to be involved with the child in the group and the family at home, for varying reasons this pattern remains the exception rather than the rule.

What, then, is the link between the intermediate treatment programme and the families of its participants? If one adopts the view that the causes of delinquent behaviour are rooted in the interaction between family members, then it would seem logical to concentrate agency resources on resolving intra-family conflict and improving the delinquent child's position within the family. Family casework would be used as the primary interventive strategy. On the other hand, where the pressures and conflicts imposed by the family are excessive, intermediate treatment might be seen as a temporary refuge.

A different approach may be required where the child's delinquency and other forms of behaviour have created conflict in the family. Where the major problem is one of control, or lack of it, and a breakdown of communication occurs between parents and children, the worker often faces the dilemma that the parents are likely to be more hostile to the project, the more their child identifies with it. In such cases attendance at group meetings or residential weekends becomes a carrot or a stick to demand compliance at home. The parents are likely to be critical of permissiveness by the workers and make charges that their children are more difficult to handle as a result of their involvement. In response to this, the worker may find himself in the role of mediator between child and parents. Especially where the child has been involved in residential forms of intermediate treatment, the workers and the parents share the common experience of handling and, at times, controlling the behaviour of the child. Workers who are involved in both residential and family casework emphasise the advantages this gives them in working within the family.

Where delinquency is seen as resulting from the economic and social disadvantages of the environment in which the family lives, then both parents and children are afflicted by the same disadvantages. These might well lead to

35

apathy or lack of energy to bring about change. On the other hand, parents and their children might be involved through the project in bringing about some change, however marginal, to their shared environment. This approach to family intervention clearly differs from those where delinquency is seen in terms of individual or family pathology.

The Influence of Residential Work

The development of special residential establishments for young offenders in the nineteenth century was not only aimed at separating juveniles from adult offenders, but was also designed to rescue children from unsatisfactory homes and 'tainted' families. Carlebach [18], in his study of approved schools, examines the effect of treating children as maladjusted or abnormal in what he calls 'moral hospitals', in that they need to look towards others, similarly labelled, for models of identification. Young delinquents, entering such institutions, were seen to have a faulty system of social norms, transmitted from their parents. These were removed through the reception procedures, which stripped them of external links with their home and community, and began the long, but often successful, process of imposing the institution's own value system on the child.

In contrast, the therapeutic community attempts to establish a set of norms which can be accepted by all members as a means of governing the life of the community. David Wills [19] has attempted to apply therapeutic community principles to work with young offenders. He argues that it is wrong to emphasise the damaging effects of early childhood experiences to the point that the individual is so constrained by his background that he is unable to determine his present behaviour or future development. There is clearly nothing that can be done to change the past; far better, therefore, to emphasise the ability of the individual to take responsibility for the present and begin to shape his future. **Members are encouraged to demonstrate their freedom** *'to rise above the bonds enslaving them'*, **and determine their own affairs within the community.** Although the community meeting is the focal point of the therapeutic community, mutual trust and interdependence must be welded through sharing a living environment and through reciprocal acts of caring for each other's needs.

It would be wrong to give the impression that either of these models is typical of residential work, but it is interesting that intermediate treatment, in its desire to rescue children from the type of 'moral hospital' Carlebach describes, has drawn from residential work some of the principles of therapeutic community practice. Recent trends in residential work towards short term, planned treatment with strong contact with the home and neighbourhood have made the distinction between residential work and certain types of intermediate treatment rather less clear.

Residential work practice has reflected the conflicting ideologies outlined in Chapter 1. The conservative ideology urges the removal of children from a society in which they are seen as disruptive, and wants to control or change them into conforming citizens. On the other hand, liberal influence is seen in the emphasis on assessment, individual treatment plans and in a more caring, or, to the conservative, a more permissive way of handling children in residential care.

Group Work

Most traditional approaches to group work with adolescents are based on the

36

application of therapeutic techniques used in adult groups, which tend to start from the assumption that the individual brings problems to the group and hopes to gain support and guidance in their resolution. The workers attempt to create an environment in which freedom of participation is encouraged and a reciprocal caring between all members is emphasised. The adolescent is often searching for an identity and an assurance of acceptance, which a supportive group can provide.

Of the several approaches to group work used in the caring professions, Button [20] proposes a structured learning programme, emphasising the importance of placing members of the group in a strong, responsible position. The programme is based on the principle that experiential learning from peers is likely to be more effective than direct teaching by adults. The focus is the self-development of the adolescent, and is based on the assumption that more will be achieved by developing the potential strengths of the members, than concentrating on the pathological nature of their problems.

A directive, treatment oriented approach is drawn from the behaviourist school of psychology. Rose [21] argues that a children's group offers more opportunities for observing and therefore reinforcing adaptive social behaviour, and is more appropriate than individual behaviour modification in response to social malfunctioning. He also argues that the reinforcement of positive behaviour can be strengthened by the use of group pressure, where the maximum rewards are only obtained if all the group members achieve the behavioural targets set. Intermediate treatment groups offer scope for such a behavioural approach, in addition to the modelling of adult behaviour, which seems to feature among the aims of many projects.

Group counselling, another feature of many projects, seems to have two major objectives. One is to help members share and receive help with problems based on family and other personal relationships; the other is to focus the group's attention on the behaviour and relationships demonstrated in the group and, by a process of reflection and at times confrontation, to help members increase their awareness of their impact on others. Some workers, who adopt a psycho-dynamic explanation of problem behaviour, may concentrate on developing insight and reflection in their group members. Others, who regard the same difficulties as part of the normal maturational process, would tend to concentrate on present relationships and observed behaviour, and seek through the learning experiences presented by the group to facilitate growth and maturity. While some of these types of group work fit comfortably under a 'treatment' label, others belong much more to the social education approach.

EDUCATIONAL APPROACHES
Social Education

'Social education' has long been regarded as the primary focus of the youth service, though it has had to compete with other demands made on the service, and has been interpreted in many different ways. Some of the prime concerns of social education were identified by Davies and Gibson in 1967: *'It is about the interaction of human beings, about their friendships and enmities, about the way these are deepened and extended and about their consequences. Its product therefore is any individual's increased consciousness of himself — of his values, aptitudes and untapped resources, and of the relevance of these to others. It enhances the individual's understanding of how to form mutually satisfying relationships.'* [22] This reflects the primary concern with the personal development and interpersonal relationships of young people in the 1960s. Although this might well be seen as the primary task today, there has been a growing concern in the 1970s with collective outcomes. In a period of high youth unemployment and continuing powerlessness, a concentration on individual development is seen as less relevant and perhaps counter-productive. Political education, increasing youth consciousness and greater involvement by youth in decisions affecting themselves are now seen as important components of social education [23].

The impact of this latter approach on intermediate treatment is at present limited, chiefly to concern and action in response to local social and political issues, but the concerns which Davies and Gibson identified for social education are certainly ones espoused by intermediate treatment practitioners. The White Paper, *Children in Trouble,* stressed the importance of handling as many young offenders as possible within their own communities, alongside their peers. Central government guidance to regional planning authorities [24] led to the wholesale inclusion of youth facilities in the early lists of intermediate treatment facilities. This policy was based on the principle that delinquent behaviour is a normal part of adolescent development, and that separating those who happen to be caught from others who are not, is likely to stigmatise the processed offender and, according to labelling theory, increase his chances of further offending.

The fact that the youth service has played a fairly minor role in the development of intermediate treatment seems due less to differences of philosophy or method, and more to organisational factors. Many young offenders have been members of youth clubs before their referral to intermediate treatment. They may have been seen as disruptive, or as a result of their offending, been excluded from the club; but in either case, the club would be seen, along with school, courts and social work agencies, as contributing to the labelling process. Many social workers have abandoned the potential resources available through the youth service for this and other reasons, and have tended to establish parallel provisions for smaller groups of problem youth. However, within these groups, they pursue similar objectives and use similar methods, sometimes with staff who have brought their experience and expertise from the youth service. For example, participation in decision making by members of the group in order to develop a sense of responsibility and an ability to influence events, seems to be drawn directly from the social education philosophy.

Compensatory Education

The Plowden Report [25] identified the links between poor educational attainment, the lack of parental stimulus and interest and the absence of adequate educational, social and recreational facilities in certain areas. In making its proposals to combat these deficiences, it recognised the principle of positive discrimination, in that extra resources should be diverted into such communities to compensate for the high incidence of negative factors, inhibiting the intellectual and social development of children.

As the 1968 White Paper stressed that juvenile delinquency was one symptom of social deprivation, it was a logical extension of this policy to provide

38

compensatory experiences *'to bring the young person into contact with a new environment, and to secure his participation in some constructive activity'.* [26] The DHSS Guide went further in saying that *'the purpose of the court in imposing an intermediate treatment requirement will have been to use the opportunity presented . . . to enrich the child's environment and assist his development'.* [27]

The compensatory approach extends beyond an introduction to new experiences and activities. Some schemes, especially those which offer more intensive contact, provide additional support and care to that received at home. Thus, when parents who have difficulty in coping with the demands of a large family are unable to provide adequate stimulus or encouragement to their older children, intermediate treatment staff working closely with the family may be able to supplement the parental role, so that the child can be maintained in his own home and community.

This approach raises the crucial issues as to whether delinquency is synonymous with other forms of deprivation. In practice, other adults in contact with the young offender, such as teachers, police and often parents, question the validity of an approach which apparently rewards the young offender by offering opportunities which may be denied to other children who have not been before the courts. If, as recent research has confirmed [28], occasional excursions into delinquent activity are normal for most adolescents, the issue is whether those who have been processed by the legal system should be singled out for special treatment.

If delinquency is seen primarily as a response from the adolescent who is frustrated at his lack of ability to succeed in an educational and career selection process which is unfairly loaded against him, then opening up closed doors and providing new opportunities for educational and social achievement may be seen as an appropriate response. It is, however, prudent to recognise that whereas society may recognise the value of positive discrimination for the handicapped and even the poor, it is notoriously difficult to gain a similar reaction to the offender, whatever his age.

THE SOCIAL CHANGE APPROACH

As one moves away from the notion of delinquency as a disease which affects certain individuals, and towards explanations based on social and economic factors, more attention is paid to the environment rather than the individual personality. The notion of treatment, in its medical sense, becomes inappropriate and misleading. The worker is more likely to see the individual offender as someone who is caught up in a changing web of family, peer and environmental pressures.

Perhaps the most damaging aspect of the criminal process is the alienation of the young offender from the majority of adults in his own community. As the responsibility for intervention is removed from the local community into official and often centralised authorities such as the police and social services, so it becomes increasingly difficult to persuade neighbours and community leaders to adopt anything other than a negative approach to offenders. Even community work projects which have been aimed specifically at delinquency prevention have found that conflicts have developed between the interests of the majority of adult residents and those of the minority group of juvenile offenders, who are seen as at worst a menace, and at best, a group which has less to worry about in terms of housing, financial and other material problems. Where local adults have been engaged with young offenders and especially where common concerns of the young people and adults in the community have been pursued, Leissner, Powley and Evans found that joint participation was a practical proposition resulting in productive work. [29]

The other side of community involvement starts from initiatives taken by the young people. The purpose of community service within intermediate treatment programmes has already been considered. A rather different approach is that of increasing the young person's awareness of the political, social and economic factors which affect the environment in which he lives. He might initially regard himself as powerless to influence his own environment in the face of strong forces of authority, which appear unapproachable or hostile. The long term aim of this approach would be to enable the young person to develop confidence and skill in his ability to handle difficulties which confronted him, and to see the potential in joint action with other members of the community who share a common concern. In the short term, by emphasising the positive strengths which the individual contributes to a shared task, the degree of stigma associated with his offending and criminal processing is reduced.

A further target for social change is the organisation sponsoring the intermediate treatment project. Where the practice and procedures of the agency reinforce negative perceptions of authority, the staff of the project, by reducing the distance between themselves and the children served by it, may identify targets for change within their own organisation. Equally, workers may find themselves advocating or mediating between their members and other agencies of social control, and as a result are likely to identify factors in those agencies which appear to be amplifying rather than reducing the anti-social behaviour with which they are concerned.

CONCLUSION

This chapter has attempted to explore various strands of thinking and experience which have contributed to the practice of intermediate treatment. That these strands are at times conflicting is not in question. As Parsloe states, *'The juvenile justice system provides a meeting place for the different approaches of criminal justice, welfare and the community . . . the system has to balance the child's rights against his needs and society's right to protection against its need for individuals who have developed to their full potential'* [30]. Intermediate treatment reflects this uneasy balance in its philosophy and aims. When it over-emphasises the welfare or treatment approach to the exclusion of the justice approach, it is likely that courts will direct children who are less seriously delinquent, but who are recognised as needing help in coping with a hostile environment. Those who have set out to tackle the more persistently delinquent have recognised the need to gain the confidence of the courts and to give attention to ways of decelerating delinquent careers. Where the emphasis is placed on a community approach, the role of the worker is more that of a catalyst, creating opportunities for young offenders to be integrated into their own community.

40

References

1   For a rather different classification of the roots of intermediate treatment, see: Tutt N. (1976), 'The development of intermediate treatment', *Social Work Service*, No. 11, pp.3-8.
2   Schur E.M. (1973), *Radical non-intervention: Rethinking the delinquency problem,* Englewood Cliffs, N.J. and London: Prentice Hall.
3   Home Office (1968), *Children in trouble,* Government White Paper, Cmnd. 3601, London: HMSO, para. 25, p.9.
4   Personal Social Services Council (1977), *A future for intermediate treatment: Report of the Intermediate Treatment Study Group* (Chairman: Mia Kellmer Pringle), London: PSSC.
5   Matza D. (1964), *Delinquency and drift,* New York and London: Wiley.
6   Personal Social Services Council, *op. cit.,* p.39.
7   Davies B. and Gibson A. (1967), *Social education of the adolescent,* London: University of London Press.
8   Wilson H. and Herbert G.W. (1978), *Parents and children in the inner city,* London: Routledge and Kegan Paul.
9   From an unpublished programme statement by Youth Advocates, Inc., Harrisburg, Pennsylvania.
10 Hood R. (1965), *Borstal re-assessed,* London: Heinemann, pp.114-120.
11 Roberts K., White G.F. and Parker H.J. (1974), *The character training industry: Adventure-training schemes in Britain,* Newton Abbott: David and Charles, pp.65,67.
12 Toby J. (1970) 'Is punishment necessary?' in Johnston N., Savitz L. and Wolfgang M.E. (eds.), *The sociology of punishment and correction,* New York and Chichester: Wiley, 2nd rev. ed., pp.362-369.
13 Home Office, *op. cit.,* para.6, p.4.
14 See for example, Reid W.J. and Shyne A.W. (1969), *Brief and extended casework,* New York and London: Columbia University Press.
15 Department of Health and Social Security (1972), *Intermediate treatment: A guide to the regional planning of new forms of treatment for children in trouble,* London HMSO.
16 *Report of the Committee on children and Young Persons* (Ingleby Report), (1960), Cmnd. 1191, London: HMSO.
17 *Report of the Committee on Local Authority and Allied Personal Social Services* (Seebohm Report), (1968), Cmnd. 3703, London: HMSO.
18 Carlebach J. (1970), *Caring for children in trouble,* London: Routledge and Kegan Paul.
19 Wills D.W. (1971), *A place like home: A pioneer hostel for boys,* London: Allen and Unwin.
20 Button L. (1974), *Developmental group work with adolescents,* London: London University Press.
21 Rose S. (1973), *Treating children in groups: A behavioural approach,* San Francisco: Jossey Bass.
22 Davies B. and Gibson A., *op. cit.,* p.12.
23 Davies B. (1979), *In whose interests? From social education to social and life skills training,* Leicester: National Youth Bureau.
24 DHSS, *op. cit.*
25 *Children and their primary schools: A report of the Central Advisory Council for Education* (Plowden Report), (1967), London: HMSO.
26 Home Office, *op. cit.,* para.26, p.10.
27 DHSS, *op. cit.,* p.14.
28 Belson W. (1975), *Juvenile theft: The casual factors,* London: Harper and Row.
29 Leissner A., Powley T. and Evans D. (1977), *Intermediate treatment: A community-based action-research study,* London: National Children's Bureau.
30 Parsloe P. (1978), *Juvenile justice in Britain and the USA,* London: Routledge and Kegan Paul.

CHAPTER 3
DEVELOPMENTS ON THE GROUND

INTRODUCTION

The way that intermediate treatment has actually developed on the ground during the 1970s has been determined not only by the social policy considerations and value orientations discussed in previous chapters, but also by organisational factors in local government, relations between the different agencies involved, and the attitudes and skills of workers. So the purpose of this chapter is to throw some light on the way these various influences have combined to affect provision, and to describe the various forms that intermediate treatment has taken up and down the country, so that the reader has a framework within which he can place the six case studies which form the core of this book.

Local Government Reorganisation

Whenever new legislation has resource implications, it invariably creates problems. It is not so much that the politicians, central or local, naïvely or cynically refuse to acknowledge the cost of change, but that they tend to operate pragmatically, usually after an experimental period in which new methods are required to prove themselves in adverse and inadequately resourced conditions. The notion that money might actually be made available prior to legislation so that adequate preparations could be made for its effective implementation is completely foreign, and consequently there is a sense in which the timing of legislation is always inopportune. Nonetheless the juxtaposition of a number of major pieces of legislation within a very short period of time did have a devastating effect.

Although the 1969 Act implied a greater emphasis on treating young people in the community and the need to obtain the active participation of the community in their rehabilitation, it was always anticipated that the children's departments would mastermind these developments. Indeed such public confidence as existed about the direction of child care policy and the effectiveness of new methods rested almost entirely on the successful reputation of these departments and the skills situated in them. It is now a matter of historical record, but nonetheless traumatic for that, that within three months of the Act coming into operation in January 1971, these same departments were dissolved and the personnel absorbed into the much larger social services departments, established by the Social Services Act, 1970. The creation of these new departments, with the responsibility for providing an awe-inspiring range of services, but inevitably preoccupied with establishing a cohesive and effective organisation, meant that the opportunities inherent in the child care legislation were not grasped with the alacrity that might otherwise have been expected. Furthermore, as if this upheaval was insufficient, it was followed by local government reorganisation, affecting both boundaries and powers, in 1974. These two major structural changes, combined with the expansion of the social work profession on a previously unparalleled scale, led to an acute shortage of experienced staff and meant that the actual implementation of the 1969 Act had to be entrusted to a largely inexperienced, rather 'shellshocked' and inadequately supported group of young workers.

Regional Planning

The 12 children's regional planning committees, set up in England and Wales by the 1969 Act, were the direct result of one of those compromises for which the British are well known. The Act represented, among other things, a significant devolution of power from the Home Office to the local authorities, particularly in relation to the administration of the former approved schools. These now became part of the community homes or residential child care system, and known as community homes with education on the premises, or CHEs for short. Most of the establishments had been set up by philanthropically minded Victorians, and consequently were not evenly distributed on a geographical basis. The fear was that, given the established phenomenon of local authorities taking their boundaries rather seriously, unrestricted devolution might mean that those authorities which inherited CHEs might fail to share them with other, less fortunate authorities. In view of the political reasons for the existence of these planning committees, it is hardly surprising that they devoted most of their energies to integrating the former approved schools into the community homes system. They did also have the task of preparing regional schemes of intermediate treatment, but these were tackled later and not completed until 1973 and 1974.

Nonetheless the simple, and apparently unimportant, decision to ask these committees to produce a plan for the community homes system separately and prior to the intermediate treatment system probably had a significant effect on the allocation of resources and the development of community care. Prior to the passing of the Act, the debate about the future of the approved school system led to its being starved of resources. Although some attempt was made to consider alternatives, the poor condition of the inheritance combined with the anxiety about 'difficult to place' adolescents almost inevitably led, particularly in a period of economic expansion, to the channelling of additional resources in the direction of residential care. Furthermore, with so much emphasis on treating the child rather than punishing the offender, one of the most immediate impacts of the legislation was an increase in the importance attached to assessment. Given the range and complexity of the child care system, it seemed patently absurd to determine placement and treatment method before undertaking a thorough investigation of the child's needs. While ritual genuflections were made in the direction of assessment within the community and peripatetic assessment teams, the planners clung to the existing model of residential assessment and initiated a massive expansion programme.

It should not be thought that social workers were any less enthusiastic than their senior managers about this building programme. Indeed, one of the many ironies is that social workers, trained to assess the needs of their clients, if nothing else, seemed so keen to have this responsibility discharged by a largely untrained group of residential workers. It may be that social workers only pretended to need residential assessment, being aware that this subterfuge was the price that had to be paid for a breathing space and, eventually, a reasonably appropriate residential placement. Certainly the former approved schools were accustomed to a screening process carried out within a residential context, namely the classifying schools, and fought hard for this safeguard to be retained in their negotiations with local authorities. Whatever the reason, the expansion of the number of residential assessment places created a vicious circle, and led to demands for more residential outlets to absorb the increased throughput. Theoretically, residential assessment did not imply residential placement; but research at Fairfield Lodge and elsewhere has shown that there could be residential, as well as criminal, careers; that residential workers were likely to be more convinced than field social workers about the value of residential care, and consequently placement in residential assessment increased the chances of that child being retained within some part of the community homes system [1].

When it came to the actual schemes of intermediate treatment, the regional planning committees were harshly criticised for producing long lists of existing community facilities, such as youth clubs, Scout groups and outdoor pursuits centres [2]. While this may have been a little naïve and shown a lack of imagination, there can be little doubt that this was in line not only with the guidance offered by the DHSS [3], but also with at least one interpretation of community care. After all, this implied not only that the community would be prepared to tolerate deviants within its midst, but would also become actively involved in their rehabilitation through methods which did not isolate them from their more law abiding peers.

AGENCIES AND THEIR ROLES
The Youth Service

Broadly speaking the social services departments, grappling with a wide range of new demands, were only too willing to accept this advice and collude with the notion that at least one of their tasks could be undertaken largely by the youth service. Particularly during the early stages, any pretensions that intermediate treatment had towards being a non-stigmatising, community based service depended to a very considerable extent on the youth service. In view of all this and the fact that intermediate treatment was heralded as a great new opportunity for co-operation between a number of agencies concerned with children and young people, it does seem germane to ask why this hope has remained largely unfulfilled. In fact, it could be argued that, by raising expectations, it has led to a worsening of relationships and served to highlight the difficulties lying in the way of co-operation. [4]

Initially, there is little doubt that much goodwill on both sides was dissipated through confusion. Too much discussion took place in a vacuum of ignorance. Social workers were unable to describe the needs of those who might be referred, simply because they were unclear about both the nature of the facilities being offered and the use which the courts might or might not make of this new provision. Equally youth workers found it difficult to describe the service they could offer until they had a more definite idea of the resources that would be made available to them and the nature of the young people they would be asked to help. As time went on, it became increasingly apparent to social workers that young people, for whom supervision alone was insufficient, would rarely have the social controls and skills necessary to survive, let alone take advantage of, most youth service provision. The youth service was divided. There were some youth workers who were convinced that they were already meeting the needs of young delinquents, and saw no need for formalising the existing arrangements or for adapting the service they were providing. There were others who feared that they could be overwhelmed by unrealistic expectations, or seduced into being a social or even a penal service as opposed to an educational one, and these sought to limit their involvement by concentrating on such issues as compulsion and confidentiality. Finally there was a significant number who saw intermediate treatment as an opportunity to gain both additional resources and greater recognition for the service.

Apart from the misgivings of both youth and social workers, one of the other factors which tended to limit the participation of the youth service was the expectation of most magistrates that intermediate treatment would represent a tangible advance on existing provision. They were not impressed by schemes which involved little more than attaching a new and glamorous term to conventional and long established facilities, which had previously failed to prevent the continuing rise in juvenile delinquency. So, rightly or wrongly, in spite of all the original rhetoric, intermediate treatment has depended almost entirely for its development on special provision by social and probation services. This has tended to take the form of social group work, where normally two or three workers are involved with eight to 12 youngsters, on the basis of either a weekly session or short term residential work. It is clearly quite possible for youth workers to set up or share in groups of this kind. Indeed it has been, and is being, done. However, while the primary task of the youth service remains the provision of recreational facilities combined with social education for the whole of the adolescent population, it has proved very difficult for the vast majority of youth workers to justify spending a fifth of their time on the equivalent of three young people, which is approximately the amount of time involved in much current social work practice.

It is sometimes argued that this form of intermediate treatment represents an expensive kind of overkill, particularly when used for children merely at risk of becoming delinquent, and that equally good results could be obtained by the youth service using more traditional methods. However this has yet to be proved and, in the absence of hard evidence, there does not seem to be any immediate prospect of either social workers or magistrates being persuaded. Unfortunately when the anticipated flow of referrals failed to materialise, some youth workers interpreted this as a vote of no confidence in their service in general and their skills in particular. Except in rare cases, this slight was never intended. It was in fact the result of a rather belated recognition by the social services of the constraints within which the youth service presently has to operate [5]. Interestingly, the immediate effect of the financial cutbacks which local authorities have been experiencing to a lesser or greater extent since 1974, was for statutory agencies to retreat into their traditional areas of work, rather than increase their mutual co-operation. Where there is virtually nil growth, money can only be found for intermediate treatment at the expense of other parts of the service, and it is this pressure which has forced social services to think increasingly about intermediate treatment as an alternative to residential care as opposed to an additional preventive service. To the extent that this policy is translated into practice, it seems unlikely that the youth service will have much of a contribution to make. On the other hand, this change in emphasis and the recognition that intermediate treatment is only cheap in comparison to residential care, could lead to a re-opening of the whole question of the youth service's role, and its potential contribution in the areas of prevention and after care, which need to be offered if intermediate treatment is to avoid creating an unrelated vacuum for itself. The tragedy is that misunderstanding, confused thinking and rivalry have so far prevented this from being fully appreciated by either service.

The Voluntary Sector

One of the interesting paradoxes is that, although the reliance on the youth service was misplaced and the army of volunteers was never recruited to participate with one or two children in such activities as fishing and motorcycle maintenance, a significant contribution has been made by the voluntary sector. Most of the policy makers expected that it would be existing community facilities that would reach out to include and help those who had previously been considered beyond the pale. In fact it was a number of small charities, set up specifically for the purpose, and some of the larger, traditional voluntary child care organisations, which have actually made the greatest impact. It is true that, with local authority cutbacks on expenditure, many of the larger voluntary bodies have been faced with a serious financial problem. However it is to their credit that they have pioneered a number of imaginative new projects, models from which local authorities have frequently borrowed, and that they have largely eschewed the soft option of using the same residential staff to operate the same regime over a shorter period. So the importance of the voluntary sector has not been so much in the number of projects or the amount of money spent as in the pioneering role which it has adopted both before and more particularly since the Act. It is no accident that voluntary organisations are over represented in the case studies which have been selected to form the heart of this book.

The Probation Service

It is a widely appreciated paradox that the more similar organisations are, the more difficult they often find it to work closely together. At the beginning of the 1970s, the probation service was subjected to two diametrically opposed pressures. On the one hand, joint training courses for both social workers and probation officers had been established throughout the country, and this increasingly meant that probation officers saw themselves as social workers rather than officers of the court. On the other hand, they had decided not to follow the example of their Scottish colleagues (covered by separate legislation), and opt into the new, large, all embracing social services departments being set up as a result of the Seebohm Report. At the same time, they were under some pressure to focus their attention on the adult offender and to identify their service more closely with the courts and the penal system.

Inevitably over the years there has been some sibling rivalry between the longer established probation service and the more recently formed child care service. The combined effects of Seebohm and the 1969 Act served to heighten this natural competition. Initially while the social services departments were attracting most of the media attention and most of the resources which they were partially designed to command, there were many in the probation service who wondered whether they had made the wrong decision. Previously the children's departments and the child care profession had made a considerable impact on both the general public and the policy makers. It was this success, and the concept that juvenile delinquents had been artificially separated from other children in difficulties, which gave rise to the policy that all children and young people should be made the responsibility of one agency, namely the children's and later the social services departments.

The ambivalence of the probation service is partially explained by the uncertainty over its role and the fact that it did not want to make an unseemly bid for the juvenile field, particularly when it looked as if the decision had already been taken and that it had lost that particular battle. The irony is that just as it had largely come to terms with its new role and was preparing itself for work exclusively in the adult field, the social services departments decided that they did not have the resources, and some would add the experience, to assume total responsibility for all juvenile offenders immediately. Consequently, nearly ten years later the matter still remains to be resolved, and the probation service continues to undertake about half of all social enquiry reports for, and supervision orders made on, young offenders [6]. With their long tradition behind them, it is not altogether surprising that some probation officers felt that they had been engaged in intermediate treatment in all but name for some time. In fact, although some group work was being undertaken, the greater part of practice in the probation service consisted of sending young people on courses at outdoor pursuits centres and participating with them on a week's camp in the summer. On the other hand social services departments expressed doubt about the value of strenuous outdoor activities, and were often reluctant to finance attendance on expensive courses. It is probably also fair to say that social services departments, initially at least, placed much more emphasis on integrating group work with casework supervision. This led to supervisors engaging in intermediate treatment with their own clients as opposed to the previously more common practice of sending them to resources provided by others.

Against this backcloth, it was possibly a mistake to fund intermediate treatment exclusively through social services departments, and this discouraged both the youth and probation services from making their anticipated contribution. The difference of approach between the probation and social services may not have been large; but this did not alter the fact that the senior service was and is placed in the invidious position of preparing projects and submitting them for approval and finance to the younger, increasingly powerful, service with the resources. Admittedly there were parts of the country where block grants were made available to the probation service, but this was not common. Money can be relied upon to put most relationships under strain. Probation officers had been accustomed to raising money for camps by approaching small charitable trusts, local industry and speaking at Rotary lunches. So there was some resentment that finance would be made available now that the major responsibility had been assumed by another agency; but much more importantly, many failed to appreciate the length of time it takes in any large local government department between the birth of an idea, the submission of estimates and the actual availability of the money. Nonetheless, in spite of all the difficulties, the probation service still makes a real contribution. It is very rare for the service to employ specialists, but, apart from a tendency to place greater emphasis on outdoor activities, probation officers run groups along very similar lines to social workers.

The Social Services

The slow development of intermediate treatment can be attributed in part to reorganisation, lack of resources and the unwillingness or inability of some agencies to make their anticipated contribution, but this is by no means the whole story. Intermediate treatment offered a challenge and an opportunity for expansion to the social work profession but it also flowed from a recognition of the limits of casework supervision alone for many inarticulate, alienated adolescents, and it did represent a criticism of the failure of children's departments to make more imaginative use of the discretionary powers given to them under the Children and Young Persons Act, 1963. In analysing changes in social policy, Hall and colleagues suggest that central government is strongly influenced by the interaction between legitimacy, feasibility and support, and the extent to which any reform passes this threefold test [7]. This framework offers some interesting insights which are equally applicable to local government departments and helps to explain why intermediate treatment, which was surely intended to be one of the major strategies for dealing with young offenders and other children in difficulties, remains so far a peripheral activity in most social services departments.

There is a general sense in which many social workers question the legitimacy of delinquency control as an appropriate role for them to assume, and find it difficult to come to terms with the very explicit way in which the legislation gives them the responsibility both for the care and the control of young people placed in care or under supervision. There may have been considerable confusion about the nature and purpose of intermediate treatment; but there was never any doubt that it was quite different from traditional casework. Consequently, in a much more particular sense, the legitimacy of group work and the feasibility of carrying it out effectively have been questioned by a predominantly casework oriented profession.

When management shared these misgivings, it often resulted in a lukewarm approach in which little or no attempt was made to reorganise workloads or provide adequate support for practitioners. On the other hand, where management *was* committed, the problem often lay not so much in lack of general approval for the idea in abstract as in persuading social workers to leave the familiar territory of casework for the virtually uncharted waters of intermediate treatment. For many of them, the prospect of spending a weekend living and working with difficult adolescents, only too ready to take advantage of their weaknesses and insecure grasp of the group work and activity skills required, was probably a real deterrent. This certainly contributed towards the early concentration on the preventive, younger end of the spectrum. However there were other feasibility factors pressing in the same direction. For instance, many social workers, particularly in rural areas, had little choice about the young people with whom they worked, because, for all the rhetoric about assessment and selection criteria, they often had the greatest difficulty in assembling a group of ten youngsters within a manageable age band.

Specialism and Genericism

It has been suggested that mechanistic organisations tend to resist change, often by encapsulating innovation, which has the effect of, at worst, decreasing the chances that it will infect the whole organisation, and at best reducing it to total irrelevance [8]. For instance, research and development sections are often prevented from carrying out fundamental investigations by the pressure of day to day enquiries, often designed to provide supporting evidence for decisions which have already been taken. Probably quite unconsciously, intermediate treatment was effectively encapsulated in many places by the device of appointing one officer at central office and placing him on the periphery of the organisation with minimal funds. It is arguable that the social work profession was so wedded to casework that management was persuaded to recruit several of these officers from outside the profession. Equally there may well have been more positive reasons, but there can be little doubt that the appointment of outsiders made it easier for reluctant social workers first to ignore and then to isolate these officers.

Given all these circumstances, it is not surprising that management increasingly opted for a policy of appointing specialist practitioners and putting many of them in residential and day centres. Management was, and continues to be, faced with a very real dilemma. It is politically much easier to develop a new piece of work by appointing a person specifically to do it , since his credibility depends on it being achieved. The alternative is to add to the number of generic workers and expect them all to share the responsibility for a new approach or additional task. This often fails, because conservatism is by no means absent in the social work profession and existing patterns of work with established client groups can be relied upon to expand to meet or absorb any available resources of manpower. In addition the education of all the social workers in a department requires more preparation, more consultation and a greater sense of direction than most senior management teams were able to offer. It is much easier to point out that many existing social workers were not temperamentally or professionally equipped for undertaking intermediate treatment and to devote one's energies to setting up residential and day centres where the actual plant helps to provide a greater degree of permanence.

The division of the social work task into a number of intelligible and mutually compatible specialisms remains an option open to social services departments; but it has to be admitted that it would have been a bold move to make soon after Seebohm, with its amalgamation of three separate departments and the birth of the generic worker. Residential and day centres for various client groups were generally expected to remain specialist, and the development of such centres for intermediate treatment posed little threat, insofar as they provided an additional resource which could be used by social workers. The introduction of specialist intermediate treatment practitioners at *area* level, particularly when this followed failure to persuade generic workers to undertake the work, often proved a very different kettle of fish. They were often made directly responsible to a principal social worker or even the area director, as opposed to a senior social worker, and this not unnaturally excited both envy and suspicion. If it was conceded that intermediate treatment was breaking new, or rediscovering old, ground, it was also argued that this luxury was only made possible by generic workers undertaking an unfair proportion of the total workload. Sometimes the hostility was so great that specialists found themselves doing work other than that for which they were appointed simply to reduce their own isolation and gain the acceptance of colleagues.

The grafting of specialist posts on to a large generic department also has career implications, particularly when those specialists do not have a social work qualification. Put very simply, if a department has a vacancy for a senior social worker post supervising generic workers, and a choice between a generic and a specialist worker to fill it, it does not require much imagination to predict the outcome. This helps to explain the difficulty which several authorities have experienced both in attracting and retaining specialist practitioners. Nonetheless the appointment of specialist practitioners, even if carried out with insufficient thought for the consequences, does represent some commitment and some determination on management's part to provide a service. In a great many places, the contribution of senior management has been limited to appointing one intermediate treatment officer. In these authorities, the existence of intermediate treatment has usually depended more than anything else on the enthusiasm of workers and their willingness to undertake what is recognised as a demanding task in addition to a normal workload. Certainly all the muddle and

confusion characteristic of many social services departments is in marked
contrast to the strategy adopted by the probation service when it was decided
that it should take on prison welfare as one of its functions. In the first place it
was not discretionary, and secondly it was made clear to every probation officer,
particularly those undergoing training, that it was almost certain that, at some
time in their professional careers, they would be expected to work in a prison.

The Courts

Prior to the passing of the Act, many juvenile court magistrates prided
themselves on the way they managed to combine the welfare and justice
principles as they exercised their role in court. Although the legislation made few
significant changes to the actual power available to the magistrates, the whole
tenor of the statute and more particularly the explanation and argument
preceding it, was towards separating the two functions. The emphasis was
placed on the judicial function of the court in deciding whether the case was
proven in the sense of offence committed or care needed; at the same time, the
social work profession was allowed an increased discretion in determining the
length and nature of the intervention required by the individual and his or her
family. Essentially this amounted to little more than the fact that the courts could
no longer send a child to a named remand home or sentence him under an
approved school order. The care order which replaced both the latter and the
fit person order did not abolish the actual approved schools, but merely gave
the local authorities greater flexibility about the children who were placed in
them and the length of time they stayed. Nonetheless it is no exaggeration to
suggest that many magistrates resented the Act and the loss of power which, in
their eyes, had been transferred to what they often thought was a young,
inexperienced and less responsible group.

Consequently, and in an equally unflattering way, many social workers
thought that magistrates would take their revenge by refusing to make use of
intermediate treatment requirements, not only because this facility would be
administered by local authorities as opposed to the penal system, but also
because it was a discretionary power, and they would have no right to insist
that it was carried out or even knowing, in most cases, whether it ever had
been. In fact statistics collected by at least one children's regional planning
committee do not substantiate this view [9]. They showed consistently over a
five year period that on very few occasions did magistrates refuse to follow
recommendations for intermediate treatment requirements; indeed, they made
far more without being requested than they refused when they were asked to
do so by either social workers or probation officers. The conclusion that must
surely be drawn is that, although magistrates may be disappointed when
requirements are not implemented, and more importantly when local
authorities fail to provide a sufficiently wide range of facilities to make it a viable
option, they cannot be blamed for the comparatively small number of requirements made. A much more plausible explanation for the slow development of
intermediate treatment is that, particularly in the early years, many local
authorities relied almost entirely on the goodwill and enthusiasm of social workers
to provide it in their spare time after undertaking a normal workload. In these
circumstances it is not altogether surprising that social workers were reluctant
to recommend requirements in their reports to the courts, simply because they
appreciated the direct effect it was likely to have on their personal workloads.

51

Apart from this, the discretionary element did create a vicious circle in some places. There were authorities which chose not to make any provision until the extent of the demand the court would make was clear; while the courts in their turn were inhibited from making requirements when they knew that they could not be implemented.

Current Levels of Provision

Notwithstanding the way in which organisational factors and the innate conservatism of the caring professions have combined to blunt the cutting edge of intermediate treatment, the fact remains that it does exist and has taken a variety of different forms. No analysis would be complete without some attempt — difficult though this is — to quantify the level of provision.

- There are no statistics published by central government of the number of young people involved in intermediate treatment, but one estimate puts the figure at 20,000 to 25,000 during the year ending 31st March 1979. Of these, probably only one in six or eight was actually subject to an intermediate treatment requirement, though maybe up to two thirds were on some kind of court order, usually the plain supervision order, and the other third or so were subject to no court order at all [10].

- The planned expenditure specifically on intermediate treatment was estimated by local authorities to be about £4.4 million, including over half a million in urban aid grants, for the financial year ending 31st March 1980 [11]. However, there are a number of hidden expenses, such as social workers' and probation officers' time, and expenditure from other budgetary headings such as preventive work under Section 1 of the Children and Young Persons Act 1963. All this means that the actual expenditure incurred, even after expenditure cuts made during the course of 1979, was probably well in excess of £5 million, particularly when the financial involvement of voluntary bodies is taken into account [12].

- The number of specialist staff increased rapidly in the late 1970s and by mid-1979 was approaching 650 for all agencies in the UK [13]. A slightly earlier survey indicated that 84% of the staff practising intermediate treatment in social services departments were not specialists, but social workers with normal or slightly reduced caseloads [14], and the proportion is even higher in the probation service, where intermediate treatment specialists are virtually unknown. This would suggest that there were at least a further 2,000 to 3,000 social workers and probation officers involved, even if on a temporary or rather intermittent basis.

Although these figures may begin to look quite impressive, they have to be considered in context: a total local authority field staff of about 28,000, plus over 5,000 probation officers [15]; a local authority budget estimate of £240 million for over 100,000 children in care, half of them on care orders [16]; a staff of over 20,000 just for those children living in community homes [17]; and quite outside the child care system, a growing number of juveniles, over 7,000 in 1977 and 1978, put into prison service institutions [18]. Alongside these statistics, the level of intermediate treatment provision pales by comparison.

A CLASSIFICATION OF PROJECTS

This section outlines some of the main models or types of intermediate treatment project. A number of different classifications have been offered. They all have their shortcomings, and the one offered here does not aspire to do anything more ambitious than provide a reasonably intelligible framework within which the reader will find it easier to locate the six case studies which follow [19].

Individual Placement of the Child

As originally conceived, intermediate treatment was expected usually to take the form of placing the child in some existing community provision appropriate to his needs in order to bring him into contact with a different environment, new interests and experiences. Four considerations may have influenced this approach, namely: to avoid further stigmatising of identified delinquents through separate provision for them; to develop new interests that could be pursued within the community after the expiry of the court order; to involve the community in coping with and helping its own troublesome youngsters; and perhaps to keep down costs, with social services paying a per capita fee, instead of the staffing and even capital costs for its own specialist facilities. Certainly part of this thinking was succinctly set out in the 1972 DHSS *Guide to Regional Planning,* which says: *'An important object is to make use of facilities available to children who have not been before the courts and so to secure the treatment of 'children in trouble' in the company of other children and through the sharing of activities and experiences within the community.'* [20] Paley describes this approach as an 'allocation' model, where the supervisor allocates the child individually to a community facility, as distinct from what he calls the 'focal' model, where the supervisor focuses and brings to bear the resources of the community on a specialised project [21].

Four main varieties of the individual placement can be distinguished:

- In the mainstream local community provision for leisure activities and social education of young people in groups, such as youth clubs and youth organisations;

- On one-off residential courses open to young people generally, such as outdoor pursuits courses;

- With an individual adult in the local community, on the basis of a shared interest such as fishing, or perhaps even for individual tutoring;

- In a work setting for purposes of work experience or community service.

The regional schemes compiled in 1973 and 1974 were based on this approach, typically the first two varieties, but this proved a false start for intermediate treatment, mainly because, for reasons examined earlier in this chapter, social workers and probation officers turned their backs on the allocation model of placing individual children in existing facilities. On the third variety, the PSSC Study Group on intermediate treatment found that schemes to attach children to individual adult volunteers in the community were *'sadly under-developed',* and attributed this partly to the difficulty of recruiting and supporting volunteers [22]. However, it probably has much to do with social workers' lack of orientation towards, or skill in, developing community resources. It is perhaps the fourth variety which now attracts the most interest, and is likely to grow, influenced by the Youth Opportunities Programme for unemployed school leavers. Nonetheless, taken together, this whole cluster of approaches does not at present amount to very much.

Special Evening Groups

By common consent [23], the predominant form of intermediate treatment has been a separate, special provision where the children are brought together by the social workers into small groups of around ten members. The group typically lasts for six to nine months, and meets one evening a week for two or three hour sessions, supplemented by one or more residential weekends or even weeks away together. It is run by two or three adults, usually social workers or probation officers, but sometimes including a youth worker, teacher or volunteer. It uses whatever suitable premises can be found, such as a youth club or an office in the social services, and involves activities of the youth club variety combined with a more or less conscious use of group work techniques. The emphasis on groups now appears to have been inevitable, given the decision of social workers and probation officers to develop their own facilities, instead of using existing resources in the community, and given their recognition of the shortcomings of individual casework with inadequate, inarticulate and sometimes alienated adolescents. A further pressure of an administrative nature lay in the fact that group work was about the only way a department could discover with its limited resources whether intermediate treatment was a viable option, warranting investment in plant and additional workers.

There are, of course, very good theoretical reasons for working in groups with adolescents [24], and it does make sense when working with inarticulate young people to use activities as a vehicle both for making relationships and pursuing social work aims; but it is at least possible that the groups are actually used, not so much to undertake social group work, which is difficult, but rather to provide enjoyable and compensatory experiences for deprived youngsters, which is much easier. Although there are good professional reasons for task centred, time limited intervention, this policy, and more particularly the low intensity of many of these groups, can be partly attributed to organisational constraints. While practitioners are expected to undertake this work with little or no reduction in normal workload and insufficient time off in lieu, it is probably unrealistic to expect them to sustain the effort for longer than nine months. The length of programme has also been influenced by the volatility of the social work profession and by the legal framework. Once it is accepted that the adult leadership of the group should remain stable throughout its life, then six to nine months is about the longest one can reasonably expect a team of three workers to stay together before promotion, resignation or secondment take their toll. In addition the legislation originally specified a maximum of 30 days (once a week for seven months), and this was in everybody's mind when plans were formulated, even though few of the children involved are actually subject to intermediate treatment requirements.

One other significant feature of these groups is that they are usually closed, in the sense that the membership is intended to remain the same throughout the life of the group. Once again professional and organisational factors have combined to bring this about; but it does not alter the fact that numerous accounts emphasise the unhappiness of many of the children when the group comes to an end. So, in many areas, intermediate treatment only becomes a reality when a small team forms to run a group, trawls for referrals from colleages, selects according to its criteria or the availability of children, and brings together an assortment of children who do not know each other. Although there are exceptions, few practitioners can claim to be working with natural groups rooted in the community, and there is always the danger that children may be plucked out of their community, thrown together for a short period and then disbanded with only minimum transfer of the benefits gained.

Day and Evening Centres

A more recent development than special evening groups is the burgeoning of day or evening centres for intermediate treatment. There are now at least 60 in England and Wales, most of them having been established from 1976 onwards, a quarter of them with the help of urban aid grants [25]. These grants have been a crucial factor because they involve central government in funding 75% of the expenditure for a period of five years, on the understanding that the local authority then assumes total financial responsibility. With these financial advantages, local authorities were more prepared to contemplate significant investment, and, at the same time, the administrators of the grants usually looked more favourably on projects with the air of permanence that premises afford, simply because they were more likely to survive the initial funding period. Most of these centres have three or four full time staff, are open during the week after school hours and in the evening, and are sometimes also used at weekends. Typically, a number of separate groups use the centre on one or two occasions each week. The majority of the centres have day programmes, usually with a structured educational component, providing alternative schooling for truanting or disruptive children, or an alternative to residential care for delinquents.

These centres have a number of advantages over evening groups run by area social workers and others. The centres offer a much wider range of resources in terms of space and equipment, greatly increasing the options available to a group programme, which can often include a meal, various arts, crafts and games, as well as group discussions and counselling in a quieter place. They also provide a base for a team of full time specialist workers, who can pool their resources and build up a reservoir of experience and skills. There is a continuity of provision which is in marked contrast to much area based work, where one group ends at its appointed time, and another can only be started if the machinery is cranked up again. This means that the young people involved not only have a place of their own, but can usually phase out their participation more gradually than is possible with a closed group.

However, centres also have their disadvantages. Although buildings and equipment can increase the options open to all concerned, the protection and management of property can absorb an alarming proportion of staff time. Unless the staff take great care, perhaps by choosing old premises and ensuring that they are used by a wide range of children and adults [26], the strengths of having a centre may also be its weakness. The structure and support which a building offers can all too readily mean that it becomes an institution, which is essentially the domain of the staff, where the young people who attend are taken, psychologically at least, out of their own community. It may well be that area based practitioners, unencumbered by plant and faced with creating their own structure each week, work with young people on a much more equal footing than specialist staff based at a permanent centre. Certainly these separate facilities inevitably create problems of liaison with field social workers, and particularly with statutory supervisors of the children.

However, these concerns have tended to dissolve in the face of one over-riding factor, which is that these centres are a prerequisite for the more intensive kinds of intermediate treatment, such as that espoused by the PSSC Report. This envisaged *'an intensive residential placement of approximately two weeks, followed immediately by an intensive daily programme of intermediate treatment'*. [27] As planners try to develop viable alternatives to residential care, it seems inevitable that various forms of day provision will increase; but every agency contemplating such a centre is faced with a crucial dilemma. It can either set up a special unit exclusively for such youngsters, drawing them from a sizeable catchment area, or it can establish a neighbourhood centre, working with a range of young people more or less intensively according to requirement, and including the small number of persistent offenders who live within the immediate neighbourhood. With the former, city-wide model, the links with the community are bound to be tenuous, and the concentration of serious or persistent offenders in one place is likely to reinforce the stigma and the increase the problems of behavioural management. On the other hand, the main problem with the neighbourhood centre is the economic one, in that so many would be required to serve one urban area.

Residential Centres

Although intermediate treatment is often described as a community based provision, and sometimes as an alternative to residential care, there was never any intention to exclude a residential component. Indeed, the original legislation actually specified a 90 day block period as one form of intermediate treatment, and the optimists hoped that this would provide a credible alternative to detention centres. Although few field social workers are favourably inclined towards residential care, many have come to appreciate the benefit of short residential periods within the context of intermediate treatment programmes. In fact this has now reached the point where it can be described as well established practice; but this section is concerned with special centres, designed more or less exclusively to provide residential intermediate treatment courses of varying lengths. Their number is not large, but they vary greatly, not only in length of stay, but also in purpose, setting and orientation. This makes classification difficult, but three main clusters can be identified, covering most of the residential centres.

1 There are a few 90 day or 30 day centres which are located in the wilder parts of Britain and take individuals referred from a number of different localities, with the groups being formed on arrival. These projects are not flourishing. They are expensive, often costing more per week than the average community home with education, and where they concentrate on outdoor pursuits, they may also be emphasising a philosophy that has diminishing appeal for many social workers. Above all, it is very difficult to link the residential course with supervision in the community, which may be a hundred miles away.

2 More residential centres are developing in or near the urban areas they serve, permitting greater integration of residential and field work. In some cases they are part of a complex providing residential or day assessment, a

wide ranging day care programme or halfway place for children returning to their own homes after a spell in a community home. In others regular residential weekends are combined with family casework during the week. There is also increasing flexibility about the length of programmes, with stays ranging from a few days to a few months.

3 There is also a growth in rural centres, some of them run by voluntary bodies, and usually offering shorter courses of a week or two. These centres take existing groups with adult leaders, which can thus take advantage of the facilities and of a permanent staff which is prepared to make its expertise available.

A few general trends can be discerned, and these include: greater flexibility in the length of stay; a blurring of the line between residential and field work, with centres as near as possible to the child's own neighbourhood; less emphasis on strenuous outdoor activities; and more attempts to devise intensive and credible facilities for the more serious and persistent offenders.

The Case Study Projects

The case studies that follow were selected partly to reflect the diversity of provision that exists. It was also important that the projects should be well established and well documented, with contributors who could prepare the kind of account we were seeking. The process of selection and preparation of the case studies is described more fully in Appendix II, but at this point it may be useful to locate these six projects within the fourfold classification just described.

There are no examples of individual placement projects, which in any case are rare. Chapelfield represents the special evening group—the type with a 'one off', time limited, closed, evening group, where a team of workers is drawn together to work with a particular set of young people, and the project dissolves when the group comes to an end. Evening and day centres are illustrated by the case studies on Pontefract, Dundee Activity Centres and Eastern Ravens Trust. The key feature is the continuity of work and team, allowing a body of experience to be built up and a process of clarifying objectives and methods to be undertaken. Eastern Ravens does not fit too easily into this category, for although it has a permanent base, it deliberately plays down the importance of working within its four walls, and it has also chosen to limit itself to one type of programme, rather than develop the range found at many centres. Among the residential centres, two very different models are represented. Tyn-y-Pwll offers exclusively short residential courses, corresponding most closely to the first of the three 'sub-types' above, while Knowles Tooth combines residential weekends at the centre with family work in the young people's own neighbourhood during the week—a rather uncommon model which falls into the second sub-type.

It is worth noting that of the six case studies, four are run by voluntary organisations. This is far from typical of intermediate treatment projects, which are overwhelmingly provided directly by statutory agencies. However, it does reflect the importance of the voluntary sector in setting up a variety of experimental projects at a time when the statutory bodies were still dabbling their toes in the water. Finally, these six projects could also be classified in other ways, according to their philosophy, clients or methods. This kind of analysis, however, is more complex, and must await the presentation of the case studies themselves.

References

1   Reinach E. *et al.* (1976), *First year at Fairfield Lodge: A children's observation and assessment centre in Hampshire,* Portsmouth: Portsmouth Polytechnic, Social Services Research and Intelligence Unit.
2   Paley J. and Thorpe D. (1974), *Children—handle with care: A critical analysis of the development of intermediate treatment,* Leicester: National Youth Bureau.
3   Department of Health and Social Security (1972), *Intermediate treatment: A guide for the regional planning of new forms of treatment for children in trouble,* London: HMSO.
4   Allard S.E. (1977), 'The contribution of the Youth Service', *Summit* (National Association of Boys' Clubs), No. 5; reprinted in *Youth Service and intermediate treatment* (Youth Service Special, No. 7.), Leicester: NYB.
5   In the second half of the 1970s, the youth service suffered a substantial decline in staffing and in expenditure in real terms, according to Smith D. (1979), *Local authority expenditure and the youth service, 1975 to 1980: A short review,* Leicester: NYB.
6   Probation was responsible for 18,031 juveniles under CYP 1969 supervision, at December 31 1977; local authorities for about 18,700 at March 31 1978. The sources, however, are unrelated: Home Office (1978), *Probation and after-care statistics: England and Wales, 1977,* London; Home Office, Table 19; and *Social services for children in England and Wales, 1976-78: Children and Young Persons Act 1969, Second Report to Parliament* (1979), HC 268, London: HMSO, Table 3a.
7   Hall P. *et al.* (1975), *Change, choice and conflict in social policy,* London: Heinemann.
8   Burns T. and Stalker G.M. (1961), *The management of innovation,* London: Tavistock.
9   Quarterly statistics on IT, 1974-78, from the East Midlands Children's Regional Planning Committee.
10 *How much IT?* (1979), 'Fact sheet'. Leicester: NYB.
11 Chartered Institute of Public Finance and Accountancy (1979), *Personal social services statistics: 1979-80 estimates,* London: CIPFA, column 101.
12 *Local authority expenditure on intermediate treatment* (1979), 'Fact sheet', Leicester: NYB.
13 *Specialist workers in intermediate treatment* (1980), 'Information' series, Leicester: NYB.
14 More W.S. (1978), *Intermediate treatment: The national picture?,* Birmingham: Priority Educational Programmes for Action and Research. (Around the time of this survey, the total number of social services IT specialists was estimated at 300 by an NYB survey, reported in *Intermediate treatment* (NYB IT Mailing), No. 2, February 1978.)
15 An estimated 27,950 field work staff in CIPFA, *op. cit.,* column 18; 5,099 full-time probation officers at the end of 1977, in Home Office (1978), *op. cit.,* Table 33.
16 CIPFA, *op. cit.,* gives a 1979/80 estimate of £243 million (column 32), for 104,900 children (column 24). At the end of March 1978 there were 101,700 children in the care of local authorities, 48% on CYP 1969 care orders, according to *Social services for children in England and Wales, 1976-78.*
17 In England alone, 22,046 in 1976, according to DHSS Research and Statistics (1978), *Staff of local authority social services departments as at 30 September 1976* (S/F77/1), London: DHSS.
18 In 1978, 7,347 juvenile receptions into prison service custody, essentially to detention centres and Borstals. Home Office (1979), *Prison statistics: England and Wales, 1978,* Cmnd. 7626, London: HMSO, Table 3.5
19 The classification used here corresponds to a simple version of the 'continuum of care' approach of Paley J. and Thorpe D., *op. cit.* For other typologies, see: Billis D. (1976), 'In search of a policy', *Social Work Service,* No. 11, pp. 11-16; Jones R. (1976), 'Getting I.T. together: Integrating intermediate treatment', *Social Work Today,* May 27 1976, Vol. 7, No. 5, pp. 130-133; Adams R.V. (1976), 'Intermediate treatment: Looking at some patterns of intervention', *Youth Social Work Bulletin,* Vol. 3, No. 2, pp. 9-12.
20 DHSS (1972), *op. cit.,* p.6.
21 Paley J. (1973), 'Two models of intermediate treatment', *Youth Social Work Bulletin,* Vol. 1, No. 1. pp. 3-6.
22 Personal Social Services Council (1977), *A future for intermediate treatment: Report of the Intermediate Treatment Study Group* (Chairman: Mia Kellmer Pringle), London: PSSC, p.53.
23 See e.g. *ibid.,* Section 3.
24 Baldwin J. (1977), 'Why groupwork?', *Social Work Today,* Feb. 15 1977, Vol. 8, No. 9, pp. 7-9.
25 Locke T.L. (1980), *Intermediate treatment centres,* 'Information' series, Leicester: NYB.
26 For intermediate treatment in the context of family advice centres, see Leissner A., Powley T. and Evans D. (1977), *Intermediate treatment: A community-based action-research study,* London: National Children's Bureau.
27 PSSC, *op. cit.,* section 8.

CASE STUDIES

TYN-Y-PWLL

Edward Donohue and Barry Todd

PROJECT DESCRIPTION

Tyn-y-Pwll is a small farmhouse set in Snowdonia between Caernarvon and Port Madoc. A former outdoor pursuits centre, it is now used mainly for children, aged 12 to 17, on supervision orders with intermediate treatment attached, or needing short term residential care. There are usually eight to ten courses a year, varying in length from two to eight weeks, and adjusted, as far as possible, to meet the needs of the individual children. In addition the centre is used for holiday groups of children in care.

More than half of the children come from the five counties north and west of London, which combine to make up Children's Regional Planning Area No. 7. Edward Donohue works as Development Officer for its committee. Unfortunately this means that they, and their social workers, have to travel some considerable distance from their homes. Although approaches are often made by social workers nearer to Tyn-y-Pwll, their applications are not always supported by their authorities, usually on financial grounds. Nevertheless a total of 17 different authorities have sent children to the centre on more than one occasion.

As most readers will be aware, there are numerous outdoor pursuits centres in North Wales and there have been quite positive links between Tyn-y-Pwll and some of them. These take the form of combined social evenings, joint outdoor activities and links between the wardens through the Association of Outdoor Pursuits Centres. Tyn-y-Pwll itself, however, places very little stress on outdoor activities as such and is primarily concerned with providing a group living experience. It is a registered charity, managed by a voluntary committee of 12 people, most of whom are connected with some branch of social work.

Origins and Objectives

This chapter covers the five years from January 1973 to December 1977. However Tyn-y-Pwll was first opened in 1960 by Edward Donohue, who was then a group and community worker in south Liverpool. In the early years it was run by the management committee of the Liverpool University Settlement, but from 1963 to 1967 had an independent management committee based in Liverpool. In 1967 it closed down because of financial difficulties and was re-opened in 1969 by the present management committee. From 1970 until 1973 most of the children came from the Birmingham area.

Tyn-y-Pwll has always been perceived by those people most closely involved as a short-term refuge for deprived children, the main objective being to offer these children an alternative, however brief, to their normal unsatisfactory living situation. The emphasis is on group living, and considerable importance is attached to the relationships between staff and children.

It was originally intended to provide facilities mainly for adolescent girls, because this seemed to be one of the most neglected areas, but both the length of the courses and the composition of the groups have varied over the years. In the first instance, the groups consisted of between eight and 12 adolescent girls; then boys' groups were introduced, and eventually, after some pressure from social workers, mixed groups were accommodated. However, it is the girls' groups which will receive most attention in the following description of the dynamics of a course. This is simply because Tyn-y-Pwll is one of the very few residential establishments which attempt intensive short term care for adolescent girls.

Tyn-y-Pwll does not pretend to make massive personality changes during a stay of any duration. It is hoped that children may see their problems in a new perspective, and may, as a result of the help given, adjust their attitudes and feelings towards certain aspects of their everyday lives. It is also hoped that children who have developed particular interests at Tyn-y-Pwll can be linked to relevant interest groups in their own communities. From the beginning of every course, the group is moved towards a process of termination, and all the children are encouraged to think outwardly during their stay. Close contact between the children and their homes and social workers is encouraged, and one of the staff acts as a liaison officer to maintain contacts after the course is completed. This, in itself, has created difficulties, as some social workers have tended to see residential courses as totally separate from their own work with the child and family.

Resources

Because Tyn-y-Pwll has always experienced financial difficulties, the main support has come from the staff themselves, who have been prepared to work at considerably lower salaries than their skills could have commanded elsewhere. In spite of this, since 1973, staff turnover has been relatively slow. Four of the original six are still directly involved with the establishment, and the majority of staff who have worked at Tyn-y-Pwll since that date have retained very close links. All full time staff have some kind of professional training, most of them in residential social work, although one or two of them have been teacher or field work trained. In addition to this, they all possess activity skills, both indoor and outdoor, and, most important of all, are prepared to live with the children on a relatively equal basis. There is also an extremely varied group of voluntary helpers. Some are social workers who have either sent children in the past or have a child on the current course. Others are students from various courses, residential workers and former students of the project leader, who help during their time off. Perhaps the most important are former course members, male and female, who having reached the age of 17 or over, feel that they would like to give something back to the centre, or experience the courses from another angle. With very few exceptions, and these have usually been students, the voluntary helpers fit extremely well into the total group.

At the present time, the only income for funding the project comes from per capita payments made by local authorities for children who attend, and any money that the management committee can raise. This means that the establishment is not only non profit making, but is usually faced with a deficit at the end of each financial year. The buildings are owned by the management committee, and the equipment is renewed as finances permit. While there has always been an emphasis on the safety aspects of equipment, there is no doubt that, compared with many of the local authority outdoor centres, facilities and equipment are no more than adequate.

Organisation

The relationship between the staff group and the management committee has, since 1969, been very much on a partnership basis and all major decisions have been taken jointly between the two groups. This has been helped to some extent by the fact that Edward Donohue is both chairman of the management committee and the project leader. The staff group has varied between four and six people and the main emphasis has been on a ratio of one member of staff to two children. This ratio is constant because the staff do not take time off during courses, but have their holidays and time off in lieu in the periods in between.

Each group decides its own programme and timetable at the beginning of the course. In the case of the short courses this is on a day-to-day basis, but on longer ones the groups get to the stage where they can work four or five days ahead although this, too, is adjustable according to the weather.

The Children

All the children have come from one of three sources, namely social services departments, probation departments, or child guidance units. The only children who are denied places at Tyn-y-Pwll are those with serious mental or physical handicaps. Others have been refused a place because of the lack of a suitable course at the time needed. All the intermediate treatment officers in Area 7 have made a point of visiting Tyn-y-Pwll and learning about the methods employed. Consequently, they are able to advise the social workers in their authority about the suitability of the centre for a particular child. In addition, Edward Donohue, the Regional Development Officer, and the member of staff responsible for follow up, can also advise social workers. All the people involved with the course see it as extremely important that the residential element should be regarded as integral to the overall social work programme, and, for this reason, contact with the social workers and their families where possible, is considered equally important. It is accepted that the distance from home can be a distinct disadvantage. On the other hand, some children have been able to say that it enabled them to see things more clearly.

There are wide differences in ability and measured intelligence, ranging from virtual illiteracy at one end of the scale to 'O' level and, in some cases, 'A' level capabilities at the other.

The social background of the children is equally varied. In many cases, the family as a stable unit is virtually non-existent, with the child being shuttled between various family members, such as grandparents or elder married siblings. In contrast, there are children who maintain reasonable relationships with their parents, but who have difficulty in carrying this over into other areas, particularly at school. As one might expect, financial circumstances also vary from family to family. In some cases, the father has a well-paid, responsible job and there is considerable material comfort in the home. In other cases the whole family is supported by the State.

The children who are referred to Tyn-y-Pwll all have one factor in common, in that they are under the supervision of a social worker or a probation officer, and it is they who initiate the proceedings which result in a child coming to Tyn-y-Pwll. Social workers send their clients for a number of reasons, depending on the circumstances of the particular child. These can be broadly categorised as follows:

1 Those children who have committed one or more minor offences, such as larceny or shoplifting, and who have appeared before a magistrate on at least one occasion. Often the child is due to return to court in the near future, and the social worker will send her to Tyn-y-Pwll for a period of assessment, and in the hope that a short term intensive residential course will allow her to show some indication that she can perform well, both socially and academically, under different conditions. The report on the child's performance at Tyn-y-Pwll is often used by the social worker to influence the magistrates' thinking at his client's next court appearance. It is explained to the child before her arrival at the centre that her visit is not a punishment, but rather an opportunity to demonstrate her capabilities under conditions more favourable than hitherto experienced. In a number of cases the experience has helped to modify the child's anti-authority attitude, and magistrates have been given a much more positive view than was previously available. For instance 14 year old Mary, who had been truanting and shoplifting, was sent to us as an alternative to residential care. She had no father and although fond of her mother, did not relate to her at all well. Aggressive and tomboyish by nature, she took readily to the outdoor activities. She kept in touch and visited us on several occasions. She is now a driver in the WRAF and seems very happy.

2 Those children whose social and academic growth is being affected by their home situation. In these cases, the child is told that the visit to Tyn-y-Pwll is a break from home, and that she will be given the opportunity to talk through problems and view what is happening at home and her role in it, from a secure and sympathetic distance. (Occasionally social workers will incorrectly, and in our view unfairly, tell a child that it is just a holiday and that no demands will be made.) Marilyn provides an illustration. She was 13 years old, more intelligent and refined than most of her delinquent siblings, but very insecure and withdrawn. She found life difficult to cope with, and the individual attention and the acceptance of adults was very valuable to her. She settled in well, and stayed for two six week periods. She now corresponds regularly from her boarding school.

3 Those children who find difficulty in forming satisfactory relationships with both adults and peers, and who are isolated from group activities. In these cases, the social worker hopes that the opportunity of joining in a variety of group activities will break down some of the reserve and hostility demonstrated. Twelve year old Tommy was a very withdrawn, quiet boy, easily rejected by his peers. His delinquency was a result of trying to impress them. He had no mother, and related particularly well to one female member of staff.

He loved working with horses. He is now living happily with his father and is due to leave school this Summer. He still writes to the centre regularly.

It should be noted, however, that these three categories are not mutually exclusive, and indeed, some children could fit into any of the three at different times. Most of the girls who attend on care orders do in fact return home, a few have gone on to hostels, and two or three have gone to community homes with education on the premises, or CH(E)s. A small proportion of children are sent for the main reason that nowhere else will accept them. Margaret, aged 14½, came directly from Holloway Prison, having been refused by more than 20 CH(E)s. She had been charged with assault, theft and causing grievous bodily harm. After a very stormy beginning, she eventually settled and stayed nine months. After leaving, she became deputy head girl in a grammar school, and took her 'A' levels. Often girls like this are victims of labelling, and only twice have such girls arrived who could not be fully integrated into the group. In one case the girl was able to stay, but needed undivided adult attention. In the other, she had to be sent away after a particularly nasty case of bullying. The girl concerned showed no remorse whatsoever when confronted by staff, despite the evident distress of her victim, and the other girls were so frightened that no further work with the group was possible while she remained at Tyn-y-Pwll.

The Programme

Courses of varying lengths and numbers were run during the period under review. The boys' courses were mainly of two or three weeks duration, the numbers on each one ranging from ten to 16. The girls' courses, however, were more experimental in terms of length, and ranged from two to twelve weeks, with numbers ranging from six to twelve girls. The length of the course could depend on how capable the staff felt of giving sufficient commitment, both to the girls and to each other, and this was always considered before the course duration was established. The general consensus of the staff is that, for most girls, four weeks is a satisfactory period. In some cases, however, this needs to be linked to a two week follow-up course, and in other cases, two four week courses separated by a short period seem appropriate. The number of girls accepted for a particular course often depends on how many voluntary helpers are likely to be available at the time. The courses for boys are more relaxed, both for staff and children, and invariably enjoyed by both. They are largely activity-oriented and not dissimilar in style and content to other intermediate treatment courses that have been documented.

The girls' courses, while still as active as the boys' courses, are far more intense in their social and emotional aspects, and because the staff involvement in the courses is total, this becomes very apparent and there is consequently far more variety in these than in the boys' groups.

In spite of these variables, certain structural factors in the actual running of the courses remain constant. Of these, perhaps the most significant is the staff involvement with the course. The permanent full time staff at Tyn-y-Pwll are available, and seen to be so, 15 hours a day for the duration of the course.

The project leader is not always able to adhere to this schedule because his work at Tyn-y-Pwll is over and above his regular full time job. However, the nature of that job allows him to spend the greater part of his time at the centre during any given course, and this is explained to the children quite clearly.

There are practical reasons for this total involvement of the staff. Firstly, in a group exercise involving children and adults equally, it is unfair to expect one section to be available and not the other. If the children are required to contribute to the group all day, every day, then they have an equal right to demand the same of the workers. It should be noted here that this proposition was first put forward by a child on the course, and is entirely consistent with the overall philosophy of the project. Secondly, this involvement enables all the staff to see much more of the children for longer periods of time, and vice versa. In other words, it provides an intensive experience in which it becomes virtually impossible to conceal one's true character or feelings. It means that manipulation of staff by girls, and of staff by staff, becomes much more unlikely.

It would be less than candid not to acknowledge that even in the most harmonious of groups, conflict arises, and such conflict often manifests itself in fictionalisation and tale telling. Extreme cases sometimes occur in residential establishments where the staff member going off duty deliberately stirs up a group of children to make the incoming staff member appear inefficient or incapable of controlling the group. The system at Tyn-y-Pwll works as a check against this kind of friction.

Finally, this system enables the staff to prepare for a course with a certain amount of confidence. Although it is never possible to predict how a particular group will react, it is of considerable help to know how the staff group will respond to any situation which may arise.

Planning

Prior to a child's arrival at Tyn-y-Pwll, a considerable amount of information about her background, abilities and problems is supplied by the social worker. Naturally the member of staff who is charged with the responsibility for dealing with the bookings, transport and finance, reads this sometimes extensive documentation. However, it is a deliberate policy, although perhaps an unusual one, that no other member of staff should follow suit. Instead they are given a brief factual resumé of the child and the events which led to her present situation. So, for instance, the fact that a girl has been enuretic and is likely to need special bedding arrangements must obviously be shared with the rest of the staff. Equally, if a child has been convicted of causing grievous bodily harm, the rest of the staff team will be informed; but unsubstantiated comments to the effect that the child is disturbed, lazy, or backward are not mentioned.

This, again, is a result of experience. In the first place, if one reads that a child is aggressive or violent or manipulative, this will colour one's attitude to the child on first meeting, albeit unconsciously. Secondly, it is inconsistent to say to a child *'You will be judged by us only on how you behave during this course'* and yet bring a set of preconceptions to that assessment. Naturally, the staff do learn about a child's history; they would be falling down on their jobs if they did not. It is the manner in which this information is gained that is important. Normally, a child will want to tell staff members facts about herself, and staff members reciprocate. If this does not happen, then a staff member may suggest to a child, after two weeks or so, that she might like to discuss the relevant documents. The child does not see her papers, but the worker will tell her the substance of comments which have been made, and offer her a chance to express her opinion, or give her own version of an incident.

In one sense, however, the statement that planning is kept to a minimum is misleading, because although the day-to-day planning is fluid, the concepts and philosophy behind each course remain entirely constant. Whatever events occur during the course, the success of the group will be judged by how closely all the group members abide by the behavioural goals which the total group established at the beginning of the course. This is explained in more detail in the next section.

PROJECT IN ACTION

Making the Contract

If we postulate a course model, then the first day is concerned with the mechanics of getting the children to Tyn-y-Pwll. As it is somewhat remote, this means, in practice, that the children arrive between noon and late afternoon. The evening is spent arranging accommodation and general orientation, and the children will be divided into sub-groups, each with its own adult group leader. The first group meeting takes place the following morning and it is here that goals are established and agreed upon. A typical meeting might decide that the group should attempt various projects during the six weeks, and it is emphasised that all group members, both staff and children, will be expected to contribute to the activity. The activity itself can be strenuous, like rock climbing, or much gentler, such as a group picnic. The important point is that each member of the group, right at the beginning of the course, has made a commitment to the group as a whole regarding the future. The children concerned find it possible to accept this contract because it is clearly a two way process.

It should be said here, that although the staff use all their skills to persuade the children to decide on suitable goals and behavioural norms, nonetheless, should a group insist on something unsuitable or even dangerous, they are allowed, within reason, to discover for themselves the wisdom or otherwise of their own decisions. Thus, those who go to bed late are still expected to get up at the same time as everybody else and do a full day's work. On the other hand, there are very real limits to this experiential approach. For instance, it was not uncommon for a small group of children to spend a night on their own, camping on the beach. On one occasion, despite the fact that there were some young soldiers camping nearby, and against the advice of staff, the girls insisted that they would be quite safe on their own.

Uneasy at the risk being taken, two members of staff decided to visit them at 9 p.m. to make sure that everything was in order. They arrived in time to find four soldiers allocating the girls between them for the night, a 25 year old corporal having chosen a 12 year old girl.

At this first meeting, the group also decides on how the day to day operation of the centre itself should be organised. The centre does not employ any domestic staff, so all the cooking, cleaning and general maintenance of the buildings and grounds is done by the group. In these tasks, adults and children share equally. Meals are communal, in that staff help prepare the food with the children, they eat at the same tables at the same time, and share the washing up when the meal is over.

The children are also told what the staff expect from them in terms of behaviour and attitude, and what in turn they can expect from the staff. The latter undertake to act in certain ways. Some of these categories are broad; for example, each staff member promises to act consistently and fairly. Other categories are more specific; for example, the staff guarantee that there will be no drinking of alcohol at any time during the course, not because the staff are teetotal, but because it would be less than fair to the other members of the group. There are some exceptions to this, such as the drinking of wine at formal dinners. Of all the promises made by staff, this is the one which elicits most scepticism among the children. Nevertheless, it is kept. It is not so much that the staff are making any great sacrifice, but that the children see that they are not the only members who are giving things up for the ultimate benefit of the group. Other considerations, such as free time for the children and cigarette smoking, are discussed, and a system agreed upon, and gradually a simple but binding set of responsibilities, rights and obligations is built up for the whole group. Basic behavioural norms are agreed upon, so the first group meeting produces a contract, or rather a series of contracts, between staff and children, between the children themselves, and, not least, between individual members of staff.

The exercise described above is meaningless without the constant monitoring and checking of results. Every infringement of the agreement must be picked up and discussed, and it is this which, during the opening days of the course, is so tedious and at times unpleasant, for all concerned. But all staff persevere with this, for unless this process of honouring obligations becomes the conduct of all, no progress can be made in the second half of the course in changing attitudes and behaviour. The legitimacy of the staff's authority derives not from might, nor from custom, but from the contract agreed upon at the beginning of the course. An adult cannot, therefore, reply to the question *'Why?'* with the answer *'Because I say so'*, or even *'Because I am an adult and you are not'*. He must say, *'You should not do this, because it means breaking your word'*.

There have been numerous occasions when individual children have challenged the right of the group to enforce their contractual obligations. This is usually resolved in group discussions when the advantages are balanced against the disadvantages, and it is pointed out that a group which is working together for the benefit of all provides a much more pleasant and enjoyable environment.

Implicit in the very idea of a contract is, of course, the need for mutual trust, and this is a prerequisite of any progress and growth of the child. If the child does not trust the staff then the exercise is futile. The emphasis on contractual obligations means that trust can be demonstrated. Rather than a child or adult saying, *'You must trust me'*, he or she must prove in practical terms that such trust is demonstrably earned and respected.

Let it be said that, as will no doubt be appreciated, there is nothing new in either the theory or the practice of the above. The theory of the contract is at least as old as Rousseau, and goal oriented behaviour models of management techniques are well established. What is comparatively new, perhaps, is their application to the residential care of children.

Methods of Control

It is impossible to understand the dynamics of a course at Tyn-y-Pwll without an appreciation of the methods of control. In other words, the contentious subject of discipline. The word itself evokes such an emotional response in so many people that it seems useful to discuss the subject in some detail. One of the most treasured moments in the last 18 months occurred during a short three day course for students about to enter their first establishments as full time residential social workers. One student was describing a week's holiday at an outdoor activities centre with a group of boys. He considered that the holiday had been a success, primarily because of the balance between the two staff members involved. *'One'*, he said seriously, *'cared for the children very much. The other was a disciplinarian'.* To the suggestion that the two are not mutually exclusive, he looked dumbfounded. Yet much emotional and physical harm is done to children by the refusal of residential workers to accept responsibility for the discipline in their establishments.

Discipline, in this case, means the safeguarding of those standards of behaviour which have been agreed upon by the group. The long term aim is to get the children themselves to monitor the action of their peers, but until the confidence which this requires is present, then the adults take up this role. Daily meetings are held, at which all present are free to express their disapproval of another's behaviour. So, although there are no punishments or withdrawal of privileges for those who break the contract, much can be achieved through group pressure. In the event of a crisis, the meeting is brought forward, if necessary. Discipline is not synonymous with punishment; rather, in a real sense, a disciplinarian is one who teaches. One of the commonest complaints made by the children who come to Tyn-y-Pwll about their own schools is *'The teacher can't control the class. He lets the kids do what they like. He doesn't care'.* It seems merely to state the obvious, that discipline is an integral part of caring for children.

In view of this, the hostility towards discipline expressed by some social workers is surprising. The simple fact of the matter is that it is more painful and more wearing to be consistently and invariably censuring breaches of the accepted code of behaviour, than it is to ignore them. It is easier to turn a blind eye to instances of bullying, intimidation and manipulation, and when this happens the whole basis of the group contract is destroyed. If all group members are equal in importance, then they should all be afforded equal care, and this is impossible in a situation where the strongest child imposes her will on the rest. Whilst it is going too far to suggest that caring equals discipline, there is convincing evidence that at the root of much chronic indiscipline is a lack of concern. One of the weaknesses of the child care system is that too much emphasis is placed on giving to the child and too little emphasis on enabling the child to learn how to give. One of the strengths of the Tyn-y-Pwll approach is that because demands are made upon children they learn, in the vast majority of cases, to respond.

The concern with discipline within the group, both, it should be stressed, with children and adults, stems not from any theoretical bias, but because it helps the project to achieve its goals. It is another way of showing that the staff are trustworthy, and this is not wishful thinking by the staff, since it is often confirmed by the children. Through living together, almost in each other's pockets, it is difficult to hide feelings from each other. Consequently it becomes patently obvious to the children that the least enjoyable part of each course for the adults is the imposition of discipline. Nevertheless, they persist, and it is only a question of time before some of the children come to understand the underlying reason for this perseverance.

This rather lengthy discussion of the framework of the course will hopefully make the description of the mechanics more understandable.

Rather than describe the actual chronological events, a number of themes which are common to all courses at Tyn-y-Pwll will be dealt with, and, where appropriate, illustrated by examples.

Decision Making

The project leader has the ultimate responsibility for all aspects of the course, and all other staff members consider themselves largely responsible to him. Apart from this the chain of command is kept as uncomplicated as possible. There are no deputy project leaders or senior staff members, and all decisions are made on a group basis. This system is not only possible but has, in fact, worked well for the past seven years. Staff meetings take place at least twice a week, and any problems are fully discussed. Due to very careful staff selection, there is little acrimony, and the group structure enables what little there is to be quickly resolved. All members of staff are capable of taking overall decisions, and in the event of a crisis, whichever member of staff is present makes the decision, knowing that he will have the support of his colleagues. Each member of staff has a particular area of responsibility, such as administration, catering, equipment, canoeing, rock climbing or camping. These responsibilities are interchangeable, and most members of staff have tried two or three of the roles.

As has been suggested previously, the overall policy for a course is agreed upon in general terms at the beginning. During the course, however, the staff meet once or twice weekly to discuss progress. The chairperson of

70

the meeting, who, incidentally, is never the project leader, draws up an agenda; minutes are kept and if any specific tasks are to be undertaken, then each task is assigned to a particular person, who gives a progress report at the next staff meeting. If any conflict has arisen during the week between staff members, this is discussed and resolved at the meeting. Details of these are also recorded in the minutes.

Staff conflicts take various forms and are triggered by a number of different causes, ranging from misplacement or misuse of equipment, differing interpretations of the rules, and differing standards in relation to the state of the showers or bed-making, through to different views and practices concerning the way children should be handled.

The day to day decisions on what activities are to take place are made at full group meetings which occur every three to four days. The guidelines by which the group makes these decisions are firstly, that each day should be divided roughly between an outdoor and an indoor activity, such as a morning of hillwalking and an afternoon of model-making; and secondly, that if conflict arises between children and adults as to the choice of activity, this is solved by give and take, so if the staff want the group to practice map reading, they may have to agree that the group should all go to the beach afterwards. This system works well and gives the staff flexibility in introducing activities which are less popular with the children but which the staff feel are important. Again, the idea of contract and obligation smooths the way.

Dealing with Conflict

There are, nevertheless, occasions when hostility and aggression are very near to the surface in the group. When this happens, the project leader holds a special meeting with the individual group and its leader, and attempts to create a climate in which all can express their attitudes and feelings. These are often connected with antagonism to the group leader, perhaps for making them walk twice as far as the other group leaders. The project leader is well placed to deal with the situation not only because he has overall responsibility, but also because he is seen as being more detached, since it is known that his involvement with the centre is only part time. Because of the very nature of the group and its situation, conflict is common, as in any similar group where the members live in continuous close proximity. Some of this conflict is no more than irritation writ large and is dealt with on an informal 'let's all shake hands' basis by a staff member. In cases where a particular staff member and one child are in conflict, this is dealt with at a whole group meeting at which the project leader acts as arbiter. Staff members must justify their actions, as must the children, and while blame is never apportioned by the project leader, he will use the situation to illustrate whatever points he wishes to make at that time. For example, he can suggest that conflict is a very common occurrence in the lives of everybody and ask for alternative ways of solving such differences. It is often fruitful to compare the conflict resolving machinery at Tyn-y-Pwll with that at the child's school or at home.

In cases where two children are in conflict with each other, the project leader will usually see them together informally and request permission to mention the subject at the next group meeting. This preliminary discussion usually ensures that the individual children can cope with a discussion of their conflicts in the total group, but this will not be done if either, or both, of the children is unwilling or unready for it. If the conflict is between child and staff, there are few problems, because the staff members can cope; if it is between two children, a little careful groundwork often eases the situation. This sort of 'falling out' is far more common among girls than boys and usually resolves itself after the first few days of the course.

There are, naturally, situations in which more violent and deep rooted behaviour occurs. A child may suddenly become extremely hostile to one or several staff members; she may manipulate others and form a gang that tries to intimidate another girl, or in some cases a member of staff. The role of the staff here is to recognise the likelihood of such a situation arising and inform the project leader. He will then deal with the situation himself. This is because, as already noted, his greater detachment makes it easier for him to handle the hostility of the children, and it is in keeping with his position of ultimate responsibility.

When the project leader feels that there is tension between members of the group, he will always attempt to bring this out into the open. Whilst there are advantages to a short intensive course, one of the drawbacks is that if progress is to be made, then the preliminary settling down period must be shortened and some conflict situations must therefore be forced. Again, the project leader takes the full responsibility for such situations. Most group meetings take place whilst the project leader is present. In his absence the meetings are conducted on a much more superficial basis, being concerned only with programme changes and activity planning.

When members of staff are in conflict, again this is discussed at the next group meeting, and here the opportunity is taken to point out that the frustration and irritability demonstrated by adults arises from just the same sources as similar behaviour in the children. The aim is for children to become confident enough to say at a meeting, *'The reason I shouted at you is because I didn't receive the letter I was expecting from home, and I had to take my anger out on somebody'.* Sometimes we succeed.

When children arrive at Tyn-y-Pwll, they are told at the first group meeting that the only behaviour which will not be tolerated is bullying. It is recognised, of course, that some degree of scapegoating is almost inevitable in any group, but this is different from persistent intimidation. Nevertheless, somebody will always try this kind of behaviour, if only to test the boundaries of the system. In order that the staff may keep the promise made at the first group meeting, that no child will be allowed to bully another, it is obvious that the staff must be aware of any incidents that do occur. As such incidents tend to take place away from the main body of the group, particularly in the dormitory, extra responsibility is placed on the staff member who is supervising the children at free times or bedtime, and if this entails 'snooping' by that staff member, then so be it. Some find it highly unpleasant to have to act in what they consider to be an underhand way; but if the alternative is that a child is able to turn such squeamishness to her advantage and intimidate another child, then the whole basis of trust and confidence in the group is destroyed. The view is taken that ignorance is no defence when it comes to preventing bullying. The temptation to believe that something is not happening, simply because it has not been seen, is considerable, especially when the unseen incident is apparently innocuous. Experience at Tyn-y-Pwll indicates that nothing destroys relationships faster than this reluctance to root out bullying and intimidation. No victim is so self controlled that his or her fear is not apparent to somebody looking for it.

To conclude, without a consistent pattern of discipline, in the sense discussed above, the likelihood of achieving any real progress is small. Only when the group has achieved stability do the staff attempt to tackle individual problems.

Activities

Although opportunities for individual counselling are made available when appropriate, it is the group which is the starting point for the discussion of problems. Because of the flexibility of the programme of activities, it is usually not difficult to create an atmosphere in which children are prepared to participate in discussion. For example, the group might attempt a strenuous physical activity which needs more than just physical capabilities. The ascent of Snowdon, which every course attempts, falls into this category. To complete the climb successfully, determination and perseverance are just as important as strong muscles. After the struggle, almost all the children feel a great sense of achievement and, as it is stressed that the achievement reflects the qualities of the group as a whole, there is often a relaxed warm feeling in the group. This can be used to bring out the themes of achievement, group work, and physical and mental determination as they relate to other areas of the child's life.

A different activity which can be used in a similar and very successful way is drama. Just as some children feel that they are not physically capable of climbing Snowdon, and are therefore very satisfied when they reach the top, so some children are very nervous about acting, and experience just as strong a sense of achievement after contributing to a 20 minute improvised play. It is after these kinds of activities that children, without any prompting at all, will talk about themselves quite openly to the whole group, secure in the knowledge that they will find just as much support as was given in the rest of the group activities.

Perhaps the most successful of all the activities which produce this climate of relaxation and trust, is in fact the easiest to organise. The hills surrounding Tyn-y-Pwll were once the location of some of the most extensive slate quarrying operations in Europe. Although these working have been abandoned, they still provide some dramatic scenery, with great mountains of slate and vast flooded quarries hundreds of feet deep. Thus, within ten minutes walking distance of the centre, there is an unusual and slightly sinister world which, after dark especially, can create awe in the most cynical of children. The group will often take a walk to these quarries late at night, and many girls, and boys, who would normally be acutely embarrassed at admitting their nervousness, will seek the comfort of an adult hand, although this will usually be quickly dropped immediately the centre is in sight! The relief at reaching the lights and warmth of Tyn-y-Pwll after the walk often produces the same sort of feelings as those described above. The significance of all these activities is that they enable children to accept the legitimacy of feelings they would rather not acknowledge. For many of them, fear equals cowardice, which often leads to foolhardy and dangerous behaviour because they do not want to be thought·'chicken'.

It should be noted here that the physical content of the courses is the same for girls as it is for boys, and there really is very little difference in the standard achieved by the two groups. It is often a source of amazement to passers-by to see a game of soccer taking place on the beach, and to realise that, of the dozen or so participants, only two or three are male. In the summer months, the evenings during girls' courses are just as likely to be spent playing cricket as rounders, and with equal enthusiasm and enjoyment. In fact, given the opportunity, the girls are just as tough and competitive as the boys. Because of years of experience, the staff accept this as a fact, and the girls are not invited to participate in a boys' activity to see how well they do, but are expected to perform as capably as the boys, which they invariably do. The male members of staff derive just as much enjoyment, if rather more bruises, from a game of soccer with a team of girls, and this is always communicated explicitly. The situation cuts both ways, since many boys enjoy, and are encouraged in, the more feminine creative arts of cookery, knitting and sewing.

Relationships

The relationship between the male staff members and the girls is vital to the success or failure of the course, as most of the girls have father-figure problems, their fathers being either dead, absent or ineffectual. There is intense curiosity among the girls about what the men think or believe, why they do the job they do, what their wives or girlfriends are like—in short, a great thirst for knowledge about the adult world they will soon be entering. In cases where the parents are divorced or the father has deserted the family, great mistrust and hostility can take the place of curiosity, and somehow the male staff must attempt to present themselves as viable, consistent alternatives. This requires great self confidence on the part of the staff and is difficult to maintain without support and encouragement. There have been many occasions when transference has occurred and the project leader, in particular, has found himself cast firmly in the father role.

There are also occasions when girls develop intense, if brief, feelings of affection for the male members of staff, and it is important that they should not be briskly rebuffed, but dealt with kindly and sympathetically. On the other hand, it would be fatal if the male members of staff were to misconstrue these situations, or worse, if they considered it to be because of their great sexual appeal. Deprived adolescent girls are constantly looking for someone to love or be loved by, and it is important that they should be able to discuss these feelings. Obviously a certain amount of prudence is necessary in this situation, but in the relaxed atmosphere of Tyn-y-Pwll, the children come to see that affectionate, physical contact is perfectly permissible as long as it is open and not exclusive. Thus, a girl who comments upon another sitting on a male staff

74

member's knee will be told that she is perfectly free to sit on the other. The evening round of bedrooms is always done by a male and female member of staff together, who tuck the children up in bed and, except where they know it will not be welcome, give them a goodnight kiss on the forehead.

For many of the girls from broken families, Tyn-y-Pwll provides a respite from the responsibilities thrust upon them at home. A girl of 14 may have five or six younger siblings that she must look after constantly, and towards whom she must act as an adult. At Tyn-y-Pwll she is given the opportunity, albeit for a short space of time, to become a child again, which means that both the good and bad side of her childish behaviour must be accepted.

Assessment

The final aspect of the courses to be described in this section concerns the methods of assessment and the resolution of the course itself. After the child has left Tyn-y-Pwll, a report on her progress is sent to the social worker concerned. The actual report form is by no means the ideal document, but it does have the advantage of being intelligible to both child and adult. It consists of 20 categories which are graded on a five point scale ranging from excellent to poor. The subjects covered by the report vary, from the straightforward, such as 'physical abilities' or 'response in discussions'; through the more complex, such as 'relationships with peers' or 'concern for other people'; to the speculative, such as 'capacity for self-awareness' or 'leadership potential'. The project leader also gives a summary of the child's performance and mentions any particular points of interest not covered by the rest of the form.

All the reports are discussed by the whole group at the last meeting before the course ends. Each staff member is assigned a specific number of reports to complete, and so the child knows who is responsible for the comments expressed. This is important because each child is given the opportunity to disagree with the grades given by a member of staff, and each child is free also to comment on grades given by staff to other children. Thus in a real way, the group judges both its performance as a whole, and the individual performance of its members. The children are invited to comment upon the performance and contribution of the staff to the course, using the same report form as is used for themselves. This form, while necessary and useful as a guide to the social worker concerned, is perhaps most useful as a means of checking how successful each member of the group has been in achieving those goals set at the very first group meeting. Naturally, everyone fails to some degree and succeeds to some degree; the important thing is that these failures and successes are known and admitted to by all members of the group and, even more important, can be seen in the context of the total living experience.

Although the experience at Tyn-y-Pwll may have some value in itself, it would be pointless unless it is related to the whole child and her total living situation.

It is vital that the social worker makes a considerable effort to prepare the child and discuss the purpose of the planned course. It is also important that the social worker and family maintain contact during the course, and that the Tyn-y-Pwll staff relate the experience of the present to the problems of the future. Good communication and relationships between the social workers and Tyn-y-Pwll are seen to be important and are actively encouraged.

EVALUATION

Evaluating the work done at Tyn-y-Pwll requires a variety of methods. None of them is particularly scientific, but then the courses have never existed to provide data for eager statisticians. During the last five years, over 300 children have attended the centre, and it has been possible to maintain some contact, however tenuous, with about 80% of them. In the case of at least 40% of the children, this has included home visits, regular correspondence and returns to the centre. For the other 40%, there has been some correspondence and occasional meetings, and in only a small number of cases has contact been entirely lost.

In the short term, the effect of the courses on individual children can be measured by comparing the comments of the social workers concerned, before and after the child's visit to Tyn-y-Pwll. If the social worker has asked the staff to work on a particular aspect of the child's behaviour, such as difficulty in relating to peers, then he can judge what, if any, changes have taken place since the child's visit. Similarly, if a child has committed a number of offences prior to her visit, and during her stay promises to try and stay out of trouble in the future, then to some extent one could judge success with this child by whether she quickly commits any further offences.

It should be pointed out here that, because the project leader's full time job is concerned with that area of the country from which most of Tyn-y-Pwll's clients come, there is less need for an extensive, formal follow-up system. He and the delegated staff member come into contact with most of the children's social workers during the normal course of events, and can therefore keep an informal eye on the progress of the children. As regards the staff's evaluation of whether a particular course has been successful or not, in the short term they have very little evidence to rely on, other than their own subjective opinions and those of the children involved. Some idea can be formed of how successful the group work sections of the course have been by the number of children who keep in contact either with the centre or with each other. The first residential short term care course at Tyn-y-Pwll in 1971 was probably the most difficult ever run at the centre, in that all the girls were rejected from other forms of care, yet nearly three-quarters of the girls on that course still keep in regular contact, either by letter, phone or visits.

There are flaws in using a measure of this kind, of course. Some children we will not hear from at all. Then suddenly, after a period of sometimes three or four years, a girl will write to Tyn-y-Pwll, to ask for advice or help because some aspect of her life at that time has revived memories of her visit. There is no way of knowing prior to the event, when or if situations like this will occur, and there is no way of recreating the conditions of one particular course in subsequent ones.

Since goals are set within each course itself, both staff and children can examine these at the end of the course and determine to what degree they have been achieved. This gives some indication of the success of the course per se, but does not necessarily have any bearing on how the child will adjust to the environment from which he or she comes. One girl, in fact, described how distressed she was after leaving Tyn-y-Pwll to find that the situation at school and at home had not changed in the least since her departure. But having been persuaded at Tyn-y-Pwll that she herself was the only person who could change her position in these environments, she found her life much more difficult than before her visit. Previously she had been able to blame all her misfortunes on her surroundings; now she was sensitive enough to realise that part of the problem stemmed from her own behaviour, and she was also honest enough to admit that this made her more unhappy than she was before she came to Tyn-y-Pwll. Her very understandable argument was that, in some cases, ignorance is bliss.

Tyn-y-Pwll has been fortunate in having a sympathetic management committee who do not continually demand evidence of the scheme's efficiency. The staff are therefore free to pursue whatever course of action seems to them to be appropriate. If actions had to be justified in terms of results, then exercises would have been invented which were easily measured, but this would have been foreign to the spirit of the course. In the last analysis there is nothing more concrete than the subjective evaluations of the staff, the social workers and the children themselves, to determine whether Tyn-y-Pwll is successful or not. It has been a very interesting and, in the opinion of the writers, a very worthwhile project. It has, however, proved very demanding for all the staff concerned, and although some of them have been involved for four or five years, others were only able to sustain the demands made by this way of life for 18 months or two years. Nevertheless, virtually all have remained in contact, and many are now serving on the management committee, which is one indication of the value and importance of the project to them.

The other main problem is financial. It is probably logical that such projects as Tyn-y-Pwll should be started by voluntary bodies, and then the ideas developed and continued by local authorities. It is certainly very difficult for a small charity to provide this kind of service without reasonable outside financial support, and it is always vulnerable to exploitation. For instance, there were several occasions when children stayed on when the course finished, sometimes for as long as a year, because the local authority was either unwilling or unable to place them elsewhere. This obviously placed additional pressure on the staff, since the period between courses was designed to allow them to assess the previous course, recover, and plan for the next one. In some cases, local authorities promised additional grants to assuage their guilt, but there was not one case where these promises were honoured.

On one occasion, the Chairman of the management committee wrote to the directors of the 17 authorities who had used Tyn-y-Pwll on several occasions, asking if any financial help was possible. The result was, to say the least, disappointing. Six directors replied promptly, two saying they would try to help and four saying that 'due to financial constraints' they were unable to do so. Six other authorities replied via someone other than the director, after a period ranging from one to four months, saying they were unable to help. Saddest of all, five authorities did not even acknowledge the letter.

What is certain in the minds of the staff of Tyn-y-Pwll is that it has been well worth the effort. While very few of the children have been provided with 'miracle cures' it is doubtful if any were harmed by the experience.

Probably the most valuable activities were drama indoors and rock climbing outdoors, since both demand a degree of self perception, self discipline and honesty. The vast majority of children enjoyed their stay, most acquired some new interests, all were valued members of a caring group, and many began to care for others.

Postscript

The staff and management committee have always been unanimous in their view that, while short term residential courses can be valuable, they should as far as possible be available within 50 or 60 miles of the child's own home. By the time this book is published, Tyn-y-Pwll will have ceased to function in the way described; but a new, more accessible centre, run along similar lines, by the same management committee, is about to open in an old coaching inn on the Powys/Herefordshire border.

EASTERN RAVENS TRUST

Val Hart, Alistair Lindsay and Keith Lindsey

INTRODUCTION

The Eastern Ravens Trust is a voluntary organisation which works with young people whose emotional needs have been substantially unmet by their families and community. It operates in Stockton-on-Tees in three fairly tight-knit communities, all with a large percentage of problem families. Eastern Ravens was started in 1961 by Roger Bradshaw who formed a group of ten boys, 10-12 years old, with which he subsequently worked on a weekly basis for six years. Over the years, 17 groups have been established and there are currently ten groups in operation.

Two of the authors of this report, Keith Lindsey and Alistair Lindsay, have been involved with the Trust for 12 years and each ran a small group of his own from 1966—1973. Keith Lindsey is now the full time worker. Val Hart is with the Trust for a year under the Job Creation Scheme and has designed and carried out the evaluation of the project reported in this chapter.

This account is based on our conviction of the increasing role of preventive work in tackling social problems. While Eastern Ravens demonstrates only one of many approaches, it seems to us to combine many of the essential elements of effective preventive work, which include: starting young enough; linking with families; using volunteers; a long-term, small-group approach; and a method designed, and refined over the years, to maximise the impact which can be made upon a group of youngsters in only a few hours a week.

While paid leaders have played a part, particularly in managing and administering the work, volunteers have been the foundation on which it is based. Using volunteers brings its own organisational problems, but this chapter aims to demonstrate that it is possible to do preventive work using volunteers, and to achieve credibility and co-operation with schools and the statutory services.

There is, in Camberwell in London, a very similar independent organisation called the Greenhouse Trust which was founded in 1956. Over the years we have kept in touch and compared notes, and it is interesting to record that we have both developed the same thinking about objectives and method, and encountered many similar organisational problems.

BACKGROUND

The Communities

The original boys' group was set up in West Street in 1961. West Street is about a third of a mile long, consisting of 150 houses, and while it joins up directly with one of the main roads into central Stockton, it is an otherwise physically isolated cul-de-sac. Built in 1928, this street had acquired a very strong internal community spirit, but its interaction with the world outside had become minimal. There were high levels of unemployment, truancy, crime and delinquency, and a large number of problem families, particularly at the closed end of the road. Broken windows were common. Fences between the houses had, in many cases, disappeared, and thoroughfares taken their place. Rubbish on the road and pavements was rife. Street lights, once repaired, were soon out of action again. The road boasted the best bonfire in town every 5th November; every house was 'open' at New Year and many were 'open' all the year round; every death was followed by a collection both in the street and the local pub. One night a house was gutted by fire, although mercifully, the mother and seven children were out. Within an hour, all of these children had been taken in by neighbours.

Since 1961 seven groups have been formed in West Street. Since 1968 five groups have been formed in part of the neighbouring Crown Estate, which had similar problems, and six years later we formed the first of five groups in a third estate, Park End. In general these three catchment areas all contained the same kinds of social problems, with a relatively high degree of mobility and inter-relationships between families. We decided to spread to another estate when we knew it well enough to establish that there were very big problems indeed. All these estates are to some extent physically isolated from the other communities; entrance by road is only possible on one side, the other sides being bounded by railway lines, fields and streams. Also the social problems on the estates seem to be greatest at the points of greatest physical isolation.

In terms of social provision these three estates were all minimally serviced, and those facilities which did exist were simply not used. In 1961 the first estate was desperately impoverished and ignored by the rest of the Stockton community. Now the houses have all been modernised by the Council and have maintained the new standard. During the modernisation, the Social Services Department appointed a neighbourhood worker to facilitate the change, who was used a lot by the community. The secondary school appointed a youth worker and established a very active community centre, which both parents and children now use. In addition the children now use, on their own initiative, the local council sports centre and the YMCA, both of which have excellent recreation facilities. The primary school also appointed a full-time home liaison teacher. We believe that many of the original problems resulted from a very poor self image, and that by helping to raise the competence and confidence levels of the estate dwellers, we have, to some extent, enabled them to benefit from subsequent improvements.

Eastern Ravens is an independent organisation, which makes it very easy to start operating in an area with no other provision and to establish trusting relationships with parents. Also it becomes a focus of attention, making it easier for other agencies to become involved.

The Young People

The young people with whom we work are carefully selected following discussions with all the agencies involved in the area. The particular problem which we are tackling is emotional impoverishment. We deliberately select young people between the ages of seven and ten, whose basic emotional needs to love and be loved, to feel important and feel they belong, and whose need for new experiences and understanding, have not been adequately met by family, community or school.

A typical child at the age of say ten, will display symptoms of gross attention seeking, disruptiveness in a group, bad behaviour in school, withdrawal such as truancy or running away from home, aggressiveness such as fighting or always having accidents, inability to maintain and keep good relationships, a very low ability to understand and relate to authority figures, boredom and lack of interest, vandalism and stealing. He has developed patterns of behaviour which enable him to cope with failure and frustration, which for him are the norm, and while very effective in terms of survival, these prevent him from finding himself in a situation which contains anything other than failure and frustration. His communication with other people is a specific example of this, being substantially non verbal with a large component of acting out behaviour. Verbal communication is very restricted. He has no ability either to describe the context and thus the meaning of what he is saying to others, or to understand the context which others describe, such as people from a background and situation he has not experienced and does not understand.

This description of the typical child with whom Eastern Ravens works is derived from observations, over the years, of the sorts of children who benefit from our approach. When we are forming a group we use it to help the schools and social workers to identify appropriate group members.

DEVELOPMENT OF EASTERN RAVENS TRUST

With hindsight there are five separate phases that can now be identified. The variables that characterised these phases are shown in Figure 1.

Phase 1: Getting Established (1961-1964)

During this phase we had only one small long-term group formed in 1961 by Roger Bradshaw, who saw some small boys putting black paint in his petrol tank. By talking to them, and having had recent direct experience of the Greenhouse Trust, he recognised their behaviour as being symptomatic of a problem he was sure he could do something about. Through a chaplain who was a member of the Teesside Industrial Mission, he contacted the local headmaster, who also happened to be a magistrate and the chairman of the juvenile bench. In discussion, it became clear that there were three problem areas in the neighbourhood of his school, namely West Street, Busby and Crown Estate, each containing large numbers of disadvantaged families.

Figure 1   Phases of development of Eastern Ravens Trust

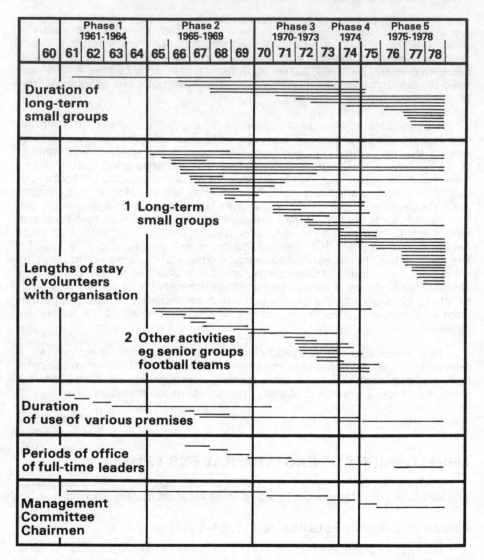

Full-time leaders

No. 1 — paid part by ICI and part by Local Authority
No. 2 — paid as part-time youth leader
No. 3 — unpaid
Nos. 4-7 — paid totally by Local Authority
Nos. 1, 2, 3 and 7 were ex-group leaders

Premises

No. 4 — Lucy Street premises.
No. 7 — 324 Norton Road.
No. 8 — Eastern Ravens Clubhouse.

Roger devised a scheme which involved the launching of a special youth club, although he saw this only as a beginning. In July 1961 he wrote a report entitled *'An Experimental Youth Club'*[1], in which he describes the aims he had in mind for the club as follows:

'1   *To supplement the home lives of a small number of boys who are either on probation, are known delinquents who have not been before the court, live in an environment conducive to delinqency or come from very poor homes.*

2   *To keep the age range as small as possible.*

3   *To allow the members a semi-free rein in planning the club's activities. Leaders to act as a steering influence. Emphasis should be on adventure, boating, camping, foreign travel and visits to local industries. Other activities to present new pastimes.*

4   *The club will be entirely non-denominational with no racial bars.*

5   *No boy will be excluded by virtue of his financial status even if the parents could afford subscriptions, since he may still have severe emotional needs.*

6   *Money will be raised to buy any necessary equipment and to finance holidays — where money from homes is inadequate — so that all the boys can participate.*

7   *To take an interest in and develop the boys' activities outside as well as inside the club.*

8   *To work in very close co-operation with youth officers, probation officers, schools, industry (at a later date when the boys are working) and parents.*

9   *To allow our ideas to pass to others so that clubs can snowball.'*

Roger decided on a group of ten boys aged 10 and 11 years from West Street and Busby. The headmaster provided a list of those he knew were in greatest need and Roger and a friend started twice weekly meetings with the group in July 1961. The friend only stayed for a few months, but Roger continued on his own. For the first three weeks the group met in Busby School, then for three months in a church hall, but neither was very satisfactory. They then moved to a disused school five miles away which they used for a year. It was the end of 1962 before Roger finally found what he considered to be a suitable building, in Lucy Street, consisting of one prefabricated condemned building, next to the school, which had been used as the school canteen. It contained two rooms, joined by a small kitchen, cupboard, cloakroom and toilets. The building's total size was 60' × 20' and proved ideal for a small group to hold a club evening.

During this phase he used his own vehicle for transport and raised money through friends and local groups while parents of group members ran jumble sales. He established a good relationship with the local authority youth officer and built up a strong personal credibility in the community where his group lived. By home visiting and having friends of his group at club evenings he got to know a larger number of families, boys and girls. He had an informal committee supporting him during this phase, consisting of the industrial chaplain, the local headmaster, the local canon and the youth officer for Stockton.

Phase 2: Expansion (1965-1969)

This phase saw three major changes occurring: many leaders joined, enabling a rapid expansion in the work of the club; the progression to a full time leader; and the club reached the size of an 'organisation' and produced more systematic ways of managing itself. The development in each of these aspects and the rapid expansion in the work overall are illustrated in Figure 1 and Table 1.

How the work grew

Three voluntary workers joined in 1965. The first, Alistair Lindsay, an engineer with ICI, got in touch with Roger through the industrial chaplain; the second, Bill Barker, an insurance agent, lived in the flat next door to Alistair; and the third was a man Alistair met at ICI called Chris Coulter, who was also an engineer. All helped Roger with his group and its friendship group for a few months, then Chris and Bill formed groups from Roger's original group and their friends. They soon merged to become the first senior group, being No. 2 in Table 1, and out of this sprang the basis of a football team which Bill ran and which attracted about a dozen extra members.

In May 1966 Alistair set up his own long term small group. Eight boys aged 10-12 from West Street were selected from lists of very needy children provided by the headmaster and Roger; these were children who were clearly going to need an enormous amount of help and support to cope and overcome the massive problems they experienced, mainly at home but also at school. His girlfriend, a nurse, and another girl, a school secretary that Roger and he had met on a youth leadership course, were to help run this group. During the summer, Keith Lindsey, who is now full-time leader but was at that time a student doing vacation work at ICI, told Chris that he and three of his friends wanted to do something useful during the summer. It was suggested that they run a week's camp in July for a group of boys aged 10-11 from Crown Estate. It was so enjoyable that the leaders and boys kept in touch; they wrote to each other and had many weekends and holidays together over the following five years. So by setting up one summer camp, we had unwittingly established another small long term group.

In January 1967 a local school teacher started a weekly meeting for a group of nine and ten year olds from Crown Estate — 16 boys and six girls. The first of our Community Service Volunteers was given the job of helping her, and when they subsequently left, the organisation decided to create three new small long term groups, each with two volunteers. Simply by giving that teacher permission to use our premises, we acquired three new groups (6, 7 and 8).

In May 1969 Alistair formed a second senior group (9) consisting of friends of his own group aged 13 to 15 years. This group quickly acquired about 30 members including four girls, and was to last for about four years. During that time some 30 different individuals helped to run it, about half of them students on placement as part of their course. It subsequently proved very difficult to find volunteers who would move from the large group to begin, or help with, a small young group. Because of this, the emphasis swung away from starting new long term groups, a process we were unaware of at the time.

Table 1   Range of activities by the end of 1969

Date of formation		Activity/group	No. of members	Sex	Members' ages when group formed	No. of Leaders	Area of members' homes	Venue of club meeting
1 July	1961	Small long term	10	Boys	10-11	1	West Street	Lucy Street
2 March	1966	1st large senior	15	Boys	15-16		West Street	324 Norton Road
			4	Girls	15-16	4	West Street	324 Norton Road
3 May	1966	Small long term	8	Boys	10-12	2	West Street	Lucy Street
4 July	1966	Small long term	8	Boys	10-12	4	Crown Estate	–
5 Aug.	1966	Football team	12-16	Boys	15-16	1	West Street	324 Norton Road
6 Sept.	1967	Small long term	8	Boys	10-11	2	Crown Estate	Lucy Street
7 Sept.	1967	Small long term	8	Boys	9-10	2	Crown Estate	Lucy Street
8 Sept.	1967	Small long term	6	Girls	10-11	2	Crown Estate	Lucy Street
9 May	1967	2nd large senior	26	Boys	13-15	3	Crown Estate	Lucy Street
			4	Girls	13-14		West Street	Lucy Street
10 July	1969	Summer camps for children not included in above groups	40	both	10-12	10	Crown Estate and West Street	

The creation of groups and the arrival of volunteers described here can also be traced in Figure 1

85

Nearly all our groups had a summer camp, which generated a lot of community pressure to do something for other children in the community. Through one of our trustees in Cambridge, who was the Director of Children's Relief International, two separate groups of students offered to run holiday camps for us. We decided to restrict them to non-members. So from the summer of 1969 for about four years, 40 children had a summer holiday. Dealing with these larger numbers of young people made it easier to get grant aid from the local authority and acted as a positive inducement to operate the variety of activities which now characterised the work of the Trust.

The progression to a full time leader

By mid 1966 Roger found himself in charge of a club with nine voluntary leaders. To give him more time to run and develop the club, he obtained one year's leave of absence from ICI on half pay, the Youth Service also contributing to his salary. This year lasted from October 1966 until October 1977. During this time, he arranged for Community Service Volunteers to work with the club, the first arriving in March 1967. He was the first of six consecutive CSV workers, each staying for between four and six months. His job was to help run groups, assist with family problems during the day, help with administration and look after premises and the minibus. When Roger went back to ICI, one of the volunteers did the job for eight months, although being paid only as a part time youth leader. She was succeeded in August 1968 by another voluntary worker who, with the approval of all concerned, filled the role of acting leader in charge, as well as his own full time job. In September 1969, the first full time worker was appointed by the local authority (see Figure 1).

How the club was managed

During 1965 and 1966, all the day to day business of the club was handled by leaders having daily informal contact with each other. In July 1967, when we rented part of a terraced house in Norton Road and had a place to meet, Roger estabished regular monthly meetings of all voluntary leaders and, for the next two years, this was the primary vehicle for managing the Trust. It firmly established the norm that all leaders, whatever they were doing, played a part in running the organisation. Meanwhile the committee slowly became more formal. It began having regular meetings every two months and acquired a few more members, one of whom took over as treasurer from Roger. Its main tasks consisted of money raising, controlling expenditure, and negotiating with the local authority for grant aid and the appointment of a full time leader.

In March 1968, the club became a trust, which enabled us to raise money by deed of covenant and also increased our standing with other organisations. Two trustees were appointed, but stayed very much in the background, not attending regular management meetings. In the early part of that year confusion was arising as to objectives, methods and areas of responsibility and in May the management committee set up a small group consisting of two members of the committee and two leaders to define and report on these items. This small group liaised with the leaders and the committee and, after many hours discussion and mountains of paperwork, a final statement of objectives and methods was produced in January 1969 which read as follows:

'1 *Objectives*
Help children from deprived and potentially delinquent homes in the West Street and Crown Estate areas of Stockton-on-Tees.

Meet their basic needs—self identity, security, significance, understanding their social framework.

Give them the opportunity of:
a *consistent relationships with adults and with each other;*
b *increased experience of people, places, situations, ideas.*

As they mature allow them to change in their attitudes to themselves, to family life, school/employment, authority, society.

Break the recurring cycle of deprivation.

2 *Methods*
Meet basic needs:
concern for individuals, encouragement, consistency and regularity.

Control environment:
start young, work in small groups with a high leader/member ratio.

Develop maturity:
emphasise experience, learning situations and relationships.

Understand and influence their background:
work with families, schools/employers, social services and particularly probation in the local community, in Teesside and if necessary, nationally.

3 *Resources:*
leaders
finance
club premises
van
camping and games equipment etc.

Within this general framework of objectives, methods, and resources there is considerable freedom. Individual leaders vary in the methods they use within their group and there is a need for both full time and part time workers. In addition to group work we need people who will take responsibility for van maintenance, secretarial work, fund raising etc.' [2].

Although this statement clearly said that working in small groups and starting young were cornerstones of our approach, it was tacitly assumed throughout the organisation that all the other diverse activities that arose from these were appropriate. This document removed confusion, and the rest of the work that was done clarified the responsibility of the leaders and the management committee. By mid 1969, we were running very short of money so new committee members were found specifically to raise funds with considerable success. We secured a gift of a new minibus from the Variety Club in September 1969, the same month as our first full time leader, paid totally by the local authority, was appointed. Significant advances were made in securing a government grant to pay for new premises in Norton Road, which had been purchased by one of our volunteers and rented to the Trust until the Trust could pay for it.

Phase 3: The problems of multiple activities (1970-1973)

During this phase there was a strengthening of the quality of our small group work, mainly because the full time leader had particular skills in dealing with individuals and small groups with difficult problems; but few volunteers came along willing to start new groups, with the majority helping with the two senior groups.

During 1970, the committee, which now had several new members, became confused and sceptical about what the Trust was doing. They wanted the money they were raising spent differently and, in particular, they wanted higher material standards around the premises. The leaders disagreed with this, partly because they saw it as irrelevant and partly because they had always been in the habit of deciding these things themselves. This came to a head in July 1970, with the resignation of the management committee chairman, who had been with the Trust since 1961. The full time leader decided to stay, although he had been on the brink of resigning too, and eventually left in September 1971 as he had always intended. This crisis brought the two groups closer together, because it sparked off better communication, leading to a better mutual understanding.

We deliberately selected a replacement leader with a flair for community work because we wanted to strengthen the other activities of the Trust. His appointment led to an influx of leaders into the senior group, and the emphasis of leaders' meetings swung away from long term, small group work to community issues. This caused problems for the leaders of the small groups, who could see no relevance in these wider community problems. This was the first indication of a rift between the leaders of small groups and the others. It slowly became greater and we were forced to realise that the differences between the motivation, needs and interests of small group leaders and the others were so great that they could no longer be managed as a unit.

The other major problem of this period was that both social services and probation became confused by what we were doing. For example, one probation officer rightly reacted very strongly when one of his clients, who was a member of a small group, of the senior group, and of the football team, was being visited at home by the leader of each to 'help him with his problems'. What the probation officer saw was three different leaders all trying to help, with different styles and different aims. This confused his client and made his job infinitely more difficult.

In November 1973 the Trust produced a major detailed report describing the method used in small group work [3]. This was written to clear up confusion within the organisation about what the small group method was, and to enable us to describe our approach to people outside the organisation. It was rapidly adopted for both purposes and since then it has increasingly been used as an authoritative statement of the Trust's method in small group work. In the same month the full time leader left, without an immediate successor being appointed.

Phase 4: Management problems continue (1974)

In this phase we began to solve some of the problems that had been building up. We obtained rent free, disused lavatories which we converted into one large room, a small kitchen, toilet and cupboard, for the use of small long term groups. As soon as it was ready, the small groups moved from the Norton Road house. This resolved the conflict of small groups and larger older groups using the same building.

We set up an executive of four people to be responsible for the work of the Trust, previously all done by the full time leader. This consisted of the management committee chairman, responsible for the management committee and financial control, and three voluntary leaders, one responsible for small group work, another responsible for family work and the third responsible for all other activities. Each co-ordinated and supported the voluntary leaders in his own sphere. In addition we advertised for a replacement full time leader, who was appointed in May 1974, to take over the role of the last member of the executive described above, his main task being to strengthen and encourage the more community related activities.

The executive was initially successful. Extra effort went back into small group work and in May 1974 we formed a new group in a new area, Park End, where there were rapidly increasing social problems. The Trust already knew about ten families in the area who had moved from West Street. Moreover, it was very close to our new junior premises. Significantly, we found a lot of support from the local schools and social services for this new group. However, the executive was not sufficiently strong to maintain its independence, and the two leader groups, who had originally been part of the management process, found this separate management even more threatening than the differences between themselves.

During the summer of 1974, we began to run short of funds again. By September we had threats to cut off electricity, gas and telephone at the Norton Road house, several court orders pending, and a lot of money owing to volunteers. This financial crisis, together with the weakness of the executive, led the trustees in October 1974 to relieve the whole management committee of its responsibilities. They called back Roger Bradshaw, now a management consultant, to do a diagnosis of the Trust's problems.

Phase 5: 1975—Present day

After lengthy consultation with both voluntary leaders and management committee members, Roger produced the following draft proposal:

1 *That the Trust should cease all activities other than long term small group work, which should maintain the same objectives as agreed in 1968.*

2 *That at the age when group members leave school, the group should no longer be permitted to use Trust premises, transport or be financed by the Trust. This is intended to help group leaders at this awkward stage to break away from group activities to individual work, which is more appropriate at this stage.*

3   *That new groups should be formed to breathe new life and confidence into the organisation.*

Roger was also invited to become a third trustee, and the three of them formed a small management committee, with a new chairman, Dave King, a JP who had been a voluntary leader himself since 1966.

As a result of Roger's first recommendation, the then full time leader found that he no longer had a job and chose to leave in May 1975. The next full time leader, Keith Lindsey, was appointed in September 1976. He had also been a volunteer since 1966. The main task during the interim period was running down and stopping the senior group. The football team survived but separate from the Trust.

In 1976 it was decided to sell the Norton Road house since it was not appropriate for long term small group work. Since Keith took over, six new groups have been formed, with 14 new voluntary leaders. Instead of acquiring more buildings we have begun to use other people's buildings within the three communities. We have continued to have our own transport, the latest being a Land Rover, which is ideal for our purposes.

A major change had come about by this time, in that voluntary leaders were, by their own wish, no longer involved in the management processes of the Trust. They continue to be consulted and have the chance to influence events, but they are not part of the decision making, management machinery. We are now clear about our objectives, methods, and scope. We have a management committee which includes four former small group leaders, and we are enjoying a period of stability and growth in which our credibility with schools, the Youth Service and social services has improved steadily. This has been reflected by a number of favourable articles in the local press.

EASTERN RAVENS AS IT IS NOW

Management, Workers and Leaders

The management committee consists of the founder of Eastern Ravens and the local community chaplain, both trustees, and seven others. They are the chairman, who is a JP, the treasurer, who is an accountant, the secretary, a local headmaster, an engineer, the full time worker and the local authority youth and community officer. The chairman, full time worker, secretary and the engineer are all ex-group leaders. The Trust has one full time worker and three people employed temporarily under the Job Creation Scheme, one of whom carried out the evaluation project reported in this chapter.

There are ten groups operating in three areas: six for boys and four for girls with a total membership of 57. The groups are led by 18 voluntary workers comprising a very wide range of people, a feature we regard as very valuable. Six of them are from the local communities and are friends of ex-group members, or ex-group members themselves. Details of the leaders are given in Table 2.

The Trust enjoys good relationships with the majority of statutory departments, which have been developed as a result of very deliberate effort. The full time worker is in regular contact with people at all levels in the local schools, social services and psychological service, and group leaders are in occasional contact with specific teachers and social workers.

Table 2   Information about Leaders as at 31st March 1978

Group	Length of time as Group Leader/s	Age of Leader	Age of Group Members	Former Member or Friend of Member	Occupation
1	5½ years	27	14-16	X	Television Installer
2	9 months	21	14-16		Job Creation with Eastern Ravens
3	3 years	18	12-14		Student at Technical College
	3 years	18			Student at 6th Form College
4	1 year	18	11-13	X	Section Leader in Bakery
	2 years	23		X	Furniture Van Driver's Mate
5	14 months	18	8-10		Student at 6th Form College
	14 months	18			Secretary
6	13 months	32	8-9		Housewife
	13 months	31			Full-time Worker at Eastern Ravens
7	11 months	26	8-9		Job Creation with Eastern Ravens
	11 months	35			Senior Educational Psychologist
8	6 months	18	8	X	Student at Technical College
	6 months	23			Garage Mechanic
9	3 months	25	11-13	X	Housewife and Shop Assistant
10	1 month	22	8- 9	X	Industrial Painter
	1 month	25			Probation Clerical Worker
	1 month	18			Student at Polytechnic
Assistants (help occasionally with groups eg as driver)					
		23			Art Teacher
		27			Maths Lecturer
		20			Student at Polytechnic

Premises and Finance

We have one clubhouse, rent free from the local authority, a small single purpose building. Other groups meet in part of a school and part of a building used by the local community. Two groups meet in their leaders' homes. We always select premises which are no more than half a mile away from members' homes and preferably as close as possible. This helps to achieve good attendance on group nights and to foster a feeling of community owner- ship. The full time leader has converted the shed at the bottom of his garden into the Trust office, complete with telephone, typing and printing equipment, filing cabinets, library and storage space for camping equipment. Three or four people can hold a meeting there. He also uses the space at the side of the house for parking the 12 seater Land Rover, which is used for transport.

Five years ago, Keith Lindsey and his wife acquired, on behalf of the Trust, a disused farmhouse called 'High House' at Scugdale in the Cleveland Hills. Two years ago, the Trust decided that High House should be managed and financed separately from Eastern Ravens.

We receive local authority grants from the youth and community service, in addition to the full time worker's salary, and from social services. We also receive donations from local organisations and individuals, and raise money ourselves through activities like jumble sales, frequently organised by the groups. The pie chart in Figure 2 shows how our expenditure is broken down.

Leader Training and Support

As shown in Table 2, our leaders have a very diverse background of training and experience and since this is very emotionally demanding work, it is essential that group leaders receive training and support. This is provided in the following ways:

1   When someone shows an interest in leading a group, he or she helps with two or three different groups; talks with the full time worker about these experiences; and is helped to think through some of the objectives and opportunities the group work presents.

2   The full time worker periodically meets with each leader or team of leaders to offer moral support and encouragement and more particularly to discuss any current problems, review the needs of the group members, discuss ideas of appropriate activities and help the leaders to set some short term objectives for the work.

3   Regular evening meetings and residential weekends about twice a year are held to enable group leaders to derive support and encouragement from each other and to think through each other's problems; and secondly, to develop skills in such fields as group work, counselling and trans- actional analysis.

Training sessions are led by our own personnel, who have considerable experience and skill from youth work and industrial management, but we have also benefited from visiting tutors, such as marriage guidance counsellors, a transactional analysis tutor and social workers.

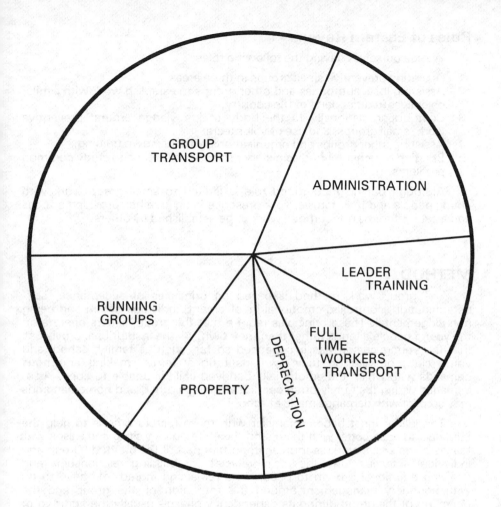

Figure 2   Analysis of expenditure 1977

(Total expenditure for 1977 : £2025)

Roles of Eastern Ravens

We see ourselves having the following roles:

1 Operating preventive small groups in three areas.
2 Assisting local authorities and other groups to establish work with similar objectives in other parts of the country.
3 Contributing nationally to the body of knowledge around preventive work, small groups, and use of volunteers.
4 Assisting other groups and organisations with their own training.
5 Bringing together multi-disciplinary professional groups to study common problems.

Although our neighbourhood role is limited to small group work with young people and their families, our presence in an area has provided a focus and a catalyst for neighbourhood work to be established by others.

METHOD

The group work method is based on principles of acceptance, self-determination, controlled emotional involvement, individualisation and being non-judgemental. These principles require that the group leaders operate on the young people's terms rather than their own. All the institutional provisions that the young person has experienced so far, such as family, school and youth club, operate on their own institutional terms, making enormous demands with which the emotionally deprived child is unable to cope. Also, demands within the family often conflict with each other, and home demands may conflict with demands made at school.

The leader must become familiar with these factors if he is to help the individual to cope better with them, and therefore home visiting and liaison with teachers and social workers form an important part of the method. Group and individual activities form the main vehicles for building relationships and enabling emotional growth to occur. The remaining ingredients have to do with boundary management around the formation of the group and the operating of the group during its dependency phase—usually the first two or three years of its life.

Boundary management

To demonstrate the need for boundaries, let us consider a family on whom we used to call at 8.30 am to help the seven children, all chronic truants aged between six and 13, to get to school. The children would creep one by one into the living room. One would open the cupboard to be enveloped in an avalanche of clothes. Each child might find his clothes. They might be clean. The food cupboard might be empty. At school the child might be late and might get the cane. At lunch time Mam might be at home, and so on. Each 'might' represents a missing boundary. Eastern Ravens' job is, on group nights, to replace these 'mights' by 'wills', not in the compulsory sense but in the predictable sense. For example: 'you will be accepted as a member of this group'; 'the group will meet every Wednesday'; 'however naughty you are you will always be welcome'.

The needs of these children had been met only partially. For them to grow emotionally and achieve a sense of identity, unpredictability needed to be replaced by predictability, failure by success, confusion by clarity, and inconsistent by consistent treatment. Group leaders see members for only a few hours each week, mainly at group meetings. It is therefore vital to take every opportunity to identify, create and maintain certain critical boundaries around the life of the group.

Forming and operating the group

As a new group is formed, a number of decisions have to be made: about the sex of the group members; about the size of the group—never more than eight; about the ages of the children—never more than 12 years old, with no more than a two year span. Group members are drawn from an area with a concentration of problem families and we ensure that the group members live within about 200 yards of each other. Since families know each other very well, the community becomes sympathetic to Eastern Ravens and supportive of resulting behaviour and life style changes among group members. This is necessary to avoid alienation or reversion and our experience is that we successfully avoid both. These decisions provide a number of boundaries between the group and its environment; they are quite clear and reduce to a manageable level the number of dynamics within the group.

To give the youngsters the opportunity to grow emotionally, it is necessary to erect a structure around the group in operation and maintain it pretty rigidly, helping the children first to adapt to it, then to grow within it. The structure consists of seven key boundaries, five of which are easy to apply, while two require a high degree of social skill.

Membership boundary. Once members have joined, group membership is kept constant. Compare the fixed group with the home where there is a continual change of family as relatives or neighbours or even Mam move in and out.

Leadership boundary. The leaders work only with their own group. This avoids the question, 'is he really interested in us or does he like them more?'

End-point boundary. This boundary is important because it does not exist. The group continues for as many years as members want it to. We try to make sure that there are no grounds for anxiety about rejection from the group.

The emotional significance of these three boundaries to the members, through their experience of the group, becomes: 'This is our group; they are our leaders; and we do belong to this group. We have tested the leaders and we know that they won't reject us'. These are all fundamental emotional needs satisfied by simple boundary management.

Time boundaries. By ensuring that the group meets at the same time on the same evening of each week, a regular, predictable and enjoyable influence is introduced into the lives of the members. This contrasts with the lack of such influences in their home environment, resulting from their inability to capture a sense of time or fit in with others.

Space boundaries. It is important that the group is clear what space it has at its disposal. We achieve this in two ways: with a small clubhouse where one group on its own will use the whole building, and with a minibus. Compare clear space boundaries with some members' homes, where they often do not know which bedroom, or bed, they will sleep in. They cannot look after their own clothes or toys because others in the family do not accept individual ownership of space. The Land Rover, late at night, gives rise to feelings of warmth and security triggering some very significant discussions. Space boundaries in that situation are crystal clear.

The remaining two boundaries require a lot of sensitivity and skill to apply.

Behavioural boundaries. Deeply ingrained in our group members is a dislike and a resentment of rules. There are probably only three rules of any real importance; don't put yourself or anyone else in danger; don't damage property; and don't damage the relationship between the group and the outside world, for example damaging the fence belonging to the farmer on whose land you are camping. Any rules over and above these are likely to hinder emotional growth, and there are many rules which should be avoided, especially those designed to meet the needs of the leaders rather than the members, such as no running, no shouting, and no boots. However, when one of the basic groundrules is broken, this must not be ignored, but should be responded to in some appropriate way. As a result of this consistency, the member will be helped to recognise the importance of these rules.

Relationship boundaries. Emotional growth is maximised by establishing as close a relationship as possible between leader and member. This is limited by the extent to which the leader can accept the member's behaviour. The relationship is less close if a leader finds his eating habits distasteful, or if he believes it is in some way wrong for members of his group to visit his own home, or regards it as right to know group members' incomes but wrong for them to know his.

After the dependency phase

Around the age of 14 or 15, and, in any case, at least two and perhaps three years after the group has been formed, the group begins to work from a dependency phase to a counter-dependency phase, a natural transition which is essential to the emotional development of the members. They will start to challenge the boundaries within which they have been operating, and it is most important that the group leaders recognise what is happening and enable these challenges to be handled constructively. For example, Jack asks the leader if he can bring his friend or a girl friend. The leader's response should now be something like, *'As far as I am concerned it's up to the group; why not ask them'*. This, at first, will seem quite foreign and threatening to Jack, who will probably ask two others, who he knows will say 'yes', and then bring his friend along and get a very angry reaction from the remainder of the group. The leader must make sure that Jack learns from this. He should now be concentrating on getting the group to assume control of itself, even if it decides on things he does not want, like meeting on their own without him.

Generally the leader will have problems of his own to cope with, for he too will have developed a dependence on the group, and rejection is one of the emotions he must learn to handle. If properly handled by the leader, the phase of challenging constraints eventually becomes a period of self government for the group, using the group leader as a resource rather than an authority figure. This can last for up to two years.

Around the age of leaving school, individual interests usually turn towards work and girl friends, and after the age of 16 or so the leader will tend to spend his time on individual and family contacts rather than group activities. Where individuals wish it, contact with group leaders can be maintained for many years after that, mostly on a friendship basis. The necessary transition around school leaving age is a very difficult one to achieve. Without positive, skilful effort the most likely outcomes are either that the leader loses contact with group members altogether, or that the group continues operating as a group with a dependent relationship on the leader. The ideal, we think, is something like the leader maintaining contact on an individual basis, with the relationship becoming one of wholesome inter-dependence based on mutual respect, help, and friendship. The Trust has achieved this with about 30-50% of members up to the age of 19 or 20, and with about 10% beyond that age.

We are clear, however, that stopping groups using Trust premises, transport and funds at the age of 16 is necessary to launch this inter-dependent phase and it must not be seen as withdrawing support. It is laying the necessary foundation for a healthier, more adult kind of support.

PROJECT IN ACTION

Richard James and Tony Harris' Group Night

This group, formed in September 1976, contained seven boys now aged 11 to 13. On 15th November 1977, Sharon had come along to drive the Landrover. It was her first contact with Eastern Ravens.

Tony and Sharon arrived at the clubhouse at 6.45 pm with the Landrover. They had arranged to collect the boys at 7.00 pm to go to Stockton Baths. There were five boys playing around waiting. Two of them said that they had been at Brian's group the night before. They asked if they could bring their mate. Tony said none of them could come because they weren't members of his group (1). By 7.00 pm three members had arrived, Darren, Tommy and Lee who told Tony the Todd's weren't coming. Tony accepted that because they usually all walk up the road together (2). They left shortly after seven and picked Richard up on the road. Richard and Tony both sat in the back (3).

In the Landrover they asked Richard where they were going (4). When he said 'Stockton Baths' Darren said he wanted to go to the Forum Baths. Richard explained they were going to Stockton because they were cheaper and by the time they got to the Forum it would be time to come out. Darren announced that when they they got to Stockton he was going to get out and go home. Richard and Tony both ignored this (5) and Darren went into the Baths. Lee said he wasn't going into the Baths because he had already been that day with the school (6). Tony noticed he had no trunks and said he could hire them but Lee decided to be a spectator.

All went into the water except Lee who went upstairs to watch **(7)**. The others played about in the water for about 20 minutes, racing, splashing, ducking, and throwing. After Richard had ducked Tommy twice he started crying and threatened to tell his father. Then Darren said he had a headache and was going out. He didn't but he sat on the edge of the bath. Tony spent two or three minutes with him, then Tommy sat with him for five minutes, followed by Richard who talked to him for five minutes then persuaded him to go out. Richard found him crying in the toilet and being sick. He helped him to get washed in the shower then got dressed **(8)**. Meanwhile Sharon had got out and was talking to Lee.

On the way home, they wanted chips. Tony explained it had cost them enough tonight to go to the baths and they couldn't afford chips. (The group gets up to £15 per month from the Trust.) The lads accepted that **(9)**. When Tony asked what they wanted to do next week they said they wanted to stop in the clubhouse.

They dropped Tommy and Lee off at their house first and went into Darren's house with him. Darren opened the door and Tony and Richard followed him in. Mrs. Robson was watching the telly and was interested in the programme. They told her Darren hadn't been well. She asked what he'd had to eat. Darren said *'nothing'* (at the club). She told the leaders he'd had egg, chips and beans for tea and asked if he had had any more chips. She asked him if he wanted to go up to bed and lie down. Darren replied with a very firm *'no'* as he leaned against the fireplace with his head hanging down. Richard said *'He's just been sick, there's plenty of room for more'*. Mrs. Robson laughed and went back to the telly. On the way out she shouted after Tony, *'By the way, Tony, is this bread going up?'* Tony turned round and said, *'I'll give you the good news first — we're going on strike three weeks before Christmas'*. From her chair she shouted *'Goodnight, probably see you next week'* and they let themselves out **(10)**.

The following morning Keith, the full time leader, saw Billy Wilson across the road at 9.00 am. Billy is also in the group but was not there the previous evening. *'Why wasn't I allowed to go to the club last night?'* he called. Keith crossed the road and went over to him. *'Why, what happened?'*. Billy said *'Darren Robson told me I couldn't go'*.
Keith *'What did Tony say to you?'*
Billy *'Nothing, he looked straight through me. I went down to the town but the Baths were closed. I couldn't find them. Then the cops got me.'*
Keith *'The cops?'*
Billy *'Yes — for trying to break into a butcher's shop. There were about four panda cars — some police ran towards us and we ran away from them. They questioned us in the police station and asked why we ran away from them. They took us home but no-one was in. One of them said 'I know you and your parents'.'*
Keith *'Where were you when the police saw you?'*
Billy *'In the church yard. I can't come to the club now.'*
Keith *'Who says?'*
Billy *'My Mam says I can't go down to the town or to the club. Anyway other people have been to the club.'* **(11)**.

Keith *'Was that why you couldn't go last night?'*
Billy nodded his head.
Keith *'Can you see Tony to tell him about this and ask him to see your Mam?'*
Billy *'I don't know where he lives.'*
Keith *'He lives in Hardwick but he's often in Norton.'*
Billy *'My aunt lives in Roseworth.'*
Keith *'I'll try to see Tony and ask him to call, but look out for him. Anyway I guess you are going to be late for school.'*
Billy *'I'm late anyway, I've got a note.'* **(12)**

Commentary on Richard James and Tony Harris' Group Night

1 An example of maintaining the membership boundary.

2 The alternative would have been to drive to their home to check out why they hadn't arrived. Might be a family problem eg. no money, or not being allowed to attend club as a punishment, a practice we discourage in parents. Might be they were late and other lads preferred them not to be there. Leader's judgement of this depends on his knowledge of the group and the families.

3 Good practice for leaders not to sit in the front. (Relationship boundary)

4 Despite the fact they had agreed the previous week to go to Stockton Baths they had not been able to retain this. Observing time boundaries helps to extend this span.

5 An attention seeking device which should not be rewarded. Ignoring it is the best way to react. (Behavioural boundary)

6 Suspect the real reason is disguised here. Most probably he had no trunks, no money and was too proud to admit either. A few pairs of trunks in the leader's kit could overcome this.

7 Lee should not have been left on his own. One of the leaders should have stayed with him—a good chance to talk or do something together. (Relationship boundary)

8 Suspect this episode is a psychosomatic reaction to emotional distress. He succeeded in getting a great deal of attention. He probably has to resort to this technique at home to get attention. Similar to **(5)**. (Behavioural boundary)

9 This group now accepts that when the leaders say *'No'*, they mean *'No!'* Eight months ago they would have argued for half an hour. (Behavioural boundary)

10 A good example of a home visit. Note the friendly relationship between leaders and parents who jointly avoid making any fuss of Darren. Darren has clearly learnt negative disruptive ways of seeking attention. Leaders have a key role in rewarding, with attention, only constructive behaviour. (Behavioural boundary)

11 Reference to believing that membership boundary has been violated shows emotional importance to group members.

12 This conversation is an excellent example of communication difficulties. Suspect Billy's statements are laced with untruths and inaccurate perceptions (he probably believes they are all genuine) caused by an emotional disturbance. This episode has to be followed up by group leaders talking to parents to find out what the real problem is.

Eileen Sanderson and Barbara Evans' Group Night

This group, formed in April 1975, contains seven girls now aged 12 to 14. When the leaders, Barbara and Eileen, arrived on 23rd November 1977, five members of the group were waiting outside. Barbara gave the key to Andrea **(1)** when they came running up shouting *'What are we doing?'* **(2)**. Andrea opened the door and Eileen and Helen put the lights on. A box of rubbish had been emptied out on the floor. Barbara said they would have to tidy it up before they did the cooking. One girl said she'd help and she and Barbara picked up all the rubbish **(3)**. They spotted the record player which Barbara had brought with her. *'Are you going to have a disco as well?'* Barbara said, *'No, but I've got some of my sister's records'*. They found two table-tennis bats. One asked *'Has anybody got a table-tennis ball?'* **(4)**. Barbara said *'No, but ask Eileen for some money out of the blue purse'*. (This is the group money. Barbara always has that purse with her; the girls never go in it; they always ask; and it is always left sitting out on the table.) Eileen gave her £1 and Andrea and Babs went with her to the shop. On return, they put the change in the purse.

Lisa, Babs and Eileen began making chocolate marshmallows in the kitchen. They let water into the bowl when dissolving the cooking chocolate, and Eileen sent Lisa to the shop, who came back with eating chocolate. Lisa refused to go back to the shop where the shopkeeper is not very pleasant. Eileen had to go herself but she waited till Lisa came with her **(5)**. While Eileen carried on with the cooking, Barbara, who lives near the clubhouse, walked home with Ann to get Ann's watch. They talked all the way; Ann told her that her Mam had won £120 at bingo, and was going to buy Christmas presents with it **(6)**. By the time they had walked about 300 yards from the clubhouse Ann was lost and didn't know where she was **(7)**. Her behaviour while she was with Barbara was very good, although whenever she was with the group she caused chaos **(8)**. Ann remarked to Barbara that she hadn't seen the phone in Barbara's house. Barbara said it was on the stairs **(9)**. While Barbara was cooking, Eileen talked to Helen and Babs about a Christmas party. They said Sharon and Jackie's group had already had one. In fact it was a Hallowe'en party they'd had **(10)**. Helen asked if they were going to do a play this year, like last year, for their Mums and Dads. She said her Mam would come. Babs said her Mam wouldn't.

The next 20 minutes were spent discussing what the play would be about. The girls decided on a funny play, but not a Christmas play. They then suggested characters that could be in it: a snobby lady, a tramp and a gipsy. Andrea said, *'If I'm a tramp I could get an old shirt'* **(11)**. This discussion was punctuated by several distractions. An argument between Ann and Lisa about the sweets they had cooked petered out when they had attracted the attention of the whole group; Ann started throwing records in the air and catching them, and turned the record player up full. Barbara told her to stop it but she didn't stop till Lisa (her older sister) told her to pack it in; Ann and Babs then sat on the bench spitting at each other to see who could spit the farthest. Eileen said, *'If you want to do that, go outside'* and they stopped **(12)**.

Barbara said to Ann, *'Why don't you be the gipsy?'* Nobody else wanted that role. Ann seemed interested but said nothing. Eileen asked her if she'd like to be anything else. *'Oh, I'm not bothered'* said Ann, and went and got the draughts out **(13)** and started playing with Babs. Ann won and a few other draughts games followed. During this, at the other end of the room, Eileen and three girls were going through a very violent dance for the Christmas party and practised it three times. Then they asked Eileen if she could teach them any dances **(14)**. Eileen led them through some rock 'n' roll. Then Helen took the lead and introduced another movement **(15)**. Eileen showed them what she did at keep fit, ending up with all of them trying to do the splits and falling. Then they did some Cossack dancing, which Ann and Helen were very good at **(16)**. The dancing session lasted about 20 minutes and ended with Andrea being invited to give a demonstration of belly dancing. She didn't manage it (they wouldn't put the lights out) but Lisa and Helen did it quite well **(16)**. The evening ended with inspection and distribution of the marshmallows. Half were set, half were floating in chocolate. They said they would cook with Eileen again. They all had five each. Ann polished all hers off immediately. The others offered one to Barbara and Eileen **(17)**. Lisa decided she didn't like the sweets and squeezed them all together in the bag **(18)**.

Helen asked Barbara *'What are we doing next week?'* and then asked Eileen the same question. When Barbara and Eileen didn't respond, Helen said *'Let's have a disco and write the play'* **(19)**. Barbara said, *'Think about it and have some good ideas'*.

Commentary on Eileen Sanderson and Barbara Evans' Group Night

1 A very small way of giving responsibility which has a lot of significance for the group members. Every opportunity like this should be used.

2 At an emotional level this is a request to clarify a framework or boundaries. The answer should describe space and time boundaries, eg. we're in the club-house all night (ie. till 9.00 pm), rather than specific activities or tasks.

3 Good leadership practice, saying what is needed (setting a standard) and helping members to do it.

4 Initiative prompted by availability of table-tennis bats and table. This girl has indicated that she wants to play table-tennis.

5 Leader helping group member to handle authority figures by not allowing her to avoid the situation and demonstrating that it can be done.

6 In a one to one situation group member is more like to talk to leader about family circumstances. It is always useful deliberately to create one to one opportunities. (Relationship boundary)

7 Demonstrates very shallow experiences of places even very near to home.

8 Evidence that this girl needs a lot of individual attention, and won't fit in well in the group till she gets it.

9 Further evidence of lack of knowledge about how others live. She may not know another home with phone and has no way of knowing where it is kept.

10 An example of confusion about time. Applying time boundaries is one way of helping group members to be clearer about time.

11 Note that they are approaching the play from where they are emotionally eg. *'How would I like to protect myself?'.* It is allowing them to build up the play in this way which meets their emotional needs as they work it out.

12 Eileen put the girls in a position of choice—going outside or stopping—and this enabled them to stop and save face with their friends. Had she just said *'Stop that',* the only way they could have created choice was by defying the leader and continuing.

13 Barbara put Ann under more emotional pressure than she could cope with but because choice of activity is permitted Ann had a way out of it—in this case playing draughts.

14 Showing that girls are free to use adults as a resource. It's important to encourage this, since normally they regard adults as a threat to be avoided.

15 An example of a group member taking the lead constructively. If there is choice of activity, there is always scope for this provided it is permitted and rewarded. It was rewarded in this case by the leader and other members following her lead.

16 Example of group members experiencing success. They are more likely to succeed when they choose the activity. A leader who dominates and directs what they do runs the risk of creating failure.

17 Example of non verbal approval of leaders. Leaders need to be able to recognise these signs to avoid feeling rejected themselves.

18 Destroying something they have created can be a way of avoiding failure—and should be allowed without fuss. It could also indicate strong emotions asociated with the object (eg. was not allowed to take part in creating it) or a very high level of frustration which could have nothing to do with the object in question.

19 Creating an atmosphere in which members feel free and even eager to express their own ideas is a vital leadership skill. This atmosphere is readily prevented from developing if leaders are too anxious to answer all the questions themselves.

EVALUATION OF EASTERN RAVENS METHOD AND PRACTICE

For a number of years we had intended to make an evaluation of the work done by Eastern Ravens for two main reasons: first, to check out the assumptions made about the basic precepts of the work, such as running long term groups for five or six years and home visiting; and second, to check the effectiveness of the work and establish some authority with which to recommend our method to other organisations or statutory agencies that wish to undertake preventive work. We were afforded an opportunity by the appointment of Valerie Hart in June 1977, for a period of one year. This evaluation took the form of:

1 A survey of the attitudes of group members, parents of members, and to a lesser extent, professional workers, towards the basic precepts of the Eastern Ravens method.

2 An assessment of how nearly the practice of the group work in the organisation matches up with the strict method which was previously set out as the ideal.

Survey of Members and Parents

Method

Three groups were chosen for the detailed study. The first was a group of boys which had met together over a period of six years with the same leader, but had disbanded more than three years previously when the members were 16. The second group, which comprised seven girls, was in the middle of its career as it was formed in April 1975. The third was a group recently formed in February 1977. This group comprised five boys who were only eight years old, since the organisation had responded to the recommendation of a group of local head teachers, psychologists and social workers, who said that children in severe need can be recognised and helped through group work, as young as seven years old. The parents of all the members of all the groups were included in the sample.

It was decided to obtain the views of members and parents on:

1 What aspects of Eastern Ravens are most important.

2 What are the benefits of membership of Eastern Ravens.

3 Any problems which have arisen as a result of membership of Eastern Ravens.

4 The Eastern Ravens group work model: small groups; long term groups; control and discipline within the group; home visiting; age of members when groups are formed.

This list was compiled as a result of workers in Eastern Ravens sharing their views on the feedback required and also as a result of some preliminary informal conversations with parents and members which also served to confirm the viability of the project.

The method for the survey entailed focused interviews, followed by the construction of an interview schedule, as described in standard texts on social research methods. For the focused interview, the members and parents in the sample were visited—the parents in their houses and the members either at home, if they were relatively adult, or individually at school, through the kind co-operation of the schools, since it was felt this was the best way of obtaining their personal unprejudiced views. The interviews were conducted in a very relaxed and informal manner. Rapport was first established with the respondent and specific questions based on the list of objectives above were slipped into the conversation. No notes were taken in the course of this interview but a recording was made as soon as possible afterwards of the specific words and phrases used by the respondents in answer to the questions.

Interview schedules were then compiled, one for parents and one for members, which were based upon the data collected during the focused inter-views. A number of fairly general questions were posed, eg. *'What are the benefits of being a member of Eastern Ravens?'* and *'What do you think of leaders coming round to your homes?'*. Each general question was then followed by up to seven possible answers, each of which had been actually verbalised by one or more people during the focused interviews. For example, two of the six alternatives presented after the question about the benefits of being a member were:

- *'Helped to keep me out of trouble.'*
- *'Able to develop friendships with other group members.'*

Following the question about home visiting, two of the five alternatives presented were:

- *'I like the leaders to come round because it makes me feel good.'*
- *'Yes—because we talk about what we do at the club.'*

Each section concluded with the open question *'Any other comments?'*

We were surprised to discover from the focused interviews that virtually all the answers we had received to our questions were positive—very few scornful remarks or bad feedback had been received. We felt duty bound to incorporate into the schedules a number of negative options so that the respondents had the freedom to identify with a written criticism.

Each parent and member was then visited again with a copy of the interview schedule. Respondents were asked to indicate which statements they agreed with, and they were then asked to indicate which two statements under each general heading they considered to be the most important. This survey thus yielded data which could be handled quantitatively. Social workers were presented with the same interview schedule as were the parents, but with a few additional questions.

Some general comments can be made on the interviewing process:

1 In all cases where the parents were interviewed, it was the mother who spoke. This was interpreted as being partly because the interviewing took place during the day, and partly because care of the kids is very much seen as the prerogative of mother. Even when the father was present, he either did not take part in the discussion or kept a low profile.

2 Only one parent refused to be interviewed. Her son was a former member and she misinterpreted the nature of the visit stating *'Our Billy's 19 now, he's not interested in coming to the club'.*

3 Another member of the same group had moved house and could not be contacted. Another never answered the door.

Results of the Survey

The importance of Eastern Ravens and the benefits of membership. An unequivocal message was received that both parents and members appreciate the work of Eastern Ravens. One of the most striking results of the interview schedule was that in response to the question *'What do you think of Eastern Ravens?'* all parents gave priority to *'Keeps them off the streets'.* It was clear that this did not indicate the negative sentiments of 'out of sight, out of mind' but rather a genuine fear that while outside in small gangs, the kids were subject to pressure from peers to engage in acts of vandalism or petty crime. In contrast, perhaps, to the typical concern of middle class parents that their children receive good education, the priority for these parents is that their kids stay out of trouble with the police.

It was felt that being in a group *'Helps them to mix and to share ideas with others'* and *'Gives them a chance to see new places and meet new people'.* One mother on social security with three lively children to look after claimed *'It helps me to know someone cares about the kids and it gives me a break'.* Another became very animated, *'Oh I think Eastern Ravens is the best thing that ever happened round here—it should become world-wide—like the boy scouts'.*

The members' answers indicated that one of the most important advantages of being a member of Eastern Ravens was the opportunity to see new places. During the initial focused interviews most of the members talked at length about the various holidays they had been on and many considered them to be the highlight of Eastern Ravens' activities. With the exception of two sisters, none of the members had been on holiday with their parents owing to prohibitive costs. All the families of the two younger groups were living on social security. This meant that the children received very little pocket money, and so activities outside their immediate environment were necessarily restricted. All members claimed that Eastern Ravens was important because there was *'Nothing to do around here'.* This partly reflects the truth in that the areas in which Eastern Ravens works are deprived in terms of accessible cultural and leisure amenities, but it also reflects an unwillingness on the part of the kids to take advantage of facilities which are offered locally.

Problems associated with Eastern Ravens. A problem often encountered is that children in a family who are not members of Eastern Ravens resent those who are. Voluntary leaders can come under considerable pressure both from the kids and the parents. Parents who indicated that this problem had arisen in their family were asked if they would have preferred their child not to have been included in a group. None agreed to this. The members were more voluble. They were asked *'What would you change about Eastern Ravens?'.* They commented on the decor of the clubhouse, said they wanted more holidays and to help at more jumble sales.

The disbanded boys' group had existed through the phase when Eastern Ravens had owned a large three-storey terraced house, and the organisation had engaged in activities other than small group work. Two of the former members complained that the club nights had been disrupted by other activities taking place in the same building. It is perhaps remarkable that, in all the lengthy conversations with the parents and members of this group, this was the only indication that Eastern Ravens had organisational problems at that time, and indicates the degree of independence belonging to each group with respect to other personnel of the Trust.

The importance of small groups. Without exception, the parents found this section difficult to answer, feeling that the altruistic response should be that large groups would be preferable because it would benefit more kids, but also feeling intuitively that small groups were of benefit to their own kids. It is a testimony to their honesty that, after expressing their initial reservations, all the parents bar one stated that they believed small groups were better. The reasons given varied, and included a practical approach to the problem. *'Small groups would be better, the leaders can only handle so many.'* *'If they're all 'owt like mine, six is enough.'* But it was also felt that *'Kids feel more at home in a smaller group'* and that *'Those who are in the group get more attention'.* Some parents did feel, however, that the group was sufficiently capable of expansion to squeeze in another of their own offspring.

The members, without exception, thought small groups were preferable. Most had experience of other youth clubs and so were in a good position to judge. One said *'In a small group you feel more like a person instead of just another number on the roll book.'* Other reasons included: *'Fighting starts when the group gets too big'* and *'You get used to the other club members.'* All thought that bringing friends should be controlled and that visitors should only have the status of guests. It was clear that members felt secure within their own group and regarded the introduction of new members on a permanent basis as a threat to this security.

The starting age and duration of the group. The parents were asked *'At what age do you think groups should start?'* and were given a list beginning at seven to eight years and finishing at 14 to 16 years. The majority of parents felt that seven to eight was the most appropriate time to start groups, mainly on the principle of 'the earlier the better'. It was felt that *'If they start at seven, they get to know it and understand it, and they have something to look forward to once a week.'* One parent who felt that groups should be formed of children between the ages of eight and ten considered that *'that's when they start to take an interest in things and would benefit most.'* The eldest age range considered appropriate for forming groups was 10 to 12. Only one parent plumped for this particular age range because *'At that age they start to hang around in gangs, especially lads'.* All the parents felt that groups *'should go on for a few years'* mainly because, *'They would feel let down if the group just stopped.'* *'It's much more use to the kids if it goes on'.*

The members were unclear about what age the group should begin, all ages between seven and 14 being quoted, but there was near unanimity that the finishing age should be 16. No-one, however, said they were too young to be in a group!

106

Home visiting. It was clear that parents greatly appreciate visits from leaders. All the parents said they enjoyed chatting to the leaders to find out more about the group activities and if the children had been behaving themselves. This latter point was stressed by most of the parents, although voluntary leaders are unlikely to complain about a child's behaviour to his or her parents.

Home visiting was a big hit among the kids. Only one was unenthusiastic — *'My mother likes it but I'm not bothered.'* Others said *'I like the leaders to come round because it makes me feel good.'* The most popular reaction was *'I like them to come round because we talk about what we do at the club.'* The overriding impression gained from the various comments about home visiting was that the leader popping round was an enjoyable experience for all the family and enhanced the child's feeling of self-importance.

Mixed groups or single sex. None of the members felt that groups should be composed of both sexes. The boys felt that the girls would always *'get their own way.'* The girls, on the other hand, did not share this sentiment but considered that members would feel more self-conscious and that it would be difficult to decide on group activities. In the past all Eastern Ravens groups have been single sex. However, it is intended to establish a group of eight — four girls and four boys, leaving open the option of dividing into two groups if it becomes unmanageable. It will be interesting to see if members were intuitively correct in opting for single sex groups, or whether their rejection of mixed groups was a conservative reaction to the unfamiliar.

Comments from Social Workers

Social workers in contact with five kids in the two groups currently running were asked to comment on the benefits of Eastern Ravens for the children and their families. They were presented with the same interview schedule as the parents, but with a few additional questions. Their answers were detailed and supportive to the organisation. With regard to individual members, the comments included:

'Elsie appears to have developed some independent sense of identity through the group, is able to enjoy activities separate from the family as a whole and from her other sisters. She enjoys her club membership.'

'Billy and Tommy both seem to enjoy their membership of Eastern Ravens for the opportunities to enjoy new experiences. They look forward to clubnight and they have some regular reinforcement about positive behaviour in different settings.'

'It provides a compensatory experience.'

In only one instance was it felt that the child being a member of Eastern Ravens had not helped the family. The enormity of the problems facing the family — the father has been to prison for sexually assaulting the kids, and the mother is educationally subnormal and unable to cope — means that the influence of Eastern Ravens is little more than a drop in the ocean. However, the social worker considered Eastern Ravens membership beneficial to the child.

Comments about the other families included:

'The mother has had an excellent relationship with the group leaders, seeing them perhaps as less authoritarian and less critical.'

'Contact with Eastern Ravens helps bridge the family's anti-authority attitudes.'

We asked if they felt the roles of the Eastern Ravens and the Social Services conflicted in any way. It was felt that no conflict had been experienced, that Eastern Ravens was involved in valuable supportive work, and the social workers had found liaison between the organisations extremely valuable at times. The social workers were also asked to comment more generally on Eastern Ravens:

'A club that is accessible to Park End children, without concern about lack of money or appropriate clothing, is vital. Usually there are too many material obstacles to club membership, quite apart from the problem of confidence.'

They felt our method was appropriate for the kids from Park End, as *'Children from more deprived environments need a sustained involvement and cumulative experiences to have any impact',* and consequently that small long term groups best met the emotional needs of the children.

Comparison of Actual Practice with the Declared Method

Time since group was formed. 1976 and 1977 saw increased emphasis on establishing new groups, five new groups being formed in 1977, with the result that Eastern Ravens now has a preponderance of younger members. This in part reflects the importance placed by the organisation on working with youngsters at an early age. However, as Table 3 indicates, a three year gap exists between groups A and B and the next group to be formed, group C. This gap corresponds with a previously mentioned crisis within the organisation.

Number of members. The average membership is 5.75. As Table 3 indicates, young groups have fewer members, and therefore a lower member/leader ratio, so that the kids can be given more individual attention. Group I has only three members—this group is centred around an educationally sub-normal child, who left group E when she moved area in May 1977, but who, it was felt, was in great need.

During 1977, groups F and H were formed of children aged seven. Previous Eastern Ravens policy had been to form groups of up to eight kids between the ages of nine and 11. A decision was made to work with a group of seven year olds, because at that age:
- anti-social behaviour and delinquency begins;
- attitudes are forming but are not hardened;
- children are beginning to work and play in small groups;
- parents still have a keen interest in their children.

Membership changes. This section indicates stability of group membership. In the first two years of the group's life, inclusion of new members is strongly discouraged. During this period the kids learn who is in the group and know that they belong to it. Of the five groups formed during 1977, the table

Table 3 Information about existing groups for year ending 31st December 1977

Groups	A	B	C	D	E	F	G	H	I
Time since group was formed	6 years	6 years	2 years 8 months	1 year 7 months	1 year	11 months	8 months	3 months	3 months
Sex of Group	Boys	Girls	Girls	Boys	Girls	Boys	Boys	Boys	Girls
Area group comes from	West Street	West Street	Park End	Park End	Park End	Park End	Park End	Crown Estate	West Street
Present age of members	12-15	13-15	12-13	11-12	9-10	7	8-9	7-8	11-13
No. of members	5	6	7	7	7	5	6	5	3
Membership changes during year	1 joined 2 left	3 joined 2 left	1 joined	1 into care	3 joined 1 left		1 had accident		
No. of leaders	1	1	2	2	2	2	2	2	1
Changes in leadership during year	0	2	0	1	0	0	0	0	0
No. of times group met	40	25 (July-Dec.)	46	47	48	49	35	10	9
Frequency of family visiting	Family connections	Irregular	Only for specific purpose Monthly	Fortnightly	Only for specific purpose Monthly	Weekly	At least fortnightly	Weekly	Weekly
Member's average attendance rate	56%	68%	67%	74%	76%	89%	84%	83%	100%
Monthly expenditure 1 on group	£6.96	£0.53	£6.55	£4.54	£6.63	£4.01	£1.15	£4.09	£1.20
2 on minibus (petrol)	£2.90	£4.75	£1.42	£5.20	£2.30	£5.72	£5.98	£2.90	£0.70

indicates that the membership of four remained constant. The exception, group E, demonstrates that Eastern Ravens' boundaries are guidelines and not hard and fast rules. In this case the member who was most in need, and required the most attention, left the area. The leaders and the full time worker felt that the remaining group members were sufficiently secure to cope with new members being added to the group. Since June 1977 the membership has remained constant and it is felt by the leaders that the group benefited from the inclusion of new members. Both the older groups, A and B, now partially control their own membership, in that they can vote in new members. They cannot, however, expel anyone from the group.

Leadership changes. The table indicates substantial continuity of leadership during 1977, only two groups experiencing a change in leadership. In group D one leader left on getting married, but a substitute leader had been working with the group for some weeks previous to this. Group B did not experience such a smooth transition. The leader left in April, but a new leader was not found until July, and the group did not meet during that time. It is easier to recruit volunteers to start their own group and watch it develop, than it is to recruit leaders during the life of a group. Experience shows that adolescent girls groups are the most demanding, and the most difficult to recruit leaders for.

Number of group meetings. Table 3 shows the number of times groups met in 1977. Inevitably leaders cannot guarantee to be available every week; holidays and illnesses take their toll. Nonetheless the table indicates a very good record for weekly meetings.

Frequency of home visiting. The table indicates that home visiting is more frequent among the families of younger group members. Leaders of younger groups often collect members from their homes, thus naturally establishing a relationship with parents and maintaining weekly contact. Although some leaders are nervous of home visiting, leaders indigenous to the communities in which Eastern Ravens works generally have no problems, and those leaders with families of their own find they immediately have things in common with parents of group members. Problems over home visiting often arise with younger group leaders, who feel that their age is a handicap in visiting parents who, in some instances, have daughters or sons older than themselves. It is interesting that group C, which is run by a girl from sixth form college, was one of the groups chosen for the evaluation project, and all parents of this group responded positively to home visiting.

The table indicates that some leaders do not maintain regular contact with the homes. This does not accord with the importance the organisation attaches to home visiting, but while it is strongly encouraged by the full time worker, voluntary leaders cannot be compelled to visit members' homes on a regular basis.

Attendance levels. The younger groups attain the highest attendance. This is because group members are often collected from home and particular attention is paid to an irregular attender. Often it is the withdrawn members,

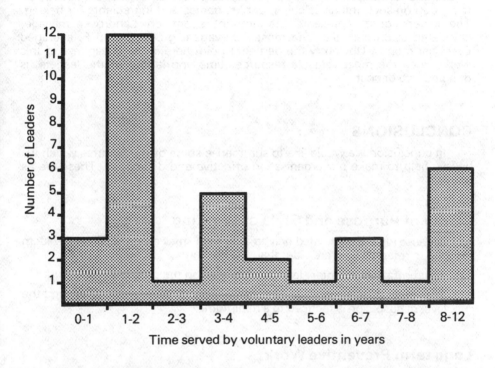

Figure 3   Periods of time served by leaders of small groups
(excluding those leaders who commenced within the last 18 months)

with difficulties in making peer relationships, who do not come. The leader will visit the home to find out why the child is not attending, and the problem is usually overcome. Once groups reach the adolescent stage, experience shows that members become less dependent on the group and the leader, and less regular attendance is often one indication of this.

Monthly expenditure. Table 3 also shows cost per month calculated as an average for the year. The top costs represent the amount spent directly on the group on such things as chips, drinks, games and ingredients for baking. The lower figure represents the amount spent on Landrover mileage, calculated at 8p per mile. The most extravagant group, group F, averaged £9.73 per month. Obviously the pertinent point here is the cheapness of this work, since the most valuable resource, time and labour of the leaders, is donated free of cost.

CONCLUSIONS

In conclusion we would like to summarise some of the features which we believe help to make our organisation effective and distinctive. These are as follows:

Clarity of Purpose and Style of Working

Because we are committed only to long term small group work, and seldom respond to referrals who are older than 11, we find:

1 That untrained voluntary leaders readily grasp the purpose of the work.

2 That other professional agencies can understand and relate to us, and the level of suspicion is reduced to a minimum.

Long term Preventive Work

A child with very severe emotional needs who is to be enabled to come to terms with and make his own choices about the delinquent sub-culture in which he grows up, needs a vast amount of support. This is provided through membership of a small group which begins before his attitudes are hard set and before problems with the law are very far advanced, and which supports him through the formative adolescent period. Significant also in this respect is the relationship built up between leaders and parents through home visiting. A corollary of doing long term work is that it takes several years fully to establish an organisation of this nature.

Volunteers

Our voluntary leaders are a very varied group from graduates to unskilled workers, but many serve for a long period of time (see Figure 3), the average being five years. We explain this remarkable achievement as follows:

1 The job itself is stimulating and interesting: people who get involved with a small group enjoy the close relationships which develop with the group members.

2 The job is a responsible one; the group depends entirely upon the skills and enthusiasm of the voluntary group leader.

3 The work develops: as members grow older the challenges and style of work changes.

4 Considerable personal training and material support is provided by the organisation and recognition is given to problems faced by, and successes of, leaders.

An industrial management consultant, Frederick Herzberg, has identified the four chief motivators: the work itself; responsibility; opportunity for advancement; and personal growth. Interestingly, working conditions and pay are not included in this list. It is significant that all but opportunity for advancement apply to our voluntary leaders.

The Community Helps Itself

There is, among the public, an increasingly prevalent attitude that responsibility for any person in need, or any problem of almost any nature, lies with the local authority or the government. The logical conclusion of this thinking is that no individual is prepared to take on any responsibility at all, not even for himself. This, we believe, runs completely counter to all ideas of personal and community growth, and thus, through using volunteers, and in particular volunteers who were themselves formerly group members, a significant contribution is being made to the integrity of the community as a whole.

Budget and Resources

We attach very great importance to owning our own vehicle, which is not only a means of providing new experiences, but also a more intimate mobile clubhouse. We lease our own club premises but use other community premises and our HQ is a shed, though a very good one, in the garden of the full time worker. Our resources are thus tailored to the needs of the work and our investment in premises is consequently minimal.

In conclusion, therefore, we reassert our conviction that Eastern Ravens is doing effective preventive work, using voluntary group leaders with a minimal budget. Some of the key factors in this work are:

- forming groups at an early age;
- running long term groups lasting several years;
- maintaining fixed membership groups;
- visiting members' homes on a regular basis;
- offering significant support and training to voluntary leaders, and having many former leaders on the management committee.

As the resources of the statutory services become even more strained, we propose Eastern Ravens as a model to be used in designing an appropriate response to the vast numbers of children and young people who suffer emotional deprivation. This approach enables them to become emotionally and socially more mature, to cope with the demands and pressures imposed on them by adulthood and society, and reduces their need to make even more demands on the statutory services.

Acknowledgements

1 The section on 'Method' is based closely on a contribution by Alistair Lindsay to *Concern* (No. 24, Summer 1977), the journal published by the National Children's Bureau, by whose permission it is reproduced.

2 The ideas in the section on the development of the organisation were, in many instances, developed at a conference on *Problems facing organisations supporting small group work,* held in Bristol in April 1977. The conference was sponsored by the Spectrum Children's Trust, and the ideas are included here by permission of the Trustees.

3 The Greenhouse Trust is a similar organisation in Camberwell, London, founded in 1956, with which we have shared ideas, experience and problems over the years and in the preparation of this chapter.

4 Paul and Helena McDowell gave very valuable support and guidance to us in undertaking the evaluation project, reported in this chapter. Both have been lecturers in social research methods at Teesside Polytechnic.

References

1 Bradshaw R. (1961), *An experimental youth club,* Eastern Ravens, unpublished.

2 From an unpublished report to the Eastern Ravens Management Committee, January 1969.

3 Lindsay A. (1973), *A small group method, aimed at alleviating emotional deprevation,* Eastern Ravens. An extract, 'Boundary management', is reprinted in *Youth Social Work Bulletin,* 1975, Vol. 2, No. 6, pp 6-11.

KNOWLES TOOTH CHILDREN'S CENTRE

Dave Evans

INTRODUCTION

The Knowles Tooth Children's Centre is one of several social work projects run by the Chichester Diocesan Association for Family Social Work. It began in 1975, with a small team of three workers, as an attempt to work with children in trouble or at risk. The programme combines a series of residential weekends with a programme of home visits, involving casework with the families of those participating in the project. Although the project serves both East and West Sussex, the vast majority of the children live no more than an hour's travelling distance from the centre. There are four groups, varying between eight and 12 in number and consisting of boys and girls aged between ten and 16, who visit the centre every fourth weekend. In addition to the basic scheme, the centre also runs evening groups, one of which is a co-operative venture with local authority social workers.

During 1974, in discussion with both East and West Sussex County Councils, a number of alternatives were considered. The decision to embark on this particular type of project and to use a large country house as a base, was significantly influenced by the steering group's visit to Northorpe Hall, at which Neil Morgan, the Director, had previously worked. At Northorpe Hall a combination of family casework and residential weekends was used, in an attempt: *'To increase self-confidence, self-awareness, and to help boys improve relationships with both adults and peers. In short the aim is not to produce boys who conform to a set pattern, but to have boys thinking more rationally and reasonably about themselves and their impact on others*[1].

Although the influence of Northorpe Hall is acknowledged, there were important differences from the start. Firstly, each child was assigned to a particular worker, who was responsible for visiting his home and taking a special interest in him; and secondly, it was decided to limit a child's involvement, in the normal course of events, to 12 months. The weekends themselves were built around activities and were intended to provide a suitable environment for developing both the social skills of the youngsters and the social work relationship with them. The home visits were designed to create a link between the residential weekend and the child's life in his own neighbourhood, and to provide an opportunity for working with the family to alleviate any problems that might be contributing to his delinquent or unsocial behaviour.

By 1976, the staff felt that the time had come to review the progress of the project, and this led to the National Children's Bureau being invited to undertake a research exercise. With the aid of a grant from the Department of Health and Social Security, Dave Evans was asked to carry out a year's study, of which this chapter is the result, concentrating particularly on the stage of development achieved during the middle part of 1977. He did not participate in the actual operation of the project but rather monitored the programme, drawing on a number of sources. These included reports and process records kept by the staff, records of weekly staff meetings, and interviews conducted during the last two months of the study with the children, their parents and social workers. This work was intended not so much to provide evidence of success or failure, but as feedback for the centre staff. Dave Evans' intention was to act as a sounding board for the ideas of the staff, and, through this ongoing dialogue, the monitoring of the programme became a cumulative evaluation of the social work processes involved.

THE PROGRAMME IN MAY 1977

Theory and Aims

The Knowles Tooth programme is based on two assumptions. Firstly, many of the problems which children have whilst growing up cannot be resolved by the complete removal from home, peer group and neighbourhood; but, secondly, neither can they be overcome by children remaining at home unless sufficient energy and resources are put into creating a dynamic relationship with them and their families. The primary objective of the project is to bring about change, not only in the attitude and behaviour of the children, but also in the family environment in which the children are developing. The original leaflet, sent to possible referring agencies and still in use in May 1977, made it clear that the staff felt that their project was appropriate for children *'who find difficulty in making relationships, who have few specific interests, and who would gain from the support of home visits coupled with their weekend experiences away from the home environment'* [2].

At the beginning of the project, the staff were anxious not to limit referrals, and consequently left both the objectives and selection criteria deliberately vague. However, as the workers became more aware of both the limitations and potential of the programme, they decided it was necessary to state the aims of the project more clearly. The following objectives were formalised in May, 1977, after two years' experience:

1 *'To cultivate the children's skills, abilities and interests in shared activities and tasks. Although varied in scope and purpose, these activities are the tools with which the staff work to create a shared experience. They may also serve as ongoing pursuits after involvement with the centre has finished.*

2 *To help children to develop and explore the ways in which they relate to others. Interaction may range from one to one relationships between peers and between adults and children, to large clusters of relationships both within the group at the centre and with the world outside.*

116

3 *To develop within the children a sense of responsibility, by requiring them to participate in decision making and problem solving processes at the centre. This may occur at individual and collective levels. Groups are encouraged to make their own pattern of rules within a flexible framework. From this rule making experience, the wider issues of what is acceptable behaviour and control may then be examined. The intention is not to impose external constraints but to build up boundaries as they arise. However, this situation cannot be maintained unless the wider parameters are perceived to be consistent, just and reliable'* [3].

Methods

The programme is based on the residential weekend combined with the home visit, and any other developments have to be seen in this context. Within this framework, the workers attempt to provide adult relationships which are different from those normally experienced by the children in question. The staff offer themselves as examples of caring adults, operating a similar system of values to that found in the wider society, but attempting to do so fairly and humanely. There is an effort to reorient the children towards accepting a society which they feel is treating them unfairly, by showing them that adults, even those in authority, can behave reasonably. Secondly, the group setting is used to teach the children how to cope more readily and reasonably with difficult situations and problems outside the confines of the centre, such as a particular authority, peer group or emotional problem.

Thirdly, this situation is used to gain insights into the individual's needs, potential and existing capabilities. By establishing a relationship with the child in the residential setting, the worker is able to use the shared experiences as a basis for working with the child and his family on their own territory. Without this home contact, the Knowles Tooth programme would be that of an activity centre, where the children are merely encouraged to develop relationships within the closed group and with the adult workers. The home visiting adds another dimension to the project. The Knowles Tooth worker is perceived by the families as the central part of the social work support to the children involved in the programme. In this way, their problems are not seen to be isolated, but a part of the real world in which they live. A mother of one of the boys involved commented on this aspect of the scheme:

'I think that the best thing about when he was at Knowles Tooth was that the worker used to come and see us at home, and helped us as much as Peter. I find that having talked about Peter with someone who really got to know him and help him, I've learnt a lot about him that I didn't know before. Although he still does get upset, I find that I can get through to him more easily now' [4].

So, Knowles Tooth does not confine itself to changing the attitude and behaviour of the child, but also attempts to influence the home situation so that a more reasonable and stable setting is provided for the child's development. For this reason, the workers prefer to take on much of the social work role with the families, if they can obtain the agreement and co-operation of the referring agency, usually the social services department. Where the family is not willing to co-operate in providing opportunities for the constructive development of the child, the centre staff must decide whether to try and compensate for a less than satisfactory home environment, or suggest the removal of the child from home.

A similar dilemma can be faced where schooling is concerned. Once the staff have got to know a particular child, it might be argued that some alternative form of educational provision is needed. This might mean a change of school or extra support at the same school. Co-operation with school and the education welfare service, and awareness of financial constraints, are especially important here. In some cases, the desired change will not be possible, and again, the decision has to be taken whether to put more effort into changing the existing situation, or to abandon the work with that particular child.

The staff have always been concerned about environmental factors beyond the family. For instance, where it becomes apparent that existing recreational facilities are not meeting the needs of an individual child, it may be necessary to attempt to influence the policy of local youth provision so that they can cater for a different type of youngster. It may mean pressing the relevant authorities to set up extra or different facilities, and attempting to have some say in how they should be staffed and run. However, the need to make changes in the child's recreational environment has been a constant source of frustration for the Knowles Tooth staff, due to both lack of time and the isolation of the centre from the youngsters' own neighbourhoods.

Resources and Structure

By May 1977, the project was still being financed jointly by the Diocesan Association and the County Councils of East and West Sussex in the ratio of one to four. There were two different methods of grant aid from the local authorities. East Sussex paid a block grant in return for a specific number of places on the programme, whereas West Sussex paid the Association for each child who was involved. By this time there had been no severe financial limitations imposed on the programme, which meant that the project team had been much freer to concentrate on working with the children than was the case in many other intermediate treatment projects. However, it should be noted that no large amounts of money have been spent on equipment for the centre, apart from the vitally important minibus. For example, archery equipment was bought from the proceeds of the sale of an antique chest, and old cars with money raised by the children themselves. The centre also has a pottery kiln, a sailing dinghy and three canoes. Within the programme, money is also available for visits away from the centre, and for holidays for the groups.

The original staff team consisted of Neil Morgan, a qualified and experienced worker in residential child care, who was appointed Director; Stephen Cathcart, who had previously worked with him, following research and teaching in sociology; and Pippa Charles. In November 1975, Wendy Cutts joined them on secondment from Brighton Area Social Services, but subsequently became a permanent member of staff. Diana Beagle was appointed as a trainee in September 1976, and remained when the post was changed to that of social worker. Having studied psychology, she had worked with children in various settings and also holds a sailing instructor's certificate. When Pippa Charles left the project in February 1977, Carolyn Phillips, a qualified teacher, was appointed to a temporary post for three months.

It can be seen that the team as a whole possesses a combination of skills and training, in both social work and activities. Where skills for a particular activity are lacking within the team, the staff use local contacts, for example, to run photography or pottery sessions. When this takes place, however, there is an attempt by the staff to learn new skills with the youngsters, not only to create a shared learning experience, but also to make the team more adaptable to the needs of the young people.

Each worker is responsible for twelve children attending the centre either at weekends or in evening groups. Two or three workers attend the weekend sessions when children on their caseloads are present, and either the Director or the Deputy Director is at each weekend. Apart from meetings held on Fridays and Mondays in connection with the specific weekend groups, the staff meets as a whole on Wednesdays. This began as a regular feature partly to provide information for this study, and it is doubtful if meetings would have been as frequent if the research had not been taking place. At the same time, staff had come to recognise the need for frequent meetings as their number had increased to a point where informal communication was inadequate.

The management committee of the centre comprises representatives of the Diocesan Association and East and West Sussex County Councils. The Director is invited to attend the committee meetings, but is not a member. Although the committee is the official link with the parent body and the local authorities, the members do not become involved with the practical running of the programme. They are, however, responsible for overall policy, and are very much concerned with the facilities and financial aspects of the project.

THE PROGRAMME IN ACTION

The Weekend Group Sessions

By May 1977, the basic Weekend Scheme had been in operation for over two years, and had changed little from the original concept. While the group was together for the weekend, the staff attempted to use the time building up relationships with the children, developing the youngsters' physical and social skills, and influencing attitudes and behaviour through personal contact and through group meetings called to plan activities or in response to crises during the weekend. The four weekend groups running at this time each had 12 members. There were no definite age limits to the groups, but one consisted of boys and girls between 14 and 16 years, two of boys between 12 and 14 years, and one of younger boys aged 10 to 12.

The groups are collected on a Friday evening after school and remain at the centre until Sunday evening, when they are taken off home by the staff. The centre workers feel that the journeys provide opportunities for observing and reaching the children in a slightly different setting from that of the centre.

The facilities of the centre are available to the groups at the weekend, but each group is also provided with a small sum of money for activities. This can be used for outings, such as swimming and skating, or saved to buy equipment for specialised activities. Under the guidance of the centre staff, the groups are encouraged to take their own decisions regarding activities and, to some extent, through fund raising events and their own contributions, to finance their own programme.

The children are not completely free to decide on their activities. Where ideas are not forthcoming from the group, the staff often make suggestions, and sometimes set up a certain programme for the weekend if they feel this to be necessary for the development of the group. They also use their influence to encourage the youngsters actually to carry out the plans they have made, in order for the group to become more cohesive and to benefit from group and individual achievements. In addition, the staff encourage the group to take responsibility for the complete living experience for the weekend. The decision making and problem solving involved in this process will often take up a major part of the weekend, and can sometimes severely curtail activities for the children, as one 13 year old girl pointed out: *'We have meetings whenever anything goes wrong. They sometimes take ages and can be really boring. Everyone moans about them and we try and put them off, or get out of them if we can. We have a big meeting on Friday night, to decide what games and things we're going to do, and which jobs everyone has to do for the weekend, like cooking and washing up. That meeting is usually alright as we need to decide what we are going to do for the weekend. In the other meetings, either everyone talks at once or nobody says anything.'*

The following example serves to illustrate some of the aspects of the weekend visits in terms of the aims of the overall programme. The weekend was chosen because it presented more than the usual number of difficulties, experienced with a comparatively new group of 12-14 year old boys.

The workers' report on the weekend stated that *'the workers' experience of this weekend in general was that it was 'up-hill' and frustrating'.* This frustration remains one of the dilemmas of the programme — that of how to provide the youngsters with an enjoyable experience, which can help to develop their relationships and skills, whilst also providing them with sometimes difficult learning experiences.

During the preceding visit jumble had been collected and a sale organised for the Saturday afternoon. The remaining jumble had to be collected on the Friday evening before the evening meal. Whilst this was going on, the group was enthusiastic and co-operated well with the staff, although interest diminished as the collection proceeded. This set something of a pattern for the weekend — whilst the group were involved in a specific activity, they were eager, even if it took some pressure from the staff to get them started. For instance, the jumble sale itself went well, with everyone contributing and working together. Even the clearing up was taken care of quickly, without complaint and with little direction needed from the staff.

During the time when no specific activities were being organised by the staff, the group was much less able to get on together, as is shown by the following extracts from the weekend report:

'At breakfast on Sunday, Charlie (staff) said that there was one thing which we had to talk about. The fire alarm in the art room had been set off, and the group was asked who was responsible. Neil admitted fairly quickly that he had thrown a dart at the alarm—this was thought to be very funny by the rest of the group and it took a lot of explaining before they seemed at all able to accept that this was not only stupid but potentially dangerous. The group was asked what should be done about the incident and they decided that they would pay for some new glass out of their £5 weekend money.

'When we had returned to the centre, after the jumble sale on Saturday afternoon, Dana and Phil discovered that their beds had been wrecked, and a meeting was called. The meeting lasted over an hour, with the majority of the group unable to listen or concentrate on why the workers thought it important to discover who had wrecked the beds. Eventually Neil said that he had done it with three others, who then also owned up saying that they had done it 'for a laugh'. By this time the group could not wait to get out of the meeting and most of the good feeling that had been generated by the jumble sale had been lost.

'Almost immediately after this meeting, Wendy (staff) discovered that a whole packet of fish food had been poured into the fish-tank with a lump of coal. Wendy called a meeting, and again three of the boys said they had done it, but then became very resentful when they were made to change the water in the tank, and said that they hadn't done it but had only owned up to get the meeting over. The staff tried to explain to them that by doing that they had only made sure that future meetings would be more difficult, but they seemed unable to take this in' [5].

At an informal meeting at the end of the weekend, the staff asked the group what they had thought about the weekend and how it could be improved. None of the group was interested in looking at what had gone wrong with the weekend, or in discussing plans for the next visit so that the children could enjoy their weekend more. In general, the staff felt that they were getting no response from the group.

It is important to remember here that the object of the weekend visit is not merely to provide the children with an enjoyable experience, but to provide opportunities, through such events as the group meetings, for discussion about stealing and vandalism as well as the personal problems of the young people. In order to provide the framework for this to take place, however, the staff need to create certain relationships with and between the children. To a large extent, this is done through the enjoyment and involvement of shared experiences. The balance between enjoyable and frustrating experiences is always a difficult one, but in this case, the staff felt that the problems which had arisen at the weekend had not been used very constructively.

The weekend was discussed at the staff meeting the following week, where those who had worked the weekend felt that much of the friction, both between boys and staff, and between the boys themselves, had been caused by half of them being much less mature than the others.

Whilst this might be remedied by an extra member of staff, it was suggested that the problems could also have been because it was only the second weekend of a new group. During the first weekend, the children had probably found the adults tolerant, and were determined to find out how far they could go in terms of behaviour. Following the discussion, the weekend was seen to have had several positive aspects, not least in deciding what work needed to be done with the group and with individuals in the time before the next visit. For this particular group, it was decided that more planning of activities was needed in the short-term, and that group meetings ought to be considered more as informal, relaxed occasions, with at least some emphasis on positive aspects, such as the planning of activities.

The Evening Group Sessions

By the summer of 1976, a full weekend programme with 48 children was in operation, so it had been decided to experiment with groups of six youngsters visiting the centre one evening per week. Although there were differences from the weekend sessions, such as less time available but more frequent meetings, and an attempt to provide a greater focus to the group's activity, the methods of working were similar and represent the Knowles Tooth programme as a whole.

The group of 14-16 year old boys had all originally been referred for weekend groups by the Brighton Area of the Social Services Department. For some, there had not been places available; one boy had a Saturday job and would not have come to the centre for the weekend. It was thought that another boy would not have been able to cope with a full weekend away from home.

The staff had originally envisaged such activities as furniture restoration and canoe building, which could be used to increase the self-confidence and sense of achievement of the youngsters. After the first two sessions, the approach was rethought, as the group did not seem to be making much progress. It seemed to the staff that it became too easy, both for the staff and the children, to have a set routine, where progress might be made within the group, without having any necessary long-term effect on the young people's development or behaviour. It was decided to throw the youngsters back more on their own resources. They would only come to the centre once every two weeks, with the intervening evening being spent in the youngsters' own locality. The following account is an example of how this evening group developed.

As half-term was due, the group asked if they could go out of the centre for the day. In the event, they decided to go to Shoreham for some canoeing. They made plans to go to a car auction to see how much they would have to spend to buy a second-hand car which they could use at the centre. The staff accompanied them, but did not share their enthusiasm for buying a car, doing it up, and painting it. At the auction rooms there was an episode in which the youngsters were thrown out, as the manager accused them of stealing a set of ignition keys from a car. They denied this, and were eventually let back in and found what they wanted would cost about £40.

At the next meeting, they talked about how they could raise £40. They were aware that a weekend group had raised about £200 by sponsorship at an earlier date. The staff told them that this would not be a legitimate use of a sponsoring event, as they were raising money for their own enjoyment. The kids accepted this, and when they suggested a jumble sale the staff agreed. They planned out the following month's activities geared to preparing for the sale, but as the weeks went by it was rather a case of the staff organising the group into doing things. The tasks were broken down into such jobs as poster making, distribution of leaflets and collecting the jumble, all of which were done over several evenings. The youngsters were, at least to some extent, involved in the decisions, such as where the sale was to be held and the design of the publicity.

When the jumble was being collected, an incident occurred which made the group want to call the collection off. One staff member and three children were collecting jumble from houses which had supposedly had notes put through their doors previously. The children had taken to wearing various articles of clothing they had collected, so looked fairly weird. Assuming that they were casing the houses in the road, someone called the police, who arrived to find out what was happening. The worker explained what they were doing, although by this time two of the children had run away, and the police were reasonable and left. The group wanted to stop collecting as they took the visit of the police as another of the warnings they received whenever they had any contact with the law. They had the feeling that what they were doing was probably illegal anyway and needed reassurance that it was not.

At the meeting before the sale they spent a long time planning both who should man the stall, and the actual stalls themselves. Of the two normal 'mouthpieces' of the group, both opted out of the selling of jumble—one decided to be on the door and the other decided to do teas. Although they were normally the natural leaders of the group they opted out in this situation which was outside their experience, possibly because they could foresee the problems of selling more than the others.

The group found themselves in the strange position of facing the possibility of being 'nicked' from, and from the group as a whole, rather than from themselves as individuals. They coped fairly well with this situation as the staff sought to face them with it. They were all very adamant about wanting to buy a car, and spent a long time reassuring each other that they wouldn't steal from the proceeds. In talking about other people coming to the sale and stealing, it became apparent that they did not mind 'little old ladies' coming to jumble sales and stealing if they were poor and needed clothes, although there was one school of thought which suggested that little old ladies were rich because they did steal things from jumble sales.

The sale was all set on the appointed evening at five o'clock, although it was not due to start until six. This caused a great deal of tension within the group, and they felt threatened, especially as a queue was beginning to form outside. In deciding who was going to take charge of the takings, they joked as to whether they could trust the workers with the money. The staff took this seriously and suggested that either they would take care of it, or one of the group should take it home, or they should split it six ways and all bring their share with them the next time they visited the centre. They refused to take responsibility for looking after the money, not because they mistrusted each other—they were all convinced that the others wanted the car badly—but because they did not trust themselves with money in their pockets which they had to keep.

At the next session after the sale, the staff attempted to organise a discussion based on the venture. The group did not seem to remember very much and had to have their memories refreshed. They had no ideas about how they could do things differently if they ever tried to organise another jumble sale.

They were preoccupied with planning the purchase of the car, having made exactly £40. They wanted to buy it the next day, but the staff persuaded them to wait a week as otherwise it would be at the centre until the evening group came out at a weekend, and in that time it might well be vandalised by the other groups using the centre.

They accepted this, but the wait meant prolonged fears about what they would end up buying, and whether they would be 'rooked'. They wanted the staff to make the decision as to what car to buy when the time for the auction came, but they refused. The staff assumed that they would buy the first car to be sold for under £40, and this happened with a Triumph Herald at £35.

No-one seemed to know whether the car was taxed and insured, and the group could not understand why the workers refused to drive it back to the centre simply because it might not be legal. The car had to be taken away by the following evening. The car did reach the centre, but when the weekend came, one of the group brought with him his new trials bike, which rather stole the show. However, as the group progressed, the car provided a focus for the visits, both in driving and on the mechanical side. Towards the end of group, the staff felt that the car was becoming too important, and they tried, with some success, to interest the lads in other activities such as canoeing.

At this stage, two of the members were sent to detention centre for further offences, and it was decided not to fill the vacancies as the group only had two months to run.

Two of the group now visit the centre one Saturday a month, partly to do specific jobs such as mowing the lawn and working on the minibus, for which they are paid a small sum, and partly to act as volunteers with the younger children. This experiment seems to be beneficial both to the group and to the two youngsters themselves, in their continuing relationship with the staff of the centre.

The Children

It is impossible to generalise in describing the children who are a part of the Knowles Tooth programme, except to say that they display a cross section of behavioural difficulties. The guide to the programme, prepared by the centre staff for referring agencies in 1977, indicates three areas where these difficulties can occur, in any combination:

1 Problems experienced within the family situation, such as large families, single parent families, clashes with 'step-parent', rejection, scapegoating, deprivation and return to home after period of residential care.

2 Problems experienced at school, such as truanting, inability to relate to peers, bullying, being victimised and conflict with staff.

3 Problems experienced in the community, particularly delinquency.

Whilst children involved in the Knowles Tooth programme have experienced problems in each of the areas mentioned, the majority of the centre's work is of a preventive nature. At May 1977, only one fifth of the children attending the weekend sessions had been referred as a direct result of a court appearance, although others had previous convictions. This concentration on preventive work is the policy of the centre, but is reinforced by the referrals made to the programme. It was the opinion of an area social worker who had had responsibility for liaison with Knowles Tooth that:

'My perception is that Knowles Tooth has most potential at the preventive end of the spectrum, with a possible limit being those kids who are in care and home on trial. One of the problems of course is that we don't get to see the kids until they have gone too far, but if we can reach them earlier, the Knowles Tooth type programmes are probably the best bet. I think to some extent, the kids they are taking now are not as 'difficult' as when they started, and I think this needs developing more.'

A 15 year old boy who had attended an evening group and had since spent some time at the centre agreed:

'Last summer, I went on holiday with one of the weekend groups. They were about the same age as me, but they weren't like us in the old evening group. They were mostly on the edge of trouble, or had problems at home. They seemed more reasonable and didn't muck about as much as we had done. It wasn't as much fun though — we had some good times in our evening group.'

The following provides an example of a typical child and attempts to illustrate some of the ways in which the centre staff aim to help children who are involved in this combined programme of home visits and residential weekends.

Colin

Colin was 14 when he appeared before the juvenile court charged with burglary in February 1975. His social worker recommended a supervision order together with an intermediate treatment requirement to be undertaken by Knowles Tooth, and this was accepted by the court. The picture presented to the centre staff by the social worker was one of a boy whose troubles stemmed from the inadequacy of the family in meeting his adolescent needs. Colin was seen to cause trouble as a means of drawing attention to himself. Also, he did not seem to be able to get on with his peers. He had a reputation for playing the clown and leading other children into trouble, but he did not seem to be close to anyone of his own age. He had been involved in various youth activities, but had left after clashes with other children.

There were two main aspects of the programme for Colin. At the centre, the workers concentrated on trying to build up his self-confidence, so that he could cope with a difficult home situation. The home visits were directed at encouraging the family to be more accepting of Colin. At first, Colin lived up to his reputation for, on the one hand, disruptiveness, and on the other, shying away from friendship, but the workers concentrated on getting him to develop skills, thereby giving him a sense of achievement. By the third visit to the centre, Colin was talking more openly with the staff and other children. In addition, when helping one of the workers to put up a partition, he was confident enough to take decisions such as what lengths of wood to cut. From talking to Colin, and from visiting the home, the worker felt that the increased self-confidence he had gained had not only helped him to cope at home, but had also been reflected by a more accepting attitude from the family.

Colin's father died shortly after the improvement had been noticed. However, Colin's behaviour continued to improve despite a setback when he was picked up for taking some wood from an industrial estate.

During his final year at school, the programme for Colin changed somewhat. Although relations with his mother varied and the family needed the support of the Knowles Tooth worker, on the individual level, the worker's energy was geared to helping Colin obtain a job by the time he was due to leave school, and it seemed that he had come through a difficult period in his life. He was keen to start work, and, in discussing his progress over the year, he said that he thought it was due to involvement in the programme, although the reason he gave for this statement was that there was nothing else he could think of to which it could be attributed.

Another boy of the same age, but in a different group, was more sure of the reason his behaviour had changed, even if only in some respects:

'I think the main thing I got out of this place was a different way of looking at nicking. People before had told me it was wrong, but I didn't really care. If you do something wrong while you're part of a group here, you can see that the people care about what you're doing, and you're less likely to do it again. I don't nick any more (although I still do things that I think are funny and other people don't like—like driving the car through the tent that was up in the field). I suppose I've got a conscience about it now. It's not just the conscience of doing wrong, but letting people down and giving the place a bad name.'

Contacts with other Agencies

Referral and Selection

At the inception of the project, statements about which types of children could benefit from the programme were left deliberately vague, in terms of the difficulties experienced in making relationships and the need for social work support in a group setting. This was because the workers did not want children to be excluded before the centre was aware of their existence.

By 1977, however, it was felt by the staff that the referring social workers were still not aware of what the programme had to offer, and what was expected of the child, the family and the social worker. A more detailed description of the project was prepared for the guidance of referring agency workers. It stated:

'The type of work embarked on at the centre means that agency workers referring children are required, to some extent, to create a situation which will enable the centre worker to become closely involved with the family. Their role while the child is involved with the project will vary depending on the individual case. In some cases it is arranged for a temporary withdrawal for the period of the child's involvement; in other cases some form of joint work is arranged' [6].

126

In addition, the centre began to use a fuller referral form, demanding more information including details about the benefits to the child expected from the scheme. Although this enables the centre workers to make more informed decisions in the build up of groups, it remains a fact that much information about the child's behaviour and attitude does not come to light until the programme is well under way. The key to success is seen as more and better liaison between agencies, and a greater effort by the centre staff to publicise the potential and demands of the programme.

Although the Knowles Tooth staff are free to accept or reject referrals, they can only choose from those which are made. Clearly the type of child who becomes involved is very much dependent on the referring worker's understanding and expectations of the scheme. Some see it as no more than extra weekend activities for the child, others think the needs of their children can be totally met by the Knowles Tooth workers. Yet others refer children on whom they need a second opinion, using the programme as an assessment for their own longer term work. The following quotations from a local authority social worker who has referred children to Knowles Tooth show aims for the programme which do not coincide with those of the centre staff.

'I had a 14 year old girl on my caseload, who came from a materially and emotionally deprived family. She was a non-school attender and there was a lot of pressure from the education authority to remove the kid from home. I felt that involvement with Knowles Tooth would be a means of staving off reception into care—the Department would be seen to be doing something and thereby relieving the pressure to receive into care. I also saw the need for some assessment of the girl's behaviour in a more neutral situation.'

'Malcolm was referred for an entirely different reason. He is attending a special school for the educationally sub-normal, and his problem is that he has not developed sufficiently as a person to cope with leaving school and starting work. He is 15 but operates at the level of a 13 year old. Maybe I'm being unrealistic, but I would like to see his period at Knowles Tooth as part of a preparation for him starting work. But anyway, I want him to have a chance to mix with his peers, rather than the children at the special school. I hope it will bring him out of himself.'

Liaison

By May 1977, there was no clear policy on liaison with other agencies, which led to situations such as a child who was involved in the programme being taken into care without the information being passed on to the Knowles Tooth staff. In other cases, where good working relationships had been built up, the workers concerned would co-operate in providing an overall service to the family.

The centre workers have always encouraged the local authority social workers to visit the centre when their children are attending. The value of seeing the child in a completely new environment is recognised not only by social workers but also by some parents. One mother noted:

'I think it's the staff there that are different—Bill will sit and talk to them, whereas he wouldn't talk to the social workers at all before. I suppose it's easier for them, anyway, as they have him out there at the weekend and

they're doing things with him all the time—not like coming round here especially to see him officially.'

However, social workers have rarely become involved in the programme unless they have been running a group in conjunction with the Knowles Tooth staff. One social worker offers an explanation:

'I feel guilty sometimes about not spending time at the centre while one of my kids is involved there, but it really is a question of priorities. Whilst Jill was involved in the programme I didn't drop my level of involvement with her and family—I saw Knowles Tooth as an extra resource to my work rather than as an alternative; but the situation highlights the need, on the one hand to become more involved with the programme in order that the child benefits to the fullest possible extent, and on the other hand my commitment to my other cases.'

Reviewing the Children

Although the value of the informal discussion about cases, plans, successes and failures should not be underestimated, three formal processes for reviewing the progress of individual children can be identified:

1 A meeting is held immediately before each weekend visit, at which the special needs of individual children and the specific aims of the weekend are discussed, as well as the developments that have taken place since the last visit of the children, based on the contacts in the intervening period. The following Monday morning there is a further meeting to discuss the achievements and failures of the weekend. Plans are also made as to when specific work is needed with the individuals before the next visit. For example, if one member of the group had a very destructive influence on the weekend, the worker concerned might concentrate on talking to the child in terms of how he or she might change behaviour in order to be more accepted by the group.

2 At the weekly meeting, the previous weekend is reported on by those staff involved in it. Through discussion with the team as a whole, new insights can often be obtained which can add another dimension to the understanding of the weekend and the ongoing programme for that particular group.

3 A formal review is conducted at the end of six months, and if the child remains with the programme, this is done every six months thereafter. The reviews are attended by the Knowles Tooth worker, the local authority social worker if one is assigned to the case, the Knowles Tooth Director, and sometimes, another representative of the local authority. Although the decision as to whether a child should finish his involvement with the programme at the end of a six month period lies with the centre, in practice this decision is taken in consultation with the local authority worker. As the review time approaches, the centre worker will discuss with the child and the family what benefits have been achieved by the programme, whether a child has obtained as much as possible from the scheme, what further progress can be made, or whether the centre is unable to provide what was originally hoped for.

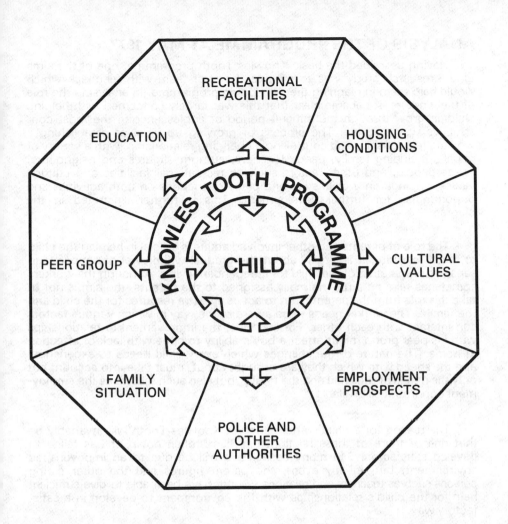

THE CHILD, THE ENVIRONMENT AND THE KNOWLES TOOTH PROGRAMME.

ANALYSIS OF THE PROGRAMME AT MAY 1977

Having described the basic Knowles Tooth programme, one of the aims of the research study was to provide the staff team with feedback which would help them in planning the developing programme. In analysing the role of the workers, it became clear that this was largely concerned with helping children grow through the difficult period of adolescence in the most constructive way possible. The process of growing up involves establishing a working relationship, and controlling a changing relationship, with a variety of people, including family, peers, teachers, authority figures and neighbours. These people, and other factors such as recreational facilities and cultural values, impinge on a child's life and place restrictions on both activities and opportunities for further development. This is further illustrated in the diagram.

The role of parents and other involved adults is crucial in helping the child to reach maturity. It is largely about the gradual withdrawal of support and sensitive preparation of the child for independent living. Although the workers sometimes take on a role normally assigned to the parents, the aim is not to take this role from the parents, but to act as an extra resource for the child and the family. The worker needs to be aware of the way in which various factors can interact with each other. For instance, the improvement in relationships with his peer group might affect a boy's ability to cope with lack of affection at home. The nature of the changes which every child needs to experience, and the speed with which they are brought about, must take into account not only the needs of the child and the family, but also such factors as the employment opportunities available.

The reason for a child's attendance at Knowles Tooth will invariably be that one or more of these relationships has broken down or has failed to develop satisfactorily. In many cases, this will be due to an impoverished environment, but, in any event, the parent figures and the other caring persons such as teachers and relations will not have been able to give sufficient help for the child's relationships with the environment to develop in a satisfactory way.

The programme decided upon for a particular child by the Knowles Tooth staff will always be geared to improving the relationships with the different aspects of the environment. This can either be in terms of changing the child's attitude and behaviour or changing some aspect of the environment in which he lives. The decision as to how to approach the problem of an individual child is often a difficult one, and a watch needs to be kept on the balance between changes in the child and changes in the environment. For example, when, after some time, the centre staff were able to persuade a boy to restart school after a long period of truancy, he was sent home for not wearing the correct school uniform. Although the centre staff agreed with the boy that this was unjust, they continued to encourage him to attend school, as they did not feel that resources would be used wisely in trying to change the school's attitude towards the wearing of uniforms. In this case, as is done wherever possible, this dilemma was discussed with the boy as part of the programme.

Assessment is an integral part of the Knowles Tooth programme, which is partly geared to finding out more about the individual's needs. Once a particular stage has been reached with a child, the staff can then move on to another aspect of the situation. For example, the initial programme for a particular boy might be to concentrate on getting the parents to accept the fact that he is growing up, and to behave accordingly. Once progress has been made towards achieving this aim, the main effort might be directed towards encouraging a more positive relationship with the peer group, or changing his attitude to attending school.

EVALUATION

The time of May 1977, chosen to describe the Knowles Tooth programme, is obviously artificial in that no social work programme is ever completely static. Changes had been taking place throughout the life of the scheme, both in the delivery of the service and in the thinking and ideas of the staff involved at the centre. It was about this time, however, that the team began to make constructive plans in two important areas.

Re-evaluation of the weekend

There is always a danger in any activity based treatment programme that the activity itself will take over the whole programme and smother the original aims of the project. Equally, in a community based intermediate treatment programme, the need to gain the support and resources for a new youth centre may leave the project completely out of touch with those groups of young people it was designed to help.

The original intention was for the weekend groups to take up half the time of the centre workers, the other half being spent in visiting the children at home, writing reports, liaising with other agencies, and staff meetings. In practice, the time needed to plan, carry out, and provide feedback from the weekend amounted to more than had been envisaged. As the time allotted to home visits and especially to developing other aspects of the centre's programme was more flexible, it was this area of the work which suffered as time went on. During 1977, it was decided to review the position of the weekend within the overall programme. For a number of reasons, the time needed to operate the weekend programme was an important factor, but also there was frustration at its isolated situation and its possible lack of relevance to the experience of the child away from the centre. Changes in attitude and behaviour whilst at the centre could be noted by the staff, but this could be seen simply as an adjustment to the Knowles Tooth programme and a response in, as opposed to, the residential setting. Apart from the attitudes shown during the weekend towards the home or school, there was no real evidence that the child was better adjusted or behaved in other settings.

Finally, it was felt that the weekend must become, to a far greater extent, part of an integrated programme. The workers needed to find out more about the child, his needs, problems and potential, before he joined the project, while at the end of the attendance period the workers needed to introduce him to other facilities in the local area, and to provide a period of support where necessary.

Liaison with other agencies

When the Knowles Tooth scheme was first established, no attempt was made to make each worker responsible for a particular area. This made liaison with social workers difficult, and the centre workers were unable to get to know the neighbourhoods where the children lived. It was decided, therefore, that the eight catchment areas should be allocated to individual workers.

This gives the individual worker more responsibility and flexibility within the area. Instead of each area office having a fixed number of places available to it on the programme, the intention is that the Knowles Tooth worker should become more involved in the referral process. Each child who is taken on at Knowles Tooth is selected by the centre worker before his first group visit. The centre worker is not only responsible for building up his or her caseload, but also for developing the contact with the area office to aid better selection by being on hand when the possibility of a child's involvement with the centre is first under consideration. The aim is also for the worker to get to know the area in terms of a deeper knowledge of the community and the various clubs and youth schemes in operation.

In terms of providing a more integrated programme, the move towards area work has another important implication in the possibility of 'feeding' children in and out of the weekend scheme. It will be possible for the caseload of a Knowles Tooth worker to include more children than those actually involved in a weekend group at any one time. Someone from the centre may be working with a child for some time before he starts to attend weekends, either to determine what sort of group programme is needed, or to bring a child to a level where he will benefit more from the group experiences. It should also be possible for contact to be maintained for a further period after the weekend progamme, or for the withdrawal from the programme to be made gradually. One contributory factor in this process has been the establishment of one or two groups in conjunction with other social workers.

One such group began to meet in September 1977. This was jointly organised and is run by one of the centre staff and a social worker from Lewes. The children, aged between 12 and 14, all live in Lewes and meet fortnightly. They have been away camping, and although none of the group is attending the centre's weekend programme, this remains a possibility if the need arises. The group also provides an extra opportunity, at field worker level, for closer co-operation with the social services department.

CONCLUDING REMARKS

The following four statements attempt to summarise the findings of the study carried out by the National Children's Bureau over a twelve month period.

Knowles Tooth Children's Centre offers a social work programme

The most significant aspect to emerge is that the project offers a social work programme. It is not something which is added to a supervision order, or to the ongoing work of a local authority social worker. Once such a referral has been accepted, the centre is capable of offering, for a fixed period of time, a comprehensive service to the child and his or her family. Within this framework, the centre staff can call on the services of more specialised workers. For example, parents might need more intensive casework than the centre can provide, a child might need special educational support, or the services of a qualified instructor might be required for a specific activity. Nonetheless, while a child is involved in the programme, it works better if the Knowles Tooth worker is, in most cases, the central social work figure in the life of the child and the family.

Although there has been some attempt by the centre staff to formalise the referral procedure, the new system depends on the relationships between the individual workers involved with the decisions taken during the period of involvement at Knowles Tooth. It was recommended, therefore, to the agencies involved, that there should be a procedure agreed between the referring agency, Knowles Tooth, and any other agencies who are working with the child or the family. It was felt that if some kind of contract could be drawn up this would facilitate the informal contacts between workers rather than make them more difficult.

In drawing this conclusion, it should be noted that a number of local authority social workers have made positive contributions to the development of the programme, and have taken the trouble to find out more about the methods employed. As one social worker, who had had special responsibility for liaison with the centre, pointed out:

'As liaison officer, I obviously needed to know about the centre, and I gained a lot from the experience of being there at weekends. Although it isn't possible for every social worker to spend time there, and it would usually be in their own time, I think it's important, if the child is going to get the greatest benefit out of the programme, for the social worker to have some idea of what the project is about.'

The residential component should remain the basis of the Knowles Tooth programme

In the evaluation of any social work programme, the difficulty often lies, not in determining whether it has been successful or not, but rather which aspects have contributed most to the outcome. In this respect, the Knowles Tooth scheme is no exception. The residential weekend component of the programme has been described in terms of building up a social work relationship with the child through the experiences of living, working and playing together. It is also a means of providing a setting where problems can be worked through with the children. The value of the residential weekend, however, cannot be viewed in isolation from the overall programme.

The essential difference between the Knowles Tooth programme and the service that can be provided by other forms of social work intervention is the type and intensity of involvement. The residential weekend, and, where appropriate to the individual children, the weekly evening groups, provide a setting which cannot be matched either by the home and office interviews, or even the informal chats in the coffee bar that the area social worker can provide. They also provide a setting which cannot be matched in the full-time residential sphere, where the nature of institutionalised care often dictates a more formal relationship.

For these reasons, it is important that the residential weekend should remain the basis of the Knowles Tooth programme. Apart from the changes in attitude and behaviour of children through the weekend sessions, its chief value lies in developing the relationship between the social worker and the client.

The Knowles Tooth programme should bear more relation to the communities where the children live

Many intermediate treatment schemes claim to be community based, but this often means that only the project base, maybe a school or a church hall, is located within the neighbourhood which the programme serves, and the scheme has no relationship with the surrounding community. The Knowles Tooth premises are not based within any of the neighbourhoods served by the centre. This places limitations on the workers in their attempts to move closer to the community, but can also help in clarifying the relationship between the centre and the neighbourhood it serves. There would seem to be two choices open to the centre staff.

Firstly, it would be possible to move directly into the communities, and run groups based on the individual neighbourhoods. Through the participation of the parents and other local people, a truly community based programme could be established, still using the Knowles Tooth premises for weekend and weekday activities. This would mean, however, that as the workers became more involved in the individual areas, the team work approach of the inter-mediate treatment programme, and the support gained from membership of the team, would inevitably be lost and would need to be replaced by some other structure.

Secondly, it is possible to remain as a centre based team, developing links with other people who are working more closely with the community, but only working directly with parents of children involved with the programme. In this case, which is the trend of existing development, it is an area of work which has not, as yet, been tackled by the Knowles Tooth staff.

The approach of the Knowles Tooth programme is not limited to those types of children who are already being helped

The staff team has discussed its selection criteria. A group has been identified as the 'heavy' end which needs some form of provision other than that which can be provided through existing intermediate treatment pro-grammes. Whilst there will always be a small number of children who are completely uncontrollable, this division is not strictly relevant to the concept of intermediate treatment. Account must be taken of two factors; firstly, the way in which the label 'heavy' is arrived at, and secondly, the differences between the approach of a programme such as Knowles Tooth and the methods employed in a programme for a particular child at any given time.

The 'heavy' label is usually attributed to a child or young person for one of two reasons. In some cases it is because the child has travelled a certain distance along a 'care' or 'criminal' career. The child will probably have appeared before the court on several occasions, and various treatment methods will have been applied. However, there is no reason to believe that a young person who has been on supervision and care orders and has attended a detention centre will have any greater or smaller underlying family problems, or will be any more or less able to relate to his peer group, than a child who is in court for a first, detected shoplifting offence.

In other cases, the term 'heavy' relates to the nature or seriousness of the offence. Thus in terms of this spectrum, the successful arsonist who causes hundreds of thousands of pounds' worth of damage will be seen to have different needs from the child who is no expert with a match.

Once a decision has been made that a social work programme is the best course of action for a particular child, the general approach can be universal. It is only the methods employed which need to be examined for the particular case. In practice, this means that no single aspect of a programme can cater for the needs of all types of children at risk or in trouble. For example, none of the four existing weekend groups at Knowles Tooth would be suitable for children on detention centre licences. This does not mean, however, that the Knowles Tooth approach is not valid for this group of young people. If they were to be accommodated within the programme, it would have to be at the expense of another group, and there would probably need to be certain changes in staffing levels and the methods employed, both in the residential weekend and in the individual work at home and in the neighbourhood; but there is no reason to believe that the approach of the centre, an integrated social work programme, using residential or evening groups, would not be as valid as for the existing groups, consisting largely of children at risk.

In conclusion, it can be said that, at this point in time and in this geographical area, the Knowles Tooth programme is an effective way of providing intermediate treatment services. It may well be a useful model, especially for those voluntary agencies developing services which are then supported financially by local authorities. The greatest danger is that, as intermediate treatment and other personal social services are developed, schemes such as Knowles Tooth will become isolated projects within wider networks of services. In this case, it is vital that the experience of the Knowles Tooth staff is used to the full before decisions are made regarding the development of other services. In general, whilst this is primarily the responsibility of the local authorities concerned, both workers and policy makers in projects such as Knowles Tooth should recognise the need for some of the workers' time to be spent in contributing to the development of intermediate treatment in the wider context of the statutory services.

Acknowledgements

The National Children's Bureau study on which this chapter is based was sponsored by the Department of Health and Social Security.

The author also wishes to thank the management and staff of Knowles Tooth Children's Centre and the County Councils of East and West Sussex.

Thanks are especially due to the children and their families whose participation made the study possible.

References

1 Hopkins P. (1977), 'Northorpe Hall Trust, West Yorkshire', in *Intermediate treatment: 28 choices,* London, DHSS, p.178.
2 From an unpublished leaflet providing guidance to referring social workers, Knowles Tooth, 1974.
3 From an unpublished leaflet providing guidance to referring social workers, Knowles Tooth, May, 1977.
4 This and subsequent quotes from children, parents and workers in other agencies are taken from transcripts of unstructured interviews conducted by the author as part of his research.
5 From worker's report on the weekend group.
6 From the referral leaflet, May 1977.

THE DUNDEE CHILDREN'S ACTIVITY CENTRES

Norman Alm

ORIGIN AND EARLY HISTORY

The Rowans Cottage and Ferry Road Activity Centres sometimes seem like outposts on the frontiers of civilised behaviour, and this can make those of us who work here feel like the Indian agents, who were expected to represent both the cavalry and the Indians, and appeared a strange hybrid to both camps. The centres are also cosy 'clubbies', where you are assured a welcome, a stable reference point in a sea of insecurity, official premises of the Dundee Social Work Department, gang headquarters, rather shabby but brightly painted houses, the scene of painful self analysis and criticism by both staff and children, places which are more related to the potential than the actual, and sites of a more or less permanent administrative and physical disarray, which only becomes bothersome occasionally.

The original purpose of this project was to design and establish a centre based activity programme, which could provide an intermediate treatment facility for young people on supervision to the Social Work Department. Norman Alm, being the original project leader, initially worked as the only full time staff member, and subsequently became spokesman and co-ordinator for the project when it expanded to include four full time leaders and two buildings.

Dundee, with a population of around 180,000, is experiencing the decline of its major industries, primarily jute spinning and weaving, and the change to a certain amount of light manufacturing. Both the older and the newer industries employ predominantly female labour, and male unemployment is traditionally high. Although the city does not have quite the colourful reputation of Glasgow, there is significant deprivation. Admittedly, during the 1960s, an ambitious building programme provided a number of community centres in the city; but the move from a youth to a youth and community service meant that the wish of many teenagers, for a place that was exclusively their own, could not always be satisfied.

In Scotland, there is at present no statutory obligation on local authorities to set up intermediate treatment. Instead, pressure comes from their duty to effect the decisions of Children's Hearings, which have largely replaced the courts in dealing with children in trouble. The philosophical basis is the rejection, in most cases, of any distinction between delinquent and deprived children. The emphasis is on looking beyond the symptoms of a youngster's trouble to the causes, and, hopefully, coming up with measures that will help.

In a sifting process, the Reporter to the Children's Hearing decides if a referred child is in need of some form of compulsory care, other than that provided by his parents. Although the system is designed to include children in need of care and protection as well as those who commit offences, it is the latter group which account for the bulk of the referrals, and of these, roughly half are considered at a hearing by members of the Children's Panel. This Panel consists of lay members drawn from the community and the hearing involves them together with the child, parents, social worker and any other relevant people. It discusses the problem and tries to arrive at remedial measures; but the area of choice is not wide. Basically the youngster can either be placed on supervision or sent away for residential care.

When our scheme was put forward to Dundee's Social Work Committee in 1972, it was on the basis that it would *'increase the range of facilities available to Children's Hearings and provide alternative methods of supervising and assisting children who come before the Panel'*[1]. The project leader's original job description was couched in general terms, but outlined a picture of a place which could be a springboard to existing youth provision in the city. It would offer a flexible range of activities, designed to interest and help hard to motivate and difficult children; it would strike a balance between disciplined structure and self expression, and it would need imagination, initiative and *'firm but sympathetic leadership'*[2]. The Children's Panel were encouraging in their support of the idea of an activity centre, and in their subsequent interest in its growth and development. At the same time, social workers were aware that it was rare for any youngster appearing before the Children's Panel to be making any constructive use of existing youth facilities, and those who had been involved in one-off activity based work with their youngsters were keen that there should be a full time facility.

For the first year of the project, the major problem was finding suitable premises. The original idea was to get an older building which the youngsters could take part in fixing up and decorating; but a combination of fire and safety regulations, redevelopment and negative feelings about the proposed use made this more difficult than we had imagined. Nonetheless, a pilot group was set up in May, 1973, using a variety of buildings, until the Rowans Cottage, formerly the matron's house in the grounds of an old people's home, was obtained in January, 1974. By this time, with the help of volunteers and one full time Community Service Volunteer, two separate groups were meeting two nights a week and Saturday mornings, while a growing number of referrals led to a waiting list being created. A detailed study of attendance patterns during the previous year uncovered the surprising fact that the average evening attendance was little more than once a week for each individual, although each group had two possible evening meetings plus the Saturday sessions. This weakened the argument that cutting down the frequency of meetings would reduce the impact of the project. Accordingly we set up another group, and the pattern eventually became separate Monday, Tuesday and Wednesday groups with Saturday sessions open to all.

The fact that the project was being largely financed through an urban aid grant for the first five years enabled the local authority to adopt a very flexible approach. However, early in 1974, the Department decided that the project had reached a stage where it was necessary to plan its future development.

Although the original intention had been to find a single, all purpose activity centre, the acquisition of the Rowans Cottage had forced us to concentrate on small groups, and the advantages of the 'small is beautiful' philosophy had become more than apparent through this experience. Consequently it was recommended that more staff should be appointed and that another small building should be obtained. Approval was given for the appointment of three more workers at the same salary as the original project leader and the acquisition of another building. After several months, the offer of a house on the edge of the city, later christened the Ferry Road Activity Centre, was accepted in the absence of anything more suitable. The map (Figure 1) shows the location of the two centres in relation to the catchment area from which the youngsters were drawn, and gives some idea of the difficult journey with which many of them were faced.

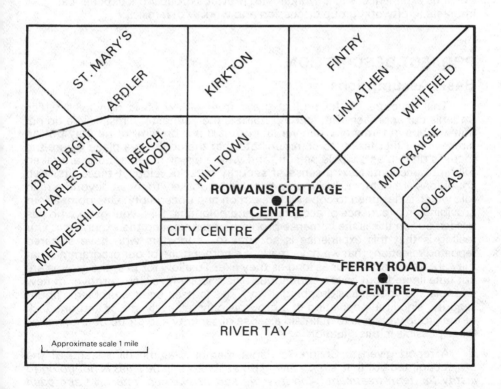

Figure 1 Sketch map of Dundee

Two of the new posts were filled in the Spring of 1975, and the third worker joined the project in September of the same year. The staff team now consisted of:

Norman: an American in his early 30s.
Previous experience: tutoring in the United States and six years working in a therapeutic community.
Interests: art, craftwork and music.

Charly: an Aberdonian in his early 30s.
Previous experience: motor mechanic, law librarian and social worker.
Interests: club cycling, motor maintenance, hillwalking, hostelling and camping.

Scot: a Glaswegian in his mid 50s.
Previous experience: Navy, working with mentally handicapped, YMCA, and running an outdoor centre.
Interests: sport, Open University, politics and church work.

Janice: a Glaswegian in her mid 20s.
Previous experience: social worker with previous group work experience.
Interests: craftwork, group discussion and work with families.

PROJECT DESCRIPTION

Basic Assumptions

The structure of the project grew from a few basic principles which underlie our approach. Our starting point is the youngster himself. We do not think of him in terms of whatever label others put on him, or he may put on himself. Our first task is to communicate that the centre is a place where the focus is on him as a whole person, and where his own perceptions are taken fully into account. Next a sense of security must develop. If these first two conditions are not met, the youngsters will be unlikely to move beyond a rigid role which is designed to cope with rejection and uncertainty. One point about providing an experience of acceptance and belonging for a youngster who has missed out on this is the immense problem of terminating the experience. Our feeling is that this experience is so vital to youngsters who have suffered repeated rejection, that we have made it a cornerstone of our programme that they are free to attend for as long as they like. To allow for this, the groups are not time limited, but have a continuous existence, with a slow turnover of new referrals and youngsters dropping away. This in itself creates problems about security, since the population of a group is only relatively static, and one task of the group worker is to maintain a sense of security and group boundaries as far as possible in this situation.

A report given to Children's Panel members at the pilot stage of the project pointed out that *'simply laying on activities and facilities is not going to justify the term treatment. And it is the sort of planned, intensive approach that this word implies that is needed in order to reach and affect children who habitually get in trouble'* [3]. Our work with a youngster can be called treatment in that it involves initial assessment, setting objectives, directed work, and subsequent assessment of progress, but the medical connotation of this word makes us uneasy. It implies that an active expert applies something to a passive client which does the client some good. However it is the importance of client participation in our programme, and in group work in general, which makes such a clear distinction between treater and treated difficult. The group itself can be an agent for change in an individual youngster; other individuals in the group can at times offer useful help in working through someone's problems; the group worker's job is often to engineer things so as to make it possible for an individual to be active and do something, rather than passive, with something being done to him by the worker. The planned and directed efforts of the group worker in relationship to the needs of an individual can be called treatment, but in our programme this is only part of a whole picture, which includes long term support for those who need it, the experience of genuinely caring and interested adults, and the existence of a stable reference point in a life which is often lacking in structure and security.

While taking the position that it is the whole youngster and his development we are interested in, we recognise that some will regard the project simply as an exercise in delinquency control. Our position here is in accord with the philosophy of the Children's Panel system, which takes delinquent acts as symptoms of an underlying need. This line of thinking is illustrated by our 1973 report to Panel members: *'The idea is to approach the care and treatment of children with behaviour problems on a more realistic basis than is possible in a residential setting, while still retaining the advantage of group experiences and learning through activities'* [4].

Youngsters are primarily referred to us when their involvement in lawbreaking or other unacceptable behaviour indicates that they need more help than they are getting in coping with their problems. We see this help as comprising support, education and treatment, in varying combinations. In terms of affecting behaviour patterns support can be seen as a preventive measure; education, in its widest sense, as a way of opening up possibilities for more appropriate ways of behaving; and treatment, as a process whereby inappropriate or destructive patterns are unwound or transformed. Our view on delinquency control, then, is that one effect of meeting the needs of the youngsters will be a reduction in their unacceptable behaviour.

Selection Criteria

This means that delinquent behaviour is not the only criterion for referral to the programme. In a document given to social workers and the Children's Panel, guidelines are given as to appropriate referrals. The paper describes as suitable, young people *'who have had trouble maintaining relationships with peers as well as adults . . . The general picture is one of failure at school, no connections with any youth club or similar activities, no particular personal interests, and no set group of friends but rather a high turnover of acquaintances'* [5]. This lack of social skills can lead directly to delinquent behaviour, seen as inappropriate moves toward quite ordinary goals, such as prestige and excitement. It can also lead to boredom and to a quite accurate sense of general failure, particularly at school. A secondary stage can be reaction to all this failure and frustration in the form of entrenched antiauthority attitudes and a mistrust of adults. The anxiety provoked by seemingly overwhelming odds can also lead to withdrawal and a refusal to compete, where one is always certain of losing.

141

Most of our referrals come from social workers' existing caseloads. A few referrals are made following a Children's Hearing; their suitability and our objectives in working with the youngsters are discussed at a weekly meeting. As well as these, we have always accepted a proportion of youngsters who come as friends or relatives of members, or because they hear about the place from others. Eventually they become as much 'part of the furniture' as anybody else at the centre, but we like to keep self referred kids at 25% of the total, in order to allow for new referrals. Self referred kids are, however, an important feature of the centres. Having even a small percentage helps remove the 'bad boys' club' label, most importantly in the eyes of the kids themselves. To the statement *'This is a place where you get sent if you are bad'*, we can always say, *'But so and so's never been in bother'.* We find it a useful confusion to foster. Also there is the point that having a biddable youngster (not that all self referred kids are) helps in getting activities off the ground, and in providing an element of what is, in fact, more of a majority viewpoint in discussions and decision making. This is not to suggest that self referred members are seen by the others as in any way 'helpers' to the staff. They are all just group members. In fact, many self referred kids turn out to have as many problems as the others, and have escaped the official 'delinquent' label only through luck.

The Children

Most attenders are aged 13 to 16. This is because this group is one most in evidence at Children's Hearings and on social workers' caseloads. For a number of reasons children's problems in coping with life tasks become more evident to society at large at this age. A professional reason for working with this age group is the possibility that in the melting pot of this change of role from child to adult there is an increased opportunity to effect lasting improvements in behaviour patterns. Both boys and girls are involved. The higher incidence of boys on Supervision Orders is reflected in the membership. Occasionally there have been all male groups, but our aim is to have mixed groups wherever possible. On one issue alone—the preoccupation of adolescents with establishing their own sexual role—the usefulness of mixed groups is clear.

As to the type of youngster we usually find ourselves working with— this is tremendously variable. The behaviour problems can range from tantrums and aggressive outbursts to neurotic withdrawal. We have bullies and victims. One could say that we do not attract happy, well adjusted kids, with a consistent set of friends and interesting things to do, although this description could fit a 'happy delinquent', well in with a set of friends, and getting status and enjoyment from delinquent escapades. This type of youngster is not frequently encountered by us, and even those labelled as 'gang leaders' so often turn out to be more manipulated than manipulating, and to be satisfying the immediate needs of their gangs, rather than their own. The common thread, however, is a strong voluntary interest in attending. If it is a cold, rainy, winter's night, whatever makes a youngster get a bus across the city to the centre or walk down, sometimes a mile or more, it is not external compulsion.

We have a more detailed picture of some of our earliest referrals from social workers (see Appendix). At the time of referral to the project, about 75% of the youngsters had been involved in delinquent acts and 33% in persistent truancy. Eight per cent were described as only having personal or family problems. More than half were from families with four or more children, and rather less than half from single parent families. A further 18% had step-parents or were in care. The boy:girl ratio was about five to one, although the actual ratio at the centres is higher than this, due to the number of self-referred girls.

Advantages of Group Work

The programme is based on an individual's long term involvement with a particular group. Working in groups has distinct advantages for realising our aims which are:

1 Creating a setting in which the youngster can experience acceptance and belonging.

2 Understanding clearly the kinds of problems he has in interacting with others.

3 Heightening his own, and others' understanding of these problems.

4 Encouraging different ways of interacting, which are less damaging to himself and others.

These aims have implications for the style of group which is necessary. For instance, a highly structured, rigidly controlled group, assuming it were possible, might achieve the first aim but would not be of value in achieving the second, third and possibly the fourth. A totally free running group, with no attempt by the worker to shape things, might achieve the second and third but would have less chance with the first and fourth.

The groups have a style which is helpful in realising these aims. The most important characteristics of the groups are:

• A high ratio of adults to youngsters—1:3 or higher.

• An accepting, tolerant approach by the adults.

• Participation by youngsters in decision making and shaping the pro-gramme.

• An emphasis on discussion, talking out of problems, and verbalising feelings.

• An activity programme that is flexible and amenable to control by the youngsters, while also capable of providing stimulation and the element of surprise.

The Programme

At any one time the overall programme will include a range of groups and sessions. Their exact shape will reflect the needs and requests of the kids, social workers, and the individual interests and strengths of the staff and volunteers. The core of our work is a set of regularly meeting permanent groups, most of which have eight to ten kids with three or four adults. One or two larger groups, 15 to 25 kids with five to eight adults, meet regularly as well. With these, more attendances per week are built in, with some individuals in a large group coming four times a week. A typical week's schedule of group meetings and sessions is shown in Figure 2.

A typical evening group session runs from 6.30 pm to 9.30 pm and includes planned and spontaneous activities and projects, casual use of games and equipment, group discussion, and a formal meeting. The latter is held to plan the programme, air complaints, and discuss behaviour and issues arising from the evening. Formal means everyone sitting down in the same place for the duration of the meeting. The atmosphere and content of the meetings can vary from the chaotic, to something approaching group therapy. It is part of the leaders' job to push the meeting in the direction of genuine analysis of problems and a search for solutions. Typically, success seems to come in glimpses, as a gem of self discovery, or group discovery, embedded in a swirl of jumbled interaction.

While the quality of the meeting can vary, in adult estimation, the members are generally eager to spend this time talking together. Our occasional experiences with starting off new groups remind us that establishing the norm of having such a meeting is usually difficult because the adults are imposing a regular and unfamiliar piece of structure on the group. An advantage of our continuous groups is that acceptance of this, once established, is passed on to newcomers by the other youngsters.

As well as attending a particular group, a youngster can also come to other sessions in the week. These are designed to allow opportunities for all centre members to get to know each other, at least slightly, and to provide a less intensive and more outward looking experience. The first is important because different groups share the same building and group workers. While the programme is designed so that on any evening only one group is present, we want to head off the development of jealousies and fantasies about the other people who use the place. So we are after a strong identification with one group, but also a general identification with the project as a whole. Each centre runs one session at the weekend at which all members are welcome.

In addition, every member is involved in at least one experience of a residential camp. Early in the project's history, contact was made with Camas, Isle of Mull, a remote adventure camp run by the Iona Community. The regime and atmosphere there seem well suited to the kind of experience we want to offer youngsters. Its primitiveness and remoteness throw a group on its resources to get through the week. There are opportunities for canoeing, swimming, and exploring a rugged and interesting landscape. We do weekend camps as well, usually closer to home. Actually living together over a period of time adds another dimension to our work with the youngsters. Developments and issues, both positive and negative, tend to be heightened on a camp. Often we find that in talking with youngsters who used to attend the centres and have been away for some time, the most vivid memories are of incidents that happened on camps.

Kids also tend to drop in whenever they think they might get a welcome, which is at most times. For individual sessions, such as tutoring, a chance to do some extra candlemaking, or a clearing up exercise, we are flexible about arranging extra attendances. If we are in the middle of a staff meeting and

Monday	Tuesday	Wednesday	Thursday	Friday	Saturday	Sunday
9.00-4.00 Dayscheme (based at Rowans)		9.00-4.00 Dayscheme (based at Rowans)				
6.30-9.30 Ferry Road Monday Group	6.30-9.30 Ferry Road Tuesday Group	6.30-9.30 Ferry Road Wednesday Group	6.30-9.30 Ferry Road Thursday Group (run by Area Team)		10.00-2.00 Ferry Road Saturday Session (all members welcome)	1.30-5.30 Rowans Sunday Session, outing to hills or beach (all members welcome)
Rowans Monday/Thursday Group (large group)	Rowans Tuesday Group	Rowans Wednesday Group (Small 'family' group)	Rowans Monday/Thursday Group (large group)			
		Rowans Wednesday outings, trips, Community Service Projects (all members welcome)				

Figure 2   Typical schedule of group meetings and sessions

145

someone looks in, he may well be put to answering the phone, or clearing out the workshop, if he is not happy just to play snooker or have a cup of coffee. For that matter, he might be included in the meeting. Extra one-off sessions and events are organised as appropriate, such as discos, parents' nights, trips in the van, individual tutoring and sports days.

Activities

Activities include a range of sports, games, crafts, cycling runs, camping and hostelling, film-making, decorating and redecorating the centres, instruction from outside experts on such things as disco construction, hairdressing, motor maintenance, gardening, hillwalking, role play, concert parties and visits to places of interest. We have an old van that doubles as personnel carrier and transporting vehicle for equipment. We try to achieve a balance between spontaneous activities and ones that need more detailed planning.

One activity that deserves special mention because of its importance in our programme is community service. Right from the pilot group stage and in spite of some initial staff reservations, community service projects have been a feature of the programme and are seen by the kids as an important characteristic of the centres. They take pride in their reputation as an action squad, ready to do a garden, hang curtains, move furniture, or whatever, at very short notice. We find this provides an ideal way to boost self esteem and give expression to the positive, creative side of a youngster. For kids who feel unrelated to the community, they provide a way back in, and so suit our intention to maintain involvement in the local community, rather than isolate the groups too much in our attempt to create a haven for the youngsters. If the project is well chosen, the results are immediate, in the form of gratitude for the help, and the clear evidence that a needed task has been performed. Usually the work is for the elderly, handicapped, infirm, or just for people in desperate need. Projects come through social workers, other agencies in the city, and sometimes from the kids themselves. We have a school release scheme which is based on community service projects. The youngsters do the projects with us two days a week and are back in school the other three. Whereas the evening groups provide social education in a number of different ways, the day scheme is built around the successful completion of the projects. The focus is narrower, but the practical relevance is high in terms of work experience and improving relationships with the school.

It is difficult to say if some particular activities are more suitable than others. Individual personalities are crucial here. An adult with the necessary knowledge and enthusiasm who has a good rapport with the kids can be the catalyst for a very successful session. Without these qualities, new activities can flounder. Usually games and activities requiring co-operation are more useful than ones emphasising competition. Competition as a group, against an outside group, is a different matter—though even here, the chance of reinforcing an already strong sense of failure makes us move carefully before organising a typical 'youth club' competition.

Activities which involve as much of the group as possible are preferable to ones that split it up. Also, it is better to have activities which allow everyone to participate all the time. Some games, for instance, eliminate one person after another, creating a row of rejectees whose role is to watch the remaining, successful people enjoy themselves. A better recipe for inviting chaos in an intermediate treatment group would be hard to imagine. We would tend to emphasise spontaneous activities which do not need elaborate equipment, because these allow the youngsters most control in shaping events. As an individual or group becomes more able to take on planning and responsibility, we increase the complexity of planning that they are asked to undertake. Figure 3 attempts to clarify the purpose behind different degrees of spontaneity in activities.

	Planned by adults entirely	Planned by kids and adults together	Spontaneous ideas of adults	Spontaneous ideas of kids
Activities	Camps Hillwalking Outside contacts Community Service Projects Instructional Sessions (Rock- climbing, Trampolining Hairdressing) ⇩	Construction projects Disco Workbench Coffee Bar Decorating Centre Horseriding Treasure hunts Film-making Tuck-shop ⇩	Made-up games Ramp bowls 3-a-side badminton Caber tossing 'Party games' ⇩	Using games equipment Piano Cooking Drawing Suggestions for trips, events ⇩
Learning possibilities — pay offs	Understanding of necessity for authority figure New experiences and challenges made possible Feeling of security and confidence in adult leaders	Necessity for limits, structure, self-discipline, group-discipline Self-esteem boosted Self-image altered in positive direction	A working demonstration of 'making do' — stimulus to own imagination, encouraging independence, hence self-confidence Depending on skill in choice and operation, could produce any of the other desirable results listed here Helps atmosphere of imaginative enterprise associated with group sessions Observing authority figures as more human and accessible	With newcomers, aid in assessment process, finding what makes them tick (or explode) Adds element of control by youngsters which is all-important Boosts self-esteem, confidence when these ideas are acted on by adults or group

Figure 3

Recording

Each session is recorded, noting who was there and what happened. We also try to include a degree of analysis and a record of the more subjective aspects, such as feelings within the group and the general atmosphere. Individual files on members contain the background information and our reports on them. We regularly do reports for Children's Hearings and case conferences and we usually appear, along with the social worker, to speak to the report and join in the deliberations.

Group records are always available for members to read. This is in fact encouraged, since it enhances the feedback effect of group membership. A useful activity is the reading through of group records, either by an individual or two or three together. Amusement and hilarity are usually mixed with a few uncomfortable moments when an incident is recounted of which the protagonist might not be particularly proud. Any reports that we write about individuals are open for them to read. Where appropriate, they are often involved in the writing of them. On several occasions youngsters have been prompted by a discussion about their report to do their own separate statement for a hearing. We have these typed and submitted along with ours.

The Workers

In describing the range of groups and sessions, the diversity created by the individual interests and strengths of the staff has already been acknowledged. The belief that flexibility and autonomy must be the operating principle of each group worker leads to a highly democratic staff structure. Assuming that there is a basic shared philosophy, our general policy is to encourage experimentation and individual initiative. This might be at the expense of uniformity, but the dividends are large in terms of the development of the project and individual job satisfaction. The usual situation is for there to be the core of long term regularly meeting groups, and around this core a changing set of short term projects and experimental schemes. Any one group worker will characteristically have one foot in the permanent groups and another in a short term venture, usually of his own devising, and often in collaboration with social workers, youth and community workers, or others outside the project. The school release community service scheme is an example of something that started off in this experimental way and became a permanent feature of the project. Other ventures have included working with one-off or short term groups run by social workers, a weekly day-time session designed to help unemployed youngsters get work and a regular day assessment session involving social workers with their supervised youngsters.

The staff structure is designed to allow this flexibility and initiative, while preserving the vital element of teamwork. The leaders form a team of four equals, with one the unofficial co-ordinator and spokesman for the project. Two leaders are based at the Rowans Cottage and two at the Ferry Road Centre. There is no back-up staff at the centres, the idea being to make the involvement of the kids in cleaning, decorating and simple repair work a real contribution, necessary to the project's operation, and not just an extra. Typing is done for us by the typing pool at the main Dundee office of the Social Work Department, but the role of leader can involve everything from preparing the estimates and working out policy, to mopping out the kitchen. This leads to a detailed overall grasp of what is going on at the centre, and an intense involvement in it. It also produces a strange feeling of creating the whole thing each day. This has a negative side. As Charly said once, 'When you put your key in the door each morning, it's like starting the project from scratch. Like if you stop thinking about it the whole lot would disappear'.

A weekly leaders' meeting takes up an entire morning, because it has to cover all the practical and planning issues of the week, as well as being the forum for a regular exchange of ideas, anxieties, and the kind of informal, honest communication and hammering out of basic agreements which is essential to anchor all this diversity. The projection of all the aggression, anger, distress and confusion felt by the kids onto the adults working with them is a well known phenomenon. The regular staff meetings with their candour, sensitivity, a professional sense of purpose, and humour help to cope with this problem. The agenda of the leaders' meeting typically includes administrative issues, planning, policy decisions, reports back of various kinds, and referrals.

The Volunteers

In addition to full time staff, extensive use is made of volunteers. We like to maintain a three to one ratio of kids to adults in a group, so a typical group would have ten kids, one leader, two volunteers, and perhaps a student on placement. Most of our volunteers have been recruited through our own and social workers' grapevines, though the arrival of a Volunteer Aid Organiser in the Department has helped. What we look for in volunteers is a genuine interest in teenagers and the ability to communicate this effectively. We hope to have a diversity of adults involved, to increase the choices available to youngsters for one to one contact, and to add to the richness of the group experience. Particular skills or talents are, of course, useful, but we find with our better volunteers that these, if present, tend to get used far less often than might be imagined. What they offer is themselves, their attention, their involvement, and their presence in the group as a whole person. For instance, it may be far more useful for a volunteer to flounder along with the kids at a skill which is new to all of them rather than be so accomplished at it that the youngster feels ashamed of his own first efforts. Most of our volunteers are more or less middle class, but we do make an effort to recruit people who might come from the kids' own areas and have had some success here. Quite a number of volunteers go on to do full time social or youth work.

Volunteers and students share in the running of the groups, in decisions made about them, and in the handling of particular situations and individuals. As well as 'talk-down' sessions after an evening group, there are weekly meetings for volunteers and students and occasional training weekends. We find these essential. Away from the hurly burly of a group session, youngsters' progress can be discussed, decisions made, questions asked, background given, and anxieties acknowledged and shared. This last part is perhaps the most important function of the meetings. One important category of volunteer consists of a number of social workers who work with us on a regular basis, attached to particular groups. There are usually two or three working with us in this way, either because they want to have experience of group work, or because they want to be involved directly in some way in intermediate treatment. If a social worker is the supervisor for one or two of the kids in the group, a new and useful dimension to the youngsters' supervision is introduced.

A YEAR IN THE PROJECT'S DEVELOPMENT

The major events and activities in the life of the project during one year, from February 1976 to 1977, are illustrated in Figure 4, and will be discussed in the following pages.

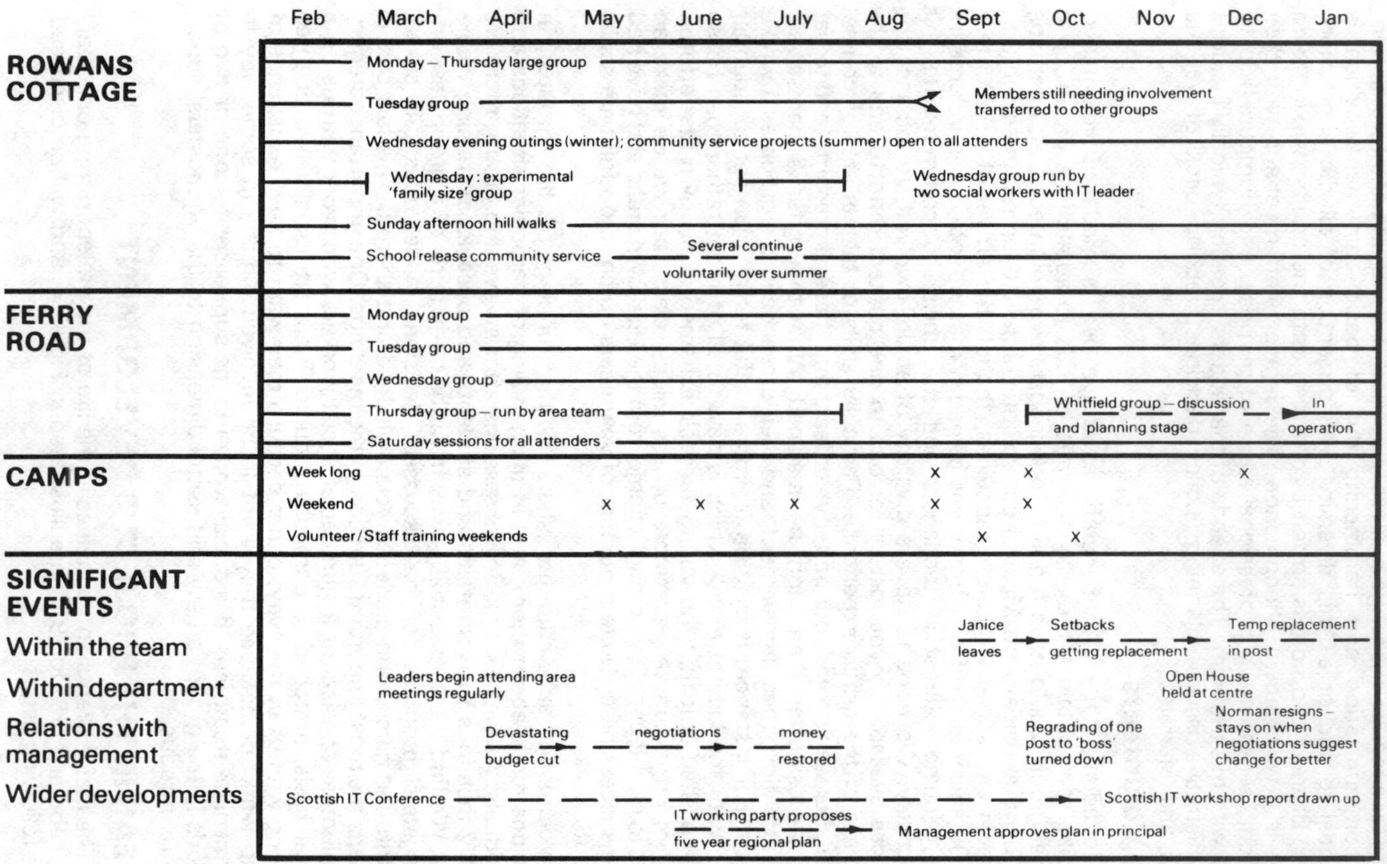

ROWANS COTTAGE

	Feb	March	April	May	June	July	Aug	Sept	Oct	Nov	Dec	Jan

Monday — Thursday large group

Tuesday group — Members still needing involvement transferred to other groups

Wednesday evening outings (winter); community service projects (summer) open to all attenders

Wednesday: experimental 'family size' group — Wednesday group run by two social workers with IT leader

Sunday afternoon hill walks

School release community service — Several continue voluntarily over summer

FERRY ROAD

Monday group

Tuesday group

Wednesday group

Thursday group — run by area team — Whitfield group — discussion and planning stage — In operation

Saturday sessions for all attenders

CAMPS

Week long   x (May) x (June)   x (Sept) x (Oct)
Weekend   x (Aug)   x (Sept)
Volunteer / Staff training weekends   x (July)   x (Sept) x (Oct)   x (Dec)

SIGNIFICANT EVENTS

Within the team

Leaders begin attending area meetings regularly

Janice leaves — Setbacks getting replacement — Temp replacement in post

Within department

Scottish IT Conference

Devastating budget cut — negotiations — money restored

Open House held at centre

Norman resigns — stays on when negotiations suggest change for better

Relations with management

Regrading of one post to 'boss' turned down

Wider developments

IT working party proposes five year regional plan — Management approves plan in principal — Scottish IT workshop report drawn up

Figure 4 Overview of one year at the activity centres: February 1976 to February 1977

Groups and Programme

In June 1975, groups from the Rowans were relocated to the new Ferry Road building, and became the Ferry Road Monday, Tuesday and Wednesday groups. This was done, firstly in order to provide a challenging new venture for the groups, and secondly in recognition of the possible difficulties of reaching the Ferry Road site, which, it was felt, the more committed, long standing members could cope with better. Once Ferry Road got established, the hope was that an interesting and relevant programme would overcome the bad location as far as new referrals were concerned. This proved to be the case.

On Thursdays at Ferry Road, area social workers run a group. This started as a two month exercise, but has been extended to run for a year, as it was thought to be very successful. Because their normal workload is not diminished, however, the group becomes a real test of the social workers' commitment and drive. The role of the project is to provide facilities with more flexibility and tolerance than a more mainstream provision. We provide premises and equipment, help with expenditure on fees, and set the place up with the necessary preparation of materials and games. Norman meets with them regularly to advise, discuss issues that have arisen, and offer support in the face of the emotional demands of running the group. After this group comes to an end, its place is taken by the Whitfield group, which is for seven to nine year old boys and their parents, the intention being to help improve the parent:child relationship. Experience with the Thursday group has shown the necessity for more direct support and commitment from the centre staff in running these groups, so Norman becomes part of this team [6].

At the Rowans a larger group meets up to four times per week, and two small groups are in operation. The Tuesday group numbers eight to ten and is run by Janice, who works closely with several of the families, with the agreement of the social worker. Otherwise its pattern of operation is similar to the groups meeting at Ferry Road. The other small group is an experimental family size group of two adults and four particularly difficult or disturbed youngsters, which lasts five months. It is a partial success in that two youngsters go on to larger groups, while two eventually go into residential care. Wednesday evenings and Sunday afternoons are given to outward looking activities available to all the members. A short term group in the summer is run by Janice with two social workers.

The large group is an attempt to move more towards a youth club atmosphere while retaining the essential planning and treatment elements of the project. Increased attendances and regular home visiting are features that are built into this approach. A group of 15 to 20 youngsters become identified with the Rowans as a whole, and with Scot in particular. Of these, a core of seven to nine youngsters are very heavily involved, coming four times a week and at any daytime opportunity. The school release programme at the Rowans consists of community service projects on Mondays and Wednesdays. Some youngsters are on placements on Thursdays as well. The projects such as grass cutting, decorating or shopping, usually benefit elderly or handicapped people. The placements are at nurseries, old people's homes or hostels, and here the staff of the place supervise the youngsters. This provides an element of work experience. The youngsters are generally very keen and many turn up during the school holidays as well.

The Wednesday evening outings tend to vary with the season. During the Winter they consist of trips to the live theatre, which are surprisingly successful, and to the swimming baths. As the lighter evenings begin, the emphasis switches to doing community service projects, particularly gardening. A high point at this time is a project cutting the grass for what seems like half a village of elderly people. The old folk are appreciative, and the local councillor turns up to thank each youngster individually and have a chat.

Both centres run weekend and week long camps throughout the year. A new development arises out of discussion with staff at Camas about their rebuilding programme. The Rowans runs a work camp there where, in return for their food, the group put in a hard week digging and laying floors. Despite the work aspect and the unlikely time of year, namely December, it goes with a real swing. All the benefits of a camp as an educational experience are still there, and it expands our camp programme possibilities within the same budget.

Relationships with the Department and Other Agencies

Within our own agency there seem to be two different sets of relationships, namely the professional and the administrative. On the professional side, the links with individual social workers continue to grow and to be generally positive. Charly proposes that each of us should have a regular attachment to a particular area and attend its meetings regularly. This is approved, and the increased contact with the whole range of area staff proves valuable. We sense that the credibility of the project is established and growing, as evidenced by referrals, discussions with social workers, interest shown by newcomers to the Department, and increasing requests for student placements. Our belief is that this credibility is based on successful work with the young people referred to us, and that the success of our work very fundamentally depends on our autonomy and flexibility.

It is these factors which can create problems when looked at from an administrative point of view. Autonomy and accountability, flexibility and departmental uniformity, are awkward pairings. When first set up, the project was directly responsible to the Deputy Director. When Dundee was absorbed into the new Tayside Regional Council in Spring 1975, the major policy making process was taken up to a higher level. At the same time, our project was re-allocated so that there were now three people over us in the chain of responsibility within the Dundee Division alone.

The first sign that remoteness plus unorthodoxy is a fatal combination comes with the start of the new financial year in April 1976. A regional decision has been taken to cut back on recreational spending for children's homes and the like. Apparently the project comes into this category and since most of our programme could conceivably be labelled recreational, most of our programme budget disappears. The £6,500 needed to cover camps, outings, fees, equipment, and materials for the 95 youngsters involved is reduced to £500. Urgent negotiations with management begin immediately, and after five months the money is restored. An important factor is that our funding through urban aid means that in order to produce £6,000 the Department only needs to find £1,500.

Another problem arises over Norman's role as unofficial co-ordinator of the project, as seen by the Department. A request to regrade his post to recognise its supervisory aspect is turned down in September. Later on in the year an issue arises about the accountability of project staff, the chain of command, and the passing of information. Norman feels he is being told to come more into line with Departmental procedures over administrative matters, while the larger issues continue to be unresolved, and this, plus the massive budget cut, raise questions about the Department's commitment to the project in general. Strong feeling about this culminates in his written resignation in January. Subsequently a series of meetings convinces him that a new beginning is possible, and that the Department is committed to the survival and continued development of the project, so the resignation is withdrawn.

Two positive events result from our difficulties in this year. When the budget cut is being discussed, the project staff are asked to join others from Angus and Perth divisions to draw up recommendations for the future development of intermediate treatment in Tayside. A five year plan is produced, asserting the value of intermediate treatment and recommending a considerable expansion, which is accepted in principle by the regional management in August. In November an 'open house' is held in order to increase knowledge about our work within and without the Department. The Chairman of the Social Work Committee attends and expresses his interest in the project.

In addition regular contact is kept up with other intermediate treatment projects in Scotland. A Scottish intermediate treatment conference, called by the Social Work Services Group of the Scottish Education Department, formalises these links, and leads to a workshop later in the year at which practitioners produce a handbook on practice and methods, to be used as a central document to help further development in Scotland [7].

The practice becomes established that project staff provide reports and attend the hearings of centre members in addition to the social workers. New Panel members are given a tour round the centres and a talk as part of their training, so that the project is recognised as part of the range of facilities available for youngsters. Links with schools are particularly strong where the school is involved in our school release programme. Contact with families is generally informal, but Scot's home visits, Janice's family casework, and the Whitfield Group's work with parents and children together are more formal aspects of these links. The project has increasing contact with the Children's and Young Persons' Psychiatric Unit, and it sometimes makes direct referrals.

Staffing Issues

During this year the four leaders operate the programme singly and in various combinations, with general harmony, although there are problems of structure, personality, and outside pressures, that are tackled with varying degrees of success.

The decision to expand the programme by having two small centres rather than one bigger one proves to be the right one for the youngsters, but increases difficulties in the areas of staff unity and morale. At each centre two people are asked to work closely together in sometimes emotionally draining situations, with neither administrative back-up on the spot, nor the support which an everyday routine provides in a more conventional structure. This puts tremendous pressure on the working relationship of each set of two leaders, and at the Rowans, the varying methods and interests of the two workers increasingly lead to major differences of opinion, which is in sharp contrast to the basic accord the Ferry Road leaders are lucky enough to enjoy. The whole issue is discussed fairly constantly both at an individual and a team level, but no acceptable resolution is achieved, and Janice leaves the project in September.

Significant Factors

Looking at Figure 4, a comparison of the Rowans and Ferry Road programmes reveals an interesting difference. Whereas the Ferry Road portion moves almost unchanged from February to January (the exception being the groups run by the area social workers), the Rowans programme looks much more complicated, both in the number of entries and the amount of explanation required. This reflects the contrast between a relatively mature programme which has bedded down, and one that is still in the process of change and evolution. Clearly the Rowans operation is also affected by the conflict between the two workers and the departure of one of them. However, although Janice leaves during this year, the staff team is remarkably stable, since the remaining members originally appointed to the project are still with it at the time of writing. However, Janice's departure, flowing as it does from unresolved conflict, highlights one of the difficulties that can be created or exacerbated by operating a staff team without a definite hierarchy. Increased pressure is brought to bear on the Rowans programme by delays in appointing a new worker. Although a temporary replacement comes in January, the national advertising is not authorised until the following June.

The year begins five months after the team is at full strength, and a number of features, which have previously been experimental, become established during the period, such as the Sunday hillwalks at the Rowans, the school release scheme and the pattern of group meetings at Ferry Road. At the same time the need for support becomes very apparent both for the project staff and for the social workers running groups at the centre. In this context, the contact with other intermediate treatment practitioners and the opportunities for sharing information and experience are much appreciated.

The threatened loss of the greater part of the budget is a devastating blow, and obviously creates considerable anxiety until it is resolved five months later. Nonetheless there are encouraging developments, the main one being management's acceptance of our working party report recommending the expansion of intermediate treatment.

THE FERRY ROAD MONDAY GROUP

To put in sharper focus the face-to-face work of the project, this section describes a year in the life of one of the groups—the Monday Group at Ferry Road. The setting in which this group operated, looking outward from the group itself, is illustrated by Figure 5. Each of the circles represents a step away from the intensity of a relatively closed group towards a more natural, but possibly threatening, free flowing experience of meeting and interacting.

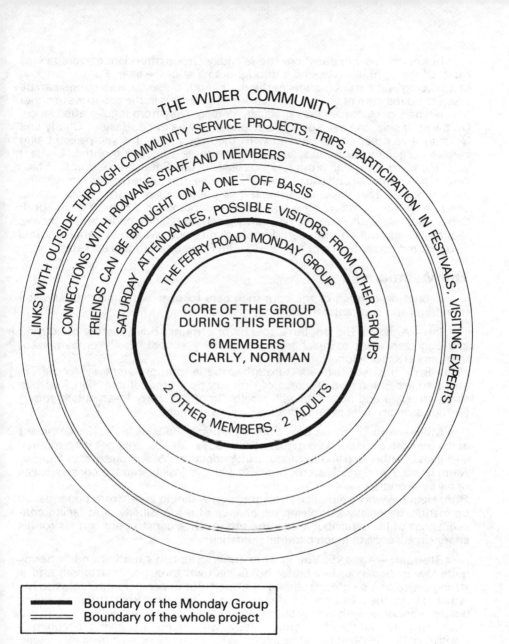

THE WIDER COMMUNITY

LINKS WITH OUTSIDE THROUGH COMMUNITY SERVICE PROJECTS, TRIPS, PARTICIPATION IN FESTIVALS, VISITING EXPERTS

CONNECTIONS WITH ROWANS STAFF AND MEMBERS

FRIENDS CAN BE BROUGHT ON A ONE–OFF BASIS

SATURDAY ATTENDANCES, POSSIBLE VISITORS FROM OTHER GROUPS

THE FERRY ROAD MONDAY GROUP

CORE OF THE GROUP
DURING THIS PERIOD

6 MEMBERS
CHARLY, NORMAN

2 OTHER MEMBERS, 2 ADULTS

━━━ Boundary of the Monday Group
═══ Boundary of the whole project

Figure 5   The Monday Group at Ferry Road

During the year in question, the Monday Group attendance average was eight. Of the eight, six were there throughout most of the year. For the purpose of analysing and describing this particular period, these six youngsters can be taken to be the core of the Monday Group. The others in the group were either new referrals or older members gradually drifting away from regular attendance. On the staff side, the average adult attendance was three. Besides Charly and Norman, five other adults worked with the group over this year, each being involved regularly for periods varying from three to seven months. Contact with members of other groups is possible in the Saturday sessions, which centre members can attend if they wish. The rule about members visiting other groups is that this is acceptable if all the members of that group agree. The rule on friends attending is that this is acceptable on a one-off basis. Both these rules were the subject of much discussion and modification by the Monday Group during this year. Joint activities and overlap at various points also ensured some degree of familiarity with Rowans attenders and staff.

The Membership

A brief description of the core members follows, setting out the reason for referral and our treatment plan.

Ian—Aged 14. Big lad, but also a bit of a 'mum's boy'. History of bullying and aggressiveness to teachers since primary school. Easily embarrassed, tantrums at school, lonely.
Plan: Build his self esteem through experiences of success, lead from here into accepting give and take of ordinary peer group interaction, improve ability to relate and negotiate with adults. Improve ability to articulate strong feelings as alternative to tantrums and aggressiveness.

Mike—Age 13. Small boy. Friend and neighbour of Ian's. Ian dominant in the friendship. Second youngest of four boys. Mother colludes with truancy and thefts. Father apparently caring, but ineffective. Mike impresses as friendly, warm hearted, and mischievous, but with a lack of insight into the consequences of his behaviour.
Plan: Help develop internal controls through weaning away from dependency on friends, especially Ian; giving experience of responsibility, and facing consequences of his behaviour in the age group. Give constructive outlets for his energy in absence of much parental guidance.

Stephen—Aged 15. Youngest of three. Stephen's mother and father of quite low intelligence, but father holds his own through persistence, and a strong sense of his rights. Stephen is similar, but in constant conflict with his father as he tries to assert independence. Problems with truancy, being bullied, unpopular with peer group. Whole family labelled as 'daft'.
Plan—Help to defuse the confrontation with father by giving Stephen a positive outlet, as seen by father, such as community service projects. Guide Stephen, within the group, to overcoming his usual scapegoat role and into tangible success, shared enjoyable activities, taking an active, responsible part.

Betty—Aged 13. Youngest of five. House dirty and in disrepair. Family regarded as undesirables by neighbours. Reaction to this has been a banding together by the children, supporting each other against outside attack. Problems from early on with truancy, lack of cleanliness, truculence, and minor thefts. Betty is much less aggressive than her siblings, but is confused and lacking in consistent guidance at home. Father respected but brutal, mother ineffectual and treated as a joke by children.

Plan—Provide Betty with consistent, caring adult contact for as long as she needs it. Be prepared for extended testing out of the commitment. In particular the availability of acceptable female help will be important. Betty has an immature, simplistic idea of authority and consequent lack of internalised controls and values. Work on developing her own sense of responsibility through exercises where she takes control and also copes with the consequences of this.

Iris—Aged 13. A friend of Betty's. Came with Betty from the start, and quickly accepted as a 'self referred' member, since her needs were obvious. Mother and father in late middle age. Older brother at home. House bleak and uncared for. Parents both heavy drinkers. Older brother in constant bother. Iris trying hard to be an island apart in the family—has aspirations to more 'normal' standards. Frustrated when blocked by lack of support from family, constant lack of even small amounts of money, sometimes well dressed, but unwashed, unaware of effect of coarse language in inappropriate setting.

Plan—Give Iris an arena to practise social skills unlearned at home. Encourage any talents as means to help her progress at school and after—she likes to draw. Encourage eventual separation of self identity from Betty, who is dominant at the moment.

June—Aged 15. Second oldest of four. Parents separated for the past eight years. Children living with mother. June is physically mature and assertive. Has trouble getting on with adults—either non-communicative and sullen or verbally abusive. Problems at school with truancy, lateness, disruptiveness. Mother worried about possible promiscuity. June not popular with peers—no firm friends or social outlets.

Plan—Create one area in June's life where adult relationships are good. Provide lots of adult interest and attention in this setting. Assumption that much of her behaviour is attention seeking. Work to improve peer relationships through improved self esteem, thus reducing the need to prove herself in ultimately destructive ways such as showing off and promiscuity.

During the year February 1976 to February 1977 the Monday Group passed through several distinct phases, which can be characterised as new beginning—chaos or dependency—organisation and creativity—another new beginning—consolidation.

New Beginning

This period is a short one of about four weeks, a natural starting point for describing some of the group's history, since at this time several older members are dropping away from the centre. The new guard, and specifically the six youngsters we have focused on, are now no longer the younger contingent and begin to make their own impact on the programme. At first this takes a negative form. Mary, one of the remaining older members, tries hard to organise everyone into suggesting activities and keeping the centre cleaned up better. She does not get enough response to satisfy her, and her strongly expressed negative feelings about the group are a feature of this time.

157

What the group does want is activity and excitement, preferably laid on without much effort on their part. Charly and Norman decide that 'pump priming' is a good idea, in order to take the momentum from Mary's loud complaints that not enough is happening, to keep the group's self image a positive one, and also to stimulate the younger members and give them a basis of experience from which they can develop the ability to suggest and follow through activities. Activities during this period include baking, film making, parlour games, community service projects and a tournament of various indoor games with the fun aspect emphasised and competition played down. The issues of boredom, apathy, dependency on adult ideas, and the projection on to the adults of Mary's hostility, aroused by her frustration at the group's lack of response, are all fodder for discussion at the group meetings at the end of each session.

While every effort is made by adults to encourage all to take an equal part in the group, Betty and Iris, and Ian and Mike are still very much two pairs, with Iris and Mike being the silent partners. Stephen and June are still relative outsiders, relating well to the adults but not fully involved with the other kids. Tentative links are growing, however, between June and the other girls. Ian is very happy with the centre at the moment, judging by the number of youngsters he has told about the place. Several who are on supervision go to their social workers to ask if they can be referred as well. This is seen as a positive step in Ian's progress: he seems to feel important through being associated with the centre and being able to act as broker for others.

One activity that carries on through this period is the outcome of discussions between Charly, Norman and a clinical psychologist, about the helpfulness of an outside assessment of what goes on at the centre. After much discussion, it was suggested that it would be interesting to analyse the youngsters' view of adults in their lives, particularly how they contrasted those at the centre with teachers, parents, relatives, and other significant adults. How the information was obtained was thought to be crucial, and the approach adopted was based on the theory of Personal Constructs, a repertory grid technique being used for the interviews [8]. This approach emphasises the youngster's own way of looking at the world and organising his experience, but the interviewing process does not depend on a high degree of verbal fluency. For the youngsters, this experience is interesting and fun, and they came out from the interviews feeling quite important. The purpose of the whole exercise is of course explained to all of them.

Chaos or Dependency

During this period the group functions well with plenty of adult guidance, but slides into chaotic and rather unhappy confusion when the reins of control are handed over. One adult task during this time is to go through this process of handing over, watching the chaos, picking up the pieces and handing over again, without reacting too personally and giving up in frustration. Fortunately the whole period is a short one of about four to six weeks.

One event that goes very well is a spooky walk. This comes about because the Wednesday Group has gone on one, and Mary complains at a meeting that they should have one as well. The idea is for the adults so to organise things as to give everyone a good fright, although of course, they deny right up to the final denouement that they are rigging any of the effects. The group are taken blindfolded to a dark wood, with a long, straight and wide path through it. As the group makes its way along, various scary noises and effects are laid on. At the end of the walk, all is revealed in the unmasking of the 'spook', Alistair, a student on placement with the group, who is supposedly at home with a cold. When the blindfolds come off at the start, Betty says *'Its just like a dream'*. She and Iris get a good enjoyable fright from the experience, and both cling tightly all the time onto Liz, an adult volunteer. Liz is a quiet, warm person, and a close bond is building up between Betty, Iris and her. June's usually loud voice is put to good use tonight, screaming and giggling hysterically, while not really being as frightened as Betty and Iris. Stephen enjoys the whole thing thoroughly and giggles gleefully whenever the whole pack, including himself, panics and runs from the latest noise. Ian and Mike are missing on this night. It transpired that Ian has broken his leg in a fall from a bicycle and will be in plaster for nine to 12 weeks. Mike did not feel able to come down leaving Ian at home. It is arranged for Ian to be given a lift down and back each week, and he is appreciative of the extra attention. Although this is a bind and causes some difficulties, Charly and Norman think it important to continue his involvement with the group.

Organisation and Creativity

In this period, the group is full of enthusiasm and willingness to take part, with a new element of self control and planning by the kids themselves. This phase covers about 20 weeks until the group changes gear with the addition of new members.

Constructive activities of this period are mural painting, a football match with the Rowans at the kids' suggestion, community service projects, repairs at the centre, designing a group badge, swimming, industrious clear-ups of the centre, candlemaking, with a display at a community festival and picture in the paper with local councillor, a disco planned and run by the group, a hill-walk, a filmed role play of a Children's Hearing, and the creation of a 'girls' room'—decorated to the girls' taste by themselves, with help from the boys and adults. Interestingly, where a session does fail to jell satisfactorily during this period, the meeting at the end usually goes very well, with lots of discussion of issues, personalities and problems.

The group is beginning to be aware of a definite identity and feels this is threatened by too many visitors looking in from other groups, so it decides to impose a ban until further notice. Ian moves this suggestion after a night which is affected badly by the disruptive behaviour of himself and two Tuesday group members whom he has invited down for a Monday visit. This seems partly an attempt to shift blame away from himself, but also use external control to remedy a problem with his own behaviour. The rest of the group are in favour of the idea, so the ruling stands. It lasts for two months, when it is modified by vote to the original rule—visiting if approved by the group at the time.

The pattern of interaction between the six core members is altering in this period. Tentative 'boyfriend-girlfriend' links are made between Ian and Iris, Mike and Betty. These are quite immature, and consist primarily of the assertion to others '. . . is my boyfriend/girlfriend'. The presence of the more experienced June may be the partial cause; she and Betty have a friendly connection now. Stephen continues to have his strongest ties with adults, and remains not quite in the centre of things with the group. In fact, a joking insult tossed at Betty on the way home one night is relayed to Ian, who reacts by threatening Stephen and demanding a fight the next week. Betty is quite pleased with the fuss. Norman intervenes strongly at the group meeting by accusing Ian of overreacting because he knows Stephen will be easy to bully, a fate he has so far escaped in the group. Ian smarts under the statement that his action is mean rather than heroic. In fact the group, led by Betty and Iris, do not agree, but Ian seems to, at least enough for the 'duel' to be off. Figure 6 shows the change in group interaction pattern.

Links with the adults are in fact quite good. It proves not difficult to develop a relationship of mutual respect with June. One special relationship is that between the volunteer Liz and the girls in the group, particularly Betty and Iris. During this period a definite 'ladies' circle' is formed, centred on Liz, who uses this to lead conversation into areas helpful to the girls, particularly boy/girl matters. Iris is beginning to move away from Betty, in that Iris is the more active one, keen to make things and join in all activities.

June lets it be known through the kids that she is pregnant by a 16 year old boy in her neighbourhood. Charly contacts her social worker and discusses what action to take, particularly since June says she has not told her mother yet. Charly and Liz have a joint talk with June, who agrees that her mother should be told. However, it comes out that she has yet to see a doctor for confirmation. This she is urged to do, with her mother. When pressed at later points over what she has done about it, June's story becomes rather variable and vague. Both staff and kids begin to get suspicious that they are witnessing an act. Conveniently, on the night of a disco, June tells the other girls she has just had a miscarriage, and that is the end of the episode. The group do not press the issue at all, and the adults decide not to pressure June into an honest discussion about this attention seeking ploy, afraid that a direct push like this might put her right back into her usual defiant, mistrustful stance. Instead, efforts continue to encourage her into successful activities, where she gets credit for her performance. She likes baking, but tends to be very slapdash—the adult role here is to ensure that the results are good, by gently but firmly helping June to stick to the discipline of the recipe and the proper method. Underpinning all this is the fact that June senses, rightly, that the adults like her, despite the difficulties she sometimes presents.

Just to dwell on this for a moment: our approach depends on generally liking the youngsters, and enjoying their company, and it is interesting to consider whether this can in any way be planned for. Selection of staff and volunteers is an obvious factor, and given a choice between someone with a cool detached interest in the problem and someone who seems warm and involved in an obvious way, we have opted for the latter. The structure of a small group with a high adult ratio works against the type of them-and-us confrontation pattern that so often exists between youngsters and adults in school and elsewhere. The relative security of a fairly consistent group eliminates much of the anxiety and fear that provoke confrontation. Consequently, it is sometimes difficult to see the destructive behaviour patterns that the group is there to help change. If the youngster gets on well in his group but nowhere else, this is obviously a cause for concern. In June's case,

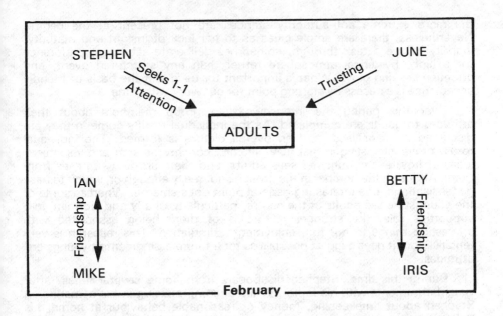

Seeks 1-1
Attention

Trusting

ADULTS

Friendship

Friendship

February

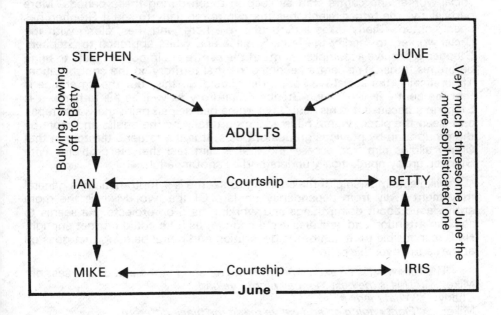

Bullying, showing
off to Betty

ADULTS

Courtship

Courtship

Very much a threesome, June the
more sophisticated one

June

Figure 6   Changes in group interaction

the more extreme anti-authority stances are not present at the centre. Nevertheless, there are ample clues as to her lack of insight and maturity, inability to see a task through, sometimes deliberate sabotage, preference for a high, hysterical atmosphere rather than any structured event, and attention seeking ploys. What is important for us is that the basis of friendly acceptance is a necessary starting point for our work with June.

Over this period the interviews with group members about their attitudes to adults are completed. As the individual results come in they are discussed and analysed, and an overall picture is formed. The individual results prove interesting in that they generally confirm the staff and volunteers' ideas of how each youngster sees adults, and there are few surprises from them. Although the number in the group is not really enough on which to base generalisations, one interesting general point does emerge. Whereas some of the youngsters see adults at the centre, particularly Charly and Norman, in a supportive role, the stronger picture is of them being associated with interesting things to do, fun, enjoyment, stimulation. This research is very tentative, but it does suggest possibilities for a future assessment of youngsters' attitudes.

During this time, Stephen disappears from home several times, after violent arguments with his father. While uncompromising in his demands on Stephen about timekeeping, money or reasonable behaviour at home, his father is quite concerned about his welfare when he is on the loose. Father, social worker and centre staff all keep in touch during these periods. More particularly, the father telephones the centre regularly to see if Stephen has been sighted. Charly takes a particular role here, and tries, along with the social worker, to modify the father's black and white approach to Stephen. Stephen's positive accomplishments at the centre are important facts to bring before his father. The centre becomes 'neutral territory' in the confrontation. Theoretically, the social worker's office could do this, but the difference is that the centre is very much Stephen's territory as well as his father's. It is Stephen's because it is his 'club', where he has helped paint the walls, repair and clean the place, where he is accepted totally by the adults and more by the group than by previous groups of peers. It is the father's territory in that Charly allows him free access and makes him feel that his problems with Stephen are sympathetically understood by another adult.

Mike's membership of the courting foursome is symptomatic of a general movement away from dependency on Ian. Of the two, Mike is the more enthusiastic about doing things and working hard on projects. He seems to soak up attention and activities like a sponge, as if he could not get enough. He is responsible for much of the decoration and mural painting that goes on at the centre over this period.

The following is an exchange from the meeting at the end of one session:

Mike: 'This is the best Monday night I've had.'
Charly: 'What made it?'
Mike: 'Plenty going on and we've made the place different.'

While aware that channeling Mike's energies is one aim, the adults discuss ways in which he can develop more internal control of his behaviour. He is given a key part in setting up and running the display on candlemaking at a local festival, and takes his responsibility seriously. In the role play of a

Children's Hearing, he opts to play the 'victim' (his word), all the rest playing adult roles. He does the part well, giving it conviction without just being himself: the boy he plays is sullen and uncommunicative. The issue of the 'no visitors' rule provides another chance to improve Mike's social skills. When the group is moving towards rescinding the rule, Mike sticks out strongly for keeping it: he has to argue his case at the group meetings, and manages to delay the change for some time. He takes quite an interest in cooking, and comments on occasion that he would like to try a particular recipe at home, where he is considered a pest and not allowed to help out. His cooking skills, acquired at the centre, help him to play a more responsible role at home.

Another New Beginning

This phase begins with a week's camp at Camas, Isle of Mull, followed by the introduction of three new members over a period of eight weeks. Two or three older members have dropped away over the summer, and the group is seen as being strong enough to cope with the influx. The camp has an accelerating effect on individual and group development, both in positive and negative ways, at least in the short term. To summarise its significance for the core group:

Ian

Enjoyed the camp thoroughly. Had some embarrassing moments in the group, however, when the more babyish side of him was apparent. Had one tantrum directed at Norman, which ended with Ian in tears, and the group both shocked and sympathetic. This did not in fact alter his growing status as a leader in the group.

Mike

Was game for anything offered but tended to get over tired. His lack of domestic training such as table manners sometimes embarrassing, but the group generally supportive.

Stephen

Clearly out of his depth. Had expected a holiday camp type of experience, despite being told the whole point was the challenge of a primitive environment. Nevertheless coped grimly with the job of getting through the week.

Betty

Made good laison with the personable female cook at the camp, and the two resident kittens. Had a rather lazy week; hard to get her to do more than the minimum chores.

Iris

In contrast to Betty, worked very hard when required and enjoyed the week tremendously.

June

Had a disastrous week, which centred on her making a link with a boy from another camp nearby, being dropped by him, and having to face the group's resentment, based on feelings that she had not thought them 'good enough' for her, with negative reaction to supposed fickleness and promiscuity. The boys were particularly brutal calling her a 'cow' and making her life pretty miserable for the rest of the week. This eventually healed over in the group after a month or two.

Shortly after the camp, Stephen leaves for Aberdeen, to train as an apprentice trawlerman. This job comes about through the encouragement of his father and Charly's help with a letter of application. Before he leaves, Stephen tells Charly he wants to give the news at the meeting. This he does, and leaves with an increased respect in the eyes of group, who still tend to regard him as a butt for humour.

Of the three new members, two are accepted fairly readily, but one has more difficulty. Joe comes from a family similar to Betty's in reputation, and it is Betty who declares *'He's not coming into this group'* when he first arrives. Joe has a way of doing irritating things, seemingly without thought, and then enjoying the consequences so much that one questions the absence of premeditation. The group is the victim of two such incidents, but in each case it exacts some sort of response from Joe. First incident: taking 12 teaspoons of sugar in his coffee, thereby running the centre out of sugar for the evening. Response: Joe undertakes to restrict himself to three teaspoons from now on. All make sure he does so. Second incident: stealing a volunteer's watch. This takes a bit of work between Joe, Norman, Charly, the social worker, volunteer, family and the group. Eventual response: watch returned, with apologies. It had to be bought back from a school acquaintance. Working through these two incidents has the effect of bringing Joe into the group, since acceptance has been on a contract basis with certain standards of behaviour expected. This acceptance process is not usually the case with newcomers, but Joe forces it by acting in a way which demands a response from the group. The adults were worried that Joe would be too much for the group to handle, and that he would be rejected from the start, but fortunately the group is strong enough to cope with Joe's demands without having its own norms swept away.

Consolidation

The newcomers are now part of the group, though Joe will have trouble integrating as long as he continues to irritate. Adult efforts are aimed at channelling him into ways of getting the attention and power he needs through more acceptable means. This proves an uphill struggle.

Over this 12 weeks, the group's activities include decorating, cooking (including making a meal for the group to share), trips in the van, swimming, boxing, building shelves for the equipment room, a Hallowe'en party, hairdressing lessons with an outside expert, community service projects, a Christmas disco, a tuck shop, and film making, including a role play of a disruptive class and exasperated teacher.

The rift between June and the rest soon mends, and she asks Norman and Charly if she can be designated a junior leader, since she is now 16. The group have no objections to this, although the adults make it clear that this means responsibility as well as a title. Certain duties are agreed on, such as arriving early to help set out equipment and reporting shortages in provisions and games. In fact this soon goes by the board, when it becomes clear that it was the status alone June wanted, without strings attached. On the positive side, she and Angie, one of the newer members, propose, set up and run a tuck shop for several months. This means handling a cash float, buying in, baking cakes for sale, selling the food and drinks, and keeping the books. Both girls manage this responsibility, and a new feature is added to Monday nights through their efforts.

Betty seems to be regressing somewhat during this time. Again the problem is partly her wish to be treated as a senior member without wanting to give any substance to the role. In a way this recalls Mary's position a year ago of wanting power without cultivating the allegiance of the others. The group frequently accuses her of laziness during meetings. She argues back, but usually concedes the point. As with Mary, her unhappiness is projected onto the adults, and this makes for some moments where adult patience is worn pretty thin. The usual pattern is that after an adult has worked hard to make something possible, Betty alone of the group complains that it is not good enough, meanwhile offering no help at any point. The adult task is to keep pushing issues and tasks Betty's way, despite her attempts to make them do all the work.

Iris continues to move apart from Betty, while maintaining their friendship. The links with Ian and Mike have faded and Iris is getting more and more involved with older boys outside the group, first a boy from the Wednesday group, later an older lad who has left the centre for the Army but visits while on leave. If her boyfriends were unconnected with the centre, she would probably be disengaging herself gradually.

Ian is going through a bad patch at school, and has been on the fringe of trouble with other centre members. This causes concern, but on the positive side, Charly has introduced him to a boxing club, where he is doing well. The coach reckons he has a natural talent for it, and the manliness of the sport appeals to him and fulfils his need to be seen as masculine and grown up by his father. Also the tie-in with developing control over his temper seems a natural one. Tackling the points of concern, Norman and the social worker contact the school, and discuss Ian's progress at the centre as contrasted with his difficulties at school. The cause seems to be his embarrassment at his lack of success, particularly with reading and arithmetic. Unfortunately neither the school nor Ian is happy with the idea of having him in a remedial class. At least the problem is aired, however. Together with the other centre members who have been causing trouble as a group, Ian is given a 'dressing down' about the consequences of his behaviour by Charly and Norman and the issue is also discussed in the group.

Mike continues to grow in stature in the group, in both senses. He goes through a rough period at home, which leads to him arriving very early for the evening sessions, and this provides an opportunity for some individual conversation and discussion about the home situation, school, the group, and Mike's plans for when he leaves school. He is still getting into some bother, none of it very serious, but cumulatively it could lead at some point to his being removed from home. The centre's reports on Mike for the Children's Hearing emphasise all his positive contributions, and urge that his mischievous behaviour be treated as such and not as criminality.

Stephen does well at the trawler school, but an argument with his brother, with whom he stays, ends with his being put out without enough money to stay on his own. He returns home and gets a job in a fishmonger's shop, and his role as a money earner eases his relationship with his father. He keeps in touch with the centre, usually by telephone, and visits occasionally. Charly and Norman encourage him not to think in terms of slotting back into the Monday group, which would be a backward step, but to develop his own social life with workmates and friends.

EVALUATION

Primary to any evaluation are the perceptions of the kids themselves, as evidenced by some of the more vivid comments and statements they have made. The viewpoints of parents and social workers are also important. A follow up survey of former centre attenders, which involved interviewing youngsters, parents and social workers, was started in Spring 1977 and a summary of this follows. Finally, there are the strengths and weaknesses of the project, as perceived by the staff.

The Youngsters' Viewpoint

New boy to an even newer one:
'Of course the centre is Scot's home, you fool. He lives upstairs.'
'I like coming from school to do the projects here, because you get treated like an adult.'
At camp, older girl to disruptive younger ones:
'Quit it. It's a shame you making Janice chase after you all the time. This is her holiday as well!'

Every effort is made to develop mutual trust and respect between adults and youngsters and create a sense of shared enterprise, leading to the feeling that this is their place, as much as it is ours or the Social Work Department's.

Introduction of a girlfriend to worker:
'Sandra, this is Charly. He goes to my club.'
Arrival of excited school release kids:
'Guess what—there's been a fire at school, and we've all been sent home.'
'Then what are you doing here?'
'What's school got to do with it? We've got to come for the projects. These people are depending on us.'
Comment when the Director drops in:
'Do you mean this boy's your boss—in charge of everything?' (To Director):
'Excuse me, do you think we could get biscuits here with the coffee?'
'Do you get paid for doing this? But we do it all!'

Once a youngster is into the routine of attending, another element becomes apparent, which is the sense of adventure, excitement and interesting things to do, which the adults try to maintain. One aspect of this challenging experience made available to the kids, is the challenge of being truly responsible for much that goes on, or does not go on. Boredom can be the preliminary to some real learning, about yourself and others.

'This is a great place—you get to do whatever you want.'
'You get a laugh here.'
'It's boring now. There used to be lots of things to do.'
'This place is a dump!'

'This place is magic!'

It is clear that for many kids, the centres are a kind of reference point, and this function carries on after they leave, particularly when their lives do not provide them with many certainties or areas of security and happiness. A boy who was apparently totally unaffected by his time at the centre still keeps in touch, from Borstal at the moment, and can recall happy incidents and events five years back with an accuracy that is strangely touching. Throughout his time in the project he was disruptive, devious, and seemingly uncaring about the group or any individuals in it. One possible viewpoint of the effectiveness or not of intermediate treatment programmes is that the kind of experience offered is in itself a good enough objective to justify the effort. In a life of unrelieved bleakness, the presence of even one isolated experience of warmth and light could well take on an importance out of proportion to the time scale of it. This point is relevant to the question *'How can one or two nights a week make any basic difference to general behaviour patterns?'* We have found, with some of our members, an attachment to the centre which is out of all proportion to the time actually spent there. We hear from a number of parents— *'He talks about that centre all the time. It seems to be his whole life at the moment.'* One factor that is no doubt important in encouraging long term contact with the centres is the presence of the same staff. If someone phones up after a year or two, the leader who used to be with the group when he attended is the only link between him and a changed programme.

Reverse charge phone call from a boy who has run away to London, and about whom there has been a great deal of worry:
'Hello Norm. This is Rab. Just phoned to see how you're all getting on.'

Follow-up Survey

It was decided to evaluate systematically how our youngsters had progressed by means of a follow-up survey of former members, in order to provide the Social Work Department with a basis for weighing up the success or otherwise of the project. This was particularly germaine since it would in time have to decide if it wanted to take on the full financial load of running the centres after the five year urban aid grant ended.

There were three levels of success by which we judged our own work:

1 Helping the social growth and development of the youngsters. This includes personal and social skills, a wider range of interests, horizon broadening experiences, and greater ability to take responsibility and control over their own lives.

2 Diverting them from further delinquency.

3 Providing social workers and the Children's Panel with an alternative to residential care.

Of these the first is the most significant to us in our day to day assessments of how members are getting on. Obviously the hope is that the second will often follow from the first. The third aim has more to do with overall policy, but it is certainly one way of measuring effectiveness, in monetary terms at the very least. These three aims were in our minds when planning the evaluation.

A follow-up of former members was chosen, rather than an assessment of those still attending, because the primary objective was to 'sell' the scheme and it was felt that this would be best served by focusing on long term effectiveness. Naturally, whatever approach is taken, there are always unanswerable questions. We cannot say how much the changes in their lives were due to this involvement, nor how the kids would have fared without us, but the survey does provide a picture of how well they had been coping when they no longer had the project to support them. The survey included all former members who met two further criteria: they had been significantly involved in the centres, measured by at least six months regular attendance; and they had come because they were on supervision to the Department, rather than self referred. At the time of the survey there were 38 such youngsters. The survey consisted of interviews, conducted mainly by social work students, with the young people themselves, their parents and their social worker, supplemented by information from Department and centre records. Fuller details of the methods and findings are reported in the appendix to this chapter, and what follows is limited to the main findings and their interpretation, relevant to the three previously defined levels of success.

First, however, a summary picture of the youngsters themselves. On average, but with considerable variations, they had been referred when nearly 15 years old, three quarters of them on supervision because of delinquency; they attended for 12 months; and had left the centre 22 months before the interviews, at which time they were approaching 18. Only 42% had both parents living at home; 55% came from families with four or more children; 40% were unemployed at the time of the survey.

For an overall assessment, those interviewed were asked whether attendance at the centre had been beneficial, and the nature of the advantages or disadvantages. For more than 90% of the sample, attendance was separately judged beneficial by parents, social workers and the young people themselves, and two thirds of both parents and youngsters named two or more benefits. Disadvantages were mentioned very rarely. One parent commented *'The centre gave him some purpose and made him happy.'* Another said *'The centre got him out to meet people and have something to do. It brought him out of himself and made him able to put up with other people better.'* Some comments from youngsters: *'It was the best time I ever had'*, from a boy presently in and out of Borstal. *'It helped me to grow up'*. *'You got to do what you wanted to'*.

1 *Helping the social growth and development of youngsters.*
This is difficult to measure through a consumer survey, but clearly many of the foregoing answers are relevant to this aim, and three other questions in the survey are directly related. Two questions were about relationships since leaving the project. Firstly, parents, young people and social workers were in agreement that the youngster's relationships with his family had improved in about half the cases, and in the other half stayed the same, with one youngster reporting a deterioration. Secondly, regarding peer relationships, the youngsters and social workers saw improvement in slightly less than half the cases, the rest staying the same. Parents were not so positive, seeing improvement in only about a third of the cases, the rest staying the same. No one reported any deterioration.

A third question was about the youngsters' use of leisure time and community facilities. Most youngsters, when first referred, were without any affiliations to clubs or community centres, whereas half of them, when interviewed, had some organised leisure interest such as membership of an activity club or centre. Informal but definite interests such as gardening, craftwork, or sports were reported by 86%, with half naming more than one interest, and for all these youngsters, at least one of their interests was a continuation of an activity to which they had been introduced at the centre.

So in the areas where we would hope to see some positive change there is evidence that it had come about: within the family, within the peer group, and in the individual's use of his leisure time to attend clubs, pursue hobbies and carry on activities learned at the centre. The leisure findings were particularly pleasing because our formal efforts to make bridges with existing community provision have usually been less than successful, and this had been seen as a weak link in the programme. We are still looking for ways of improving the 'weaning away' process, but it is heartening that so many kids seem to have made use of what they had learned, at their own pace and without much structured help from us.

2 Diverting them from delinquency

Three quarters of the group were known to have been in trouble with the law previously, since that was one of the reasons for their being on supervision at the time of referral. Of this group almost half stayed clear of trouble up to the time of the survey, which was almost three years on average after joining the project. Of the remaining kids, referred for other reasons, there was one case of subsequent trouble, so that taking the entire group, 42% were in some further trouble after leaving the centre—mainly for breach of peace or crimes against property, and in only two cases for crimes against the person. Four boys were sent to Borstals or young offenders' institutions, specifically because of delinquency.

School behaviour and attendance had been one of the reasons for supervision for nearly half the group originally. Nearly a third of the entire group had left school by the time they left the centre; of the rest, three were referred to the Reporter for truancy or school misbehaviour, with two of them going into care. For the others, the school situation was judged by social workers to have improved or stayed the same, with no deterioration reported.

Given that the kids were passing through an age when delinquency and school trouble are likely to increase and peak, the overall drop in offences and the general stabilising of the school situation were encouraging and indicated some effectiveness in diverting them from further trouble.

3 Providing an alternative to residential care

At the outset, the centre was not particularly seen as an alternative to care, and in only four cases did social workers give this as a reason for initial referral; though for these and a further four, 21% in all, they said subsequently that they had hoped the centre would contribute to keeping the kids in the community. However, ten youngsters, or 26%, did in fact go into care or custodial provision and three were still in care at the time of the survey. The reasons were sometimes multiple, with offending listed eight times, truancy twice, and family breakdown four times. For a group who all started out on supervision, we regard this neither as a particularly poor record, nor as highly successful. This is an aspect of the centre's work which is gradually strengthening with time. The programme had to develop credibility in order to figure as a true alternative to List 'D' school. In the two years since this survey was done, it has become clear that there is a definite downward trend in the number of Dundee youngsters being sent to List 'D' schools, dropping from about 90 in 1973 to a current level of about 60. Of course, there are many possible factors at work, not the least being an overall drop in reported juvenile offences in the region. Nonetheless we are convinced that our programme has been a highly relevant factor.

In conclusion, the findings are mixed, but generally encouraging, in view of the problems faced by the youngsters and the kind of predictions one would have made for many of them at the time when they joined the centre. We are conscious of the limitations of such a survey with small sample size, and the difficulties of measuring 'success', let alone ascribing it to the centre's influence. Nonetheless, intermediate treatment is under increasing pressure to justify itself, which is quite proper, and we found this survey sufficiently useful to plan another one with a subsequent group of youngsters.

The Staff Viewpoint

Looking back, it was by no means certain that the project would be viable in the form first proposed, since it was an enterprise that depended on the positive co-operation and participation of difficult youngsters for it to work at all. Conceivably a few disasters could have led to a recasting of the project into a safer, but less ambitious mould. This did not happen because the project was seen to operate reasonably well.

In fact we have been able to hold the interest of most young people, with over 70% of those referred attending regularly for six months or longer. Those who come regularly show a high degree of identification with the project. Having been built slowly, through trial and error, it has a firm base of proven methods and ideas. The response of the youngsters while involved with us, and their subsequent careers, indicate that the project is offering both immediate and longer term help to the young people who take part. Many self referred youngsters have also benefited from the programme, both in the long term groups and with one-off or short term schemes. The involvement of these youngsters has meant that the project has avoided the label of 'bad boys' club'.

We have devised a way of coping with continuous referrals. We have good liaison with the Children's Panel, and our familiarity with the youngsters' problems, their performances at the centre, and the benefits to them, have kept the project's credibility high with it. Within the Social Work Department regular attendance at area meetings has ensured good links with area teams as a whole, and provided a way of keeping new social workers informed about the project.

An emphasis on flexibility and initiative has meant that we have had a constant series of exploratory ventures running and can respond to changing needs. An example of this is our growing commitment to working along with social workers in running groups.

The project, compared to residential care, is cost effective. At the present time about 80 kids are involved in the programme, which means the cost per head is about £7.50 per week.

The major shortcomings of the project seem to grow out of its strengths. Its relative autonomy has meant we have had little apparent impact on our immediate management structure. Mutual lack of information, with consequent mistrust, has been unfortunately common. Within the project itself, working relationships have been generally harmonious, but the lack of hierarchy and dependence on personalities rather than structure has caused occasional discord and loss of direction. An unstructured setting allows deeper issues to surface. Where these are negative and involve personal clashes, it is harder to deal with them and impossible to ignore them. The whole area of staff support is so far underdeveloped. Administrative, training and consultancy support need to be developed in a way that avoids institutionalising the project too much.

Afterword

A number of indirect results of the work are worth commenting on, since there is a relationship between them which has implications that go beyond intermediate treatment.

The issue of compulsion was much discussed in the planning stages of the project, but in most cases turned out to be a red herring, as the problem often lay in keeping the numbers down. Our operating base—small groups, high ratio of adults, emphasis on participation and control by the kids themselves—attracts the great majority of youngsters referred, and interests far more, judging by the numbers who have turned up at the door. All this throws a serious doubt on the label 'unclubbable'. It may well be that part of our programme, leaving aside the more intensive individual and group work, reproduces an old fashioned 'make do or mend' youth club approach, which contrasts favourably with what the kids see as the more impersonal facilities available now. An even more interesting speculation is that this rosy picture of the good old days is largely fantasy, and that such imaginative facilities for kids were only the occasional product of luck and individual personalities. If this is the case, it could be that part of what intermediate treatment schemes are about is to establish such environments for kids on a planned, consistent basis. In our scheme the daytime school release projects suggest that another label could bear with close scrutiny. Many youngsters who are considered disruptive in the school setting have with us performed arduous, demanding tasks with eagerness and good humour. It would be a reasonable guess that ways could be found of working with these youngsters without total removal from the school.

While we do not emphasise work with families, a fair amount has in fact been undertaken—regular home visits, family casework in a few instances, the Whitfield parents/children group, and continuous informal contact with parents of members. The result of all this is that, in general, we link with families as often as the social worker. This often helps us in getting a hearing from the parents, or in effecting a change of attitude or decision, where it impinges on the youngster. At times we have wondered if an important, implicit fact about us in the eyes of parents, in contrast with others who try to advise the family as professionals, is that we have actually shared with them, in some small measure, the experience of living with their child. Where anxieties run high about a youngster's behaviour, this shared experience may be a key part of our relationship to, and influence with, the families. Where residential workers are close enough to visit families regularly, no doubt the same sort of relationship is possible, but it might be that one would have to work against the strong feelings produced by the child's enforced removal from home.

Just as the youngster sees us as alongside him, rather than keeping our distance, the families can see us as working with them, rather than just talking to them. So both the youngster and the family are potentially partners in the enterprise. Our job is to co-ordinate and guide an enterprise in which we offer ourselves, our skills, and any resources we command, to a partnership arrangement with clients, where the value arises from movement toward mutually agreed goals, with everyone contributing what he can to make it work.

APPENDIX: FOLLOW-UP SURVEY

1   Sample of Young People
The sample consisted of 38 former members, 32 boys and 6 girls, and included all the youngsters who met the following three criteria:

a   They had been significantly involved in the project, which was defined as at least six months of regular attendance.

b   They were young people for whom the Social Work Department had a responsibility, in that they were attending as part of their supervision rather than on a self referral basis.

c   They were no longer attending.

All were on supervision to the Department at the time of referral, for delinquent behaviour (74%), truancy or school behaviour (47%), family problems (29%), or personal problems (84%), usually in some combination. A third had been involved with the Department for at least a year prior to referral.

Average age at time of referral: 14 years 11 months. Range 12–17 years. Average age at time of follow-up: 17 years 9 months. Range 14–20 years. Average length of attendance at centre: 12 months. Range 6–38 months. Average length of time since leaving centre: 2 years 2 months. Range 8–41 months.

2   Procedure
A form was designed, to be completed partly from agency and centre records, and partly from interviews with the young person, the parents and the social worker separately, using open ended questions. On a few items, information was tabulated from the best available source. In all but a few cases the interviews were carried out by social work students, rather than by centre staff. Tracking everyone down for interview proved to be difficult, and in some cases impossible, and the survey managed to reach no more than 69% of the youngsters, 72% of the parents and 97% of the social workers.

The findings reported here are only those related most directly to the points raised in the last section of the chapter. In those questions which asked for 'consumer' assessments and compared these with workers', the sample is reduced to the 29 young people (76%) for whom we had interviews with either the youngster or a parent. For five of these we had one or other interview, but not both; however, these are included since parents and children tended to agree on their judgements—in 83% of 96 pairs of responses, with three response alternatives.

3 Characteristics of the Young People

At the time of the survey, or according to latest information:

a Family Situation*

	No.	%
Both parents at home	16	42
Single parent at home	15	40
Step-parent at home	4	10
In care	3	8
Total	**38**	**100**

*55% of the youngsters were from families with four or more children.

b Current Occupation

	No.	%
School pupil/student	6	16
Armed forces	4	10
Apprentice	1	3
Unskilled work	4	10
Semi-skilled	3	8
Skilled	1	3
Residential care	1	3
Borstal	2	5
Unemployed	15	40
N.A.	1	3
Total	**38**	**100**

4 Views of 'Consumers' about Value of Centres

a *'Do you think attendance at the centre was beneficial? If so, what were the benefits? If not, what were the disadvantages?'* *

	Parents No.	%	Young People No.	%	Social Workers No.	%
Nothing gained	2	7	2	8	0	0
Uncertain	0	0	0	0	2	6
One benefit mentioned	7	26	6	24	9	35
Two or more benefits mentioned	18	67	17	65	15	58
N.A.	2		4		3	
Total	**29**	**100**	**29**	**100**	**29**	**100**

*The disadvantages named were too few for tabulation.

b *'How have you (has she/he) got on at home and with friends since leaving the centre?'*

	Parents' opinion No.	%	Young People's opinion No.	%	Social Worker's opinion No.	%
With parents						
Better	13	48	12	48	11	46
Same	14	52	12	48	13	54
Worse	0	0	1	4	0	0
N.A.	2		4		5	
Total	**29**	**100**	**29**	**100**	**29**	**100**
With peers						
Better	7	29	11	44	10	43
Same	17	71	14	56	13	57
Worse	0	C	0	0	0	0
N.A.	0		4		6	
Total	**29**	**100**	**29**	**100**	**29**	**100**

5   Current Leisure Pursuits and Interests

	Organised No.	Organised %	Informal No.	Informal %	Activities carried over from centre No.	Activities carried over from centre %
None	15	52	4	14	4	14
One	13	45	9	31	12	41
Two or more	1	3	16	55	13	45
Total	**29**	**100**	**29**	**100**	**29**	**100**

Activities mentioned include sports and other outdoor activities, crafts, decorating, mechanics. 'Organised activities' refers to membership of clubs, Territorial Army, community centres, etc.

6   Truancy and Unacceptable School Behaviour

Reason for social work involvement at time of referral:

	Truancy/ School behaviour	Other	Total
Subsequently referred to Reporter for truancy or school trouble	2	1	3*
In the view of social worker, also drawing on school records:			
School situation improved	6	2	8
School situation unchanged	4	8	12
School situation worse	0	0	0
N.A. — left school before leaving centre	6	9	15
Total	**18 (47%)**	**20 (53%)**	**38 (100%)**

*Two placed in residential care, partly on account of truancy.

7   Delinquent Behaviour

	Reason for social work involvement at time of referral:		
	Delinquent acts	Other	Total
Further trouble with law since leaving centre*	15**	1	16 (42%)
No further trouble with law	13	9	22 (58%)
Total	**28 (74%)**	**10 (26%)**	**38 (100%)**

*In nearly all cases, this was for breach of peace or crimes against property without violence.

**Of these, three went to List 'D' school and four went into the penal system.

Note: to minimise undercounting of further delinquency, hearsay evidence was used on this item. If a boy was not interviewed, but some other source reported that he had been in trouble, the boy was classified accordingly.

References

1   From the project proposal submitted to the Dundee Social Work Committee in 1972.
2   From the project leader's original job description, 1973.
3   Alm N. (1973), *The Children's Activity Centre Project in Dundee*, Dundee Social Work Department, unpublished, p.2.
4   *Ibid.*, p.1.
5   Alm N. (1974), *Children suitable for referral to the Children's Activity Centre*, Dundee Social Work Department, unpublished, p.1.
6   Alm N. and Whitaker A. (1978), 'The Whitfield group: IT for children and parents', *Social Work Today*, Vol.9, No.40, 20th June 1978, pp.16-18.
7   Scottish Education Department, Social Work Services Group (1979), *Intermediate treatment in Scotland.*
8   On personal construct theory and the use of repertory grids, see Kelly G.A. (1955), *The psychology of personal constructs,* New York: Norton. See also Bannister D. and Fransella F. (1971), *Inquiring man: The theory of personal constructs,* London: Penguin.

CHAPELFIELD INTERMEDIATE TREATMENT PROJECT

David Ward

INTRODUCTION

The Chapelfield Intermediate Treatment Project was set up by a group of social workers and probation officers as a direct response to the appearance in court of a group of teenagers, from the small mining town of Chapelfield, for a series of related offences. The project was shaped around the needs of these identified offenders and a larger friendship group, and lasted for a period of approximately 12 months. It is this period of intensive and wide ranging social work activity, together with its prior planning, which forms the subject of this study. The writer was one of the workers involved in planning and running the project, and the intention is to describe and evaluate their attempt to meet the needs of a natural group of adolescent delinquents, who were all friends drawn from the same neighbourhood. This is a familiar situation, often experienced, but rarely tackled, by social workers.

The workers adopted an integrated approach which they believed was not only unusual but also had a number of positive effects. Much of the work took place in two separate groups of young people, but it has not proved possible to evaluate developments separately and comparatively. Instead, except where explicitly stated, material on both groups has been combined into a single presentation.

BACKGROUND
Setting

Chapelfield is a rather isolated town of some 23,000 inhabitants, located in the centre of a large Midlands coalfield. Amenities were very limited, with the inhabitants having to look to neighbouring towns for anything beyond essential goods. Historically Chapelfield depended on two industries—mining and railways; but in the late 60s the main colliery closed and the railway sidings and depot became redundant. In due course, new light industries moved in, bringing with them a skilled labour force, and now many miners commute up to 30 miles to other pits. An effect of these changes was to undermine the focal role previously exercised by the Miners' Welfare, and residents related stories of the secretary of the Miners' Welfare rounding up children in the streets after dark and taking their parents to task. Although criticism of official responses to economic and social changes was widespread, there was little movement to bring about change.

With its industrial background Chapelfield remains a working class town, comprising a number of distinct residential areas peripheral to a central shopping and industrial area. At the time of the project there was no cinema, disco, coffee bar or indoor sports facility open in the evening; just pubs, clubs and bingo for the adults, and for the young people a statutory and voluntary youth service, reckoned to be offering less than half the minimum desirable level of provision. Attended by all secondary school children in Chapelfield, the comprehensive school was inconveniently located on the very edge of the town, involving many of its 2,000 pupils in long journeys to school. The appeal of the youth wing was severely limited by its proximity to school and inconvenient location, and at one time it was closed because of damage to the school by club members. The school was highly structured and streamed academically. Damage and truancy ran at a high rate, and the 'Comp' was noted for a very high staff turnover.

Both Probation and Social Services were located in neighbouring towns, and typically, social workers would drive in, or clients would have to travel out to see their workers.

Origins

While acting as a duty probation officer, the writer noticed that, during a period of little more than a month, 11 children from Chapelfield were due to appear in court, most on more than one occasion, to face charges arising from seven separate offences. It quickly became apparent that there were links between the children, as each of the offences involved several of the accused. Accordingly, the police were approached for details of their investigations, and, as well as gathering personal and family information for the 'social enquiry reports' on the accused, workers made particular efforts to acquaint themselves with full details of both offenders and associates in the escapades.

These investigations revealed that a much larger group of children had been involved in the offences. Many of these either had not been apprehended or had not received cautions from the police, who had brought to court those whom they assumed to be most seriously involved. In fact, it seemed to the workers that the accused were those who had previously appeared in court, were known to the police or were jointly charged with such a person. Certain features distinguishing the whole group readily emerged. All the children, boys and girls aged 13 to 16 years, were acquainted, but did not present a picture of a closely knit gang—rather, a much broader association in which offending had become a frequent activity [1]. There was a nucleus of regular offenders, with the remaining children more intermittently involved. The offences themselves, mostly burglaries, were not of the impulsive type. For example, the burglary of a local sports pavilion involved elaborate organisation of look-outs and break-in strategy, followed by the disposal throughout the group of the stolen sports equipment and sweets. Further striking features were that all the children attended the town's comprehensive school, all lived in two distinct areas of National Coal Board and council housing, and few attended an organised youth club regularly.

It became apparent to the probation officers and social workers preparing court reports that neither the offending itself nor an individual child's participation in it could be understood without reference to the group and the wider social environment in which the offences occurred. It was agreed that recommendations to the court could not ignore these factors, and should urge

178

that on this occasion the children be helped, but **not** as isolated individuals. Of the 11 accused, four were already on supervision to the Probation Service. However, they had reported individually to the office in a neighbouring town, and consequently most of the supervisors knew little about the mutual friendships that existed. Similarly, although workers made frequent reference to Chapelfield as a debilitating environment, this was considered to be outside the scope of professional assessment for the courts and subsequent social work intervention.

In order to bring the full range of factors to the attention of the court, a supplementary report was prepared in addition to the individual social enquiry reports. Also outlined in this was the intention to set up a project aimed at preventing the recurrence of offending among this group of children. It was suggested that this would entail working with the whole group of offenders, including the friends of those brought to court, and offering specific help to individual children and families where necessary. The project would also involve looking further at the community from which the children came, with a view to assessing how far conditions there may have contributed to delinquent activity, and attempting to change those conditions where possible and appropriate. When the 11 children appeared in court, eight were placed on supervision and 'advised' to attend the project. Two children were committed to care and one was acquitted. However the full group, including those identified by parents, teachers, police and the children themselves, constituted a total of 41 children who would become involved in the project during the following 12 months.

From the outset it was realised that an integrated, multi-method approach might be required, rather different from the individual and family casework orientation of the local social work agencies. Therefore, in addition to convincing the court, it was necessary to persuade Social Services and Probation that the project had sufficient potential to justify financial and other kinds of support. Papers were prepared by interested workers and direct negotiations took place at a local level between the Area Director of the Social Services Department and the Senior Probation Officer. It was eventually agreed that a project should be sponsored and funded by both agencies for 12 months, with the understanding that the workers would make every effort to extend the available resources by obtaining contributions from participants where appropriate, tapping other sources and recruiting volunteer helpers. Each service made available three workers to the project with all that this implied in terms of time and administrative back-up, and the Area Director agreed to use his good offices as trustee to secure the use of a hall in Chapelfield as a base.

PROJECT DESCRIPTION
Theory and Methods

In the final proposal prepared by the workers, the focus was this natural group of peers, within which, it was felt, socialising processes had led to delinquent behaviour becoming established as the norm. The central selection criterion would be association with this group, and treatment was to be fashioned around its needs. Three stress areas were distinguished as roots of delinquent activity and hence as considerations in treatment: the home background and relationships within the family; the individual's personality and abilities; the socio-cultural factors such as relative economic deprivation, limited opportunities for betterment, poor housing and lack of recreational facilities.

Taking these into account, the workers decided that any constructive treatment approach had to be multi-dimensional, including:

a Casework—an onging process with individuals, designed to provide a relationship within which learning can be reinforced and reflection encouraged as a back-up to group work.

b Group work—working with the peer group through the medium of activities and group discussion in both community and residential settings, the latter offering opportunities for more intensive work.

c Group work—working with family units and bringing parents together, so that they can consider their children's problems in the context of home and neighbourhood and be involved in bringing about change.

d Community work—assessing the needs of the area and tackling material and social problems conducive to delinquency through the mobilisation of both material and human resources.

Thus, it seemed possible to link an analysis of causative factors directly to a treatment approach. The theoretical stance was that for each group member there were problem areas, either personal or related to peer group and family dynamics, that impinged on each other and also existed within the wider context of social, material and economic provision. This is illustrated in Figure 1. It was intended that the behaviour of the group as a whole, and of its individual members, would be tackled by harmonising casework and family work within a group work context, supported by community work in relation to neighbourhood problems. For practical purposes the latter was identified as local provision directly affecting the young people, such as recreation and schooling, and the workers were specifically concerned with the development of normal community facilities to which the children could move once they had gained a greater sense of identity and resolved some of their more serious problems.

Within the workers' own agencies, procedures for dealing with young offenders relied mainly on individual and family casework. The workers were dissatisfied with these: they believed that their planned approach would be more constructive and appropriate to the youngsters' needs, and hoped that it would offer a useful model for other practitioners in the field, and new procedures for their own agencies.

Within this multi-method approach, group work was to have a key role. The underlying assumption was that, through controlled group learning experiences and achievements, delinquent norms and anti-authority attitudes could be replaced by more socially acceptable behaviour and better relationships with adults, particularly those in authority. Discipline and decision making were to be based as far as possible on democratic, therapeutic community principles [2], and while aware of the difficulties and limitations, the workers intended to develop horizontal relationships with the children and involve them in decision making. Group work was seen to have further advantages as preparation for individual work [3] and for making assessments [4], and through the integration of group work with casework and family work it was envisaged that varied levels of treatment could be offered, including the very intensive kind required by habitual and serious delinquents [5].

Figure 1   Theoretical framework

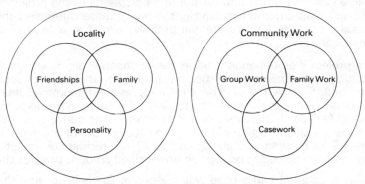

Assessment based on interlinking stress areas developed into intermediate treatment approach.

From the outset it was decided that activities were fundamental to the group work with adolescents in the project, since they provide a natural format for meetings, they enable relationships to be made more easily with both adults and other children, and they create opportunities for verbal as well as non-verbal communication. They also provide new interests, an outlet for energy and aggression, and alternative opportunities for achievement. Not least, they develop self-confidence and the security to trust and rely on others because one is valued oneself. Initial suggestions, ranging from the most strenuous to the more sedentary, included rock music, drama, free painting, adventure pursuits and discussion of local events.

The preparation for the project had entailed discussions with a number of agencies serving Chapelfield, and it was decided that the initial thrust of the community work element should be in the area of developing and fostering working links with the Youth Service and the local comprehensive school, and links between the two in relation to the project. Before the project started, considerable efforts were made to explain its purpose to the parents. The majority of parents welcomed it as a means of 'keeping them out of trouble'; but a few feared contamination and others found it difficult to accept the possible value of an apparently pleasant 'punishment'. It was intended to maintain frequent contact with parents and also to bring them together as a group so that they could learn more about the project, discuss their feelings about it and their children, and hopefully become more closely involved. Where necessary direct help would be provided to families. It was considered that one form of such help—family therapy—should be undertaken ideally by an outside social worker. However, it was recognised that shortage of man-power would sometimes make this impossible and a project worker might have to work with both the family as a unit and the child in the treatment group.

Resources and Structures

When the project finally started in May 1973, 34 children had been identified. They were divided into roughly equal mixed groups according to known friendships and family relationships. Despite the division, the groups were still larger than usual for social group work, both in size and in child:staff ratio. The weekly two hour group meetings, with their activity based group work. served as the springboard for the other elements of the project, as well as providing treatment in their own right. Among these other elements were five weekend or week long residential periods, aimed at a total of 30 days during the year.

The project was dependent upon the sponsoring agencies for finance, workers' time and administrative support. In addition the project sought a link with the Youth Service, not only because it represented an immediate resource but also because it was the only agency with the capacity for expanding the recreational facilities in the area. As far as finance was concerned, the Social Services made available a sum of £530, with £100 for rent of premises, £160 for equipment and running expenses, and £270 for residential activities. The Probation Service agreed to provide an unspecified amount towards the rent.

It was suggested that a base was needed in Chapelfield, and that these premises should not be identified with institutions of authority, such as school, church or local government. The base should include a large room, a small room, kitchen, toilet and storage facilities, with playing fields nearby. The hall that was finally secured through the good offices of the Area Director seemed ideal.

At the time the project was being planned, co-operation between the Probation and Social Services was minimal, with each agency demonstrating little appreciation of the other's responsibilities. Tension between the two Services seemed to be reinforced by experience over referrals made by one agency to the other. Fortunately, in both agencies there were recently qualified workers who had gained some practical experience of both Services during training. In addition, a community worker had just been appointed by the Social Services Department, and had as yet no fixed role definition. In the initial discussions a shared appreciation of the range of factors underlying social problems in Chapelfield emerged, together with a desire to practise social work in a more broadly based way than was conventional for the area. The community worker co-ordinated the ideas and drafted the proposal, which was approved by both agencies.

The project involved the allocation of two probation officers, three social workers and the community worker, and it was calculated that the exercise, including planning, supervision, recording and evaluation, would make a weekly demand of four and a half hours from each worker for a year. Although the project was seen as one entity, the workers were divided into two groups, with one woman and one probation officer in each group of three workers. Their links with their own agencies—at the outset, at least—and the links between the two agencies were of the usual kind in hierarchical organisations (see Figure 2), with the exception of the community worker, who was directly responsible to the Principal Social Worker. However, within the project the workers wanted to establish an alternative to this hierarchical structure and adopted a democratic model for decision making, not only with the children on the actual running of the groups, but amongst themselves on issues of planning and administration. It was expected that specialist roles would emerge during the course of the project. In fact the community worker assumed a strong administrative role from the start, partly because he had easier access to the Area Director.

Figure 2 Links between sponsoring agencies

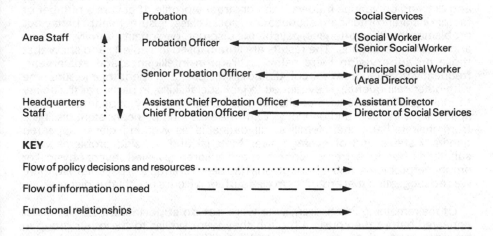

	Probation	Social Services
Area Staff	Probation Officer ◄──────────►	(Social Worker (Senior Social Worker
	Senior Probation Officer ◄──────────►	(Principal Social Worker (Area Director
Headquarters Staff	Assistant Chief Probation Officer ◄──────► Assistant Director Chief Probation Officer ◄──────► Director of Social Services	

KEY

Flow of policy decisions and resources ·····························▶

Flow of information on need ── ── ── ── ── ──▶

Functional relationships ──────────────▶

It was decided that recording, planning and evaluation would be a weekly activity to take place after group meetings—but not on the same night. At additional meetings all the staff from both groups would share and compare findings periodically. Being fairly inexperienced as far as an integrated, multi-method approach was concerned, they appreciated the importance of staff support, but recognised that there was nobody within either agency capable of providing appropriate supervision. Barr has pointed out that, in the development of a new treatment method, it is impossible to provide either consultation or teaching from within the agency until some pioneers have gained some first hand experience [6]. The workers came to the conclusion that they would have to provide mutual support and supervision for each other, and it was agreed that a critical evaluation of the way staff exercised and developed their skills would need to be an integral part of recording. It was understood that a high level of mutual respect, confidence and trust, as well as a certain amount of individual security, would be required for this form of supervision to be successful.

The Young People

It was considered justifiable to work with a natural group, both for practical reasons and because there are no reliable methods of predicting which children will become seriously delinquent. While a single method of intervention implies rigorous selection, the greater flexibility afforded by an integrated multi-method approach meant that it should cover the needs of all the children. It was, however, accepted that children whose behaviour was so damaging that the public must be protected, and those diagnosed as mentally ill, should be excluded.

The workers were in favour of obtaining as much background information on the children as possible in addition to their knowledge of the neighbourhood and peer group, but it was accepted that, for children and families not already known to either department, full assessment and the planning of treatment programmes would only take place once the project was under way.

A picture of the group before treatment can be presented, using information available at the start of the project in interview notes, files and court reports, and drawing on various models [7] to construct a profile. It covers a number of factors including intelligence, education, social class, leisure, health, behaviour problems other than offences, psychiatric disorder, personality, family, material and housing conditions. The results are summarised in Table 1, and show that those **on supervision** were below average in intelligence and attainment, frequently truanted from school, did not join clubs, and spent their leisure time with other delinquents. They tended to lack social skills, in particular the ability to make relationships with adults, and in personality they appeared anxious, apathetic, withdrawn and unhappy. With the exception of inconsistent discipline from their fathers, their families, all definable as working class, appeared generally stable and of average size. Material and housing problems were substantial but not extreme. None of these children revealed severe physical or emotional problems, and, although one had been referred to a psychiatrist, there was no suggestion that any of them was suffering from a psychiatric disorder.

Of the remaining 24 children, who were **not on supervision,** 22 had never appeared before the court. Although they were similar to the other group in many respects, there were some striking differences in that outward going personalities predominated, and generally speaking, they were more intelligent. Of course, in certain cases personality and family factors stood out and there were exceptions to the general profile. However, the following illustrations, one from each group, are not untypical of the information available at the beginning of the project:

Albert—aged 14, on statutory supervision

'Albert was placed under supervision for a number of offences of burglary, theft and handling, mostly committed with children younger than himself, but some on his own. He is the eldest child of a large family but the only one not the child of his stepfather. A likeable but rather apathetic, slow, unintelligent lad, Albert seems to get satisfaction from little in his life—truanting from school, bored in his spare time, and at times very unhappy at home. A follower, Albert's offending may have been partly group inspired but there are also some indications of seeking relief and escape from home. Looking forward to the group.

'Marital relationship seems stable: mother impresses as fond of her children but unintelligent and can offer little in the way of constructive guidance and stimulation. Father seems totally uninterested—particularly in Albert, but is not actively rejecting.'

Tommy—aged 15, not on statutory supervision.

'Tommy initially came to attention when N... Prison asked for a visit to the family prior to the father being granted home leave, as he was convicted of offences of violence against Tommy's two younger brothers.

'Since then, Mr. Jones, Deputy Headmaster at Chapelfield Comprehensive School, has referred Tommy to social services. He was truanting and very depressed in Bristol Social Adjustment Test. Having had several interviews with Tommy I've found him to be withdrawn and reticent. He assures me that he is not concerned at the thought of his father's release this summer, and his mother does not appear worried about him, saying that he has always been 'a quiet boy'. It seems that Tommy 'knows' boys rather than being friendly with them and he

Table 1   Summary of profile of project members

Characteristics		Children in Project (41)	Children not on Supervision (24)	Children on Supervision (17)
Social Class	—1	0	0	0
	—2	0	0	0
	—3	12	6	6
	—4	20	11	9
	—5	9	7	2
Accommodation	— Council/NCB House	32	21	11
	— Old property	25	14	11
	— Overcrowded	11	5	6
Family Size	— 1 child	2	1	1
	— 2 children	6	5	1
	— 3 „	16	8	8
	— 4 „	10	7	3
	— 5 „	2	1	1
	— 6+ „	5	2	3
Family	— Intact (2 parents) at present	32	19	13
	— Broken at some stage	14	7	7
	— Interested parents	32	19	13
	— Overindulgent parents	11	7	4
	— Defective paternal discipline	37	22	15
	— Maternal affection	33	20	13
	— Cohesive family	34	20	14
	— Child in conflict with parents	16	10	6
	— Parent or sibling with criminal record	12	8	4
Material Problems		19	12	7
Health	— good	36	22	14
Physique	— sturdy	33	21	12
Intelligence	— below average	19	7	12
School	— attainment below average	31	16	15
	— truancy	32	18	14
	— unpopular with teachers	26	15	11
Friendship Pattern	— with offenders	41	24	17
Leisure Pattern	— 'unattached' to organisations	39	22	17
Behaviour Problems	— other than crime, e.g. sex, drugs	5	4	1
Diagnosed psychiatric disorders		0	0	0
Social Skills	— easily influenced	29	17	12
	— lack of foresight	35	19	16
	— lack of responsibility	34	18	16
	— poor capacity to relate with adults	17	5	12
	— lack of verbal skills	26	12	14
Outgoing Personality	— attention seeking	21	10	11
	— careless disregard for others	22	16	6
	— unreflective	27	19	8
	— seeks immediate gratification	26	19	7
	— projects blame	28	21	7
	— impulsive	27	19	8
Inward Personality	— anxious	18	6	12
	— withdrawn	15	4	11
	— apathetic	17	6	11
	— unhappy	18	6	12

Table 2 Significant events and group development

Date and Meeting No.	Significant Events	Model of Group Development
		Early Stage Features
		Anxiety, stereotyping of others. Boundaries tested. Complaining, confrontation. Reliance on previous experience to adapt to new situation. Individualistic behaviour. Existing friendships identifiable.
May, 1973		
1		Little sense of group cohesion. Inhibited behaviour among some members, disruptive among others. Only activities generate interest. Discussion a complete failure.
5		
8	Residential weekend in Peak District	
14	Residential week in disused Leics. farm.	
Oct. 1973		
23	Residential weekend at barn in Peak District.	
26	Confrontation with group of young people not in project, who try to force their way into group meeting. Damage to hall and surrounding property. Police intervene.	
28	Equipment stolen from hall between meetings.	Sense of demoralisation in the group. Attendance of older members wavers. Some damage done to premises during meetings, but raffle tickets sold enthusiastically to raise funds. Following eviction, activities focus on commercial facilities like skating. Although attendance remains high, there are instances of destructive behaviour such as theft during library visit. Staff feel they are struggling to contain group.
Jan. 1974		
32	Evicted from hall, following complaints. Meet in car park till new premises found.	
34	Theft from fine box at library.	
36	Three members apprehended by police.	
38	Residential week-end in Peak District youth hostel.	
40	Move into new premises — Scout Hut.	
41	2 boys committed to care as result of previous arrests.	
April 1974		
43	Residential week at Youth Centre in Yorkshire Dales.	

Early-Middle Stage Features	**Late-Middle Stage Features**
Strangeness wears off. Tentative attempts at cohesive action. Subgroups form. Testing out of staff. Increased frankness and intimacy. Backward movements common.	More secure alliances develop. Greater freedom to express initiative and share. Able to analyse what has happened and gain insight into individual and group behaviour. Greater sense of security. Occasionally external threats re-activate conflicts and failings, but more often produce greater unanimity.
After half day trip out, beginnings of group life appear. Spontaneous family role play with staff as parents. Staff interest and authority repeatedly tested. New members rejected, and meetings become important. Strong subgroups emerge along boy/girl, older/younger, withdrawn/outgoing lines.	
	Cohesive group identity emerges—initiation rituals for new members. Members attempt to organise activities themselves. Meaningful discussions about organisation of premises, additional members, relationships with parents, teachers, police, and methods of controlling behaviour and resolving disputes between members. Staff working **with** rather than merely containing group.
Group reacts to invasion of its premises by retreating under wing of leaders into side room. On arrival of police, group splits— younger cling to staff and older taunt police.	
Discussion re-emerges as way of resolving problems and examining issues. Insight developing as to implications of group behaviour. Weekend eagerly anticipated and planned for by members, who conduct themselves creditably, accepting rules and completing morning chores.	
	Members talk of value of club to them. Spontaneously take responsibility for chores. Relationships open and supportive, subgroups weak.
	Removal of two boy leaders greeted with unanimous anger. Talking through leads to self examination.
	Two older girls emerge as leaders, mothering the group. Sexually intimate boy/girl relationships do not take place as group adopts taboo on such relationships. Group becomes self-regulating, planning and organising activities and devising sanctions. More formal relationships, with staff used now as a resource for advice rather than previous more active role.
	Staff feel group has developed norms, structure and skills to function acceptably and constructively on its own. Later a letter is received from the Centre commending the group on its behaviour—contrasting this favourably with a group of teachers the week before!

has no particular interests. The only time I have seen him animated is when disputing a marbles game with his brothers.

'During the Easter holidays, Tommy was missing from home for two nights, after an argument with his mother. Later he said he was frightened to return because of this and also in case he might be taken by the police for 'hedge-hopping'. So far he has not been in trouble with the police. The group would give an opportunity to see how Tommy relates with others of his own age, and with an adult male figure' [8].

PROJECT IN ACTION

The two project groups began to meet some four months after the offending came to light. These groups formed the central element of the integrated practice model. In the year that followed, all the parts of this model — group work, including residential activities, casework, family work and community work — were practised broadly as planned. On occasions the methods all pursued a single, limited objective, particularly at times of crisis, whilst at other times a multiplicity of objectives was being pursued within the broad aims of the project.

Development of the Group as a Whole

Instead of a narrative of the group work aspect of the project, the significant events during the year are briefly presented in Table 2. Owing to the fact that full records were only kept by one of the two groups, this table is based on the experience of only this group. It illustrates the group's development by setting features of group meetings against the model of group development from Tom Douglas' *'A Decade of Small Group Theory'* [9]. Although the validity of thinking in terms of developmental stages can be questioned in relation to a natural group, it seems justified on the grounds that this group was subjected to a special experience through its programme of activities.

It can be seen that the group quickly moved from early to middle stage patterns of functioning. However, the movement was fluctuating rather than steadily progressive, with more mature functioning gaining ascendancy as time passed. Regressions occurred at times of crisis, but these became less severe and of shorter duration the later they occurred in the time span of the group.

The five residential experiences, two full weeks and three weekends, were themselves analysed according to the Douglas model. Four general points emerged.

1   Each of the first three residential experiences was a microcosm of the group as a whole. Initial anarchy was replaced by self organisation as the prospect of interesting activities overrode the initial attraction of freedom to be chaotic, which members said rapidly became boring. Nonetheless, an initial period of aimless milling around, or 'exploration' as the children called it, was an established feature of all the residential periods, providing a transition between everyday life and a total experience centred on the group.

2   A forthcoming camp seemed to inject extra enthusiasm into normal meetings.

3   The residential experience was more intensive. It not only helped to develop cohesiveness more quickly, but also provided a range of opportunities for

working through situations experienced with the family, school and neighbour-hood.

4 The final two residential experiences maintained secure and productive 'late-middle stage' functioning throughout. It seemed that, with increasing maturity, residential experiences came to fit naturally into the group's life.

In the course of the year, there had been some change in membership, and by May 1974, 41 children had been extensively involved in the two project groups —26 boys and 15 girls. Some of those who had failed to attend at the beginning subsequently joined. On two separate occasions two members were removed into care by the courts following further offences; one member left when his supervision order terminated, and a few others dropped out through parental pressure or opted out themselves.

Developments within the Group

Initially, children came to the group either as individuals or within existing friendship groupings, but even these were divided on fairly conventional lines between boys and girls, and older and younger. In the early period, the group was dominated by the older boys, who spent a certain amount of their time bullying the younger boys and vying for leadership. However, by the fourth meeting, a certain number of pairings between boys and girls had taken place, and older boys who would provide leadership could be identified. Within four months, the younger boys began to assert themselves and stand up to the older boys in a number of ways, including refusal to hand over games equipment. During this middle period of the group, a number of identifiable subgroupings emerged in both activities and seating arrangements in cars. For instance, there was a mixed group which enjoyed cooking, an older group of boys who engaged in physical activity, and a younger group of children who played table tennis and other games.

During the crisis periods of disturbances and arrests, the subgroup boundaries were secondary to cohesion in the face of a threat to the whole group. Subsequently, when the established leaders were removed into care, many of the leadership positions were assumed by older girls, who had previously supported the boy leaders. These girls played an important role as maternal figures, supporting, appeasing and holding the group together. It was during this later period that the younger members came to receive protection and consideration, with their apparent failings being accepted as reflections of age and lack of experience. Another feature of this period was a significant move towards integration, with the more isolated and 'scapegoated' being drawn more fully into the life of the group. It is interesting that this process seemed much easier with the younger scapegoat, probably because it was more difficult for dominant members to make allowances for their contemporaries. The last barrier to go was that between the older and younger children; but the final structure which emerged seemed appropriate for a cohesive and effectively functioning group—fluid relationships, with subgroups forming around functional requirements, and contributing to a strong family atmosphere.

Relationships with Staff

Once again the group went through a number of phases. The first was marked by suspicion, with the children being co-operative but remote, putting the staff firmly in control and relating to them as an outgroup. It moved fairly quickly through a testing out period at the end of the first month to a middle phase, which was marked by growth and learning within the group. During this period, the children were very ambivalent, often demanding and monopolising the staff, with fairly marked dependence, but at other times testing boundaries, neutralising and rejecting staff. The workers were used in reliving experiences of other relationships with parents, siblings and teachers; this included testing out gender roles and behaviour such as aggressiveness and compliance. They were also used for exploring ways of interacting with other people, especially such authority figures as parents, teachers and police. While the older children were looking for models, the younger ones used the workers to explore a range of feelings within a safe and secure relationship.

The final period involved the separating of members and staff to form relationships based more on task objectives, practical skills and knowledge on the part of the workers. The children no longer denied the separate identity of the workers, and were far less attention seeking. This contrasted starkly with the previous phase in which intense and emotional needs were being met by the personal characteristics of the staff and their skills in the use of relationships.

Although the group's passage was far from smooth, this analysis of the available material indicates that, as a group and individually, the participants moved to a more mature, constructive and responsible level of functioning. This is particularly important since it was a natural group.

Methods and Techniques of Intervention

Group work with the children was combined with residential periods to allow more intensive work to take place. In addition it was recognised that, in the case of children who were either very withdrawn or aggressively anti-authority, individual casework could be valuable. As it turned out, particularly in the early period of the group's development, it was activities such as table games, painting, cooking and outdoor pursuits which provided the major vehicle for individual and group expression and achievement.

A regular discussion period at each meeting proved impossible to sustain, but more informal group discussion was encouraged wherever possible. For instance, during the summer camp the group was invited to attend a local youth club. Some of them behaved rather arrogantly and a confrontation developed with local youths. Neither staff nor youth leader intervened and eventually a rather hurried and premature departure by the group was required. In the mini-bus staff were abused by some members for not intervening on the side of the group! Other members pointed out how a potentially good evening had been spoiled by provocative behaviour. It was also clear that there was now some apprehension as to how staff would react. They, however, put it to the group that members must bear some collective responsibility for 'goings on' during a group event. A lengthy discussion ensued on responsibility to self or group, and the behaviour demanded in different situations. Staff found themselves doing little more than prompting and reinforcing material coming from the group. They had taken a calculated risk in not intervening, and felt that the learning brought about by the uncomfortable experience and subsequent discussion was of immense value, and would not have occurred had a controlling line been taken in the club or minibus.

As the group developed, activities were expanded spontaneously both by the children and the staff, and provided opportunities for relations in which social learning could take place. The children became more tolerant, remaining involved without disruption, even if no activity proved to their liking. Educational visits were arranged, spontaneous dressing up and role plays occurred, and residential living provided a wide range of experiences, in particular opportunities for giving and receiving care, as well as for success and achievement in more challenging outdoor pursuits. Although the activities proved valuable in a number of ways, the staff felt that the advantages were not always realised owing to lack of planning and insufficient variety. The staff were also ambivalent in the sense that too many activities appeared to fragment the group, whilst absence of activities often resulted in worsening behaviour, and the staff feeling threatened by loss of control.

In conclusion, after the opening stages of the group, activities became more than an attractive entity in themselves: they provided a vehicle for developing relationships, for channelling aggression and encouraging tolerance, for gaining insight into oneself and other people, for extending practical and physical skills, and for widening the members' knowledge and horizons, thus bringing about changes in behaviour and attitude.

Although activities were very important, the workers considered that if they were to help the children to develop less hostile and suspicious attitudes towards people in authority, and also to become more socially competent, then decision making skills were vital. In the group these developed around internal matters such as rules to govern behaviour, or external issues such as activity planning. The staff were concerned to promote:
- effective two-way communication between everybody involved in the group;
- creation of democratic decision making machinery;
- development of a group culture in which the attitudes and beliefs of all participants were valued.

It was anticipated that the democratic nature of such a group would prevent members projecting responsibility on to others, since those members would themselves have helped determine both the activity and the rules. Also, the fact that authority was shared would help members to accept that adults are open to question—as Thorpe notes, *'a powerful antidote to any assumption about the nature of authority figures'* [10]. In practice this meant that none of the adults involved had any special privileges of food, sleeping arrangements, or evenings off duty on residential activities to go the pub! *'Where adults participate in small groups with delinquents, sharing activities and accommodation alike, the (delinquent) subculture development is minimised'* [11]. The approach also involves bringing problems to the group for a decision: *'. . . if the leaders themselves are open to change—because they too are involved—then the clients will reciprocate'* [12]. In the group, discussion became more acceptable, both for planning and organisation and for resolving difficulties, with the children themselves calling meetings. At the same time shared decision making and acceptance of responsibility for group behaviour become more prominent and effective. Putting such techniques into practice put a great deal of stress on the workers involved. Nevertheless, in retrospect it was felt that this approach to decision taking played a not insignificant part in any success the group may have had.

Casework was another planned component of the multi-method approach. The workers came to feel that effective casework depended on the development of a secure group, in which both children and workers felt sufficiently comfortable to be able to concentrate on a one to one relationship. It was well into the group's life that this situation arose, although one to one contact had been important in assisting individual children to integrate fully into the group. Two other major factors inhibited the development of casework as planned: first, individual treatment plans were not consistently produced and reviewed, except for those on statutory supervision; and secondly, the first reaction to pressures experienced by project workers seemed to be a curtailment of any work with individuals outside meetings.

Nevertheless, noteworthy developments were observed among individuals, very similar to the analysis offered by Margaret Miller-Smith on the ways in which individuals may use groups[13]. Tensions associated with family difficulties were resolved through role plays or dressing up activities. The aimless found interest, extended their horizons and discovered new skills and abilities. The lonely and disorganised, although sometimes remaining isolated, demonstrated by their consistent attendance the discovery of that sense of belonging which then enabled some to come out of their shells. Those in crisis found in the group a situation where their emotions could be expressed safely, accepted and if necessary controlled, but never rejected. The safer outlets of words instead of action appeared to be learned by many in the course of the project, and in maintaining a commitment to the group, personal skills of self-control, tolerance, and co-operation were acquired.

Work with Families

While there was consistent oversight of all the families, based on getting consent for activities, intensive intervention in the families of group members was limited. Of the families concerned, three received help through conjoint family therapy, and 12 more received direct intensive assistance. In some cases such direct help involved support over practical problems which parents brought to the workers or which emerged on visits, such as housing complaints and financial difficulties. The group became a convenient referral point for family problems, many of which would not otherwise have reached social workers, but both agencies were ambivalent about this development, which increased demand on already overstretched resources.

The workers felt that their consistent contact meant that family crises were handled more adequately. For instance, short term support was offered to families where there were emotional difficulties, or when further offending and consequent court appearances occurred. This limited intervention could lead to more intensive work either by a project worker or one introduced from the outside. On one occasion, when a relatively stable group member committed offences which seemed related to disturbances within his family, a project worker and an outside worker undertook conjoint family therapy. The two workers involved saw in their experience advantages to this joint approach, in that the work seemed to have greater pace and improvement in family functioning appeared to be achieved more quickly.

As regards the parents' group, two meetings were held, but despite considerable 'selling' by the workers, very few parents, all mothers, turned up. In line with Barr's[14] findings it was the parents with intact relationships but lower intelligence and inferior circumstances who did **not** come; the parents who responded were either the most capable, or at the other extreme, the most distressed, perhaps seeking help for themselves. With workers, and perhaps also the mothers, disillusioned by the lack of response, the parents' group did not develop, although as individuals these parents displayed a high level of interest in the project. One parent regularly attended as a volunteer leader in the later stages of the group and others called in more sporadically.

Work with the Community

Basic to the workers' philosophy was that the local community should be encouraged to accept responsibility for the existence and prevention of delinquent behaviour in its midst, but apart from this there were more practical and immediate issues. Firstly, the project's premises were situated on a quiet street of owner occupied housing from which none of the children came, and they were shared with sedentary adult organisations. Thus, as Mays has pointed out[15], they were plainly not suitable for a project of this nature. Secondly, as the mere setting up of this project created an additional youth facility in Chapelfield, contact with a wider range of children than those initially invited had to be handled. This, together with a recognition by the social workers of their own lack of group work expertise and limited facilities for activities, pointed towards developing a relationship with the youth service. Finally, the preparation of the project itself had entailed discussion and co-ordination with a number of agencies serving Chapelfield.

Until the attachment of a student social worker, community work involvement was limited to the parents' group, the development of liaison with the youth service and the school, and co-ordination between the sponsoring agencies. As regards the youth service, the project was given support and registered as a youth facility. A condition of such registration was the formation of a local advisory committee—a project requiring direct work with local people which was suspended until the student arrived. With the school, information on the children was exchanged, and the project explained to interested teachers. There were also visits by the project workers to the remedial unit where many of the children were placed.

Besides these developments, there were other more immediate factors influencing the direction of the work of the student when he arrived in January 1974. The group had been expelled from the premises it had been using and new premises were a vital necessity. Also the group of outsiders who had invaded the club and damaged nearby property the previous November prepared a petition with 250 signatures, adults' as well as children's, and presented it to the youth and social services calling for more youth facilities.

Figure 3 shows how the community work developed and how far stated objectives were achieved. The long term goal became the setting up of a youth club which could accommodate former project members and the unattached young people who had come to notice. The aim was that this club should be supported, as regards professional personnel and finances, by the youth service, but with considerable support from the residents of Chapelfield in the form of material help and volunteers. By the end of the year, the structure for the new club had been set up, except for the securing of long term premises.

Relations between the Workers

Working in a setting where their own skills and knowledge were very limited, the workers found group work both exhausting and stressful. They felt further

Figure 3 Development of Community Work

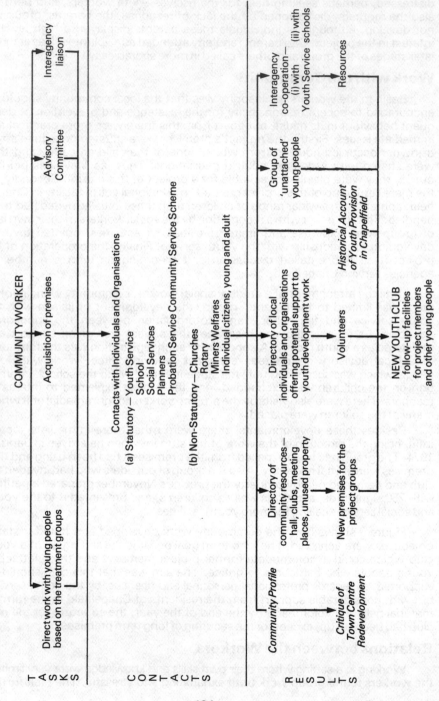

TASKS

Direct work with young people based on the treatment groups

COMMUNITY WORKER

Acquisition of premises

Advisory Committee

Interagency liaison

CONTACTS

Contacts with Individuals and Organisations

(a) Statutory — Youth Service
School
Social Services
Planners
Probation Service Community Service Scheme

(b) Non-Statutory — Churches
Rotary
Miners Welfares
Individual citizens, young and adult

RESULTS

Community Profile

Directory of community resources — hall, clubs, meeting places, unused property

Critique of Town Centre Redevelopment

New premises for the project groups

Directory of local individuals and organisations offering potential support to youth development work

Volunteers

Historical Account of Youth Provision in Chapelfield

Group of 'unattached' young people

Interagency co-operation — (i) with Youth Service (ii) with schools

Resources

NEW YOUTH CLUB follow-up facilities for project members and other young people constrained by lack of activity skills, time and money, and considered that they were not using the group process or the activities effectively, but rather, practising casework within the group setting and dealing with situations ad hoc. These factors, together with the high ratio of children to staff, created a bias in favour of the more demanding and attention seeking children.

Staff minimised anxiety by working in ways in which they felt most comfortable rather than by responding to the children's needs. This often entailed confining themselves to small subgroups of children, and the fragmentation thus caused was recognised but not easily avoided. There were occasions when anxieties about the intensity and emotionally charged nature of interactions resulted in meetings becoming too structured. In addition there were differences stemming from varying views about the ability of the group to participate in decision making and about the kind of behaviour that required control.

As Morrison has pointed out, *'conflict and contradictions in staff roles and rivalries between different types of staff reduce the effectiveness of the treatment approach'* [16]. However, overall, the workers felt able to discuss and reconcile their different patterns of working, their needs to adopt a particular role, and the conflicts over control and intervention. Such issues were analysed immediately after they had arisen: in the nightly staff discussions during the residential periods; and otherwise at an outside venue after a weekly meeting or during the next recording session. They felt that a range of role models could be presented to which the children could relate, ranging from the warmly maternal to the strongly masculine, from permissive to controlling. Nevertheless, they also felt an urgent need for further training to improve their skills, and for time to study, evaluate, and plan group and personal experiences for the children.

The staff of both groups seemed to develop strongly traditional male and female roles, and interestingly there was much tension in one worker group where the woman member assumed a strong leadership position. It was followed for a time by a high turnover of male workers, two leaving the area for new posts, and a replacement leaving after only a few weeks due to pressures of other work. Little was attempted beyond weekly meetings with the children and communication problems between the workers were greater.

In contrast, a number of features emerged where the staff group remained stable. A regular pattern of meetings developed for recording, evaluation and planning, and a greater depth of understanding seemed to be achieved, based on more thorough recording. There was a more concerted effort to maintain the multi-method approach, and there were more residential experiences. Worker contact increased through meeting socially outside the project, and greater knowledge and involvement with each other seemed to widen the possibilities for intervention.

Specialist workers were introduced for community work and family work. Thus, a student who was placed with the project was directed towards the task of stimulating community involvement, which was a planned aim of the project, to relieve pressure on the workers. Even so, the development of the project demanded increasing time and energy from the workers. The initial time involvement was increased in the light of experience, but was still inadequate for various reasons:

- the effect of fragmentation on the rest of a day's work;
- work related to the group meetings, due to unpredictable crises or spontaneous visits by children or family members during office hours;

- increasing contact with school and other agencies as liaison became more effective;
- planning and preparation of periodic residential activities.

However, because of other obligations, the agencies were unable to support a greater commitment of workers' time to the project. The workers' response varied with the stability of the staff group—either to restrict involvement to little beyond the weekly meetings, or to try and maintain the development of the project by increasing their time spent 'on the job'. The latter proved impossible to maintain, and conflicts arose between workers and their agencies because of the priority they continued to give to the project, even after cutting to a bare minimum time spent on worker meetings, recording, planning and activity preparation.

As pressures grew on those involved, co-ordination did not develop as effectively as had been intended, and only one of the intended bi-monthly meetings for all project staff occurred—after six months had passed! The result of this was that the sharing of learning, particularly necessary in the absence of outside supervision, did not take place. Within the groups only one kept recording up to date, the other falling behind and eventually abandoning recording altogether. For the first group, recording sessions became the focal issue in the conflict with their agencies over time given over to the project and helped maintain a sense of solidarity. They also had practical value in facilitating consistent evaluation and planning.

Relations with and between Parent Agencies

As Miller has suggested, *'the process of introducing a new organisation into a field of existing organisations will often activate aspects of the system which ordinarily remain latent, but which will manifest themselves when the status quo is challenged'* [17]. This is a factor which often receives scant attention when projects are planned, yet it can have a profound effect on their development. While the general objectives of helping children in trouble or at risk initially attracted support, it was the methods and philosophy underpinning the objectives which were novel, and perhaps radical, in the eyes of the sponsoring agencies. Nevertheless, these matters had initially been aired without adverse comment.

In practice, difficulties developed in a number of areas. The project appeared in two ways to disturb the traditional and established pattern of relationships and decision making in statutory agencies (outlined in Figure 2). Firstly, the Area Director of the Social Services Department held the financial resources allocated to the project by his agency, although these needed to be accessible not only to social workers but also to probation officers involved in the project. Within the project team, responsibilities were divided so that the community worker would be responsible for financial liaison, but strict adherence to this was not always possible. Secondly, there was no senior worker from either agency supervising the project. Thus the community worker dealing with finance would liaise directly with his Area Director, and a probation officer seeking resources would liaise directly with the same Area Director, not through his senior probation officer.

The effect was that a number of people, both at central offices and area levels, were unaware of developments. A further change occurred in the relationships between and within the agencies, when the Area Director reacted to the complaints of residents near the hall by blocking further acquisition of resources from the Social Services Department. The probation officers in the project responded by reverting to the traditional lines of communication up their own hierarchy. Discussions at a very senior level in the two agencies revealed that there was more support in the Social Services Department's central office than was being shown at area level. Consequently the Area Director was circumvented and instructed to release the available funds. He reacted to being outmanoeuvred by reimposing hierarchical as opposed to direct communication and by putting pressure on the social workers to do work outside the project, so threatening their continued involvement.

For the agency managers, especially in the Social Services Department, liaison based on administrative matters took the place of discussion and consultation. Although copies of recordings and minutes of project meetings were formally supplied to the Area Director, little was effectively communicated to senior officers about the development of the project. No agency official ever attempted to test, explain or resolve fears or disagreements by attendance at project meetings, reading the records, or meeting the project staff group, until crises occurred. Inevitably, both knowledge and perceptions of the project, based on such communication, were incomplete and negative. Frustrations grew in the workers when they saw hierarchical and out of touch organisations, on whom they were dependent for the provision of resources, constraining them apparently arbitrarily. On the problems of change in organisations, Wilkins suggests that *'it will be . . . difficult for hierarchical systems to adjust to change or to build into their own structure any learning devices for self adjustment, except from the top of the hierarchy'* [18]. This project presented a challenge from the bottom.

It should be added that communication within the Probation Department improved greatly after the theft at the library took place, because the agency happened to be negotiating about use of library facilities elsewhere in the county at the time. Nevertheless, the general point remains: had communication been considered an important issue at the planning stage of the project, a system more effective in meeting the needs of both a hierarchical agency and the project could perhaps have been created, with senior area workers involved in a supervisory and consultative capacity.

Relations with office colleagues tended to reflect those with management. In the Probation Department the project was frequently discussed and a degree of support was felt as a result of this interest. In the Social Services Department, where most workers seemed to feel swamped by the immediate demands of crisis referrals, the project workers quickly felt distanced from their colleagues, becoming the objects of misconceptions and some resentment. It is perhaps noteworthy that as workers from the Social Services Department left the project, they were not replaced by colleagues, and one group was staffed exclusively by probation officers for a period, until a social worker moved over from the other group.

Tension developed also between the sponsoring agencies, particularly between the two area teams, where most cross boundary transactions took place, and this was reflected in a return of traditional, stereotyped suspicion and withdrawal behind strict statutory responsibilities, after a period of co-operation

Table 3 Factors affecting inter-agency relationships

Area of Difficulty	Probation (P.S.)	Social Services (S.S.D.)
Operating Philosophy	1 Orientation of P.S. to offender and his family as against the width of intervention planned for the project.	1 Group work viewed as voluntary by agency where emphasis is on working with individuals.
	2 Increasing emphasis in P.S. on control and surveillance of offenders contrasts starkly with the permissive/democratic work philosophy of the project.	2 Because of pressure of statutory work where there is emphasis on authority of the social worker, i.e. child care, permissive work philosophy does not fit into S.S.D. as readily as might be expected.
	3 Involvement of 'non-identified offenders' gives project image of being 'preventive'. P.S. considers it has neither responsibility nor resources to do more than very limited preventive work with juveniles.	3 S.S.D. also feels it has insufficient resources to make extensive commitment to 'non statutory preventive' work.
	4 Tradition of individual worker/client responsibility in P.S. as against worker team responsibility for clients in the project.	4 Tradition of individual worker/client responsibility in S.S.D. as against worker team responsibility for clients in the project.
		5 Personal feelings and pressures on Area Director because of his position as trustee of premises used, transformed into agency policy towards the project.
Organisation and Methods	Project emphasises teamwork and decentralised decision making.	Decentralisation of decision making implicit in the project contrasts starkly with hierarchical decision making process in S.S.D.
Jurisdictional Domain	No direct conflict but the project seen by P.S. as going beyond its desired sphere of operation in a situation where P.S. is trying to get rid of its responsibility for juveniles.	No direct conflict but S.S.D. resisting accepting responsibility for juveniles beyond a very gradual rate of transfer from P.S.
Exposure of Failings		Project exposes lack of resources, material and personnel, to provide adequately such services as the project attempted, and to meet extra demands arising from project's accessibility to the public.

The 'areas of difficulty' are nominated according to the model of Miller, Baum and McNeil [17] in the early days of the project. This reaction appeared to be linked with the fact that the project required a high level of co-operation at all levels between the two agencies. This was not always forthcoming and there was an alarming level of ignorance about the objectives and methods of working of the other agency. Furthermore, there was not always either a shared acceptance of the assumptions and methods underpinning the project, nor the accordance of a high priority to it within agency tasks. In fact each agency seemed to approach the project solely from the point of view of its own primary purpose or purposes, and the more immediate tactical objectives which stemmed from these. Some of the factors affecting the relationship between the two agencies are analysed in Table 3.

Delinquency is only one of a wide range of concerns for social services, whereas it is the major concern of probation. The Probation Service was perceived to have unrealistic and unreasonable expectations of the Social Services Department in relation to delinquency, and probation officers tended to get frustrated at the low priority given to delinquency by social workers. Indeed the Social Services Department viewed the Probation Service, because of its more clearly defined clientele, as being under less work pressure, and consequently as having more time and resources to undertake such 'experimental preventive' projects. When pressure was increased on the social workers in the project, probation officers were expected to carry more responsibility and give more time.

At the outset, group work was accepted as an integral part of social work by the Probation Service, and their workers involved in the project were given a workload allowance. In the Social Services Department, the project and its group work were considered to be voluntary on the part of the workers because statutory demands did not allow time for preventive group work. When the social workers imitated their probation colleagues and took time off in lieu without official consent, Social Services area management blamed the Probation Service for 'disruptive influences'.

Basic grade social workers seem to have less decision making authority than their probation counterparts in apparently similar situations. Consequently close contact between the basic grade workers of both departments in the project tended to reinforce dissatisfaction among social workers over their own department's structure. Again, close involvement with the Probation Service came to be perceived as threatening by area management.

Beyond this, there seemed to be an element of more general threat to the Social Services, that of exposure of their inadequate service to clients caused by pressure on their resources. Their lack of commitment to the project reveals not so much material resource deficiences, as excessive pressure on area field-workers, working in cramped conditions, restricted to crisis work and burdened by high caseloads. Close involvement with the Probation Service highlighted this problem, since workers became aware of the more limited caseloads and better working conditions enjoyed by their colleagues.

Within both parent organisations, the project workers began to detect a desire to withdraw from the project, their explanations hinging on the limited resources which restricted their commitment to preventive work. There was also the wider issue of responsibility for juvenile offenders, until then the province of the Probation Service but due to be handed over to Social Services, as laid down by the Children and Young Persons Act 1969. Neither side wished to stretch its resources into increased work with juveniles, and although both departments paid lip service to the value of the project, each placed responsibility on the other for difficulties, with mutual accusations of failure to show commitment. The project workers came to feel like pawns in an inter-organisation war game.

EVALUATION

Recording

Considerable attention was given, when the project was being planned, to recording, planning, evaluation and supervision. The difficulties which surrounded supervision have already been examined. As regards recording, planning and evaluation, these were to be a weekly commitment for each of the leadership teams, with meetings of all the project workers to share and compare findings, on a bi-monthly basis. The failure of the bi-monthly meetings to become established has already been mentioned, and in practice, recording was given a high level of commitment by only one worker team, while the other responded to pressure on its time by eventually dropping ongoing recording, evaluation and planning.

It was however generally agreed that weekly recording was a very important commitment. Even without the extra meetings, it presented an opportunity for some evaluation and planning; it was symbolic of the continuance of the project; and it provided a focus for decision making and for the workers' own learning and support. Without recorded material, co-ordination of such a complex project would have been difficult; moreover, no consistent and purposeful experience could have been provided for the group and its individual members, and no strategies towards the wider targets of intervention—members' families and the residents and institutions of Chapelfield—would have been formulated.

With this in mind a recording structure was devised, comprising:
- **Activities:** essentially a factual record of group meetings and work between meetings.
- **Group interaction:** a description and evaluation of processes within the group.
- **Individuals:** a person by person account and evaluation of the performance of the young people; periodic assessments of change to be incorporated into this section.
- **Staff:** a critical examination of staff roles and performance, seen as a very important commitment in view of the absence of outside supervision.
- **Conclusion/future plans:** an overall evaluation of the previous week; any salient observations; exposition of intentions for future work.

A further note of interest is that, towards the end of the year, the group members began to show an increased interest in recording, particularly on residential experiences when the worker team would tape its thoughts after lights out. The first group recording session that was attempted around a tape recorder was chaotic, but during the final residential week of the project group recording became an opportunity for members to examine both their experiences in the project and their personal developments. These sessions certainly were not chaotic, were taken seriously, and reckoned to be worthwhile, if challenging, by staff and members alike.

Engaging Participants in the Project

As regards the young people, the project proposal claimed that: *'despite compulsory factors . . . we shall seek to develop horizontal relationships . . . and make decision taking as democratic as possible . . . working towards normal community activity'* [19]. Although there was an element of compulsion in attending the project for members on supervision, for many others attendance was voluntary. Moreover, it was central to the project that the children be involved as fully as possible in its development, and that it should prepare them for normal youth activities.

Attendance registers were kept. In the course of the year, 41 children were extensively involved, and attendance was maintained at a steady 75%-80% of potential membership. For the group as a whole, attendance seemed to vary with:

- The nature of the particular meeting in the early stages: later on, the type of activity did not seem to affect attendance.
- The stage of group development: attendance improved with the development of group cohesion.
- Residential attendance: those who missed invariably came along to the next community based meeting.

Within the group, individual attendance seemed to be related to:

- Sex: girls were more inconsistent than boys.
- Personality: initially, withdrawn kids were bad attenders. Their attendance improved as group cohesion and sub-groupings developed, but subsequent absences tended to be linked with instability within the group, e.g. member/worker confrontations.
- Newness: new members tended to miss their first residential experience.

Within these generalisations, some individuals were consistently regular attenders, a few came only occasionally, others were intermittently absent. For the individual child, attendance or absence seemed to be related to outside matters such as problems at school, home or further offending. For children on supervision, involvement of the supervisor in the project seemed crucial. Seventeen members were on statutory supervision during their period in the project. Only three of these were on supervision to a worker outside the project team, but the attendance of two of these was very sporadic until supervision was transferred to one of the project workers. Six children out the 34 initially selected failed to come along to the first meetings and three of these were on supervision to a worker who was not directly involved in the project.

Noticeably, attendance was not affected either by a change in the worker team, unless a supervisor was involved, or by disruption from outside, such as the invasion of the meeting hall by non-members.

Translating Intentions into Planned Intervention

It will have become apparent in the descriptive sections of this study that in broad terms the project utilised and pulled together skills, methods and strategies from community work, group work and casework, much as intended.

The focus on the natural group of friends was maintained, and the year's programme of weekly community based meetings and a total of 30 days in residential activities was completed.

As regards the group, movement towards a more mature and responsible level of functioning seems to have taken place and this group as a whole, and its members individually, became less of a threat or a nuisance to other people. The main deficiencies within the programme lay in its being less versatile than the workers had hoped, as a result of limitations in resources, both in the material sense and in the sense of worker time, professional skill and practical expertise.

Work with the parents developed only in part as intended. A considerable amount of work with families did occur, but the rather disappointing level of involvement in the parents' group was probably brought about in part by confusion caused by seeking to develop community action by parents, alongside child focused group work. The former stressed the need to change the environment, while the latter involved helping the child to adjust to it.

The community work intentions for the project were rather ambitious, and while it cannot remotely be suggested that they were entirely fulfilled, nevertheless there were considerable developments in this area (see Figure 3). Much research and assessment were done and resources for voluntary youth work were identified. Some of these resources were used in the project, but more significantly they formed the basis of the follow-up youth facility.

Community work generally failed to develop at a grass roots level in encouraging the community to *accept its responsibility to prevent delinquent behaviour'*, to *'prevent circumstances arising that are conducive to delinquent behaviour',* and to realise that *'part of the solution lies in housing and amenity provision'* [20]. Beyond those people contacted about the new youth club, who did represent a fair cross-section of the community, and beyond irate neighbours of the hall, it is unlikely that the project rated in the life or thoughts of the Chapelfield man in the street. Given the resources of the project it was probably unrealistic to think that a significant grass roots impact could be made. For instance, the time available did not permit work with the wider group of unattached youth to extend beyond assistance in preparing and presenting a petition. However these limitations should not detract from the fact that preparing the ground for a new youth club constituted a considerable achievement.

Where the project clearly did not develop as envisaged was in the area of work specifically focusing on the sponsoring agencies. While workers intended the project to demonstrate a more effective way of dealing with young offenders and of making professional decisions, they had not anticipated the dysfunction this would produce in their own agencies. Indirectly this must have had a significant effect on the treatment programme offered to the children, because of the commitment of time and nervous energy this agency focused work drew from the workers.

The most successful project development occurred in the areas which involved direct work with the children and their families. This is perhaps to be expected as it was predominantly expertise in these areas which the workers brought to the project. Reorientation had to take place most markedly in the areas where the workers were very much novices — working with the community and within their own organisations. A degree of effectiveness seems to be indicated both by the setting up of the follow-up youth club, and also in that the project completed its action programme. A blemish on this picture is however of some note. Undoubtedly the process of introducing a new organisation into a field of existing organisations was challenging and discomforting, and at the end of the planned year of operation it was unlikely, at local area level, that either sponsoring agency would readily support a similar project again. However, among senior management there seemed to be higher regard, and workers from the project were invited to talk about the project to wider audiences of academics and practitioners regionally and nationally.

The Young People

An area of great importance in evaluating this project is the pattern of offending and reoffending among the members. Bottoms and McClintock point out that such projects are *'not to be seen as a more effective way of stopping delinquency and nothing more'*, but rather as *'an attempt to come to grips with some of delinquency's causes, . . . fewer convictions becoming a welcome consequence rather than an overriding aim'*[21]. Nevertheless, it has to be accepted that this is the criterion by which the value of the project is likely to be judged by the public, the courts, and indeed by some within professional social work.

No further large scale offending by the group, like that which prompted the project, has come to light. The following statistics in Tables 4 and 5 enable the offending that did occur among the membership to be examined more closely, over comparable periods both before and after the project. While court appearances do not show the number of offences committed nor indicate their seriousness, there are authorities who suggest that those who show up in court do in reality commit more serious offences more frequently[22]. In fact, police cautions have been included in the statistics so that some 'hidden' delinquency can be accounted for.

On examination of Tables 4 and 5 it can be seen that there has been:
- A dramatic reduction in the number of appearances made by the whole group.
- A reduction in the number of children from the group appearing in court.
- A drastic reduction in the number of children appearing repeatedly, i.e. twice or more.
- An increase in the children not appearing, particularly among supervisees.
- An increase in occasional offending, meaning one appearance only. This increase is accounted for by movement of some repeated offenders into this category, but also a continuation of occasional offending among some members, and others appearing for the first time.

It is the results in relation to the repeated offender that seem to be of greatest interest. Six of the 14 children who had appeared twice or more before the project started did not reappear. Yet it is this type of offender who is most likely to continue offending[23] and to end up in an institution. In this project they tended to be already on statutory supervision, and Ryall[24] suggests that it is they, as opposed to the occasional offender, who pose real problems for society and for treatment. Any stemming of repeated offending, therefore, would seem to constitute an outcome of considerable importance. Of concern to the workers

Table 4

Number of project children appearing in court, and total number of appearances, in two 18 month periods — 1972-73 and 1973-74, before and after the start of the project.

	Group as a whole		Children on supervision	
	1972-73	1973-74	1972-3	1973-74
Children **not** appearing	11	18	1	6
Children appearing **once**	16	19	4	9
Children appearing **twice or more**	14	4	12	2
Total number of children appearing	30	23	16	11
Total number of children	41	41	17	17
Total number of appearances	55	28	40	13

Table 5

Number of project children appearing in court in two 18 month periods — 1972-73 and 1973-74, before and after the start of the project: comparison of the number of (re)appearances after with the number of appearances before.

	Appearances	1972-1973				
		Nil	1	2	3+	Total
1973-1974	Nil	7	5	4	2	18
	1	4	9	4	2	19
	2	0	1	0	2	3
	3	0	1	0	0	1
	Total	11	16	8	6	41

204

was that the tariff system in the courts hampered the recognition of such progress as far as the individual child was concerned. Policy in this Social Services Department was that a care order for an offender should entail a residential placement, and four children from the project were placed in care while it was in operation. Three of these had made two or more appearances in the period before the project started, and were made the subject of care orders after one further appearance in court following the start of the project. Social workers had recommended continuing help in the community partly on the grounds that their rate of offending had been stemmed.

Even if it could be argued that the occasional offender is not too great a problem for society, the continuance of any offending is of considerable concern, particularly in the case of erstwhile non-offenders where contamination could be a possible explanation. As regards the persistent offender for whom it may be said that offending has become a habit [25], it would be unrealistic to expect it to cease instantaneously, especially if it is remembered that the impact of intervention is cumulative. In relation to the first offender, it is not possible to know whether the offence would have occurred if the child had not been involved in the project. No doubt some would have appeared, but in the light of the marked decrease in appearances overall, one would like to speculate that it would have been more.

In conclusion it it postulated that one further offence during intervention does not necessarily demonstrate failure, and, moreover, the reduction of offending among repeated offenders is an achievement of some significance.

Ideally a measurement of change in personality characteristics should supplement consideration of offending. Unfortunately, no test measuring personality traits was used in the project, and the content of the project records is too haphazard for them to contribute anything more systematic than impressions. Nevertheless, the section of the records on 'Individuals' does provide a sufficiently consistent source of information on individual members to be able to describe developments that were noted by the workers in particular children. In following up Albert and Tommy, the two boys described earlier, it should be remembered that no one individual is representative of any other — Albert and Tommy are just illustrative examples.

Albert
Albert was the pale, awkward 14 year old who had offended together with much younger children. On entering the group, he was isolated and withdrawn, always outside the main stream of group activities. Gradually, with patient staff support, he found activities in which he could participate, learning to enjoy them and eventually hold his own with his contemporaries. From then on, entering into the main stream of activities and discussions, he found he could assert his individual preferences and opinions and still be accepted. Albert became a pivot of stability in the group, a sort of reference point for many of the more assertive members from whom he initially cowered and withdrew. By the end of the project Albert had begun work, but he still attended the follow-up club occasionally. His appearance improved immeasurably, he acquired a girlfriend, and went camping with friends on his own. No further offences have come to light.

Tommy

Tommy was the boy from a family with a violent father who, it subsequently became apparent, was alcoholic. Also Tommy's problems were more serious than at first thought. He was considered unmanageable at school from which he truanted. Soon after the project started he was placed on supervision on theft charges. At this time in the group he would burst out unpredictably with destructive behaviour, usually aimed at property in the premises where the group met, but also involving physical confrontations with male workers. Tommy was intelligent and physically strong but to little constructive purpose, and beneath a superficial admiration most members feared his unpredictability and violence. On residential experiences, Tommy found satisfying physical challenges and became interested in wildlife. He, and the group, also found that his intelligence and physical capacities could be used for the benefit and comfort of all. When the established group leader was removed into care, Tommy and another member naturally stepped into his role, co-operating in a joint leadership pattern. However, outside the group further offences of theft and one of assault were reported, for which Tommy's supervision was extended. These had been committed by Tommy on his own after family eruptions. He left school officially shortly before the end of the project, and proceeded to hold down, without difficulty, a physically demanding job. He continued to attend the follow-up club regularly, advising and assisting members towards constructive ends. In many respects Tommy appeared to develop considerably in stability, maturity, and social competence, although the workers were only too aware that the dynamics of his family were a critical variable on which little impact had been made.

Families and the Community

Tommy's case leads naturally to consideration of the impact made by the project on families, and in terms of support and practical help the project seemed to provide a worthwhile service. There were a number of families, like Tommy's, where the workers felt that family dynamics played a considerable part in producing problems among their offspring. However, except where conjoint family therapy was employed, there was no impression of significant change occuring, the apparent conclusion being that it takes more than indirect involvement to bring about improvement in family functioning.

Finally, although little was achieved in the way of alleviating the massive problems of this locality, there were observable changes directly related to the community work objectives of the project:

1 A new club for young people was set up in Chapelfield, so that youth facilities were increased.

2 Through the wide ranging contacts made in Chapelfield in the course of this project, a large number of people, both ordinary citizens and professional workers, gained a clearer perception of the problems facing this town. Through some of these people, the following developments took place:

   a Contacts were established between voluntary organisations, statutory welfare agencies, youth service and school, and through these fieldworkers came to realise that many problems were commonly identified, and a beginning was made towards co-ordinating work.

   b The formation of a group of volunteers to work in the new club brought together individuals who were previously isolated and ineffectual, although concerned about their community and in particular the children within it. It was a constant revelation and source of inspiration to the workers to find real appreciation and support for the project among lay people contacted.

3 The *Community Profile,* the *History of Youth Provisions,* and the *Critique of the Town Centre Redevelopment Plan,* together with impressions gained in the course of the project, were disseminated amongst local government officers and volunteers. It is not possible to say whether this influenced a considerable increase in public investment in Chapelfield, in the form of town centre regeneration. This was planned to include a school providing a range of recreational facilities, and the establishment of social services and probation offices.

CONCLUSION

As a one-off project it would seem fair to make a tentative claim to success in a number of respects:
- in stemming recurring offending by 'hard end' delinquents;
- in generating more mature and socially acceptable behaviour among a group of young people, definable as delinquents or at risk, both as a group and as individuals;
- in engaging residents and institutions in a constructive response to the unmet needs of young people in a locality.

However, while it is gratifying to be able to identify success, areas of failure should not be ignored. These can be identified readily enough and include the breakdown of agency links, disorganisation among the workers, and failure to engage the parents of group members. A common factor in these areas of failure appears to be that they occurred where different value stances, largely implicit and unidentified, met in practice.

The approach that the workers adopted involved viewing the behaviour of the children as caused by a number of interlinking stress factors outlined in Figure 1. A multi-method intervention strategy appeared to be a logical development from this and the workers were surprised when it came to be questioned in their agencies. Their reaction was to attribute most of the difficulties they met to resistance to innovation.

However, such a perspective to assessment does not identify the cause of the children's offending but merely a range of areas in which contributory factors may lie. In fact the workers also shared a view, not closely examined nor spelled out, which was more specific — that the behaviour of the children should be seen as a response to the circumstances in which they were living. Such a position would suggest an approach geared to changing those circumstances. While some of the community work undertaken with the project could well be said to fit into this stance, much of the individual and group work was geared to adapting the children to unchanged circumstances.

There is an inherent illogicality in integrating approaches geared towards such contradictory purposes. To prove that offending can be stemmed and behaviour improved by such child focused intervention can only detract from the credibility of assertions that such behaviour is a response to structural forces, and from developing intervention with this in mind. Thus, it seems that rather than having a coherent purpose, the project in fact had fundamentally divergent objectives, with varying degrees of appeal to those involved as workers or sponsors. It is not surprising, then, that mixed feelings should prevail about the project, gyrating apparently wildly, but perhaps understandably, from commitment to rejection.

However, even with such an appreciation of these conflicts, it is likely that these workers would still have pursued such an approach. Faced with young people whose lives appeared to be careering to ruin, immediate child focused action was required on humanitarian grounds, even if appearing to 'blame the victim'. The process of achieving more meaningful change is inevitably long term. Accepting that successfully achieving short term pragmatic goals can have an undermining effect, this longer term process involves engaging clients, their peers, family members and other residents collectively in enterprises, such as setting up the youth club, which achieve concrete results and demonstrate an alternative perspective on problems and their solution. By this means a process is begun in which established attitudes are reviewed, and alternative responses tried out.

The purist would probably discount such an approach. However, progressive social work practice invariably involves balancing short term humanitarian and longer term social change goals, and the Chapelfield project would suggest that with an integrated methods perspective a feasible strategy can be devised and pursued. While problems arising from inbuilt inconsistency may be inevitable, the extent to which such an approach will be able to meet its range of objectives will depend heavily on the clarity of purpose and on the level and range of practice skill among the workers involved.

References

1 Scott P. (1972), 'Gangs and delinquents in London', in Mays J.B. (ed.), *Juvenile delinquency, the family and the social group,* Longmans.
2 Thorpe D. (1974), 'Therapeutic community techniques', *Youth Social Work,* Vol. 1, No. 4, pp.7-9.
3 Sohn L. (1952), 'Group therapy for young delinquents', *British Journal of Delinquency,* Vol.3, pp.20-33.
4 Gordon Z. (1971), 'Group work and juvenile offenders', *Probation,* Vol.17, No.3, pp.81-86.
5 Ryall R. (1974), 'Delinquency: The problem for treatment', *Social Work Today,* Vol.5, No.4, pp.98-104.
6 Barr H. (1966), *A survey of groupwork in the Probation Service,* HMSO.
7 Bottoms A.E. and McClintock F.H. (1973), *Criminals coming of age,* Heinemann.
   Davies M. (1969), *Probationers in their social environment,* HMSO.
   Glueck S. and E. (1965), 'Varieties of delinquent types', *British Journal of Criminology,* Vol.5, pp.236-247 and 388-405.
   McQuaid J. (1970), 'A personality profile of delinquent boys in Scottish approved schools', *British Journal of Criminology,* Vol.10, pp.147-157.
   West D.J. (1967), *The young offender,* Pelican.
8 Taken from notes on Albert and Tommy, written for the project by referring social workers.
9 Douglas T. (1970), *A decade of small group theory, 1960-1970,* Bookstall Publications, pp.29-32.
10 Thorpe D., *op. cit.*
11 *Ibid.*
12 *Ibid.*
13 Miller-Smith M. (1974), 'Grendon outpost', *Social Work Today,* Vol.5, No.1, pp.3-6.
14 Barr H., *op. cit.*
15 Mays J.B. (1971), *Intermediate Treatment of the young offender* (Charles Russell Memorial Lecture), reprinted in Mays J.B. (ed.) *The social treatment of the young offender,* Longmans, 1975, pp.312-322.

16 Morrison R.L. (1967), 'Individualisation and involvement in treatment and prevention', in Klare H. (ed.), *Frontiers of criminology*, Pergamon.
17 Miller W.B., Baum R.C. and McNeil R. (1966), 'Delinquency prevention and organisation reaction', in Wheeler C. (ed.), *Controlling delinquents*, Wiley, pp.61-100.
18 Wilkins L.T. (1964), *Social deviance*, Tavistock, p.258.
19 *Project proposal:* paper prepared by workers and approved by management outlining the methods and objectives of the project.
20 *Ibid.*
21 Bottoms A.E. and McClintock F.H., *op. cit.*, pp.263-264.
22 Elmhorn K. (1965), 'Study in self reported delinquency among school children in Stockholm', *Scandinavian Studies in Criminology*, I, pp.117-146.
23 West D.J., *op. cit.*
24 Ryall R., *op. cit.*
25 *Ibid.*

PONTEFRACT ACTIVITY CENTRE

Robert Adams

BACKGROUNDS AND ORIGINS

'What we're aiming for in this place is just detached youth work with a roof on' — project leader.

'It's not like a school . . . where you can get on top of the kids . . . here they're on top of you all the time' — evening helper.

'I suggest you get this graffiti off the walls and introduce some discipline' — visiting teacher.

'It's great this place . . . it's ours and we built it' — 18 year old customer.

Introduction

Since 1973, the Pontefract Activity Centre has been a listed intermediate treatment facility in the terms of the 1969 Children and Young Persons Act, though it began in 1960. Referred to locally as 'the Club', it is also familiarly known to children attending as 't' Fruity', a reference to the name of the founder, Martin Rowntree, and the fruit gum manufacturers.

It is a non-residential centre, staffed by a group of workers from several different disciplines, including social work, youth work, community work and education. An integral part of the life of the Club has concerned its use of volunteers and the help of parents. Although pioneered by Quakers, who brought in a management committee of local representatives, it was taken over in 1974 by Barnardo's, who were therefore managing it during the period covered by this study — 1974 to 1977.

This was a period when new staff with new ideas were attempting to develop a community based programme, which involved moving away from offering activities linked to casework for individual boys, and towards working with natural groups of children from various neighbourhoods. The rationale lay in the notion that some of the problems experienced by individuals might, in the process of work with a mixed disciplinary team of workers, be viewed as issues to be tackled with, and on behalf of, a whole group. Thus neighbourhood based groups of young people might focus on issues affecting their own problem status, rather than being treated as the problem themselves. The project leader was particularly interested in providing referred children with helping roles, or what Priestley has since called *'realistic escape routes'* from the dead end situations which seemed to face many of them. [1] As one 16 year old boy said: *'If anything happens in Ponte . . . it's always us lads that does it . . . you're guilty before you even speak with these coppers . . .* **and** *the staff at school* **and** *these bloody social workers . . . you've no chance.'* [2]

The author was leader of the project during the three year period described. The study uses records kept at the Club during three years, and in the section on

211

the young people's views, it also draws on a study carried out by Carole Smith, research and development worker at Barnardo's. [3] It remains, however, largely the project leader's personal account of efforts to develop community based work with delinquents and near-delinquents, and to offer an alternative to the individual treatment orientation found in the bulk of the literature on intermediate treatment.

The Setting

The Club is situated almost in the centre of Pontefract, the core population of which just exceeded 15,000 at the last census. Most participants lived within two miles, although occasionally young people and their families travelled in from as far away as three or four miles. In theory the population served by the Club approached 100,000 people, but in practice regular participants came from an area populated by about half this number. The work of the Club has always been primarily with children and families from council estates in Pontefract, though during the period since 1974 work was developed on a more formal basis in two neighbouring towns, with those living on estates occupied mainly by miners.

This part of West Yorkshire is dominated by pit shafts and slag heaps Social and physical mobility has not been high in the past, which means that in some of the more depressed areas, where mining is on the decline, or where sickness or other factors have prevented the earning of full wages, extended families may be living in cramped conditions and experiencing a multitude of housing, economic, medical, educational and social problems. [4]

The particular brief of workers was to work with problem children and those 'at risk'. Workers were aware in 1974 of the range of difficulties faced by 'labelled' children 'in trouble', if they wished to break out of the vicious circle of disadvantage and stigmatisation, and these were emphasised and compounded in Pontefract by the fact that the local Housing Department had for some years followed the practice of placing 'difficult families' in one or two well known streets on local housing estates.

'The residents across the way have petitioned us to have a wall built round that street... it's a constant embarrassment to us' — councillor.

'Just because we live up Redpath Avenue we're just scum to them... t'neighbours are always on to you as well... it's like... being tret like animals' — boy living in Redpath Avenue.

The Birth of t'Fruity

In 1960 a local probation officer, Martin Rowntree, became concerned about the inadequacy of traditional, office-bound supervision of boys on his caseload, so he invited half a dozen of them to join forces with him in developing some kind of activity together on one or two evenings a week. As a member of the Society of Friends, he was able to make use of the Quaker Meeting House, and the present Club has developed on the same site, although the actual premises have gone through several radical changes. The first group of boys were encouraged to bring their friends, so that about a third of the membership consisted of referred or identified offenders, between the ages of 10 and 16, and two thirds of self-referred or invited members.

By 1971, the Handicraft club, as it was then known, was offering craft, judo, woodwork, and outdoor pursuits activities to 60 or 70 boys, on three evenings a week in a loosely structured setting, staffed by several youth leaders and further education instructors. [5] There were insufficient resources to pay a permanent full time leader and apart from the supervision offered by Martin Rowntree on an intermittent basis, the likelihood of any sustained social work involvement in the activities seemed remote. A tradition of volunteer and parental involvement was established over the years, but the Club was desperate for financial stability to ensure its survival.

As a result, the management committee invited Barnardo's to take an interest in the programme, and Barnardo's agreed to make an increasing commitment from 1971 until it assumed full control of the management in January 1974. By 1974 it was responsible for one full-time outdoor pursuits leader and two part-time social workers at the Club. The period 1974-76 saw the steady growth in staff numbers to five full-time workers; however, for the first year of this study, the activities were run by two full-time and two part-time leaders.

The Changing Philosophy

In 1971, Martin Rowntree saw the Club as providing a caring community with a programme of challenging activities, community service and outdoor pursuits, linked to casework with individual boys. His philosophy envisaged the relationship developed between boys and adults as the means to remedial work, and activity as a means to this end, rather than an end in itself.

The period discussed in the present case study marked a new phase in the life of the Club and was in some ways a radical departure from its traditions. The philosophy which governed the change was rooted partly in the conviction that since more treatment-oriented approaches had failed with these young people, an approach was needed which would encourage them to invite the adults into their own world to share their difficulties, and which would thereby enable them to develop their own rules for more acceptable behaviour on the basis of genuine group participation.

Another feature in the change of philosophy was the shift in focus from individual to peer group to community: the 'problem' was seen to be located not so much in the young people individually as in the community, of which they were part and to which they had much to contribute. Club-type activities and outdoor pursuits would continue, for a time at least, but would need to be justified much more in terms of furthering relationships and community action. In 1974, the workers had not fully sorted out the implications of developing a neighbourhood based programme, but it was to become clear later that a focus on the local community would mean supplanting or entirely replacing the previous emphasis on outdoor pursuits.

There were a number of reasons for this departure from tradition:

- The 'take over' by Barnardo's, a very large voluntary agency, in 1974;
- The employment of several full-time staff, some of them social workers, which meant the possibility of a more intensive development of the programme;
- The recruitment by the project leader of workers with a community work

213

orientation, who added a new dimension to the casework-linked activities which had been an established pattern in the Handicraft Club;

- The particular interest of the project leader in trying to provide referred children and young people with helping roles in the Club, as a route to community action locally.

Working through Change

In January 1974, when Barnardo's assumed responsibility for managing the Club, the influx of new workers was instrumental in initiating the changes which are the main focus of this chapter. Once appointed, they were left by Barnardo's to determine their own philosophy and methods of working. Because they came from very different backgrounds and disciplines, they often had to work extremely hard to establish a common way of seeing a situation, and the main task in lengthy staff discussions was how to use individual differences in orientation constructively, instead of regarding them merely as problems to be surmounted.

The major constraint in every area was the established tradition of work at the Handicraft Club, and new workers were conscious at the time of the anxieties of existing workers and long-term supporters who remained on the former management committee when it was reconstituted as an advisory panel.

It was obviously imperative to preserve consensus with these groups about the philosophy and practice of the work, but this was only achieved at the expense of a gradual turnover of sessional staff, some of whom said they found it difficult to adjust to the changes. The main strains involved in the changes were as follows:

- There were difficulties between Barnardo's and the new advisory panel, as each party learned to cope with the new situation. The project leader operated as an intermediary, more often than not representing the views of the panel to Barnardo's. The committee's loss of executive power was the main anxiety, combined with fears about what Barnardo's, like some 'big brother', might do to alter policy at the Club.

- Children and young people using the Club often resented changes in the programme, such as girls being admitted to the building from summer 1974, and the trend away from pure activity in general, and combat sports like judo in particular.

- Some staff also expressed anxieties about change, and those with most reservations were, perhaps, those who had worked at the Club before 1974. For example, many were doubtful about the wisdom of allowing girls into the building. Mary, the canteen assistant, said, *'There'll be young lasses wi' babbies before you've finished',* and to the extent that such anxieties were conveyed to the children during the first 18 months of the new orientation, that period was rendered that much more unsettled.

The changes in philosophy, aims and methods of working were negotiated mainly with local people and agencies, whilst Barnardo's divisional office provided equally important, but more distanced, administrative and professional support. The project leader sought to help all involved to cope with change by ensuring that as many decisions as possible were reached through a consensus between workers, volunteers and children.

214

THE PROJECT IN OVERVIEW
Orientation and Aims

The workers were concerned in 1974 to develop an approach to working with children in trouble which took account, not just of their living situation, but of the wider problems experienced by their families in their own neighbourhoods. A further concern was to try and help children labelled either as delinquent or near-delinquent, to develop non-deviant roles and definitions of themselves. The workers were unhappy in many ways with the term 'intermediate treatment', their doubts centring on:

- The risk that if the Club was identified as an intermediate treatment centre, the programme would just become a part of the general labelling of young offenders;

- The essentially individual orientation of many statements trying to link intermediate treatment with supervision, within the context of either casework or group work;

- The risk that a potentially exciting concept might become an essentially punitive form of social control, masquerading as liberal treatment.

In 1975 the aims of the Club were described in an annual report in the following terms. The first was *'to involve in the life and activities of the Centre children and families who are identified by local agencies—social services, school, probation, child guidance, etc—as facing 'problems'. In the case of children that generally means 'in trouble' or 'at risk' in the terms of the 1969 Children and Young Persons Act.'* [6] Inherent in this broad statement were two specific objectives: one was to promote a reduction of delinquency and truancy, by setting up programmes which retained the participation of referred and self-referred children, largely through activity and discussion groups; and the other was to give support to children and families seen as 'at risk'.

Secondly, the Club aimed *'to enable them* (the children and families) *to develop collective solutions to problems in their neighbourhoods. This entails staff participation in a variety of community-based projects, which develop from group work within the Centre.'* [7] It therefore involved the workers in enabling Club members to develop helping roles, either individually or in groups, and in building up some aspect of community activity which the members themselves saw as helping to keep children out of trouble.

The third aim was *'to develop where possible, and without interfering with the above, a range of 'community centre' activities.'* [8] This reflected the long standing tradition at the Club of not further stigmatising members by running activities solely for 'bad boys'.

These aims were set down by the project leader in the autumn of 1975, and so represented the outcome of his first 18 months' work on the project, as well as being a statement of intent. A year previously it had been recognised that the general approach of the Club raised some problematic issues. As the annual report of 1974 pointed out, *'Its approach, therefore, may cross and recross boundaries between social work, youth work and community work.'* [9] That this did in fact happen is shown by the following quotes from two workers at the club:

Ken (community worker): *'The trouble with Sid is . . . he's still looking on these kids as individual problem cases.'*

Sid (social worker): *'It's all very well running these projects out of the Club on the estate but someone needs to be there to pick up all the problems some of these children have got . . . There's no-one else to do it.'*

It was such thinking that led to the recruitment of a youth and community worker, Joe, to replace Fred, the outdoor pursuits leader, when he left in Autumn 1975, and also to the creation of a community work post for a fifth full-time worker in the winter of 1975. Further, the often abrasive interaction between workers with different stances—for example, the individual and the collective as polarised by Sid and Ken above—indicates a dilemma between individual remediation and community development, between individual care and neighbourhood action, on which the project was permanently poised.

Resources

Funds

Whilst Barnardo's was reponsible for the major revenue costs of the programme and for any capital expenditure, grants were also made by the Wakefield Social Services Department, which was meeting 25% of the costs by 1976, by the Youth Service, which also seconded youth leaders for evening activities, and in kind by the Further Education Department, which seconded instructors.

This bland statement about how the Club was funded conceals the massive anxieties each year about whether escalating costs would be met in a period of straitened finances in the local authority. Between 1974 and 1977 the annual budget more than tripled, from about £10,000. Whilst Social Services increased its contribution from £500 in 1974 to about £10,000 in 1977, the Youth Service halved its input of sessional leaders, on the grounds that what the Club was doing was closer to social work than to youth work.

Staffing

Although full time staffing was gradually increased by Barnardo's and reached five by 1977, the Club depended very much on part time helpers and volunteers from a wide variety of backgrounds. This is illustrated by the following extract from the staff list:

Full time (all pseudonyms except project leader)

Rob	Project leader 1974-78, formerly six years in the Prison Service, aged 30
Sid	Social worker 1971-78, over 28 years in residential work with Barnardo's
Pen	Social worker, ex-probation officer, early 20s, left in 1975
Ann	Social worker, ex-probation officer, late 20s, replaced Pen in 1975
Fred	Outdoor pursuits leader, ex-mountaineer and Alpine guide, left in 1975
Joe	Youth and community worker, early 20s, replaced Fred in 1975
Ken	Community worker 1975 onwards, with local working class, unemployed background; recruited as, and saw himself as, something of a 'new careerist'

Paid sessional (1-3 sessions each week)

Andy	FE woodwork instructor, daytime manager of factory
Jim	Youth leader, daytime teacher at school for ESN children

Alec	FE games instructor, residential worker in community home with education
Ned	FE woodwork instructor, daytime manager of training centre for mentally handicapped
George	Youth leader, daytime headmaster of school for ESN children
Mary	Local mum and canteen organiser at the Club
Mick	Handyman, daytime labourer

Volunteers

Jen	Parent of several referred boys and girls
Ted	23 year old former offender and attender, now a miner
Peter	Referred from court after an offence and paid as outdoor pursuits leader as well as doing voluntary evening work
Allan	Ran guitar class, daytime research chemist
Jeff	Daytime hairdresser

Premises and equipment

The rough, tough premises of the Club, with their extraordinary mixture of ramshackle cupboards, corners and small rooms, were described by the project leader as *'a converted battleship, turned inside out'*, and Mary, the canteen assistant, was fond of telling visitors that in winter, *'It's that cold in 'ere, it'd freeze the balls off a brass monkey.'*

The project leader felt that children using the building should associate Barnardo's arrival on the scene with the effective handing over of day to day maintenance to the children. The electrifying graffiti that developed tended to preoccupy visitors, especially those who were under the illusion that the Club provided a kind of evening school. One room was dominated by a mural featuring Dennis the Menace, whilst in another, a wall was so covered with names that the workers called it 'the register'. The feeling of children and families was that it was very much their club, built over 14 years by many of the older brothers of current members.

'Heaven help us', said a former activity leader, *'if we ever finish building this place . . . it'll be the end of our work with these kids . . . we'll have to knock it down and start again'*. And as Sid added: *'Each wall in this club has been moved around at least three times since the boys originally built it'*. This process was perceived by the project leader in terms of the need for the programme to be de-institutionalised or de-organised at intervals and to be allowed to build up again. [10]

The Club had little equipment of a permanent kind, apart from the woodwork room which was well equipped with benches, lathes and tools. A jewellery making group flourished for a year in 1976, and bought a cutting and polishing machine with money raised at jumble sales; but other art and craft materials tended to be improvised and bought in an ad hoc fashion, depending on the project in hand. The motor mechanics group in the basement operated out of a single toolbox, of which the contents cost less than £20, and would buy old cars from a nearby garage, for £5, or motorbikes for not much more. It was the view of workers generally that it was not so much the physical assets acquired by a particular group that counted, but rather the personal relationships which developed and, perhaps, the way the project reached out to the more marginal attenders and involved them in what was going on. But the Club had one luxury

—a Land Rover which was adopted and cherished by members and proved immune from any form of deliberate damage, perhaps because it came to represent mobility, freedom and enhanced status.

Shortcomings in resources

There were several ways in which resources at the Club were less than adequate during the period. Until early 1977, the probation service used the building, for three complete weekdays, as a day centre for adult probationers, and this inhibited the development of daytime projects with out of work young people, as well as holiday projects with those still at school.

In 1974, when the project leader arrived, there were three other workers, two of whom were very much part time and based at Barnardo's Leeds office. So in the first 18 months, the implementation of an area based group programme was hampered by the lack of a stable, full time staff team. In one sense, this was of positive value, since it encouraged the development of work through sessional workers and volunteers, but there were times when the programme suffered. For example, when a volunteer driver left in February 1975, the evening group of young people who came in from Pitside declined and broke up, because the transport on which it depended could no longer be provided.

The changes in orientation of the project were initiated by the project leader at a time when none of the workers had experience or training in developing community programmes. Thus, many of the shortcomings in the work of the Club may be attributed to the lack of skills of the staff themselves, rather than to any inherent deficiencies in the philosophy. This was particularly true in the case of the project leader, who had little social work experience outside the Borstal and prison setting.

Internal Organisation and External Links

Figure 1 indicates the range of people involved at the Club. During the year 1974 to 1975, meetings of all workers were held fortnightly, but their frequency was then reduced to half termly meetings. Full time workers tended to meet to review particular aspects of the programme as required, and quite often policy changes discussed would follow, or be followed by, meetings with children during the evenings. Most administrative work was left to the project leader, though in 1976 a part time clerk was appointed.

The Club represented one of three community based projects administered and supported from Barnardo's Yorkshire divisional office in Leeds, and given the distance, full-time workers tended to make varying use of the informal support offered. Barnardo's had some difficulty at first in adapting administrative procedures to the needs of the project. However, they showed considerable flexibility in modifying their national policy, both on annual budget estimates and on fund raising. In the first case the project workers were spared the require-ments to specify in advance exactly how money would be spent, which allowed greater freedom of development and action. In the second case, local, as opposed to national, fund raising was allowed, and a local bank account retained. This was crucial, both to the community based ethos of the Club, and to the self-respect of the advisory panel.

This advisory panel included parents, magistrates, a local councillor and representatives from virtually all the statutory agencies concerned with young

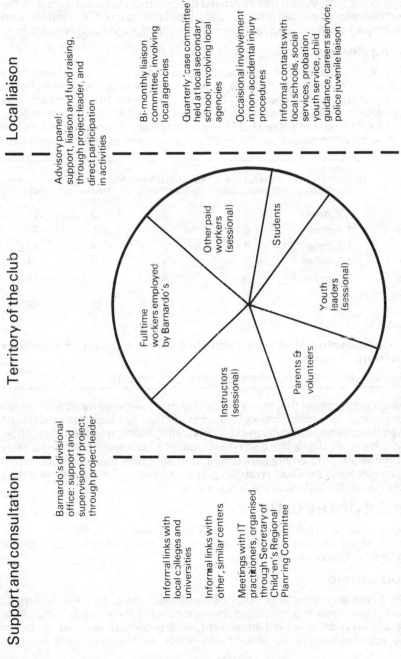

Support and consultation

Barnardo's divisional office: support and supervision of project, through project leader

Informal links with local colleges and universities

Informal links with other, similar centers

Meetings with IT practitioners, organised through Secretary of Children's Regional Planning Committee

Territory of the club

Full time workers employed by Barnardo's

Other paid workers (sessional)

Students

Youth leaders (sessional)

Parents & volunteers

Instructors (sessional)

Local liaison

Advisory panel: support, liaison and fund raising, through project leader, and direct participation in activities

Bi-monthly liaison committee, involving local agencies

Quarterly 'case committee' held at local secondary school, involving local agencies

Occasional involvement in non-accidental injury procedures

Informal contacts with local schools, social services, probation, youth service, child guidance, careers service, police juvenile liaison

Figure 1 External links for supervision, support and liaison, and adults working in the Club

Note: the pie chart segments are roughly proportionate in size to the number of hours spent in activities at the Club by each group.

people. From the autumn of 1975, it met every two months. At least, that was the intention. In practice, attendance by local youth and social services agencies tended to be intermittent, and parental and local councillor support became increasingly important. Whilst this improved the community based nature of the project and deprofessionalised local support, it did reflect a social distance from some statutory agencies — which was perhaps healthy for a voluntary agency.

The Young People

In 1976, about 220 children and young people, aged five to 22, attended the Club. Most of these were not in trouble, although a large proportion were felt to be at risk by virtue of the area they lived in. The most focused work was undertaken with five groups, discussed below, which had a total of 65 members, aged 13 to 17. Of these (see Table 1), 30 were on statutory supervision orders and a further 16 were either on voluntary supervision or were in official touch with probation or social services.

Name of Group	Average Distance from the Club	On Statutory Supervision	On Non-Statutory Supervision	Others	Total
Redpath	½ mile	9	3	3	15
Bellvue	1 mile	6	6	10	22
Pitside	1 mile	5	2	4	11
Tipstone	1 ½ miles	7	2	2	11
Blackton	2 miles	3	3	0	6
TOTAL		30*	16	19	65

Table 1   Composition of groups according to the number of members on supervision.

*Includes 6 with an IT requirement in their supervision order.

In practice this meant that many of them were considered by all with whom they had contact as archetypal delinquents. Social workers and probation officers had the greatest difficulty in even persuading them to come to the office, and when there, their disruptive behaviour created a fair amount of havoc. They were, on the whole, extremely expressive, and although there were no direct assaults on workers at the Club, rival gangs from neighbouring estates often had pitched battles at, for instance, the bus station.

THE WORK OF THE CLUB

'Ye can 'ave a good laff at t' Fruity' — 14 year old boy.
'It's the only place we can have a good discussion about — you know — things an' that' — 15 year old girl.

The Programme

In 1974, the emphasis was upon doing things. Over the next two years there was a move towards providing more opportunities for group and individual talk, but activity still remained important, and indeed it seemed to be an inevitable accompaniment to almost any work with young people which occupied more than an hour. The one important exception, with no obvious explanation, was a girls' discussion group, which is described more below.

Regular activities provided in the building included woodwork and craft work, music making, art, indoor games — including a form of indoor football with skittles — and from 1975, motor mechanics in the garage basement. These disciplines may conjure up a vision of craft training, or instruction in small groups, but whilst boys would often produce small items of woodwork or jewellery, the emphasis was generally on ad hoc activities. Attempts to undertake longer term projects, like obtaining and making roadworthy motor bikes, were exceptional. One focus of evening activities was the canteen area, which was very much an informal talking shop, largely because of the expansive, maternal personality of Mary.

The workers decided to exclude nightly discos, in order to encourage members to look to the statutory youth facilities in the area for piped music and other more conventional resources. This was accepted by members in a surprisingly agreeable way when the rationale was discussed with them, and it was made easier by the existence of flourishing music making groups between 1974 and 1976, using a variety of instruments such as oildrums, African percussion, guitars and old piano. This policy proved effective in reducing casual attenders, and without loud music, it became physically possible for people to talk together almost anywhere in the building. It should be noted here that the workers and helpers attached paramount importance to chatting with the children, more or less casually, and often one to one.

Working with Groups

In early 1974, the new project leader noticed that the Club was attracting boys in gangs, or natural groups, from several areas in and around Pontefract. These areas are referred to in the study as Redpath, Bellvue, Pitside, Tipstone, and Blackton. In April several of the Tipstone boys, and in the summer several from Redpath, appeared in court for group offences. The Tipstone group, in fact, all came from one estate in the town, and together comprised every juvenile supervision case on that estate, so the idea of working with these natural groupings suggested itself. In the autumn of 1974, workers began to meet with these groups separately, in what were then called 'workshops.' Working with these groups took various forms during the period of this study, but was seen as central to focused work with the most problematic young people.

Workers distinguished three basic kinds of group.

1 **Closed groups.** For instance, a number of boys drawn from one particular housing estate, Tipstone, all of whom knew each other, met together on Thursday evenings as a closed group for nearly two years. During this period, movement in and out of the group was minimal. At the end of the life of the group, activities for all members terminated.

2 **Semi-closed groups.** The Wednesday evening Bellvue group, for example, was formed in May 1975 from an original list of ten boys referred by local agencies. They were invited to bring their own friends with them to the first meeting. A social worker later commented:
'The first night of the Bellvue group we wondered what was happening because the ten kids we had invited didn't appear, but seven or eight others instead . . . They were much bigger boys and we suddenly realised that they had come down to 'sus' the place out whilst the others waited up at the bus

station till they got the all clear . . . Eventually they came down and it was amazing because all of them stayed on for the next 18 months or so . . . We realised the boys referred were part of a wider and larger subcultural group which was quite cohesive, and which we would have failed to locate if we had only taken those referred as in trouble.'

Thus, whilst the members of the closed group seldom exceeded a dozen, membership of the semi-closed groups tended to number between 15 and 20 weekly. The principle of self referral was combined with that of simple referral by agencies as a way of enabling the workers to establish links with the natural groupings on the estate.

3 **Open groups.** On Monday evenings, for instance, the Club was opened to a large number of children and young people including a small proportion of referred children, and attendances of 40 were not uncommon. This provided fewer opportunities for focused work with any sub-groups, and the atmosphere was like that in a youth centre. This open group setting was seen as involving minimal worker control over membership and as perhaps attracting young people who might be at risk. It was noticeable that some members travelled two or three miles to attend the open group on Monday evenings, in addition to the closed or semi-closed group which catered exclusively for their own neighbourhood or estate.

The five area based boys' groups are the focus of this case study, and their development is described in the next section. There were, however, other groups at the club, including a mum's group, a mother and toddler group, and those for chidren aged five to nine and nine to 13 respectively. Of particular interest was the weekly two hour discussion group for girls, which the girls themselves began in 1976 and ran for over 18 months. Discussions covered a broad range of their experiences, including problems of many kinds. A few of the girls had been in court for under age drinking, but none had had any contact with social work agencies. They were not seen by workers as 'at risk', although one had received counselling and help with arranging an abortion just before she left school. The group arose from pressure put on one of the cleaners at the Club by the girls to create a meeting for them, and it is arguable that the absence of a 'disco scene' made it possible.

Work with Individuals and Their Families

Casework with the families of individuals referred was carried out by social workers at the Club, though on a decreasing scale from 1974 to 1976. Children referred to the project were allocated to one or other of the social workers in the staff group, and whilst all workers were involved in review meetings, these individual workers took on the responsibility of maintaining liaison with statutory supervisors, schools, and families. On occasions they would attend court when asked to do so by the young person concerned.

Particular importance was attached by the workers to the way in which court appearances were approached. In general, they tried consistently to keep up a stance that reflected their positive experience of a child at the Club and was linked generally with optimistic recommendations on how further involvement would be a justifiable alternative to some kind of residential or custodial court order. It is interesting that on no occasion between 1974 and 1976 did the court reach a decision contrary to the recommendation made by the worker. This was attributed by the staff to the fact that recommendations like this were usually discussed beforehand with the child (who therefore agreed in court), and tended to be based on some tangible plan for specific activities over a period of time. It was also the case that the Club had developed a very positive image with the magistrates, largely due to the credibility built up in the 14 years before 1974 through the work of those involved at that time with Martin Rowntree.

The boys, and increasingly the girls—after they had become established attenders—came more and more to bring their personal, and often intimate, problems to the workers for advice. This growth in the area of individual counselling was so marked in 1975 and 1976 that the workers considered for some time whether there was a need for some kind of drop-in advice centre for teenagers in the town. Eventually, it was decided that such a resource was better based in a building, like the Club, which was open for most of the hours between 9.00 a.m. and 9.00 p.m. From 1976 onwards, staff sought to ensure that a worker was available during the daytime to see anyone who dropped in for help or advice on individual problems. The kinds of difficulties which were raised by young people covered a wide range of educational problems, like school refusal; employment problems such as choosing work, finding jobs, and interview preparation; domestic issues such as where to sleep when thrown out of home; and sexual problems, including venereal disease and abortion.

Some of the parents of children attending the club either made use of facilities for individual counselling themselves, or brought their friends down. The mums' group seemed a convenient focus for such work. A few mothers and fathers came because of difficulties with children, but mothers also asked for help with financial problems like debt and disputes with local social security offices, as well as with relationships within the family. The project was also used by families in the locality to provide resources like transport and workshops where furniture and other items could be repaired or made. Those who were moving, or who needed particular items of furniture, like an extra bed for ground floor care of a sick relative, could be given practical help.

Residential Work

Workers set out to provide different intensities of involvement with children and young people. In 1974-75 this was achieved largely through residential weekends with small groups, and the boys in the area-based groups made about four trips a year. They used a farmhouse at Semerwater in the Yorkshire Dales, until its closure for renovation between 1976 and 1978. Whilst such weekends put an emphasis on traditional kinds of outdoor pursuits, the opportunities they gave for developing close, informal relationships in a small group were valued by workers and enthused about by boys.

One boy wrote: *'it's magic, Semerwater . . . ye can go boating . . . canoes an' that on the lake . . . it's great with Fred, he goes midnight swimming with us . . . he lets ye make camps an' that . . . in t' evenings we play dominoes an' Scrabble an' those things . . .'*

Another wrote: *'it was raining when we got there, it was raining. So we had to put the tents up in the rain but it was fun. Durring (sic) a duty day we had to make the food and wash the puts . . . but we had time to swim and play crickett and canoeing. One night we all sat round a camp fire and sung and sung songs . . . I went canoeing it was good. On the whole it was very good and I enjoyed it and I think every body else inJoyed . . .'*

The declining use of residential weekends after 1975 reflected the growth of local community projects, and the opportunity for some, at least, to be involved fairly intensively in the Club during the week, for instance in the daytime activities for the unemployed as well as the evening sessions. It also reflected the fact that the existing groups were all well established: if a fresh group had been started at that time, a good case would have been made for residential activities, as a means of securing group cohesion early in its life.

Community Projects

The new project leader had discussed with other workers the notion of an integrated approach to social intervention, and this led to the idea of developing neighbourhood projects, alongside more traditional individual and family based social work. These projects were seen by the workers as a way of helping young people themselves to identify, and find collective solutions to, problems in their neighbourhoods related to their own difficulties.

They were encouraged by the fact that the Bellvue group, soon after it was formed, seemed to be aware of the kinds of issues that might be focused on in community programmes. Other groups, even after running for a year, showed no interest in looking outside the group to any kind of community project. It needs to be borne in mind that these were boys who were largely defined as educational drop-outs and as not much good to the local community.

The Process of Involvement

A child or young person might be referred by agency, school, parents or others; alternatively, he or she might be introduced by a mate, already attending, or might come along and ask to join in activities. Although some children simply attended on a casual basis, more focused work with others entailed some kind of contract, and a group activity tended to be initiated at this point. Where they were referred by agencies, an effort was made to meet and discuss with them the reason for attending, usually the reduction of their problem behaviour. Often, this meeting involved their supervisor, either probation officer or social worker, and in two cases, parents who did not like the idea of referral to the club.

The workers felt that a clear understanding, by all parties concerned, about the reasons for the referral, was a precondition of effective involvement at the Club. This was not always achieved, or only with difficulty where the youngster or his family were reluctant. Thus, it took three meetings to establish a contract with John and his family, though in the event he stayed three years. The social worker's notes record:

'Met John's family with him and his supervisor in the club tonight. It went better than the last home visit when he jumped out of the door and spent the rest of the meeting outside the window listening. This time he ran out but came back later, and we talked about what he might do at the Club and left it that he will join in the workshop next week and see if he likes it.'

Introducing new members to an existing group or evening meeting could be difficult and initially they were given a hard time by the others. Workers tended to hedge delicately around questions of why a boy was referred. Existing members did not. They would challenge a newcomer, exposing the sensitive nerves of the stigma-conscious workers. Thus, when a worker carefully introduced Jim to a group, a leading figure rounded on him at the first chance: *'What are you on then? Probation?'*

While the work was carried out mainly in the context of the groups, individual young people sometimes continued to participate at the Club, after their group terminated. In fact workers thought it was essential to offer them opportunities for continued involvement, although the older they were the more they were encouraged to seek activities elsewhere. Older former members who showed signs of commitment were found jobs as helpers. Some workers found it difficult to accept them as co-workers, and others found it confusing to be encouraging older children to seek involvement elsewhere, on the one hand, and to be inviting them to be helpers at the Club on the other.

In the 1975 Annual Report the sequence of group involvement of members was identified as follows:

a Initial invitation to children identified by (statutory) *agencies as 'in trouble'.*

b Invitation to children to bring a mate.

c Setting up of activities which bring them initially into co-operative relationships with adults as well as peers.

d Getting to know individuals, their peer groups, and nature of interaction between them.

e Reinforcement of any positive moves the group make toward socially acceptable organised activity.

f Encouragement of community problem-solving programmes'.[11]

The degree to which this sequence accorded with reality can be judged from the following section, which describes the development of the groups, within the Club as a whole.

DEVELOPMENTS IN THE CLUB

This section provides a selective account of developments in the Club during the three years from the spring of 1974 (see Figure 2). The focus is on the work with referred, 'problem' boys in the area-based groups and Tipstone in particular, at the expense of omitting many developments in the work with parents and other children, though these were an essential context to the former.

During this period the life and work of the Club underwent major changes. Some of these involved physical aspects, like the 1976 improvements to the building and the consequent eight month disruption of the programme; others involved human resources, like the increase in the number of full time workers from two to five. The nature of the work with young people changed too, as the emphasis shifted towards community projects and discussion combined with activity. Some of the adults and children doubted the value of certain of these changes (for instance, the admission of girls), and a large part of the project leader's task was to manage these changes and sort out their implications for the different individuals and groups using the Club. However, it is clear that a good deal of the change was an ad hoc response by the workers to demands made on them, exigences of one kind or another, or a form of opportunism; and similarly, many of the results of the work during this period were not anticipated.

Main Phases of Project Life	Commentary		Chronology of Groups

1974

Formative	Jan —	Transfer of management to Barnardo's.
	April —	New project leader started work.
		Several children referred following court appearances, some on IT orders.
	July —	
		Bellvue playscheme. Early exploration of notion of community projects helped by 'problem' children.
Formal group		Four area-based groups set up: 'workshops'.
	Oct —	
		Christmas re-organisation of evening programme at club, giving area-based groups more focused resources.

1975

Discusson/activity grow	Jan —	Area-based move from discussion to activity-discussion.
Transitional	April —	Two playschemes. Adventure playground project.
		Staff shortages lead to transport problems and Pitside group ends.
	July —	
		Outdoor pursuits leader leaves. Gradual shift towards locally-based activities.
Experimental	Oct —	
		Planning period for latchkey club, with Tipstone boys as helpers.

1976

Intensification of action and crises	Jan —	Inter-group rivalry and hostility grows. Work with all groups intensifies.
		Decision to cease group work with Redpath.
	April —	
End of group life		Holiday playscheme at Tipstone and working holiday programme at Club.
		Club disrupted through refurbishing.
	July —	Tipstone, Bellvue and Redpath groups end.
Aftermath		Tipstone summer playscheme.
	Oct —	Unemployed individuals from three groups continue to use club during daytime on casual basis and given help finding jobs. Day programme develops and runs till all have found work in February 1977.

Chronology of Groups (right column): Pitside Group, Blackton Group, Tipstone group, Redpath Group, Bellvue Group.

Figure 2   Phases of development and group chronology

The Formative Phase: April—September 1974

In the months following the appointment of the new project leader, workers were engaged in examining the goals of the Club and assessing what kind of children and young people were attending. To test ideas about neighbourhood projects, two small ones were set up in the summer of 1974. The first was a planned attempt to involve boys aged 13 to 15 as volunteers in a local play-scheme, which the Pontefract Council for Social Services was organising. The workers attended preparatory meetings in May and June and had to persuade the organisers to accept a small number of volunteers from the Club, alongside those from International Voluntary Service. This was by no means easy, since Club members *'might more usually be thought of as troublemakers by the community, or at best as* (clients) *on the receiving end of help.'* [12] When the project was reviewed in October by the agencies involved, it was decided, in spite of reservations expressed by some local helpers, that the Club volunteers had behaved responsibly, and that the Club would be invited to take part in future play schemes.

On the basis of this moderate success, the workers attempted later in the summer to involve some of these volunteers in an informal promotion of sports and games in a field at the back of the houses they lived in. This exercise was an almost total failure. The workers judged that it was the proximity of the project to the homes of the participants that was responsible for the problems encountered.

However, the organisation of sports and games near the Club did enable the workers to introduce local girls into the play activities quite naturally, and to bring them back to the Club after the session had finished. Until that point, girls had not been admitted, and the workers wanted to break the monopoly of the boys as early as possible. By the autumn the tradition of girls attending was becoming established, although they still had regular skirmishes with boys at the entrance to the building.

During this period, a number of boys aged from 12 to 15 appeared in court for various offences and were referred to the Club. They came from two separate areas, Redpath and Tipstone, and many of them, or their mates, had already been taking part in Club activities for some time. Before the court hearings, the workers had discussed with the boys what kind of Club involvement could be put clearly to the court, and it was agreed that group discussions, as well as activities, were to be part of a programme that the boys themselves would develop, aimed at helping them to reduce their delinquency and truancy. This explicit reference to the reason for the programme was held by the workers to be crucial at this stage.

Formal 'Workshop' Meetings: September—December 1974

Intensive work with the referred boys and their families resulted in the formation of four groups, serving Redpath, Tipstone, Blackton and Pitside. As noted earlier, the process of involving the boys was not always straightforward, and the groups themselves differed in 'openness' to others. During the autumn, the groups met for half an hour each week in what were called 'workshops'. In a paper written that October, they were described as follows:

'Workshops have been held for six weeks. They consist of meetings . . . of boys from four catchment areas, . . . each composed of 10 to 15 boys

'at risk' . . . some on supervision . . . Meetings are voluntary, and generally last half an hour. Staff attempt to close the meetings when they extend beyond this limit. Between one and two staff attend each meeting. Meetings are open for supervising officers to attend. Boys can bring their friends, providing they live in the same area. Volunteers can attend meetings. . . . The tasks of workshops are defined by staff as being 'to discuss things of current concern to members'.

'The role of staff in workshops is to act as a supply of resources to other members, and to maintain the boundaries of sessions. They do this in several ways by setting temporal, behavioural and spatial limits, as they think fit. This usually means stopping meetings after half an hour, preventing fights, and suggesting that interlopers leave. The staff function as enablers, rather than as doers. . .

'The emphasis in meeting is upon experiential, rather than insight gaining, aspects . . . Continuity from session to session seems to be maintained by boys rather easily. They refer back to the earlier meetings regularly. Staff make a brief summary of previous meetings, and usually limit this to a couple of sentences. This recording is not intended as a cross-reference to the behaviour of individuals. It is the kind of record the boys might keep themselves. Meetings are not held in camera, but the contents of meetings are not freely broadcast by staff.' [13] In fact, workers' records of groups were available to all members.

Three of the groups—Pitside, Tipstone and Redpath—managed to meet very regularly during the ten weeks until Christmas, but the Blackton workshop was amalgamated with Redpath halfway through term. Blackton was the least successful of the groups; interestingly, it was one whose members did not normally go around together, but had been formed by the workers. The groups arranged a number of activities, with or without staff, in addition to the workshop meeting. These included outings, residential trips, parents' evenings, and time spent improvising music and help in the production of a film. The Tipstone parents' evening enabled the boys to display new-found dramatic talents in an improvised horror story in drag, based very loosely on *Murder on the Orient Express*.

The Pitside and Tipstone groups each had residential periods away, including five eventful days at Semerwater for the Tipstone group, which greatly increased its cohesion. During their stay, a purse was stolen from Jane, the statutory social work supervisor for three of the boys, who had invited her along. The following extract from a boy's diary indicates how the incident was handled by the workers—neither punished nor ignored but resolved in group meetings, and how it had become incorporated with more mundane events in the shared memory of the group, including workers, rather than recalled as a grievance by the boys alone.

'On Tuesday Jane's perse went missing and someone had Stolen it and Tom accused Joe of pinching it. And we all serched the house top to bottom, and then we serched the garden and the building out side and then we all had a meeting in the house and we searched again and then Lee admitted that he knicked it in the river near the lake and Dave, Mick, Tom Tom and Lee went down to look for it, and then they came back.

*And we had another meeting inside about what we were going to do about
it and we decided to all put in and give her nine pounds when we got back to
the club. after the meeting we all went to build the bonfire and we to the
landrover and we got in and went down to the jety were canoos are and after
the bonfire we had a game. Some had a torch and they had to find them
then we went to Haws for some fish and chips and it was closed and then
we went in the park for twenty minutes and We ran to the pub for Fred . . .'*

Meanwhile, evenings at the Club were characterised by a good deal of
rivalry between the dozen or so group members taking part in a workshop
meeting, and the large number, perhaps 70 or 80, attending other activities. The
latter felt excluded and sometimes tried to force their way in to find out what
was going on. This is illustrated by a record of the seventh meeting of the
Tipstone workshop, dated 14th October 1979:

*'There wasn't a lot of time for chatting somehow tonight. I didn't get down
until there had been a coffee throwing session and Jim and burnt his hand
on someone's fag. Frank came up to fetch me when the drinks were
organised, and Jim came back in. Some members perched up on the
shelves and the sky kept raining coffee. Eventually we had to go upstairs
because the other boys burst in with sticks and I think everyone was a bit
disappointed that we couldn't really have the meeting.'*

Discussion — Activity: January — April 1975

Workers had decided that the structure would have to be modified to take
account of the feelings of children and young people excluded from the workshop
settings. They were convinced that more resources needed to be focused on the
small number of young people who were identified by agencies and others as
being 'in trouble'. The question was how to deal with them in a way that did not
further label them as delinquent, whilst not running a programme for all the youth
of Pontefract who cared to come along. In the weeks before Christmas, a
number of meetings were held involving all members, workers, volunteers and
other helpers, in order to recognise the structure. The overall aim was to try and
reduce the number of members from over 90 on an average winter evening, to
something between 20 and 30. The new weekly evening programme which
emerged from the meetings allowed pairs of neighbourhood groups and their
peers use of the building on one night each, children under 13 an evening to
themselves, and one free-for-all evening. A drop in numbers was in fact achieved
quite easily, probably because the workers refused to have piped music on the
premises, which encouraged those who were capable of graduating to one of
the youth clubs in the area to do so.

A marked change occurred in group meetings in January 1975. As soon as
the reorganisation reduced the numbers of children attending, members seemed
much less inclined to participate in a half hour group discussion. The workers
gradually realised that one of the reasons why workshop groups had developed
high cohesiveness was the very fact that other children, outside the group, were
attempting to disrupt it. So the pattern of development during the spring period
was one of relaxation, and to some extent a retrenchment to more activity.

Another consequence of the reorganisation was a dramatic increase in the
adult:children ratio. With the Tipstone group this was almost one-to-one on some
nights, and since they were now spending two hours an evening at the Club two

evenings a week, with almost one hundred per cent attendance, there was a great deal of interaction between adult and children. It was noticed that the behaviour of members of this group moderated during this period. When they were referred, supervising officers had suggested that they were beyond control and likely to finish up in care fairly shortly. They were reported to be difficult to interview. When they first came to the Club, a favourite activity was sitting on the roof of a nearby building and tossing small items of debris on to the road and garden nearby. The police were in fairly regular contact with them for minor offences which were constantly being investigated. The improvement achieved may have been due in part to the increased time and resources devoted to them from autumn 1974.

Transition towards Community Projects: April — September 1975

The spring of 1975 saw the demise of the Pitside group because there were no staff available to ferry them the couple of miles back and forth, but some members continued to use the Club individually. About this time, a new group was started for young people from the Bellvue Estate, consisting mainly of 11 to 14 year olds. but including some boys a year or two older. The suggestion to form it came from a school counsellor and from social workers. Starting in the summer, the Club was also opened on a limited basis during the daytime for some of the unemployed school leavers.

Throughout this period there was a gradual shift in emphasis, away from outdoor pursuits activities and towards locally-based community projects. The transition culminated in the appointment of a youth and community worker to succeed the outdoor pursuits leader when he left in August — a change that was far from popular with the young people at the time. The aims of such community projects were described in the Annual Report in the following terms:

'1   *To involve children and young people as helpers and as positive resources in the community, rather than as clients.*

2   *To enable groups of young people to be seen by the general public as contributing to, rather than detracting from, the neighbourhood . . .*

3   *To initiate projects aimed at areas of need, identified by young people as linked with the causes of their own difficulties.*

4   *To offer groups of young people opportunities for action within a broader canvas of community development in the community.* [14]

In April 1975, the workers invited teachers at a nearby secondary school to discuss the possibility of mounting a joint project on an estate in Tipstone, the idea being to capitalise on time which several children, whom they wished to involve, would otherwise spend truanting. The aim was to extent an adventure playground on the estate under the guidance of the playleader. Teaching staff suggesting that the project be integrated into the school curriculum as part of community studies, and it was agreed that two mornings a week would be set aside for practical work by a group of boys, who would be working with staff and volunteers from the Club throughout the summer term. The project entailed some heavy work erecting a framework of telegraph poles, but was successfully completed over a ten week period, despite the drawback that the site was two miles from the Club and the homes of most of the boys.

During 1975, it became apparent that parents were as keen as their children to raise money to finance activities and buy equipment. Happily, Barnardo's now agreed to amend its national policy, and allow funds raised locally to be used locally. The Advisory Panel, which now had a revised constitution under which parents of members participated actively, stimulated a number of fund raising events during the year. There were three jumble sales and a flag day, and whereas in the early stages most of the organising was done by the workers with one or two parents helping, in the latter stages the reverse was the case. Money raised was used to buy equipment for activities and thus a direct link was established between what the members chose to do during the evening, and the effort they put in to raise the money. More importantly, as parents commented at the time, these locally funded activities blurred the edges between providers and those provided for.

Planning and Experimentation: October-December 1975

The period after the appointment of the youth and community worker in August 1975 was one of adjustment to the more explicit emphasis on the Club as an integral part of the local community, rather than as simply offering escape routes from it. Thus, workers and boys from the Tipstone area joined with parents on a local management committee in planning a weekly club for five to 12 year olds at a hut the parents had themselves built on their estate. The previous year, these boys had been strongly resistant to the idea of undertaking any such activity and preferred to travel over to the Club in Pontefract several times a week. This new development was a very practical test of the ability of the workers to integrate the group back into the estate. In the event, this project was not a success: some of the group had little interest in being helpers in work with younger children; moreover, they were not seen locally as helpers but as troublesome teenagers for whom the age restrictions on play had been unfairly relaxed.

In the autumn of 1975, daytime workshops were begun with school leavers in the area-based groups until they found jobs. This successful experiment was repeated in the following two years.

Throughout that autumn, tensions were rising between different area based groups using the building and there was a fair amount of sabotage by one group of another's activities in the building. For example, the Tipstone group's motor cycle was damaged by the daytime activity group for unemployed school leavers from the Redpath area. Rivalry was particularly intense between the Tipstone and Redpath groups, which were the only ones remaining of the original four workshops. Interestingly, the Bellvue group, although under pressure from the Redpath boys, was managing to hold its own, partly because some of them were very tough and aggressive and could match threats with equal weight.

By this time, offending by the Tipstone boys had almost entirely disappeared. Instead, it was the Redpath group whose delinquent activity was at a high level, with an upsurge during the Christmas period when they were responsible for a spate of assaults and thefts in the town, and a series of thefts and break-ins at the Club. They already had an unenviable reputation in the town, and were increasingly the subject of overt police activity; it was common for them to be picked up in the street and taken to the station for questioning as prime suspects when any thefts were committed in their area. It was apparent to workers that they were committing offences, but that they were also becoming targets for an excessive degree of official harassment, and were consequently in danger of being pushed into an alienated position where they would feel compelled to live up to their 'hooligan' label. In rankled with them to find that even though newspaper reports of court appearances did not mention them by name, all their neighbours and acquaintances knew to whom they were referring.

It was suggested that they might get involved in projects at the Club which could attract some positive newspaper reports, and one boy, due in court after Christmas for an offence committed several months previously, was particularly keen on the idea.Two programmes resulted from this, the first being a scheme to chop up and deliver firewood to old age pensioners, and the second a sponsored swim for Dr Barnardo's in which they were prominent helpers. Firewood deliveries fell away sharply after Christmas, and it was felt by the workers that the loss of interest, despite the positive newspaper items, arose from the fact that they were largely initiated and organised by the workers.

A change, however, later took place in Redpath that dwarfed the effect of the Club's work with boys from that area. In September 1975 the local housing department began to rehouse families living in the Redpath Road area of Pontefract, and scatter them over the town. This process was largely completed by Christmas. In assessing the ultimate impact of the programme on the Club, account must be taken of the major impact of this environmental change on the lives of the boys and their families. It provided opportunities for them to break out of the ghetto streets in which they had been living as labelled 'problem families' for many years, and increased the possibility for those on the fringe of the group to make new friends.

Intensification of Activities and Crises: January—April 1976

During this period some strikingly contradictory trends emerged. First, the rivalry between the different groups referred to above was intensified. Eventually the Redpath boys won out over Tipstone in the territorial rivalry. The workers dealt with the situation by meeting with the Tipstone boys away from the Club, on their own patch, and arranging activities from there.

Secondly, even whilst the Club reverberated to the aggressive challenges issued to members and workers alike by the Redpath boys, the spate of offences which they had committed throughout 1975 had suddenly fallen away to nothing. It was clear to the workers that some kind of transition was happening but it was not easy to discover the nature of it. It was clear, too, that the mounting aggression of the Redpath boys over the previous year had been somewhat thwarted by the non-aggressive response of the workers, who refused to reject them even when they were at their most destructive. The approach of the project leader was to attempt to involve them in group meetings about these problems, and to try and understand what was going on, which was a very demanding situation for all concerned. By Easter, however, no problem behaviour was occurring, with the exception of one of the Redpath group who was sent to detention centre for a theft during the spring, and one member of the Tipstone group who was taken into care following repeated problems both at home and school.

A crucial decision, taken in April 1976, was felt, in retrospect, to have had a positive influence on the behaviour of the Redpath boys. The workers considered that their delinquent behaviour over an 18 month period had worsened as the cohesiveness of the group had improved. So, it was decided to try to use staff resources to identify and work at tasks, discussion or activity, with individuals as far as possible.

End of Group Life: May—July 1976

Two successful projects were held in the Easter holidays, one based at the Club involving the youngsters in decorating and gardening activities, and the other in Tipstone involving them in organising play for younger children.

Almost all meetings with the Tipstone boys took place away from the Club on various evening excursions. These terminated in July, by which time most had left school and got jobs. Members of the Bellvue group accepted the end of their group life without much comment. Several indicated that they would come back on an informal basis in the autumn, but this seemed unlikely in most cases, since they were rapidly growing out of school and into work. Only two out of the ten referrals had committed offences since May 1975. One was made the subject of a care order and went to live with his aunt on a nearby estate but still attended regularly and did not re-offend.

The groups were all wound down by July because the building was due to be closed for several weeks whilst a new heating system was installed and other alterations took place. This followed a long term decision of Barnardo's to improve the premises and bring them into line with fire and other regulations. Unfortunately the contractors brought in after Easter to scrape the asbestos roof caused dust to settle throughout the building, this at a time when national concern was rising about the danger of asbestos dust. It took several weeks to rectify the situation, and in the meantime much of the Club was closed to groups. Most of the boys in the Redpath and Tipstone groups were unhappy about the interruption caused to their activities, but it was generally accepted, like an earthquake over which one has no control. The girls seemed to be less affected by the crisis. They met in smaller groups at lunchtime, and did not require facilities for activities like indoor football.

Aftermath: August 1976—February 1977

Several boys who had not found jobs turned up at the Club on a daily basis as September drew near, and it was apparent that they were feeling more and more depressed about not having a job, once the initial elation at their release from school had worn off. Accordingly, a group was formed to cater for half a dozen boys who were in this situation. All the boys were from the Redpath group, so in a sense the existence of this group was prolonged until February 1977, when the last of them found work.

Although in terms of its outcome this programme was a success, its day to day functioning was often precarious, poised between the all too often inconsistent, faltering ambivalence of the boys regarding many of the unattractive jobs offered to them, and their requests that the workers should try and guide them into work.

Postscript

This account is not intended to reflect the Club as it may be now. There may have been changes since 1977. In early 1977 the present writer was preparing to leave, the small group programme was finishing and there was a hiatus whilst other workers looked at new developments. In particular, workers felt that more intensive day, evening and weekend facilities were needed in the community, run much more by than for the children, and plans were being formulated to develop a day centre programme in conjunction with Wakefield Social Services Department. The day centre was not conceived as an alternative to school for truants, but rather as a social educational facility for those delinquents whose truancy was also a problem. The rationale for this was encapsulated in a comment about Lee, reckoned by workers and boys alike to be the most troublesome of the Tipstone group in the early days: one of his teachers said in retrospect,

> 'He never got anything out of school . . . he was hardly ever there . . . I never heard anyone say anything good about him . . . It would have been better for him if you'd kept him at the Club all the time . . . all day long . . . If he stayed out of trouble it was a miracle.'

Lee stayed out of trouble, and in early 1980 was married and holding down a job as a miner. It was not a miracle, but in 1977 it was tempting for workers to suggest that in the absence of major changes in the schools to accommodate difficult boys like him, the Club could extend its facilities to provide novel routes to acceptable behaviour.

The difficulty with this thinking was that it let the education system off the hook and also renewed the pressure on boys like Lee to adjust. But workers felt justified in their judgement that this would be the starting agenda for future workshops with children and community programmes, and the possibility of exerting pressure from that base to change local institutional and educational practices should not be ruled out.

EVALUATION

Attainment of Aims

This section first gives the writer's view of the achievements or failures of the Club in terms of the aims set out in 1975 (see p.215 above); this is followed by a review of the perceptions of the Club held by other people, such as parents, workers in other agencies, and the young people themselves. To recap, the aims were threefold: to involve in the life of the Club young people referred because they were at risk or in trouble, as a step towards reducing their delinquent and truant behaviour; to involve them in developing community projects focused on problems they identified in their own neighbourhoods; and to develop at the Club a range of community activities. These are dealt with in turn below.

Maintaining involvement in the Club

The five area-based groups had a total of 65 young people who were members from the time when they were formed (see Table 1). This included 46 whom the workers regarded as the core membership, because they were on supervision orders or otherwise on the books of the statutory agencies, and in all cases referred because of delinquency, truancy or both. Of the total, all maintained their involvement through the life of their particular group, except for a handful, three of whom left the neighbourhood. The workers attributed this continuing involvement to the fact that they were already members of a natural peer group around which the Club workshop was formed, or else that, at the time it was constituted, they were placed in a group in which they already had friends, or were brought along by mates.

By contrast, of the ten boys referred and placed in a group after its commencement, only two continued to attend. Two others opted out immediately after their introduction, in spite of an agreement they had made with workers to attend for a trial period, and the rest left after a short time. Workers took pains to try and minimise the problems arising when new boys were referred, but felt that the time spent by referring agency and project workers was still not enough to prepare for their introduction. Those who were brought into a group that was not their natural peer group quickly lost interest, and further factor was the rejection of new members by existing ones. Only the more stable and resilient could weather this period.

Amongst the many self-referred children, the main difficulty was that a number were seen by the workers as not particularly in need of special help and support. The problem here was the delicate one of retaining contact with a core of members and with a certain surrounding group of self-referred children, while keeping the boundaries of group membership fairly loose, yet not so diffused as to make focused work difficult or impossible. This was something which workers managed with varying degrees of success at different times. What became apparent over a long period was that the children themselves, when the issues involved were discussed with them openly, exercised a good deal of control over the boundary of membership in each group. This was thought by the workers to be the most satisfactory way of resolving such issues.

The workers feared that too many children would become attracted for the Club to cope, and there seemed to be obvious dangers in laying on extensive activities which could have been provided better by local youth clubs. However, these concerns conflicted with the expressed youth service view that success was proportionate to the numbers catered for, and so the workers felt at the same time that they had to engage in the numbers game if they were to retain the levels of staffing adequate for working more intensively with the more demanding young people.

Reduction of 'problem' behaviour

The effectiveness of the Club could be measured in several ways, for instance by comparing its cost with that of alternatives, or by trying to assess the extent to which the boys' behaviour changed. The question most frequently asked of workers was whether the Club reduced the 'problem' behaviour of those attending. Over the period from the inception of the area based groups to mid-1977, workers made the following assessments in relation to the 46 boys who made up the core membership:

Considerable change: former offender and now no longer offending	26
Some change: former offender and now offending intermittently	10
Little or no change: still offending much as before	10
Total core membership	46

Of course, this represents a very crude measure of change and in no way could be claimed to demonstrate a causal relationship between what went on at the Club and the subsequent behaviour of the children attending. In fact, workers felt that three main factors influenced this improvement in behaviour.

1 Growing up and leaving school, the graduation to some kind of work, and the move from a more predatory boys' delinquent group to pairing off with

a girlfriend and 'going steady'. These were changes which seemed to occur largely independently of any intervention by social agencies.

2   The rehousing in September 1975 of 90% of the families living in the Redpath area. This was the direct response of the housing department to repeated complaints over the years about the housing of problem families in a kind of ghetto.

3   Whilst workers felt that the above two factors weighed most heavily in any success associated with the Club, they also considered that the intensive work with individuals, families and groups in the community over a period of several years had had some effect on the very dramatic improvements in behaviour and attitude of the boys. Whilst the actual nature of the process can only be guessed at, the fact that in the majority of cases chronic delinquent records fell away to non-delinquency in a period of two and a half years cannot be denied. Of the core members, only two were sent to institutions for offending during the period under review. What also cannot be denied is that in 1975 offending in the Redpath group actually increased at a time when staff work with the group had increased in intensity. It was almost as if working with the group exacerbated group delinquency. This phenomenon did not occur in any of the other groups.

Reduction of labelling

The role of workers as negotiators on behalf of those with job problems, difficulties with teachers at school, and police investigations, was often instrumental in reducing the mutual 'stand-off' these young people had reached with the adult world. They were, in a sense, their own worst advocates, and many were into a spiral of degenerating relationships with teachers, police, parents and others, which neither party seemed willing or able to reverse. Sometimes the situation was ambiguous. For instance, when some members of the Redpath group thought they were being oppressed by the police purely because they were known to have records, the view of the police was that their response was legitimate, since the group were committing so many offences. The view of the boys was that this constant pressure was predisposing them to offend out of sheer frustration. In any event, there seems to be some evidence that this group felt consolidated in the delinquent image that grew up around them, at least during the year when the offending was at its height. But overall, the impression gained by the workers was that the Club helped to prevent the 'problem' label of children getting any worse, rather than improving it markedly in any direct way.

The way the Club publicised statistics of outcomes for individuals seemed to be associated with the politics of justifying the project to those outside it, including funding bodies, and reassuring workers that they were doing a good job. What still needed working out were some of the practical implications of the move towards a more community based work style.

Involving young people in community projects

As the above account has emphasised, the thrust of the changing philosophy of the Club after 1974 was towards working with referred young people in their neighbourhoods, by involving them in community projects. There is no simple criterion by which to judge such activity — as a means of helping individual children, as an aspect of group work, or as a development in its own right. Workers mainly adopted the latter view.

From the summer of 1975 they saw these projects increasingly as an alternative to outdoor pursuits activities, though not necessarily as a substitute for them. It was recognised that to the extent that outdoor pursuits had formerly been a way of offering children exciting diversionary challenges, such outlets existed in the locality, if only the focus of participants could be adjusted to perceive them. Further, the advantage of building up local activities lay in the possibility that children might be able to continue them independently of the workers, even after the formal programme had ended, and they seemed to offer the opportunity of providing urban solutions to difficulties originating almost exclusively in urban environments.

This area of work was opened up for further exploration rather than demonstrated as a success, and more was learnt from the mistakes than from some of the achievements. An example is the difficulty of running programmes from one centre for several area-based groups, which was compensated for only partially by the opportunities it gave for working with groups as they came into contact with each other at the Club. It pointed to the necessity to develop outposts on the territory of each group as a local base.

In the early stages of the life of a group, much time was devoted to relationships between members. In fact, one or two of the groups had been running for more than a year before it was possible to get members interested in looking outside the group at any kind of community project. Self help projects, such as work on an adventure playground, were generally found to have more appeal than community service, like delivering firewood.

It also proved easier in the early life of the groups to involve members in helping programmes away from their own neighbourhoods rather than 'on their own patch', as in the Bellvue and Tipstone projects. In retrospect, it seems questionable whether this simply reflected the limited motivation of the children. The evaluation meeting on the playground project noted that some of the boys who took part complained that they were not doing anything useful which kids in their own area could use. It seems likely, therefore, that such programmes could have been oriented towards the home areas of children, if the workers had had the necessary skill and experience at the time. Other factors which posed difficulties were the views that others held of the young people, and the low opinion they sometimes had of themselves.

Developing a range of community centre activities

This aspect of the Club lies outside the scope of this case study, but some brief observations can be made in passing. One rationale for encouraging a variety of centre activities was to avoid the Club being seen locally as a sin bin for the 'bad kids'. In this it was only partly successful. Nevertheless, activities like the open club night on Monday evenings showed how a whole range of young people, including some who were seen by many people as uncontainable in a normal school or youth club, could enjoy themselves in a relaxed setting.

Moreover, during the period of this study, the Club developed activities for most members of the family, including two Mums' groups, and two groups for children who were too young for most youth clubs. The programme as a whole provided opportunities for helpers to be recruited from one established activity or group to help in another, and in fact some of the Redpath boys helped out in the group for five to nine year olds. However, there were few occasions which brought young people and the elderly together in co-operative projects in the building. Efforts to involve fathers in activities with their children were also unfruitful, with the notable exception of three or four fathers who were recruited as volunteers with the groups.

In concluding this discussion of the implementation of the Club's aims, it should be pointed out that at times they conflicted, or were given conflicting interpretations, according to the stance of the worker. Thus, in shifting towards community projects, the Club did not abandon the pattern of individual referrals, treatment and subsequent assessments of progress, but this led sometimes to uneasy compromises rather than resolutions. With hindsight, it is arguable that the workers had not thought through the pitfalls of the philosophy adopted. It was relatively straightforward to set out aims and objectives. It was less easy to work out their implications for practice.

Perspectives of Children and Other Participants

In 1975 Carole Smith, Barnardo's research worker, gathered the perceptions of children, parents and supervisors about the Club, by means of structured interviews. [15] These were carried out with children participating in three of the area based groups. They are supplemented in the following discussion by extracts from interviews carried out by the writer two years later.

The children and young people

Two thirds of the interviewed children in these groups associated attendance at the Club with being in trouble, although they were not clear exactly what kind of connection it was. Ten per cent of them recognised that they had to attend the Club as a result of going to court. There was a more general recognition that attending the Club was meant to keep them out of trouble and a third of the children said their parents wanted them to attend for this reason. There was a general feeling that they could not get into trouble whilst at the Club, and some saw it as providing them with an alibi.

The children thought that the groups, which started in September 1974, were a good thing, partly because they were an escape from the general noise and hubbub of evening activities, and partly because they enjoyed talking and were keen on planning activities. The reorganisation undertaken around Christmas 1974, which facilitated area based groups having an evening shared with just one other group, was confirmed in its value by the views of most of the children.

Other data available on the reactions of young people indicate that the vast majority of them had positive things to say about the Club. The following is typical: *'It's a good place t' Fruity . . . ye get trips out an' that . . . ye can do woodwork an' that there'.* But the responses of girls indicated that they resented the presence of boys, who disrupted their group discussions, and many boys felt the girls were intruders. This, despite the fact that it was two years since girls had been introduced to the Club, and workers made no attempt to encourage activities on a single sex basis.

More important, a number of the older boys were very critical of the Club, maintaining that it offered them little, and was very rejecting just when they needed it most, as when they wanted to get off the streets because the police kept picking them up. The workers took the view that the boys needed to accept that the building could not accommodate more than one group at a time. Added to which, the building was still rented to the probation service for three days a week, thus severely curtailing any effective daytime work with young people.

The hostility of these boys was qualified, however, by their warmth towards individual workers: *'He's alright . . . lets ye sit in t' driving seat of t' Land Rover when we're out.'* And again: *'Ye can have a good laff with him . . . he's a good bloke.'* This underlines the value of close relationships with an appreciative adult, as opposed to the relative unimportance of the equipment or the activities themselves. Children asked for particular workers when they came into the building, rather than a particular activity.

Parents

Half the parents interviewed in 1975 expressed the desire to be more involved in activities at the Club. They seemed to feel the necessity of showing more interest in activities outside the home. However other parents felt that children should be allowed to get on with activities without adults from home interfering. The latter attitude has a bearing on the efforts made by workers to get parents more involved.

Whereas parents generally knew about the outdoor activities, like Semerwater weekends, perhaps because workers had been accustomed to seeking written consent for children to participate, they often had only a vague idea of what actually went on at the Club. Most of them did not know about the workshop groups even when they had been running for several months. When the rationale for these groups was explained to them they generally felt they were a good idea.

Most significantly perhaps, parents did not recognise that their children had been referred to the Club for positive intervention, but thought that the job of the Club was to provide a setting which would engage a child's interest. In more general terms, the participation of parents as members of the Advisory Panel over two years led to a small number developing a more active role in managing the project. These parents, and those who took on fund raising, usually developed a clearer view of what the Club was all about, and saw themselves as more part of what was going on. This represented a considerable improvement on the situation in 1975.

Supervisors and workers in other agencies

In 1975, although local social workers and probation officers stressed the importance of relationships between children and adults, they did not specify exactly how such relationships could be used to help those attending the Club. However a number of these workers saw the freedom and relaxed atmosphere of the project as providing a necessary feeling of acceptance. Supervisors felt that the residential weekends provided an invaluable opportunity for the development of shared living experiences. Most of them liked to keep in touch with what was happening at the Club, but they did not see it as necessary for them to attend. Some said that lack of time prevented this, but one worker made the point that being present might inhibit the child's enjoyment of activities.

The police view in 1976 and 1977 can be summed up in two contrasting comments by different policemen, justifying their reason for keeping out of the Club. One said: *'We're a bit wary of interfering with what you're doing . . . I'm a bit worried that if I appear it will stop them from being themselves.'* And a constable commented: *'I tend to let well alone . . . what you do in there is your affair but if they tried that on with me up in town I'd clobber 'em.'* It should be borne in mind, though, that for short periods both a juvenile liaison officer and a community constable each worked in the Club as volunteers—the former on a motor cycle group project, and the latter in the woodwork area.

Although the Club maintained reasonably close links with a local secondary school, this was through the school counsellor rather than a large staff group. The school counsellor had referred boys, and had been largely responsible for persuading workers to initiate the Bellvue group, but did not feel able to attend the activities himself: *'If I was to attend t' Fruity myself I think a lot of the value for the kids might be lost . . . because they might see me as bringing a part of school and that's what I feel they need to get away from.'*

GENERAL ISSUES

The Nature and Level of Involvement

It is clear that the case study covers a period when an outdoor pursuits tradition was being replaced by an orientation towards community projects. Does this point to the irrelevance of weekends away in the Dales climbing hills? Perhaps the clue to the usefulness of such activities lies in the greater intensity of interaction they facilitate. Thus, as the use of residential weekends declined at the Club, there was a move towards providing more daytime activities, particularly in relation to the unemployed. This meant that some children were only attending the Club for two hours or so weekly, for an evening group. Others were attending for an evening group and a regular succession of residential weekends, or, latterly, involvement in a community project. Still others were attending on a daily basis for much of the day and were also returning to the Club most evenings during the week. Providing different intensities of involvement was seen to fit with the views of workers and the young people themselves about how much at risk they were.

It was noticeable that the unemployed boys in particular tended to ask for activities which would keep them off the streets, because they claimed they were much more likely to be harassed by the police if they were seen to be walking around the town.

In part, the reduced emphasis upon residential activities from 1976 reflected the fact that the boys in all the group activities at that time had been involved for at least a year. It seems arguable that if a fresh group of newly referred children had been established at that time, a good case would have been made out for recourse to residential activities, as a means of securing early group cohesion.

Self help and participation

An earlier section attempted to evaluate the workers' efforts to involve young people in community projects. But they were equally concerned to develop a self help and participatory approach within the Club itself. The most striking example of a self help initiative was the girl's group, which, interestingly, was frowned on by the professionally trained social workers in the Club but remained highly valued by the girls themselves. The expressed anxiety of these workers revolved around the fact that the cleaner at the Club, whom the girls had approached to run the group, had no training in group work and tended to foster dependence. Others had anxieties about the girls spending a considerable time talking about their sexual problems. One girl expressed a typical view: *'It's our group . . . we started it . . . we can talk about anything we like there . . I can say things there I can't tell my mam . . . Where else is there ye can talk about your problems and that?'*

The participation of young people in managing the Club was restricted to middle range issues like timetabling the evening programme, but given this overall constraint, the workers took great care to involve all those using the Club in discussion of each issue as it arose, and in the decisions as to what should be done. This led to some rather stormy meetings, but also to some marked changes. The reorganisation of the programme which evolved after 1974 was an outcome of the feelings of the majority of members, and specific programmes like those for the unemployed boys during the day arose directly out of requests for that group. However the young people were not involved in any of the formal reviews of the work of social workers with individuals.

An underlying issue here was the degree to which power could be shared with any of the participants, whether young people or local adults, on issues of policy, use of resources, and project development. The indications are that locally and nationally Barnardo's were unable or unwilling to do this. Despite the involvement of parents on the Advisory Committee and the various consultative meetings held with children, neither parents nor children were given access to key areas of executive power in the project, like decisions over the refurbishing of the building or allocations of the annual expenditure budget.

Nevertheless, these efforts, limited though they were, to involve young people in Club management, and also to employ some as additional workers, reflected the concern of the workers to explore the extent to which it is possible to break down the caste division which often separates workers from young offenders. They felt that their efforts to blur the distinction between themselves and clients made control more difficult, but that this was a good thing, since it meant that adults had to negotiate progress rather than impose it. Further, the often conflicting interests of children and adults were made explicit. All the experience of the workers indicated that this process was more stretching for the adults, but more just for the members.

Thus the emphasis on participation and on self help within the Club, like the shift towards community projects, was consistent with a move towards a 'rights' approach and away from a 'needs' approach. It implied a perspective on delinquency radically different from the treatment one, and this had ambiguous implications for social workers. In fact, they never did resolve the implicit inconsistencies involved in viewing the children as referred 'in need of treatment', and yet wanting to offer them resources to work out, jointly with staff, a negotiation of their 'problem' status.

'Unacceptable Behaviour': Appreciation or Control?

Crises were regularly experienced in the Club. As one worker wryly put it, *'If nothing is going wrong no-one is learning anything'.* It became clear to workers over a period that although each incident, major or minor, needed to be appreciated and understood in its own right, over a period of weeks or months, certain patterns emerged which demanded explanation and action. Where possible, incidents which occurred were discussed immediately with the children and young people concerned. Sanctions were not imposed but they were faced with the natural consequences of their actions. The style of working in such conditions is best illustrated by an example.

One evening in the Autumn of 1976, the Tipstone boys were having one of their weekly meetings, when five Redpath boys found their way into one of the two basement discussion rooms through an ill fitting fire door. Too late, workers realised they were there, when they heard furniture being thrown around. By the time they reached the basement, the Redpath boys were disappearing into the night with catcalls and taunts, leaving chaos behind them.

There were four workers upstairs, including Mary who was making cups of tea in the canteen. A way needed to be found to talk with the Redpath boys immediately rather than the next day. The problem was to create a way to do this, suppressing first reactions to expel them if they turned up again, and to encourage them to talk whilst not seeming to reward their behaviour by responding to it. Further, it was difficult to envisage doing this without breaking into the programme of the Tipstone boys, which, the Redpath boys were making it clear by this behaviour, was the main purpose of their efforts.

Half an hour later the opportunity arose. The Redpath boys arrived at the front door, whilst most workers were elsewhere, walked quietly in and began talking to Mary at the canteen in the foyer. It could have been the signal for instant rejection and righteous reproof, but Mary was very good, in such situations, at providing continuity and softening jagged edges of interaction, whilst other workers sorted themselves out. So, far from showing them the door with a bill for compensation, the third worker left the Tipstone boys with the other two members of staff and sat down on the bench in the foyer behind the Redpath boys. They turned and became rather aggressive, and seemed to be inviting a fight to throw them out, although this had a ritual quality about it, redolent of a series of such incidents: *'Aren't ye going to kick us out then? Up the road they ban kids at Jim's for less than that.'*

The dialogue developed. Their grievances began to get an airing. Workers already knew that they were feeling sore about not being able to use the building when it suited them, irrespective of any other events going on. On this particular evening they articulated it particularly clearly. They felt it was unfair that the programme which gave Tipstone an evening to themselves left them to walk the streets of the town centre where they were subject to police harassment and were more likely to get into trouble. It was put to them that the present evening arrangements were the outcome of all the groups using the Club pooling their views, and they were persuaded to go downstairs to talk about it, with workers and the Tipstone boys, in the discussion room.

This was opportune, since they now were led into the room they had just looked like wrecking, and before it could be used again for talking, the chairs and cushions had to be set to rights. This was done remarkably quickly, and a 40 minute meeting developed from a very quiet and tense start into a dialogue of unprecedented length between Redpath and Tipstone boys. The closest they had been before to talking as two groups had been shouting mutual jibes across the bus stands in the local bus station. Its conclusion was a kind of agreement between them concerning limits within which either group could legitimately encroach on the other group's evening. In subsequent weeks, such limits were broken several times and redefined; but the important transformation achieved on this occasion was from unilateral physical aggression to verbal negotiation between those concerned. Further, workers felt they had moved the situation from crisis and confrontation to a reformulated contract with the groups concerned, without rejecting Redpath on the one hand, or ignoring the consequences of their actions on the other.

The project leader felt that when young people were 'high', this acceptance of difficult behaviour was particularly important, but the maintenance of this approach necessitated a tolerance of extremes of behaviour, which meant that intensive support for workers was needed. It did help workers to be able to vent their anger on the project leader, but the positive aspects of each situation lay in understanding how an incident had been triggered off, it being invariably linked with an aspect of worker behaviour.

Break-ins at the Club occurred sporadically, but there were two main outbreaks. These both seemed, to workers, to express anger and frustration with an aspect of policy, since both involved boys who soon afterwards volunteered information about what they had done. With rare exceptions, such break-ins were followed by informal tip-offs to workers about who was involved, and on many occasions nothing was actually taken. The second outbreak, however, coincided with the period when the Redpath boys were most alienated from the workers, yet most cohesive as a group, and several thefts occurred.

This last case apart, workers felt that in general misbehaviour at the Club did not just reflect the way a particular situation had been handled, but also how the young people, in particular the boys, were perceived and dealt with at school and in other youth facilities in the area. It was noticeable that the end of November in each year represented something of a nadir. The boys talked of rows and violent scenes at school, and of being thrown out of youth clubs in the town for their behaviour. At such times they clearly wanted to use the Club as some kind of refuge, where they were largely accepted as they were, but nonetheless they spent this time criticising the Club and nagging the staff to remove the few basic rules which maintained the use of different parts of the building for different area based groups at different times. The significance of this behaviour may lie in the fact that it reminded the workers to keep their distance. The boys were only in the building to escape 'aggro from the law', as they put it. It was not a sign of coming to heel and they were still a force to be reckoned with.

There was a sense in which the workers faced the aggressive defensiveness of the Redpath boys with some awe. After all, there was always a genuine danger that the next threat to 'get done over' might be real, although in fact workers were never assaulted directly, only indirectly with a well aimed 'accidental shot' from a football. There was a sense, too, in which workers wanted to see that very aggressiveness preserved. It seemed to be the kind of armour the boys would need to get them through the next few years of unemployment or pit work—both representing a different aspect of capitulation and demoralisation, though the latter was tempered by decent wages. The guts of counselling the unemployed young offender, or boy at the bottom of the working class pile, consisted of biding one's time till the demoralisation of seeing

243

all his mates in work left him feeling relatively happy about going for anything, as long as there was good money in it. Success tended to be synonymous with ironing out disparities between a boy's job aspirations, and what he could expect to get.

The crucial dilemma

David Matza [16] has referred to two stances which he feels represent alternative perspectives on deviant behaviour: the correctional, which is oriented towards modifying the behaviour and controlling it, and the appreciative, which concentrates upon trying to understand it.

The workers at the Club were, to some extent, caught between their motivation towards appreciation and the imperatives of maintaining behavioural boundaries, so as not to undermine the social work goals, or threaten the future of the organisation. Thus, the question of being understanding about thefts does not solve the problem of what to do when, all the equipment having been stolen, there is nothing left to do, and the remaining children become frustrated as a consequence.

In the event, the project leader tended to oscillate between the two stances. In practice this involved always attempting to identify individuals responsible for breaking behavioural boundaries, facing them with the consequences of what they had done, and asking them to help sort these out. The police were called for major breaches of the law such as theft, but in general a non punitive, non rejecting approach was always attempted. This was often difficult, since the reaction of many adults and other children using the Club was usually punitive — *'Kick 'em out and don't let 'em in till they've paid for it.'*

Neighbourhood groups and territorial aggression

It was predictable that different area based groups using the same building should, as they developed a sense of belonging, begin to challenge the right of others from different neighbourhoods and estates to use the premises. The workers, rather than trying to impose controls, brought them together to discuss differences and, where possible, to resolve them. They were aware that the groups using the building were engaged in mutual hostilities from time to time, in such places as the bus station in the town, where the police were quite likely to pick them up. The Club was a place where natural interaction between individuals and groups could be mediated by adults, and even occasionally worked out, in ways which preserved the dignity of different boys without necessarily exposing them to physical attack. This is not to say that the workers believed that anything was better than a good scrap, but work at the Club could not continue with different groups, unless they themselves were willing to reach mutual accommodations. They were only successful to a limited degree, and that mainly because the Pitside boys' group terminated early in 1975, and because Bellvue and Redpath boys were fairly evenly matched, which prevented Redpath making ultimate challenges in terms of *'off my territory or I'll flatten you'*. The Tipstone group, mainly 'immigrants' from Scottish and North Eastern mining families, were smaller in stature, and, for other reasons perhaps, less aggressive, so they lost out in the face of the territorial claims of the Redpath boys.

This experience raises questions about the viability of establishing neighbourhood based groups in a central setting where, as a group increases in cohesion, its territorial sense may increase to the point where it is expressed in active hostility to others. Perhaps the solution lies in providing smaller resources based within territories, rather than a single large centre for several neighbour-hoods.

Resource Aspects

Both the demands of change and the stresses of the work itself, in particular with the very demanding Redpath group, pushed the workers to the limits of their personal resources. They were in contact with young people on a daily basis, often as intensively as in any residential setting, and the Club had few of the organisational barriers field social work keeps between clients and workers, like reception desks and waiting rooms. Boys who wanted to talk *now* could, and did come into the Club through one of the ill fitting fire exits at any time, and present themselves as a group, to discuss a problem which had just arisen, such as police harassment. Since the policy was not to reject, or to apply any sanctions like banning people from the premises, workers needed to acquire skills in order to survive!

Linked to this question is the fact that at crucial points human resources tended to fall short of what was needed. Thus, the Pitside group folded up because there simply were not enough workers to provide continuing help with transport. Further, the leader felt that the project was perhaps not flexible enough, in that a strong case for more workers could be made out to Barnardo's, the employers, but it was difficult to put the operation into reverse. Perhaps what was needed was agreement to employ more workers, on short term contracts, within the framework of a long term plan to employ less, as the self help pro-grammes became established.

Resource limitations taught workers to be opportunistic in responding to crises. They did not sit down and make rational plans in a vacuum. Events occurred and they were used in as creative a way as possible. Thus, in 1975 the growing budgetary crisis in local authority financing made it very likely that sessional help would be cut back, and this stimulated workers to recruit volunteers. The general shortage of resources helped to stimulate fund raising, which was itself an important source of cohesiveness during 1975 and 1976.

However, the biggest succession of crises occurred in 1976, when the refurbishing of the building was scheduled. The work, which was to take six weeks, dragged on from May until December, and made the workers extremely frustrated. However two positive aspects came out of it. First, it provided workers with an opportunity to phase out the groups, which had already reached a terminal stage. Second, it provided an important source of cohesiveness amongst the members. In a strange way, some of the divisions were actually reduced by the fact that now there was a common enemy to grumble about. This externalisation of conflicts gave a respite to some workers and children, and enabled some personal 'refurbishing' to occur.

Role of the voluntary agency

The question needs to be raised about whether social workers or probation officers working in statutory agencies are sufficiently free from the climate of officialdom to be able to undertake this kind of role. Most of the full time workers had previously been employed as statutory workers, and although none felt there was much change in their use of authority in adult/child transactions, all were agreed that the worker/child transactions were crucially altered. Abandoning the rhetoric of therapy and searching for alternative rationales for activity has considerable implications for the changed role of workers. At Pontefract some hesitant steps were taken towards self help, but there is scope for many other strategies to be explored. The workers may need to be much less distanced and yet remain true to their role. Initially, they need to lean more towards an appreciative stance, in order to gain access to the world of working class delinquent youth; but that world is so dissociated from the adult world, that appreciation may at times conflict with the workers' correctional responsibilities. It needs to be recognised that the advocacy role required, if hard core delinquents are to be kept in the community, may necessitate the redefinition of social work relationships with police and magistrates, and that such work needs to effect links between 'problem' children and their 'problem' environment, and provide them with the power to change it. Whilst that may be difficult for workers in statutory agencies, it may be almost as difficult for those in voluntary ones. Or perhaps a cynic would say—just as impossible.

CONCLUSION

'We know best'—or do we?

The staff gained a perspective on the problems and predicaments of working class youngsters growing up in an environment which progressively denied them the trappings of acceptability. Work with the Redpath boys emphasised the vicious nature of their social interaction with adults. Starting with truancy in the early teens, and the odd offence committed by the group, their relationships spiralled down into a total dissociation from the older generation in their neighbourhood, which came to reject these particular boys as if they were not just desperados but lepers too. At this point, where their positive contacts with just about all adults elsewhere had shrunk to vanishing point and the offending was at its height, workers at the Club were going through the most intensive period of working with them.

But the most notable erosion of the 'we know what's best for you' syndrome, which reaches its purest forms in the treatment model which the workers were doing their best to break away from, was the establishment of a style of working with the area based groups which involved much more participatory activity on the part of the boys themselves. It was out of the demands made by the members of Redpath group that the day programme for those out of work was run in 1975, and again on an extended basis in 1976. This was a significant move, since it implied that the Club needed to provide young people with more intensive facilities, alongside the evening and weekend programme. Moreover, this move had grown out of the perspective of the users themselves, rather than being dreamt up by the providers, with the characteristic condescension of adults.

If there is any one conclusion to this kind of experience of work with delinquents and near delinquents in a community setting, it is the need to listen to their experience more, and to our own experiences, prejudices and professional ideologies less. Then when we have gathered something of the depth and intensity of the predicament of the outcast adolescent, and have recognised the inadequacy and inappropriateness of what we have to offer at present, perhaps there is just the ghost of a chance that we shall be able to work out with them somewhere fresh to go, rather than continuing to provide more of the same.

Acknowledgements

I should like to record my thanks to all workers, parents, other helpers, children and young people involved in the Club, without whom this study would not have been possible. The comments on this case study by Beryl Davies, Nora Dixon, Kathy Foster, Ted Vowles, Allan Siddall and Derek Spicer—all of Barnardo's—have been invaluable, as has the help of Martin and Mary Rowntree. Any inaccuracies and misrepresentations remaining are, however, my own. R.A.

References

1 Priestley P. (1975), 'New Careers: power sharing in social work', in Jones H. (ed.), *Towards a new social work,* London: Routledge & Kegan Paul.
2 This and other quotes from workers and young people are taken from the diary kept by the writer unless otherwise indicated.
3 Smith C.S. and Adams R. (1978), 'Towards a community approach to intermediate treatment: A research note', *British Journal of Social Work,* Vol. 8, No. 2, pp. 197-199.
4 See, for example, West Yorkshire Metropolitan Council (1977), *Structure plan.*
5 Rowntree M. (1971), 'An introduction to intermediate treatment', *Probation,* Vol. 17, No. 1, pp.18-21
6 Adams R. (1976), *The work of the Pontefract Activity Centre: Annual report to December 1975,* Pontefract Centre, section 1.1.
7 *Ibid.*
8 *Ibid.*
9 Adams R. and Foster K. (1974), *Pontefract Handicraft Club and Activity Centre: Report for year 1974,* Pontefract Centre, p.20.
10 The project leader's thinking was influenced by Schon D.A. (1973), *Beyond the stable state,* New York: Norton.
11 Adams R., *op. cit.,* section 2.2.
12 Adams R. and Foster K., *op. cit.,* p.18.
13 Adams R. (1974), *Workshops: Structures, supports and communications,* Pontefract Centre, unpublished paper.
14 Adams R. (1976), *op. cit.,* section 2.3.
15 Smith C.S. and Adams R., *op. cit.*
16 Matza D. (1969), *Becoming deviant,* Englewood Cliffs, NJ: Prentice-Hall.

COMPARATIVE ISSUES

CHAPTER 10

OBJECTIVES

INTRODUCTION

Each of the projects described in the previous section developed independently of the others. There has been no national prescription as to what should constitute intermediate treatment, and central government guidelines have been broad enough to allow a great variety of practice. In selecting projects for inclusion in this book the editors sought as wide a range of established facilities as possible. In effect, the range was rather more limited, but nevertheless, in terms of basic philosophy and objectives, in organisational structure and in actual practice, the impression is one of considerable diversity.

In this and the following three chapters we examine certain issues that arise out of the case studies or are illustrated by them. These are issues selected by the editors because they highlight aspects of philosophy, policy or practice that we consider important; there is therefore no attempt to discuss all the topics covered in the case studies. On many of these issues, we consider any common ground or convergence between the six projects, but we also point to clear divergences in approach or practice and to areas in which individual projects have been innovative. However, we have not systematically compared all projects on each point, and we have been very cautious about making broader generalisations, given the limited number of projects and the manner of their selection. References to the projects reflect the stated positions of the case study writers.

In handling these comparative chapters, we have inevitably interpreted the material drawn from the case studies according to our own perspectives. In doing so, certain conclusions will inevitably be implied. We have, however, reserved for Chapter 14 our conclusions on certain key issues raised by the case studies.

The purpose of this chapter is to identify the differences in orientation and approach in each of the projects and some of the assumptions made by the case study writers about the children with whom they are working, and the changes which they are attempting to bring about through their work. More specific objectives of the projects will then be considered, grouped under broad headings, but with differences of emphasis and priority noted.

Orientation Towards Delinquents

The orientation of the projects will be reviewed firstly in relation to a continuum which at one end has a preventive focus in work with children who have not been processed as delinquents, and at the other a concentration on work with young offenders on supervision or care orders referred by social work agencies.

At one end of this continuum, the Eastern Ravens Trust places the strongest emphasis on prevention. The project begins to work with children at the age of seven, drawing its membership from certain neighbourhoods in

Stockton rather than from statutory agencies of social control. It provides the security of long-term, small groups which support and stimulate the child's development through crucial phases of his or her life. At the opposite end of the continuum, Tyn-y-Pwll draws its group members entirely from the caseloads of statutory social work agencies. In providing short-term refuge for adolescents, away from the pressures and conflicts of their home environment, the project seeks to provide an opportunity for them to concentrate on their own developmental needs and to become more able to cope with their home environment on their return. The remaining projects appear to fall between the two extremes on this continuum. All of the rest take both adjudicated offenders and children who are considered to be at risk. Pontefract, Chapelfield and Dundee all draw a proportion of their members from the general population they serve, and the rest through referral agencies. Dundee recognises the importance of its self-referred kids in helping to remove the label of 'bad boy's club' (p.142), but also admits that many of them have only escaped the delinquent label through luck.

Apart from Eastern Ravens, Knowles Tooth takes the largest proportion of children at risk, rather than identified delinquents, and in 1977, only one fifth of its referrals were a direct result of court action, although others had previous ·convictions. It emphasises work with children who are experiencing problems within the family or in school, and this emphasis is seen as preventive in relation to the possible breakdown of the family or the exclusion of the child from school — either of which might lead to care proceedings. To that extent, this project is on the preventive end of a continuum concerned more with the need for care, rather than with identified delinquency.

Theoretical Assumptions

Little direct reference is made in the case studies to the ideological positions of the writers or their colleagues, although the reader may draw inferences from the objectives and methods adopted. With ideology classified as conservative, liberal or radical, we may say that none of the writers would happily wear the conservative mantle, most appear to adopt a liberal stance, and a couple — Chapelfield and Pontefract — consciously explored more radical positions.

It was suggested in Chapter 2 that a useful classification of intermediate treatment objectives was between justice, treatment, educational and social change approaches — related, though by no means simply, to the three ideologies above. Here this classification is applied to the overall orientation of each project, and in the subsequent sections to the particular objectives stated.

None of the projects is based totally on the justice approach, though several have elements, considered below, that would fit with this. The treatment approach, which associates delinquency primarily with individual or family pathology, seems to be most evident in the Tyn-y-Pwyll and Knowles Tooth case studies. The staff at Tyn-y-Pwll hope that children will see their problems in a new perspective and, as a result of their involvement, adjust their attitudes and feelings towards certain aspects of their everyday lives. They do not expect to achieve massive personality changes, nor are they in a position directly to affect the environment to which the children will return. They do, however, recognise any positive attributes and try to reinforce these so that the children can survive and flourish despite the handicaps imposed within the family or social environment. The Knowles Tooth project aims to bring about change, not only in the attitude and behaviour of the children, but also in the family. The major focus of the work is therefore twofold: responding to the developmental needs of the children involved, and trying to create a more stable and stimulating family environment.

Eastern Ravens Trust seems to be the best example of the compensatory education approach, emphasising the need for long-term support and stimulation to children and their parents living in a disadvantaged neighbourhood. Dundee is perhaps the most eclectic of the projects in that it adopts a three-pronged approach involving support, education and treatment. The staff are unhappy about the medical connotations of the term 'treatment', but state their own working definition, which involves assessment, setting objectives, directed work and evaluation. They are also conscious of their responsibility to the Children's Panel in particular and society in general in accepting the need for delinquency control. But the predominant tone in the case study is one of social education.

The Chapelfield team based its work from the start on a multi-method approach, including individual counselling, family casework, group work and community work. Its application to the field of delinquency is based on two assumptions, which David Ward, the author of the case study, spells out: first that delinquency is the product of various conditions and forces in the social environment of the children; and secondly that the objectives of the different methods employed are not in conflict with each other. In the evaluation of the project, he casts a very real doubt on this second assumption, by pointing out that a child- or family-centred approach leads towards adaptation to the environmental conditions, which had been identified with delinquency, but that the community work approach seeks to bring about structural changes to that same environment.

Robert Adams also gives attention to this central issue in the Pontefract case study. During the period covered by the study, the project moved away from an individually-based approach, incorporating challenging outdoor pursuits and caring interpersonal relationships, towards neighbourhood-based community work, the aim of which was to enable the members to become involved in projects affecting their own neighbourhood. This change was based on a different perception of 'problem youth' — one which recognises the shortcomings of the environment in which the young people live, and which also underlines how official intervention by law enforcement agencies reinforces the deviant status of the young offender. This approach attempts to remove the negative effects of the 'delinquent' label, by offering opportunities for the young person to enhance his image — in his own eyes, and in the eyes of the community in which he lives.

CLASSIFICATION OF OBJECTIVES
Elements of the Justice Approach

Apart from its overall theoretical orientation, each project states a number of specific objectives, and these deserve more detailed comparison, using the same classification. In Chapter 2, certain roots of intermediate treatment were identified under the 'justice' approach. These may be summarised here as those which emphasise delinquency control, surveillance of leisure time, character building through challenging activities, and reparation through some

253

form of service or repayment to society. This approach views an offence from a moral standpoint, where the appropriate reaction is to punish the offender according to the seriousness of the offence. An associated aim would be to deter the offender from repeating his actions.

While none of the case study writers would regard referral to their project as a punishment, they might well see as one of their aims, perhaps their primary aim, that of preventing a repetition of delinquency. The case studies give varying degrees of emphasis to the task of delinquency control. It is interesting that Pontefract, which had the strongest commitment to social change, also considered that one of its aims was to *promote a reduction of delinquency and truancy.'* (p.215). Chapelfield and Dundee recognise the demands placed on them through their referrals from juvenile court and children's panel respectively to exercise themselves with the task of reducing the amount of delinquent activity of their members. Dave Evans sees the main thrust of the Knowles Tooth effort directed at problems in family, school or neighbourhood which might be contributing to delinquent behaviour. Although Tyn-y-Pwll received the highest proportion of children under social work supervision — though not necessarily for delinquency — less emphasis is placed on delinquency control in the case study, perhaps because of the short-term nature of the work, but also, one senses, because of the strong emphasis placed on the central objectives of care and refuge, which are uneasy bedfellows with delinquency control.

Although control of behaviour within the project does not necessarily reduce the likelihood of committing offences outside, several projects aim to encourage a pattern of self-control by learning from the consequences of anti-social behaviour. Edward Donohue stresses the importance of control as an essential part of the caring relationship between staff and children at Tyn-y-Pwll. The aim is to help the children to monitor the actions of their peers in relation to the standards of behaviour which have been agreed by the group. At Pontefract, the workers were often confronted with the dilemma of either maintaining behavioural boundaries and seeking out those responsible for breaking rules, or adopting an 'appreciative' stance in trying to understand the behaviour. Knowles Tooth groups are encouraged to make their own system of rules within a flexible framework and to discover from experience what is acceptable behaviour to the group and what controls are required. They use group sessions to try to resolve problems which occur, rather than apply arbitrary rules. The intention is to help members understand, from experience, the effect of anti-social behaviour and to achieve a greater degree of self-responsibility for individual behaviour.

Surveillance is a word which does not appear frequently in accounts of intermediate treatment. It involves the supervision of a child's leisure time, on the assumption that delinquency is a response to boredom. In the earlier days of the youth service, keeping youth off the streets was seen as a significant contribution to delinquency prevention. In that all of the projects described occupy and supervise their members for a given number of hours per week, they also remove potential offenders from the arenas in which they are likely to commit crimes. Moreover, some projects try to introduce their members to a range of activities, in the hope that the young person will take one up as an interest and pursue it subsequently in some community group, or indeed on his own. Dundee introduces probably the widest range of activities and the staff regard it as one of their achievements that about half of the participants claimed membership of some club after their involvement in the project, whereas few of them had any such affiliations at the outset; nearly all were pursuing an interest first developed at the project.

Enthusiasm for outdoor pursuits appears to have declined since the early connection which magistrates and social workers made between intermediate treatment and the benefits of fresh air and vigorous, challenging activities. To an extent, this is reflected in the case studies. Tyn-y-Pwll, close to the Welsh mountains, plays down the importance of outdoor pursuits and is more concerned with providing a positive group living experience. Pontefract demonstrated its shift of emphasis from an activity-oriented centre to one more concerned with social change, by reducing its regular weekends in the Yorkshire hills and replacing the outdoor pursuits specialist with a community worker. In spite of this fairly general trend, many projects, including most of those represented here, continue to use outdoor pursuits, albeit in a modified form. Perhaps this is not because they have any inherent value, but because, as David Ward indicates in relation to Chapelfield, they provide a useful vehicle for developing relationships within the group.

Another reaction to crime is that which requires or encourages the offender to make appropriate amends or reparation for his wrongdoing. The development of community service by offenders has been welcomed not only by conservatives who adopt this view, but by those who recognise the positive attributes of the offender and the opportunity to play a different and non-deviant role in society. Norman Alm states that the Dundee community service programme provides *'an ideal way to boost self-esteem and give expression to the positive, creative side of a youngster.'* (p.146). The youngsters involved see themselves as an *'action squad'* with a reputation of providing a speedy and valued service. Each of these perceptions seems to be based as much on philanthropic as on reparative motives. The quality of the work carried out, and therefore any improvement in the credit balance between the young person and the community, might be enhanced if there is a voluntary, rather than an enforced commitment to the task. The Pontefract project used two forms of community service. Insofar as other people are seen as the beneficiaries, the rationale would be either philanthropic or reparative, depending on the motivation of the participants. In the other form, which was focused on the neighbourhood in which the young people lived, the motivating force is one of self-help, in that those carrying out the service hope to benefit directly themselves, their families and their neighbours.

Treatment Approach

Intermediate treatment has inherited from a century's experience of working with young offenders the assumption that delinquent behaviour is pathological. Even where a project establishes a very different view of delinquency, children may be referred to it by social workers who expect some form of treatment to be provided in response to the needs which they have identified. Prominent in the treatment approach is a concern for improving personal relationships, on the assumption that these have been problematic in the past and need to be changed. Several objectives in the case studies are about improving personal relationships with adults and with other children; usually these originate from a treatment perspective, though some may partly reflect a social education approach to personal growth and maturation.

Edward Donohue stresses the value of mutual trust and open communication between children and adults at Tyn-y-Pwll. This is especially important for children from broken and unstable families, where the child is seeking to regain confidence and security in relationships with adults. The constant availability of staff, and the sharing of the same rules and living conditions are directed towards achieving such a relationship. The volunteer leaders at Eastern Ravens Trust have a much longer period of time in which to establish relationships with their group members, although the contact is less intensive; the dependence and security of this relationship are regarded as a key element of the Eastern Ravens approach. While Norman Alm at Dundee stresses the importance of security and acceptance, he also adds the importance of the mutual enjoyment of relationships with the members through shared company and activities. The ability of a staff member or volunteer to relate warmly and become involved with members is regarded as a more important attribute than a cool, detached interest in the problem. David Ward examines the way in which group members used the relationship with the Chapelfield staff in different ways, for instance to relive experiences of relationships with other adults, to test out sex roles and authority, and as the project developed, to achieve certain personal objectives or specific skills through contact with staff members. This range of objectives involving adult-child relationships is directed at three ends: maintaining membership through friendship rather than coercion; compensating for defective or weak adult relationships; and giving opportunities for exploring appropriate adult role models.

The Knowles Tooth project aims to help children develop and explore the way in which they relate to their peers. It provides many opportunities for this testing of relationships through residential weekends and group sessions. The Dundee group discussions are also seen as a safe place in which to explore relationships and new patterns of behaviour which are more conducive to maintaining rather than destroying relationships. By keeping group membership stable over a long period of time, the Eastern Ravens leaders are concerned to provide a security of relationships with peers as well as adults.

As several projects point out, it cannot be assumed that improvement in relationships within the protective environment of the project will automatically lead to better relationships outside. At Eastern Ravens the group members are all drawn from the same neighbourhood, and so the impact of membership on external relationships and behaviour is likely to be greater than in a group whose existence is related only to the project. In other cases opportunities have to be created to test and evaluate the improvement in external relationships. Knowles Tooth attempts to do this by bringing members into contact with others in the community in a way which allows staff to monitor progress and problems. The Pontefract project made demands on members to handle new adult relationships in its activities, some of which required members to work alongside adults in the community to achieve the objective of environmental improvement. The Chapelfield leaders used the contact between their group members and other youths as opportunities for learning. An example of this was the discussion that followed a confrontation with local youths on a visit to a youth club during a summer camp. Those projects which create opportunities for a range of contacts with the community have a better chance of monitoring relationships between their members and external adults and peers.

Many of the objectives of group work fall within the realm of a treatment philosophy, although others may be more appropriate to a social education or social change approach. Knowles Tooth, for example, aims to share responsibility for resolving conflict and other problems, such as stealing, through group sessions, called in speedy response to the occurrence of a problem. Tyn-y-Pwll uses group sessions to express hostility, when this appears to be about to erupt. The leaders attempt to create a climate in which attitudes and feelings can be expressed, even when these are antagonistic to the adults. Where conflict has arisen between a member and a leader, this is also discussed in the group, and an attempt is often made to relate this to the child's home or school experience. At Dundee, group members are encouraged and feel free to evaluate the progress of their fellow members and to relate this both to their behaviour in the centre and to external problems shared by members within the group.

Social Education Approach

Social education emphasises the normal process of maturation through adolescence. This is most clearly stated by Dave Evans in identifying the role of the Knowles Tooth workers in *'helping children grow through the difficult period of adolescence in the most constructive way possible.'* (p.130). He recognises the need to develop an ability to relate to a variety of adult figures, and to gain specific social skills in handling these relationships. The developmental needs of children referred to Knowles Tooth are seen as no different from those of other adolescents, although the obstacles to meeting them may be more difficult to overcome because of the lack of support, security or stimulus in the child's particular environment.

Perceiving the whole child and attempting to see the world from the child's perspective are important starting points in adopting a developmental approach. This seems to be the basis of the educational strategy identified in the Dundee case study as a way of opening up possibilities for more appropriate ways of behaving. This is further spelt out in one of the specific aims of their group work, *'encouraging different ways of interacting which are less damaging to himself and others.'* (p.143). The emphasis is on eradicating negative behaviour, but the assumption seems to be that this can best be done by finding new, more constructive ways of interacting.

Several other objectives stated in the case studies seem to fit a social education philosophy. For instance, most of the projects introduce activities in order to broaden the horizons of the members and give them the opportunity to develop particular interests in the community once their involvement with the project is completed. Thus Knowles Tooth aims to *'cultivate the children's skills, abilities and interests in shared activities and tasks.'* (p.116). David Ward regards activities at Chapelfield both as a vehicle to open up communication with adults, and as a means of providing new interests, an outlet for energy and aggression and alternative opportunities for achievement. The connection between success in activities, whether individual or collective, and increased self-confidence is stressed in several of the case studies.

Most intermediate treatment projects also involve their members in planning the programme and in other decisions affecting the life of the group. The intention behind this is to increase the responsibility of the members for the development of the project, and to give them some experience, however limited, of using power in the decision making process. The Pontefract staff tried to erode the 'we know what's best for you' syndrome, which is common to both an authoritarian and a treatment approach, by involving their members in planning, at a rather more fundamental level than deciding between two alternative activities. Thus, for instance, the demands of the Redpath group led to a day programme for unemployed youth being run in 1975 and 1976. Members were also involved in decisions about the type of community action project in which they should become involved. One of the aims of the Chapelfield staff was to create a democratic decision making process between adults and members, so that members would not be able to blame others for failure or disappointment. Such a process allowed the members to question the authority of adults and also to take the initiative in calling meetings, either to resolve difficulties or to promote new developments in the project. These attempts at power sharing are also recognised as valuable opportunities to develop skill and experience in preparation for decision making outside the life of the project. The limitations and external constraints on the democratic process within the project also parallel the constraints placed on the individual in relation to social institutions in the wider community.

Compensatory Approach

The compensatory philosophy does not emerge too clearly in the objectives of the projects, except Eastern Ravens Trust, which in 1969 stated that its first objective was to *'help children from deprived and potentially delinquent homes'* (p.87) in certain areas of Stockton. A further aim, stated boldly, was to *'break the recurring cycle of deprivation.'* (p.87). The emphasis is similar to the ideal prescribed for 'educational priority areas' by the Plowden Report and for the 'Headstart' programmes in the United States, namely to compensate children for the disadvantages of a deprived neighbourhood by providing additional resources. Because of the neighbourhoods and families from which their members are drawn and the types of programmes operated, some of the other projects such as Dundee and Chapelfield also apply principles of positive discrimination in their work. One of the obstacles to open expression of this approach in relation to work with offenders is the opposition of many significant adults, such as teachers, magistrates, police and often parents, to giving special priority to children who have committed offences over their 'non-delinquent' peers or siblings.

Eastern Ravens is concerned to compensate for emotional, as well as social or economic deprivation, and this view of compensation is also evident in the Knowles Tooth and Tyn-y-Pwll case studies. These projects are especially concerned with children from unstable or broken families. The primary objective of Knowles Tooth is *'to bring about change, not only in the attitude and behaviour of the children, but also in the family environment in which the children are developing.'* (p.116). It attempts to do this by regular home visits and family casework, and also by helping the child, through his relationship with the project staff and experience during the residential weekend, to cope more effectively with the pressures and conflicts of his home environment. This is expressed in rather different terms by Tyn-y-Pwll, which seeks to provide a period of respite from the pressures of home and an opportunity for children to see their problems in a new perspective and to return home strengthened in their survival skills.

From the consumer reaction studies undertaken by some projects, the sense of enjoyment and attachment to the project are two of the benefits seen by participants. It is difficult for projects drawing their membership and their resources from social control agencies to state explicitly the aim of keeping children happy or providing them with memorable experiences in childhood. If, however, the children had been referred because of mental or physical handicap, or because their homes had been disrupted, no doubt these would be acceptable and explicit aims. This discrepancy seems to be an indication of society's demand that offenders must be punished or controlled and of the assumption that the latter aims are incompatible with enjoyable, memorable activities.

Social Change Approach

Of the four major approaches, this has the least impact at the present time on work with problem youth. Although several of the projects are clearly aware of the social and economic conditions which play a significant part in the delinquency of their members, few attempt to bring about change specifically directed at the improvement of those conditions. The Pontefract staff recognised the effects of structural disadvantages on delinquency, and the powerful impact of labelling offenders through official intervention. The search for neighbourhood based projects was motivated both by the possibility of some immediate improvement in the environment and by the desire to demonstrate that changes can be brought about by those who had previously regarded themselves as powerless. At the same time, successful change efforts would increase the self-confidence of the agents of change, in this case labelled delinquents, and so offset the damaging impact of that negative image. The Pontefract case study includes several objectives in relation to its social change philosophy. In its 1975 statement of aims, the project intended *'to enable them* (children and families) *to develop collective solutions to problems in their neighbourhood.'* (p.215). This required the staff to become involved in various community based projects, with the ultimate aim of helping the young people to share with other community members in efforts to improve their common environment.

Although no other project is so clearly directed towards social change, several are aware of the importance of achieving change in the community. The Eastern Ravens Trust is concerned to raise the competence and confidence level of the estate dwellers, many of whose problems are associated with a very poor self-image. The workers attempt to do this not only by helping to prepare their members for adulthood, but also by involving parents and other community members in participation and leadership of the organisation. One of the conclusions of the case study is that through the use of volunteers, several of them former group members, and others drawn from the local community, *'a significant contribution is being made to the integrity of the community as a whole.'* (p.113).

Part of the basic philosophy of the Chapelfield Project was that *'the local community should be encouraged to accept responsibility for the existence and prevention of delinquency in its midst.'* (p.193). This, many practitioners have found, is a very difficult task, and runs counter to the prevalent tendency to ostracise the deviant members of a community. The Chapelfield team found the task beset by many obstacles, but with the assistance of a community work student, this part of their work was directed mainly towards the specific goal of developing a youth club in the community, which could accommodate not only the project members but other young people who had been excluded from the project.

Social change effort can also be directed at the systems and agencies concerned with handling offenders, such as the courts, the police and social work agencies. Although several projects had to negotiate with their agencies to achieve certain changes of procedure to accommodate their plans, only the Chapelfield staff set out with this as a specific objective. They recognised that both of the parent agencies, Social Services and Probation, were accustomed to dealing with young offenders through individual and family casework. The system of referral and accountability assumed that the work would be undertaken on a one worker-one child-one family basis. In adopting a planned multi-method approach, drawing staff and resources from both agencies, the project realised from the outset that changes would be required in agency procedures.

The case study writers are rather cautious about offering their projects as an alternative to residential care, although this has been recognised as desirable in statements of social policy at national and local level. For this to become a reality, further resources would need to be directed into community based programmes, and influence brought to bear on the policy of the juvenile courts and of the professional social workers who control the flow of referrals. Where a court is faced with a young person who returns at frequent intervals and with whom other means of intervention have failed, there may seem to be no alternative to incarceration, especially where public tolerance of the offending has been strained to the limit. In these circumstances, intermediate treatment could be seen as an alternative to incarceration, if the courts, agencies and the public have sufficient confidence in the community based services available.

In the light of the origins of intermediate treatment and its ties both with the courts and social work agencies, which tend to adopt either a justice or a 'treatment' approach to delinquency, it is perhaps more surprising that projects should be thinking of putting social change theory into practice than that the attempts have not so far penetrated our social institutions very deeply.

CONCLUSION

When the objectives and practice of the projects are compared, there is a greater degree of consensus than one would expect given the ideological positions of the workers. The liberal tradition is a powerful one, both in the training of personnel and in the structure and procedures of the agencies involved. While the case studies embrace a considerable range of approaches, the major thrust of most of the projects seems to be within the liberal tradition, whether this is more attuned to the treatment model or to a social education approach. Nevertheless, some projects have made planned and recorded efforts to develop or shift their practice towards a social change approach, in accordance with their understanding of the nature of the problem of delinquency and the appropriate response to it. In order to do so, objectives have to be clearly expressed and agreed, and a structure and plan then worked out to implement them. Such a planned process of change is difficult to achieve, given organisational constraints and the varied demands and expectations of those who control the supply of funds and referrals. To these issues we now turn.

CHAPTER 11
ORGANISATION
INTRODUCTION

Over the years, practitioners have become increasingly aware of the way in which environmental factors have influenced the young people with whom they are dealing; but, human nature being what it is, they usually find it much more difficult to recognise the way in which organisational issues affect themselves and their work. The interaction between values, organisation and practice is complex . When practice does not seem to flow logically from expressed values and defined objectives, one of three factors may be responsible: either the practitioner lacks skill; or the values and objectives are not being genuinely held or pursued; or else their attainment is being obstructed by organisational constraints beyond the control of the workers and, in some cases, the managers as well. This chapter considers some of the issues raised by the case studies about the organisational environment of intermediate treatment projects, their internal structures and their resources, and the ways in which these interact with the particular values that characterise much intermediate treatment.

Project Autonomy

The six case study projects are at first sight quite diverse in organisational terms. Tyn-y-Pwll and Eastern Ravens Trust constitute independent voluntary agencies with their own management committees; Pontefract and Knowles Tooth are both parts of much larger voluntary agencies; the Dundee Children's Centres and the Chapelfield project are run directly by statutory agencies — the latter jointly by Social Services and Probation. These features might suggest corresponding differences in the autonomy enjoyed by each project, but other forces may override these distinctions. In particular, there is the influence of those who ultimately control the funds and the referral of clients, and there are the claims of the workers for professional autonomy vis-a-vis their managers.

One of the most striking things to emerge from the case studies is the strong desire for professional autonomy, together with the equally strong need for the project to be better understood and supported by its own parent agency or by other agencies on which it is directly or indirectly dependent for referrals. Intermediate treatment workers have clearly developed definite aspirations towards professional autonomy and the right to make decisions through the exercise of professional judgement. Yet this is an area of work where such tendencies might least be expected, since the usual conditions for them to flourish are surely lacking, namely a well developed knowledge base, and a set of values and principles to guide practice which are agreed and shared by all members of the profession.

Indeed the traditions and structures of local government do not sit comfortably with professional autonomy in any field, and the controlling mechanisms normally operated by hierarchic organisations usually have a chain reaction, ending up with the client or consumer of the service provided. It may well be that this provides at least one of the clues. If, as in intermediate treatment, workers want to provide more freedom and choice for the young people involved, this can usually be achieved only if the workers sacrifice some of their own power and limited room for manoeuvre. In some cases, this may account for the workers then demanding more space from their own management, in compensation for that surrendered to the clients.

Norman Alm makes the bold assertion that *'the success of our work very fundamentally depends on our autonomy and flexibility'*, but he is very aware that *'autonomy and accountability, flexibility and departmental uniformity, are awkward pairings.'* (p.152). The Dundee project illustrates the way in which a place of work, once it has moved beyond the initial, sensitive experimental phase, can be absorbed into the structure of accountability applied to other aspects of the department's work. Admittedly local government reorganisation is an additional factor in this case, with the net effect that Norman Alm, originally responsible directly to the Deputy Director, finds that there are three people placed over the project in the chain of responsibility within the division alone. David Ward describes a situation in which the workers, whether by design or by default, secured a very large measure of professional autonomy. Unfortunately this did not go hand in hand with administrative autonomy and consequently proved to be something of a Pyrrhic victory, with workers becoming increasingly frustrated by an organisation which apparently did not understand what they were doing, but on which they were dependent for resources. Almost by definition, the Chapelfield project represented a criticism of the way the two parent agencies were currently dealing with young offenders. It was intended to establish a democratic decision making process, in what the workers perceived as a telling contradistinction to the hierarchic organisations to which they belonged. It is not difficult to imagine that some insecure managers would find themselves uncomfortable with this peculiar new manifestation or even see it as a direct challenge to their authority.

Knowles Tooth provides an example of a partnership between voluntary and statutory agencies, since, although the actual centre is owned by the Chichester Diocesan Association for Family Social Work, both East and West Sussex County Councils are represented on the management committee in recognition of the fact that they provide 80% of the current expenditure. Apparently the management committee concentrates on overall policy and financial matters, and allows the staff a considerable degree of autonomy as far as the actual operation of the project is concerned, and no mention is made of any supervision or advice being offered. One of the essential differences between Knowles Tooth and Chapelfield is that the former was set up on the initiative of senior management and with the consent of those holding the purse strings. Nonetheless, in one important respect, the professional autonomy of the project staff was more apparent than real. Theoretically the power to accept or reject referrals was vested in them; but they could only accept from among the referrals which statutory social workers, with their different expectations, chose to make, and there was a limit to the number they could reject, particularly when the two local authorities involved were paying for a specified number of places.

Management at Eastern Ravens Trust

Eastern Ravens started very much as a result of a piece of private enterprise; but Roger Bradshaw recognised the need for support and set up a small informal committee. However, in the early days, the real power lay with the voluntary leaders on the co-operative principle that the twin roles of management and operation should be vested in the same individuals. As the work developed, the committee acquired new members, became more formal, and concentrated on fund raising, controlling expenditure and negotiating with the local authority for grant aid and the appointment of a full time leader. It is worth rehearsing the main features of this candid account, simply because the shifting fortunes of the various groups involved and the struggle to find an effective and acceptable way of managing and operating the project illustrate so well the issues at stake.

With the diversification and further expansion of the project, its identity changed and confusion resulted. The response was to set up a working party, with representatives from the management committee and from the group of voluntary leaders. Although this group apparently clarified the aims and increased the sense of well-being, it endorsed the diversification by assuming that everything being done was appropriate, and consequently failed to resolve what was later to be recognised as a basic conflict. Following this report, the committee was further expanded and proved very effective in raising money; but it wanted the money spent differently, with higher material standards, and once again found itself in conflict with the voluntary leaders. This difference of opinion was exacerbated by the fact that the full time leader concentrated on wider community issues, for which he had been deliberately chosen, but which the leaders of small groups found irrelevant. The committee attempted to resolve the matter by co-option, but the leaders of both small groups and of other activities found this more threatening than the differences between themselves. This problem, made worse by a serious financial crisis, led the trustees to intervene, relieve the management committee of its responsibilities and recall the pioneer, Roger Bradshaw, to assess the situation. The solution — 'final' would probably not even be claimed by its architects — was for the trustees to form the new management committee, inviting a voluntary leader to join them as Chairman. The functions of management and leadership are separated, with the vast majority of the leaders, apparently at their own request, not involved in making policy decisions. At the moment, the management committee consists of four former voluntary leaders, including the present full time worker, plus six other representatives drawn from the community and local authority.

Tyn-y-Pwll is a small charity, where the project leader is also the Chairman of the management committee. It enjoys a large measure of professional autonomy, but this position has not been achieved without cost. The viability of the project, and consequently the freedom of the workers to determine its actual operation, has been entirely dependent upon its capacity to attract sufficient referrals. The willingness of the staff to work in the unpopular field of difficult adolescent girls probably did more than anything else to ensure this autonomy. It is interesting that the two small charities, Tyn-y-Pwll and Eastern Ravens, should have developed such similar structures, even if they came to them by very different routes. Eastern Ravens Trust is much more dependent on grants in aid and consequently has local government representation; but both committees have a very significant block of either existing or past workers, and this probably helps ensure that the committee does not get out of touch with the workers or run the risk of developing different objectives from them.

The organisational permutations seem endless, and Pontefract is different again, starting life as a small voluntary body and then becoming part of a large national charity. The transition was not without pain, and Robert Adams suggests that initially, at least, the project did not sit very comfortably with all the other jewels in the Barnardo's crown. Being part of a larger organisation does impose constraints simply because the impression created by one project can reflect well or badly on the whole organisation. In distributing power, a large organisation must take care lest the objectives of a particular project conflict with those of the parent organisation, and this is illustrated by Barnardo's refusal to allow the local advisory committee any real power. Moreover, large organisations are bound to be less flexible, since they develop systems to make the job of management possible. So Barnardo's should be given credit for its flexibility in modifying its national policy in order to allow fund raising for a local project. This was an important concession since it is difficult enough to persuade demoralised people that they do have a latent pride in their own community, and quite unrealistic to expect them to have any loyalty to a national organisation. For a variety of reasons, including distance from divisional office, the workers seem to have been allowed a fair degree of autonomy.

Liaison with Other Professional Workers

It is often claimed, perhaps unfairly, that social workers and their clients are insatiable devourers of resources, and that, however weak the evidence of need, facilities have only to be provided for them to be oversubscribed. Few inter-mediate treatment projects that rely upon referrals have been afflicted with this problem. Most social work still depends upon the relationship made with the client, so it should not be surprising if some social workers who could make referrals fail to be convinced that a different method of work will have anything to offer their clients, or if others do not want to risk the discovery that it is more effective than their casework. It may also be that hard pressed social workers are influenced by more mundane considerations, such as whether taking up a place for their client will involve them in more or less work.

The explanation is probably less important than the fact, already apparent through the case studies, that autonomy is linked very closely with the number of referrals. The claim to autonomy has a rather hollow ring if, through lack of clients, the workers have no justification for their existence, and staff are usually only too well aware that a manager can undermine any project simply by influencing the number of referrals. The net result is that project staff, if they are not in a position to recruit directly the young people with whom they work, find themselves making considerable efforts to improve the understanding of referring agencies and to increase the number of referrals. In this way they hope to ensure that the project remains viable and that they have a greater opportunity to exercise professional judgement by selecting those whom they feel will benefit most from the programme they have to offer.

The nature of the Knowles Tooth project means that it is dependent on referrals from statutory social workers, and, although it may have contributed to the misunderstanding by being 'deliberately vague' over selection criteria, it obviously had some difficulty in establishing credibility and good liaison with social services. While the project staff did have a central role with many clients and had definite aspirations towards becoming the key workers in relation to all the young people involved in their programme, some of the referring social workers preferred to see the project staff as an additional resource rather than colleagues involved in a joint endeavour. This attitude is illustrated most obviously when a young person involved in the project is placed in residential care, without the staff being informed, much less consulted. In an effort to improve the situation, the workers decided to give each member of the team responsibility for liaison with one or more areas. This strategy, combined with the appointment of a worker who had previously been employed in one of the referring areas, probably helped to overcome the suspicion and mistrust which are frequently experienced by voluntary bodies, particularly in the early stages. However there is a sense in which the only reason for good liaison is to generate referrals, because, although the project apparently welcomes social workers at its residential weekends, it is actually felt that *'it works better when the Knowles Tooth worker is, in most cases, the central social work figure in the life of the child and the family'.*(p.133).

The Chapelfield approach reduces the likelihood of conflict or competition between the child's social worker and the intermediate treatment practitioner, simply because in many cases these were one and the same person. However, experimental work of this kind can only be undertaken if colleagues are prepared to undertake an increased share of the traditional workload. Reference is made to the Area Director bringing pressure to bear on social workers to do additional work outside the project, and, although this may not have been done at the behest of colleagues, it does not appear to have aroused their active opposition. Interestingly enough, far from the project staff wanting to arrogate unto themselves all the social work involved, David Ward alludes to the possible confusion caused by family therapy and intermediate treatment being carried out by the same person, and indicates the advantages of conjoint therapy where resources allow.

Although Dundee claims to enjoy very good relations with area social workers and goes to considerable lengths to foster them, including the mounting of joint projects, it is clear that the staff had to fight for full recognition of their role. For instance it is mentioned in passing that it became established that project staff would provide reports for hearings in addition to those prepared by the young person's own area social worker. Later Norman Alm suggests that the project staff sometimes have more contact, and a better relationship with families than the area social workers. He attributes this to the nature of the work and the fact that they have in some small measure shared the experience of living with their children. In view of the very wide catchment area served by Tyn-y-Pwll, liaison presents special problems, and reference is made to the way in which some social workers mislead the centre about the child, and the child about the demands that will be made of her. Edward Donohue indicates that the strenuous efforts made to overcome the problem of distance by allocating one member of staff to act as liaison officer, maintaining contact with children, their families and social workers after the course is over, are not always welcomed. *'This, in itself, has created difficulties, as some social workers have tended to see residential courses as totally separate from their own work with the child and family.'* (p.62).

Pontefract does not mention any such difficulties, dwelling instead on the conflicts within the inter disciplinary staff team as it struggled with the problems of change. However Robert Adams does refer to the practice of involving the child's social worker in the initial interview so that all three parties are clearer about the provision being offered and the expectations demanded. He also mentions that the social services department had not at that time established any procedure for regular joint reviews of children attending the Club, and that this was initiated by the project staff, although he admits it often took a rather rudimentary form. Eastern Ravens appears to have been the project where the interface between the staff and area social workers was the most trouble free, largely perhaps because it does not often exist. The Trust appears to do most of its own recruiting, and since most of the children are very young, there is much less likelihood of statutory involvement. It may also be that with all the leaders being voluntary, the burden of liaison falls upon the one full time worker. In this connection it is interesting that the survey, extended to cover social workers, asked about the benefit to the child rather than about the desirability of sharing information and working together more closely. Nonetheless one occasion is mentioned, when the Trust was less sure of its direction, where one youngster, who was attending three separate groups, was being visited by three different leaders with different styles and aims. The probation officer is described as reacting very strongly to a practice which was making his own job infinitely more difficult.

Physical Resources

With intermediate treatment, the focus is normally placed on the relationship, and it it very easy to underestimate the part played by premises and equipment; but most of the case studies confirm the significant effect which the meeting places used can have on the work undertaken and the sense of cohesiveness which it is possible to engender in the group of young people involved. Chapelfield was concerned that the premises should not be associated with institutions of authority such as school, church or local government. With experience the staff discovered that the hall chosen, initially thought ideal, was in fact highly inappropriate in that the building was situated in a quiet street of owner occupied houses, from which none of the children came, and which was shared by a number of respectable and sedentary adult organisations. For the residential weekends, considerable efforts were made to secure the exclusive use of the premises chosen. Admittedly the invasion by other young people not allowed to join raises issues for all exclusive groups, but it also underlines how important it is for many adolescents to have the security, at least for a period, of belonging to an exclusive group, and having a place of their own.

This conclusion is reinforced by the Pontefract experience, in which Robert Adams suggests that the main attraction, if not the viability, of the workshops could be ascribed to the fact that other young people were denied access. The rivalry between the Redpath and Tipstone boys was often expressed either in a desire to have exclusive use of the premises or in challenging the right of any other group to such exclusive use. Indeed this rivalry became so intense that the only way the staff found of coping was to have most of the meetings of the Tipstone boys away from the club, thus colluding with or acknowledging the territorial victory won by the stronger group. Pontefract had the advantage of owning its own premises, and this meant that the staff were in a position to allow the young people to stamp the club with their own character and culture. At the same time it could be argued that the existence of one central building was an obstacle to the community based approach which the staff were trying to promote. Eastern Ravens also experienced, in a rather less dramatic form, a similar kind of rivalry between older and younger groups using the same premises. With their concept of boundary management, the leaders have become convinced that it is essential for every group to have exclusive use of its premises, at least during the period that it is meeting, and the Trust has gone to considerable lengths and used all its ingenuity to find a variety of meeting places that are never more than half a mile distant from those who use them.

In Dundee, finding suitable premises proved to be a major problem. However, having once experienced the advantages of a comparatively small building, Rowans Cottage, the staff became disenchanted with the original idea of finding a single, all purpose activity centre, and opted for two separate small centres. Although the staff were worried about the location of the Ferry Road centre and the difficult journey with which many of the youngsters would be faced, this does not, in the event, appear to have proved much of a problem for the young people. However it did create a management problem and meant that the two members of staff working at each centre were very dependent upon each other. The location of Knowles Tooth probably had even more important implications for the project. As the staff increased their liaison work and recognised the virtues of a more community based approach, they found the geographical position of the centre and the time it absorbed a very real constraint. Nonetheless, on balance, they considered the residential component, which the centre made possible, the cornerstone of the project upon which all the other aspects depended. As for Tyn-y-Pwll, the location did not apparently affect the work detrimentally once the children reached it; but it did make liaison difficult and community based work impossible. The fact that the centre has been sold and the proceeds used to establish another one nearer to the user authorities speaks for itself.

Financial Resources

In the last analysis, the main control exercised over any project is the financial one. Traditionally it is usually claimed that voluntary bodies experience greater difficulty in obtaining resources than their statutory counterparts, but enjoy more freedom in other ways, such as the capacity to innovate and be flexible. It is also worth considering whether there is an inverse relationship between the amount of funds provided and the degree of freedom or autonomy which the staff have in spending it. It would certainly seem reasonable for management to devote most of its time to those aspects of the agency's work which absorb the greater part of the available resources.

Certainly Tyn-y-Pwll, with its very large measure of autonomy, suffered from the financial insecurity often associated with small charities. Indeed the project appears to have owed its survival to a generous bank manager and the willingness of the staff to work for considerably less than they could have commanded elsewhere. It also proved vulnerable to exploitation by local authorities, which cajoled and pressurised the project to take very difficult children with promises of additional finance which were never honoured. At Eastern Ravens, the other small charity, Roger Bradshaw was sustained in the early days by friends and jumble sales organised by parents, and it had its fair share of financial crises in subsequent years before reaching the comparative equilibrium enjoyed today. The staff at Knowles Tooth feel they have fared reasonably well considering the economic climate; but Dave Evans describes a situation in which they needed to raise money for equipment through their own efforts and those of the children. Whether this is an advantage or disadvantage is another issue, but it does indicate a resource situation which is not commonly experienced by those working in statutory agency projects. Pontefract, under the umbrella of a large national charity, actually expanded very considerably during the period described. Nevertheless, Robert Adams refers to the acute anxiety which the staff experienced every year, as they expanded whilst all around them other projects were being contracted.

In his account of the project in Dundee, Norman Alm demonstrates that the fact that a project is funded by a local government department offers no guarantee of financial security. Indeed the whole venture is nearly destroyed when its budget is slashed, apparently because its unorthodox role, combined with the ignorance of those with power in the organisation, means that it is categorised as a recreational facility. It is a somewhat surprising turn of events, given that the setting up of the project was an agency decision taken at the highest possible level, and that the project leader was directly responsible to the Deputy Director in the initial stages. The only explanation is that all parties concerned underestimated the effect of regionalisation, and insufficient effort was taken to acquaint the new line managers with the purpose and objectives of the project. In some ways it is easier to understand the way finance was used as a weapon in the Chapelfield project. David Ward describes a situation in which the project and workers involved not only came to represent a contra culture, but also demanded an increasing proportion of the area's resources. The power struggle is a fascinating one in which the intermediate treatment practitioners win the battle rather than the war. They manage to circumvent the Area Director and obtain higher authority for the release of the funds allocated to them, but increasing pressure is brought to bear on workers to take what the Area Director would no doubt have termed a fairer share of the traditional workload.

Staff Roles and Staff Development

Intermediate treatment represents not so much a method of working with young people as an attitude towards them. There are many strands in this attitude, but it commonly includes a determination to reduce distance between workers and clients and to create a climate in which it is possible for young people to participate in the course and direction of their growth or rehabilitation. Sometimes this causes difficulties. Most of the case studies reveal a conscious effort to devise internal structures within the project which would assist in the achievement of these goals, and some of them were intended to be radically different from the hierarchic organisations from which staff accepted referrals or for which they worked. To the extent that intermediate treatment practitioners are critical of the current strategies for dealing with young people and anxious to demonstrate the practicability of a more democratic system than that prevailing in their own agency, it is not difficult to understand why they are so reluctant to accept supervision by what they perceive as an antipathetic organisation.

Traditionally workers have structured their relationships with clients and used distancing techniques to survive the onslaught which troubled and difficult children have frequently made upon them. Paradoxically the abandonment of some of these defence mechanisms in order to establish more honest, egalitarian and reciprocal relationships actually makes managerial support more, rather than less, relevant. It hardly needs mentioning, but very few social workers, youth workers or teachers are equipped either by training or experience to undertake the kind of intermediate treatment described in the case studies. The laissez faire approach adopted by many managers, combined with the naïvety of some practitioners, surely accounts in large measure for the alarmingly high proportion of enthusiastic workers burning themselves out in two years or less. Obviously some managers can lack imagination and sensitivity and place administrative convenience before the needs of both clients and workers. However there is a high price to be paid for freezing managers out, because the political reality is that, if practitioners genuinely want intermediate treatment to be taken more seriously and to become an essential part of mainstream social work, youth work and teaching, they will have first to gain managerial interest, support and commitment.

Although it is rarely made explicit in the case studies, the demands made upon many intermediate treatment practitioners are very heavy. For instance the staff involvement at Tyn-y-Pwll could hardly be more total in that all the workers remain on duty throughout the period of the course on the grounds that it would be less than fair to offer a smaller commitment than they are demanding of the young people involved. Many projects either cannot afford auxillary staff or eschew them for therapeutic reasons. Norman Alm points out that this means that a worker can be involved in everything from preparing estimates to mopping out the kitchen. This reduces institutional features and makes it easier for participants to see the human being behind the role. It also increases anxiety by demanding rapid changes of role and removing the structure of coffee breaks and routine which auxiliary staff provide. He quotes a worker's description of this situation: *'When you put your key in the door each morning, it's like starting the project from scratch. Like if you stop thinking about it the whole lot would disappear.'* (p.148). Robert Adams in Pontefract describes some of the inevitable tensions which arise when you bring together in one team staff from different disciplines, shaped by different basic training and used to different methods of working. David Ward describes the Chapelfield staff taking no privileges in connection with sleeping arrangements, food or time off. This shared living does help to break down barriers between adults and children, but it also makes unusual demands. The group meetings described in the Knowles Tooth project demonstrate that involving children in decision making and self regulation is very exhausting, particularly when the children concerned are not used to, and do not actively seek, participation and the implied responsibility which goes with it.

It is not only children who find the sight of authority figures endeavouring to be egalitarian, initially at least, rather bizarre and confusing. Workers, whatever their theoretical beliefs, are also usually accustomed to structure, and often find the democratic approach difficult to handle in relation to both colleagues and children. Knowles Tooth seems to have the most traditional structure with a Director and Deputy Director. Both Pontefract and Tyn-y-Pwll have a recognised leader, but there is no differentiation made between the other staff, with interchangeable roles in the case of Tyn-y-Pwll, and there is a more diffident acknowledgement by both of the authority vested in the project leader. In the Dundee project, Norman Alm's situation was much more ambiguous. This was partly as a result of the staff team's determination to give every individual worker space to develop and initiate within the framework of a shared philosophy. Ironically, although the workers come to recognise the need for one of their number to be acknowledged as the official co-ordinator and regarded accordingly, the department refuses to grant this request. The unity of the team is placed under further pressure by the fact that the two centres operate almost as separate, autonomous units. A serious personality clash between two members of staff, unresolved by numerous staff meetings, taken together with other factors, leads Norman Alm to the conclusion that an unacceptably high price has been paid for the absence of a definite hierarchy. However, the absence of a hierarchy is no guarantee that power will be shared, as Chapelfield demonstrates, where a female worker is described as assuming a dominant leadership role in one of the groups and contributing to the departure of three workers in rapid succession.

In spite of the pressures experienced and difficulties described, there is little reference to staff support or development, except for its absence. Significantly, perhaps because of its almost total dependence on volunteers, Eastern Ravens appears to have devised the most comprehensive pattern of support, with a system of apprenticeship, regular supervision sessions and a continuous training programme. In the Chapelfield project, although records of work undertaken and minutes of meetings held were formally sent to the Area Director, neither of the sponsoring agencies had a supervisory or consultative role, seemingly because the project involved workers from two agencies and represented an unfamiliar method of working. At the outset, the staff recognised that adopting a multi-method approach, of which none of them had much experience, would place considerable strains upon them, and make the need for support even more important than usual. However, they came to the conclusion that there would be nobody within the organisations involved either capable or willing to offer the appropriate level of supervision. Nonetheless, with hindsight, David Ward is convinced that if the staff had appreciated the difficulties they were going to encounter, they would have found some way of obtaining an outside consultant.

CONCLUSION

The case studies have highlighted a number of organisational issues, which present as a series of interacting paradoxes. The demanding and still experimental nature of intermediate treatment means that practitioners need a degree of flexibility which many of them believe can only be secured by increasing their professional autonomy. On the other hand the survival of intermediate treatment, let alone its expansion, depends very largely upon the conviction of managers and administrators, the very people whom the practitioners often wish to exclude. The same tension surrounds the interface between practitioners and professional colleagues, because the former usually think it appropriate to have the dominant role, but nevertheless remain dependent upon the latter for referrals and other support. Buildings provide a further dilemma. They are important to young people in terms of their need for exclusivity and the sense of security afforded by the familiar, but as far as the work is concerned, they both open and close options. They provide the structure and support which make it more possible to develop skills and concentrate on the primary task; but they also tend to reduce flexibility, and, unless small and localised, draw many young people out of their own communities. Finally consideration was given to the extent to which intermediate treatment represents a real shift in the power relationship between worker and clients, and consequently demands a different organisational framework within both the project and agency, than that provided for the management of other more traditional work with young people.

CHAPTER 12
PRACTICE

INTRODUCTION

Most of the projects described in this book have been able to consolidate and maintain their programmes by learning from their early experiences and gaining the confidence of their own agencies and of the courts. They have not remained static, but have responded to change as a result of experience and ongoing discussions in staff groups and elsewhere as to the most appropriate means of achieving their objectives. The purpose of this chapter is to examine some of the important elements and issues drawn from the case studies in relation to the practice skills and methods required in intermediate treatment. They include issues surrounding a young person's entry into the project, the programme and activities which are intended to facilitate the achievement of the project's aims, the skills and methods required by the workers, the question of control, and finally some issues about ending the young person's involvement.

Patterns of Intervention

The projects differ considerably in the pattern of intervention they make in the lives of their participants. On the one hand Tyn-y-Pwll works intensively with children in a residential setting for quite short periods, between two and eight weeks. The high level of intensity is illustrated by the fact that staff work full-time with the children during the courses, and only take time off when there are no children in the centre. On the other hand, Eastern Ravens Trust works with a child for a few hours a week over many years. The project starts with children from the age of seven, and continues for as long as they need the group, which may be seven years or more, covering various 'crises' in the child's life such as change of school and the start of adolescence. The community based centres at Pontefract and Dundee have no set time limit, and length of involvement varies according to the individual participant. Often, those involved have contact with centre staff two or three times a week. The 'continuum of care', developed by Paley and Thorpe [1], refers to the *intensity* of involvement, so that Tyn-y-Pwll would be seen as the most intensive and Eastern Ravens Trust as the least. However, this concept fails to take into account the *length* of involvement: the degree of intervention by a project depends on both intensity and duration.

Moreover, this intervention need not be limited to direct work with the young people. Knowles Tooth, for example, offers residential weekends at monthly intervals for the children, and also regular contact between staff and families in the intervening period. The total combined contact time with family and children would probably place this project towards the more intensive end of the continuum. In the Chapelfield project the time structure appears to be typical of many community based groups, with a weekly group meeting plus several weekend residential periods. However, if one includes the additional work with families and the efforts to bring about organisational change, the contact time during group meetings alone does not adequately reflect the impact of staff time in the project overall.

Selection Criteria and Assessment

In spite of the differences in the intensity of the programmes, there is a fair degree of consensus about the stated criteria for selection. A criterion given by several of the case studies is the difficulty experienced by young people in making and sustaining relationships, both with their peers and with adults. The guidelines prepared by the Dundee project for the benefit of the Children's Panel indicate that young people *'who have had trouble maintaining relationships with peers as well as adults'* (p.141) would be suitable for referral. The Chapelfield profile showed a tendency for the young people in the group not to be able to relate well to adults outside their own family. The Tyn-y-Pwll staff find that even where the young person relates adequately to the parents, she has difficulty in carrying this over to other adults, especially at school. The Knowles Tooth case study also emphasises the importance of the school setting in identifying relationship problems, as evidenced by bullying, being victimised by other children, or conflict with staff.

Another common selection criterion used by the projects is a sense of failure to achieve. The Eastern Ravens case study presents a profile of a typical child who joins one of the groups. In identifying a series of symptoms, such as gross attention seeking and disruptive behaviour or withdrawal from school, the writers suggest that many children develop a defensive armour to cope with their sense of failure and frustration. The voluntary group leaders see their task as one of providing for certain basic emotional needs, such as a sense of belonging and a feeling of importance, which many of the children lack when they join a group. Tyn-y-Pwll takes children whose social and academic growth is being inhibited by the pressures or inadequacies of the home environment.

A third selection criterion which is sometimes implicit rather than explicitly stated, is the demonstration of some type of behaviour that others, whether parents, school or courts, have defined as problematic or unacceptable. Insofar as most projects accept referrals largely from agencies which supervise children on court orders, delinquency or non-school attendance will be seen by the child as the prime reason for referral, even when other criteria are emphasised by the referring agency and the project. In some instances, the problem of anti-social behaviour is expressed in terms of hostile or unco-operative attitudes towards authority. For example, the Dundee case study regards the development of mistrust of adults as a reaction to the failure and frustration which the young person feels about the educational and leisure facilities available to him.

It would be misleading to overemphasise the common elements in selection criteria to the exclusion of significant differences. Thus, the Knowles Tooth project invites referrals of children with serious problems in the family relating to large size, conflict with step-parents, rejection and scapegoating, whereas the profile of the young people in the Chapelfield project presents a picture of fairly stable and average sized families. Whereas Tyn-y-Pwll caters entirely for children who are referred because of specific problems already identified by their social workers, Eastern Ravens Trust concentrates its attention on children at an earlier age, whose basic developmental needs are not being adequately met by family, community or school.

The other important distinction, which is not always apparent from a comparison of selection criteria, is the severity of the child's problem or need. As regards, for example, the ability to relate to adults, it is arguable that any young person has room for improvement, as this is a task of normal adolescent development. But if an adolescent girl finds herself in such serious and regular conflict with adults, such as parents, teachers and police, that she is in imminent danger of committal to a residential institution, then a project is required which will give immediate and specific help with this problem. The Tyn-y-Pwll case study gives an example of an attempt to do this with a girl who might otherwise have been committed to residential care.

Because of the relativity of most selection criteria, the process of referral to a project is seen as crucial by several of the case studies. For instance, the Knowles Tooth staff, who had previously left the selection criteria deliberately vague, recognised by 1977 the need to be more precise in their description of what the programme could offer and also began to use a more detailed referral form, including a question about expected benefits which a child should gain from participation. Although the Chapelfield team felt they could work with a fairly wide range of young people because of their multi-method approach, they asked for as much information as possible on the children already known to social work agencies, but recognised they would have to make their own assessment of self-referred children in order to set plans for them. A different view of received information is taken by the staff of both Tyn-y-Pwll and Pontefract. In the former case, staff do not have access to the information about the child's background, as this would affect their perception of her during the early, contract making phase of the programme. The Pontefract staff were concerned about the possible labelling effects of the well documented written referral in creating pre-conceived images and also prescriptions for individual treatment. The staff preferred to have a discussion with the referring social worker about the rationale of the project and what an individual might gain from participation.

Compared with residential care, with its heavy commitment of resources to the assessment of children, intermediate treatment has not generally adopted a pattern of specialised assessment facilities. Assessment is usually seen as a continuing process, starting with the referral of a child to a facility, and developing as further knowledge of the child is gained through participation. The emphasis given to the assessment of individual children varies considerably among the six case studies. Tyn-y-Pwll is sometimes used by social workers to determine the best future placement for a child who is remanded by a court or referred by a social worker for this purpose. Generally the referring social worker is said to attach considerable importance to the report on the child's response and progress during the stay at the centre. The early part of a child's involvement in the Knowles Tooth project is seen as a continuation of the assessment process, and during this period the staff are prepared to review their plan of work with the child as they gain more knowledge of his needs. In liaising with the referring social worker, staff are also willing to offer information about a child's progress and guidance on future plans.

While individual assessment is a central part of a programme of intervention that uses a treatment approach, it is less relevant to either a social education or a social change approach. For example, the staff at Dundee regard the starting point of work with a young person in terms of his perception of the world about him. They aim to see the individual as a whole person and to provide a planned, purposeful intervention which will help the child develop away from the destructive ways he has used formerly to cope with problems. Although none of the projects fully espouses a social change approach, less emphasis on individual assessment is given in the Pontefract case study. However, when a child is referred by a social worker in response to an assessment of need, there is an expectation that work will be undertaken by the project staff in response to those needs. When the ideology of the project staff differs from that of the referring social worker, there is a risk that lack of clear communication between the two will lead to confusion for the child. A clear expression of the philosophy and objectives of a project can help to safeguard against this.

Programme and Activities

Some intermediate treatment practitioners appear to regard their programme and activities as incidental to the real core of what they are trying to achieve. The activity is seen as the vehicle for the relationship which they hope to build. As an adjunct to individual casework in the office or the home of a young 'client', the advantages of a shared activity in enhancing communication are considerable, but this would not merit the development of new structures under the umbrella of intermediate treatment. We would argue that the programme and activities of a project should be more than an attempt to distract the child while counselling him. They are quite central to the aims of the project.

A good example of the relationship of programme to aims is found in the Pontefract case study. The centre had been well established as an activity centre, to which young people were referred by social work agencies to participate in a wide range of acitivities, some carried out individually but the majority in groups. One of the most popular and well used aspects of the programme was the residential period based in an outdoor pursuits centre in the Yorkshire Dales. When it was decided to change the orientation of the project towards neighbourhood involvement, certain structural elements of the programme were seen as inappropriate. The fresh air and vigorous activities of the Dales weekends were seen as an escape from, rather than involvement in, the deficiencies of the neighbourhood in which the children lived. Perhaps the crucial decision, though resented at the the time, was to replace the member of staff who had led many of the outdoor activities by a youth and community worker with a specific brief to develop projects in the community. Too often, aims seem to be constrained by the available resources. In this example, resources were redeployed to match the revised aims.

In re-examining the Knowles Tooth programme, staff felt that the rural base, separated geographically from the main catchment areas from which children were drawn, was limiting their scope of work. Evening groups were started with alternate meetings at Knowles Tooth and in the members' own community. These usually began with a particular activity introduced by the leaders, but it was then decided to throw more of the responsibility onto the members for planning their own programme. A parallel development has led to the start of a joint area-based group, co-led by a social worker and a Knowles Tooth staff member. Eastern Ravens, in evaluating their work, found that the focus on one particular method they had developed, of working with small groups over a long period of time, was being deflected through the varied use being made of their large headquarters, and the range of demands placed on their resources. They decided to revert to their previous concentration on small groups, using premises in the children's own neighbourhood.

Just as the overall programme should be designed to allow the best chance of fulfilling the project's aims, so individual activities can be chosen to enhance them. In the early stages of the Dundee project, the intention was to focus on small groups, where the group life itself was the vehicle for 'treatment', and where individual activities had a place as a means to an end. With the experience of a wide range of activities, the Dundee project is able to classify the activities and their associated learning possibilities, and to evaluate them in terms of the participation and co-operativeness generated. The choice of activity now takes on much more significance than is implied by 'a means towards an end'. For instance, a member who makes a model on his own may gain a sense of achievement if it is recognised by the workers and the rest of the group. However, it is unlikely to test or enhance his ability to co-operate with others, which would be demanded of him in a camp or a group film-making project.

A further aim in choosing activities is to develop interests which can be carried on outside the project. On these grounds, activities requiring mountains have been criticised for young people living in lowland cities. Others which are very expensive might be vetoed for the same reasons. Of the projects reported in this book, Dundee probably offers the widest range of activities and has tried to match them to its aims for individuals and groups. The follow-up survey found that whereas few youngsters had an affiliation to clubs and organisations before contact with the centres, half of them had some organised leisure activity at the time of the study, and five out of six were continuing informally in activities they had been involved in at the centres. This encouraging outcome may in part be due to the links forged with other community leisure resources, but also seems to indicate that the choice of activity is important insofar as it can capture the imagination of the young person and be carried on outside the project.

Although it is very rarely included in a set of aims for intermediate treatment, enjoyment of the activities and of the whole programme is an important facet of maintaining membership without coercion. 'Enjoyment' as an explicit ingredient is probably excluded out of fear of criticism from those who see intermediate treatment as a court imposed sanction, which if not actually a punishment, should at least be concerned with the serious matter of behaviour change. But in the abcence of coercion, changes in behaviour are unlikely to be achieved except through positive motivation to learn new patterns of behaviour.

METHODS
Group Living

One of the effects of recent emphasis on the advantages of community based work with adolescents has been the devaluation of residential work, which this has seemed to imply. The 1976 White Paper on the 1969 CYP Act was at pains to make a distinction between institutional and residential experience, [2] and any negative connotations were intended to apply to the former rather than the latter. In fact, the emergence of intermediate treatment has re-emphasised the value of short periods of group living, and is matched by converging developments in residential work, with an emphasis on five-day care, and shorter, planned periods of care in certain community homes.

It would, however be wrong to imply that the residential components of intermediate treatment were merely shortened versions of residential care, or that all projects use the residential period for the same purpose. Within the case studies, there is considerable variation. Thus Tyn-y-Pwll might be seen as the nearest to short-term residential care, with the significant difference that its staff are on duty for the whole of each course. Stress is laid on the appropriate need to provide a secure environment emotionally, and on the combination of care and control. In other projects, typified by Knowles Tooth, the basic purpose is the development of closer, more informal relationships between adults and children, which form the basis of continued work within the centre and at home. The weekend programme at Knowles Tooth also seeks to develop the youngster's physical and social skills and to influence his attitudes and behaviour through personal contact and group meetings. Each group is encouraged to share responsibility for the group living experience, including domestic routine as well as planning the programme of activities. The particular weekend illustrated in the case study shows that shared responsibility can be frustrating, and that children often prefer adults to take the decisions. If staff did so, however, this would defeat one of the primary purposes of the residential experience— helping the group members to learn how to take decisions, cope with setbacks and conflicts, and thus develop a greater degree of responsibility.

The Chapelfield project, which included a number of residential weekends, found that these were a microcosm of the total life of the project in terms of group development. Thus the early phase of anarchy, in response to the experience of freedom, was replaced fairly quickly by self-organisation. The weekends also served to accelerate group cohesion and provided frequent opportunities for learning about behaviour and relationships through the more intensive inter-action during the residential period.

Group Work

As the method of intervention most commonly associated with intermediate treatment, group work is often regarded as any contact with more than one other person. The PSSC report, however, makes the distinction between 'group work' and 'working with groups'. [3] In line with that distinction, this chapter adopts a restricted definition of 'group work', to mean the deliberate use of group interaction and experience as a means of achieving the aims of the project.

The Dundee case study presents an interesting picture of a group struggling to gain an identity and then to make the rules which its members feel they need. Norman Alm describes this as *'organisation'* emerging from *'chaos'* (p.158), as the Monday group seeks to find its own identity by imposing a ban on visitors. He emphasises the importance and difficulty of establishing a regular group meeting and gaining the group's acceptance of this. An advantage of the continuous group with changing membership is that the existing members transmit the norm of holding a regular meeting to the new members. The task of the group leader is seen as steering the group towards a genuine analysis of problems and a search towards solutions. Success in achieving this is spasmodic and character-ised by moments of self-discovery.

The Chapelfield project was able to chart the group's development according to a particular theoretical model [4]. As the group members were known to each other before the start of the project, a role structure was more quickly formed. In the early stages, the older boys were fairly dominant and also vied with each other for leadership. During the middle phase of the group, various sub-groups and pairings had developed, and the younger boys were more prepared to assert themselves. In periods of crisis, when external events threatened the whole group, there was a tendency for the group to regress to earlier stages, but also to develop a degree of cohesion in which four of the older girls assumed leadership roles. In the later stages the group were able to integrate previously scapegoated members and sub-groups formed around common interests, which indicated to the staff an appropriate degree of maturity.

Group work implies that at some time all members and staff will meet together and share in both activities and discussion. Many practitioners have found difficulty in establishing a regular pattern of group discussion. Younger or more active members find the concentration required for more than a few minutes less appealing than boisterous activities. Older members many not see the point, or claim they are bored. Few will have been socialised into the procedure of group decision making. The most common focus for group discussion is in planning future activities. Both Tyn-y-Pwll and Knowles Tooth place stress on involving young people in shared responsibility for the daily living routine. Dundee has a 'formal' meeting, in which everyone sits down in one place, *'to plan the programme, air complaints, and discuss behaviour and issues arising from the evening.'* (p.144). The reasons given for involving members in decision-making are to increase responsibility, to reduce dependence on the workers and to increase the motivation of members for the activity. David Ward goes further in regarding shared decision making at Chapelfield as a crucial aspect of the change strategy, *'to help children to develop less hostile and suspicious attitudes towards people in authority, and also to become more socially competent.'* (p191). He cites the principles of therapeutic community practice in relation to decision-making. If the leaders involve the members actively in decision making, and are themselves responsive to change, group discussion becomes more acceptable, not only for planning and organisation, but also for resolving problems which the members themselves bring into the group discussion.

Other projects pay more attention in their group sessions to behavioural or relationship issues. This requires the whole group to legitimise the contribution which all members can make in helping to resolve these issues. The detailed account of the life of one group in the Dundee case study demonstrates the readiness of members, in the group's more mature stages, to bring such issues to the group. In some instances they are prepared to give support and in others, criticism and evaluation of their fellow members.

The Knowles Tooth staff have developed a two-fold pattern for group discussion: the one in relation to planning has been mentioned; the other is in response to crises. In a self-critical account of three consecutive incidents, each of which led to a group meeting being called, the frustration of the staff emerges from the refusal of members to take the incidents seriously. There seems to be a danger that meetings only called in response to crises turn into 'witch hunts' for the culprits. On the other hand, it is important that the established machinery of decision making or problem solving is not overturned by testing out behaviour, for which the group meeting presents an ideal 'gallery'.

Some groups have recognised the valuable contribution which members can offer each other, by moving towards a self-help approach. Perhaps the best example of a self-help group is provided by the girls' group at Pontefract. The girls invited the cleaner to lead an informal discussion group. Although this created some hesitation on the part of professional staff, the initiative taken by the girls led to a strong commitment and high value being placed on this group. This was the exception in group formation, but several other projects stressed the value of encouraging, even demanding, active participation from the members of the group.

Individual Counselling and Advocacy

Because the setting for most intermediate treatment practice involves groups, it is sometimes assumed that individual counselling has little part to play. On the contrary, many social workers see group activities and residential experiences as an opportunity for more effective counselling than is possible in the office or home setting. Most of the projects in this book recognise the important part individual counselling plays in their work. With the shift at Pontefract away from an individual orientation, individual counselling might be expected to have had little place in the revised approach. In fact, the demand for this actually increased, so that consideration was given to the need for a specialist 'drop in' advice centre in the town. The centre continued to offer this service, often to non-group members, who brought a range of problems, personal and practical. However, the focus of individual work at Pontefract seems to have been more on advocacy for young people, and opening up access to other services.

At Dundee, in selecting staff and volunteers for particular groups, attempts are made to match on the basis of mutual attraction for each other. This is a recognition of the importance of the personality of the staff members and volunteers, and the potential for direct modelling of behaviour by the young person on the adult. Apart from encouraging an active role in the group, Dundee staff also offer long term support for individuals who need it, and provide a reference point for lives often lacking in structure and security. They try to move away from the treatment relationship, and its connotations of the expert curing the passive patient, by requiring participation from the youngster not only in group activities but also in planning his future involvement in the project.

The interaction between individual children and staff members is conveyed quite clearly by the examples and commentary on the two group evenings in the Eastern Ravens case study. The handling of Darren illustrates the behaviourist influence on their approach. Starting from the principles of boundary management, this approach depends largely on the positive rewards or negative reaction of staff to the behaviour of members. Despite the focus on small group work, the emphasis throughout the case study is on adult leader—individual member interaction. This is explained partly by the emotional needs and the age of many of the members and also by the style of leadership, which depends very much on the consistent and relatively permanent relationships developed between staff and children.

The Chapelfield workers regarded casework as an integral part of their multi-method approach. Rather than group work emerging from individual casework with several clients, the development of effective individual casework needed a secure group setting, in which both adults and children felt sufficiently relaxed to discuss on an individual basis family relationships or problems. Although the development of individual work was hindered by the absence of treatment plans on many of the children and the pressure on staff to concentrate on group activities, perhaps this had the advantage of allowing the child to bring a problem to an adult when he felt ready to do so, rather than be pressured into disclosing it in response to systematic questioning. Children in the Chapelfield project used adult relationships to test out sex roles and aggressive or dependent behaviour, but opportunities were also sought for exploring the interaction with other adults in the community, especially authority figures. Where the project is seen as a workshop in human relationships, it would seen important that any learning achieved from this setting should be translated and monitored in external relationships, but few projects were in a position to do this.

Working with the Family

Chapter 2 noted that the relationship between the project and the families of children involved in it was often indicative of the perspective held by workers on the causes of delinquency and of the general orientation of the programme. The case studies describe a wide range of practice with families, and they vary in the importance attached to it. It occupies a central place in the Knowles Tooth project, where the same workers are involved in direct work with the children and with their families, while for Tyn-y-Pwll, the distance of the centre from the catchment area makes direct contact impractical. However, both of these projects have in common a perspective of delinquent behaviour rooted primarily in family pathology.

The Knowles Tooth worker is seen by some families as the key figure in the social work support system. It is therefore possible to link the child's behaviour in the residential centre and in his own home and community, and also to help the child cope with any difficulties created in the home environment. Moreover, the workers attempt to influence the family situation so that a more stable and caring environment can be provided for the child's development. This is in contrast to the notion of partnership with children and parents perceived by the Dundee staff. They see that they have in common with parents the experience of living with the child, and this gives them, along with many residential workers, an advantage denied to the field social worker. Eastern Ravens also recognises the advantages which close, long-term work with the children gives the project over social workers from statutory agencies. The case study notes as well that the volunteers who live in the same neighbourhood as the children have more opportunities for access and that they gain ready acceptance from the families.

Although the majority of parents welcomed the efforts made by the Chapelfield team to keep their children out of trouble, some feared contamination from known offenders and others were confused about the pleasure gained by their children from what they saw as a form of 'punishment'. The nature of the work with families varied from obtaining consent for activities to conjoint family therapy in a few cases. Although parents were prepared to raise problems unrelated to their child's membership of the project with the workers, there was a lack of enthusiasm from the statutory agencies supporting the project for the additional work pressures this might create.

The Pontefract example given by Robert Adams of the partnership between workers, boys from the Tipstone area and their parents in a management committee to plan a club for younger children on their estate, typifies a more radical approach to intermediate treatment, which sees both parents and their children as facing the same socio-economic disadvantages, rather than the child's delinquency being seen as a result of parental conflict or inadequacy.

Community Involvement

The concept of community care loses its sense of direction if institutions are replaced by groups of referred clients drawn from different communities and brought together in a setting far removed from their own environment. Those projects which are based in the community from which they draw their members are unlikely to ignore their local environment, but each approaches this part of its work in a rather different way. The emphasis of Eastern Ravens is directed towards enabling their members to cope with the stresses imposed by the environment, and in some instances helping their families to cope with immediate material or environmental problems. The Dundee project included community service as part of its programme in order to build up the young person's self esteem and to help re-establish disaffected young people in their own community. Media coverage of their activities — here and at Pontefract — gave community members an opportunity to review their stereotypes of young offenders.

The Chapelfield project developed partly because of the convictions of the founders that the delinquent activities of young people from a certain community cannot be isolated from the social and economic conditions of the environment and from the resources — or lack of them — directed towards young people in that community. The workers were brought into contact with the original referrals through the court system and the agencies responsible for supervising offenders in the community. The original broad aim of *encouraging the community to accept its responsibilities to prevent delinquent behaviour'* (p.202) was in fact narrowed down to the specific task of developing a new youth club in the area. This was due in part to the demands of those excluded from the specific project for similar resources to be open to them. It was also due to a recognition that the resources of the Probation Service and Social Services Department were limited in relation to this project, and that its members would also need an open youth club, when the project itself ended. David Ward, while accepting in his conclusion the value of the groundwork done for the youth club, also states that the impact of the project on the local community was limited.

One of the four aims of the community involvement aspect of the Pontefract project was *'to initiate projects aimed at areas of need, identified by young people as linked with the causes of their own difficulties.'* (p.230). This forced staff and young people to examine their own community for suitable projects. Robert Adams evaluates a number of different community projects and draws the conclusion that those which grow out of the experience of the young people are likely to be more successful than those conceived for them by adults. With the co-operation of a local school, one group was engaged in extending an adventure playground in a project integrated into their curriculum. At first, it was easier to involve young people in projects away from their own neighbourhood, but a later project, involving boys and parents in planning a club for younger children on their own estate, enabled the workers to assess the integration of the group members into their own neighbourhood. The young people's commitment to this was eventually greater than to the community service projects which the staff had initiated in order to reduce the hooligan label attached to many boys associated with the centre.

It might be argued that involving young offenders in the community through a specialist project increases the risk of further labelling and rejection by the community. In terms of achieving increased acceptance from the local community, there is the dilemma of deciding whether to place a young person directly in a community facility, as the early DHSS guide for planning intermediate treatment advocated, [5] or to create motivation and opportunities for the specialist group to be received back into its own community, through community service or through other means. From the limited evidence available, it seems that the further he is removed by the labelling process from his own community, the more likely he is to require involvement in a specialist facility in order to regain acceptance.

Handling of Conflict and Control

'Control' is a word that has been eschewed by many workers. It is seen to be associated more with detention centres and attendance centres than with a 'treatment' regime, and to be a barrier to establishing close, informal relationships with children who may have rejected other forms of authority. However, experience has shown that the lack of control or the failure of workers to agree on a system of control has led to much floundering and the inability to pursue the aims of a project. Edward Donohue stresses the importance of control as part of the caring process at Tyn-y-Pwll. This is clearly stated as a responsibility of staff in providing a secure environment. The Eastern Ravens project, in developing the principles of boundary management, also recognises the need which children have for limits to be seen and experienced. One or two other projects, while not denying the need for control, adopt a rather different approach. Robert Adams tried to gain acceptance from the Pontefract staff that sanctions would not be imposed, but rather that children would be faced with the natural consequences of their actions. Thus, if a door handle was damaged, it would not be repaired until the person responsible had taken the initiative to repair it. At Knowles Tooth, the group meeting is used to handle conflict or misbehaviour. This is often a lengthy and at times more frustrating experience for both adults and children than direct adult control. Dave Evans points to the opportunities for learning and development of responsibility as the justification for this approach to handling conflict.

Two other types of rule are identified in the case studies. Rules which are introduced by the staff and explained to the children at the start relate to property and safety but would also include the 'no bullying' rule at Tyn-y-Pwll. There are other rules agreed by the staff and the children, including arrangements about daily living routines, such as cleaning and washing up. They may be set in response to some incident which has disrupted the group's smooth running and for which members see a need. As illustrated by Dave Evans in the Knowles Tooth case study, the whole group is involved in resolving a breach of such rules.

No system of control or boundaries can predict every incident which arises in an intermediate treatment project. Workers have to react spontaneously and speedily to the deliberate testing out by members. In such cases, the ability to gain and maintain control depends very largely on the relationship already established between the adult and the children, on the action taken and on the support received from colleagues. The longer term aim of the staff at Tyn-y-Pwll is to help the children develop self-control and monitor each other's behaviour, but until this is achieved, the staff must identify, rather than ignore, breaches of agreed conduct and must prevent actions, such as bullying, which are likely to destroy the basis of the group contract. Where the staff team hold certain basic principles relating to control, these should be expressed in language which the children understand. There seems to be a tendency to undervalue such principles in favour of a 'democratic approach', but the Tyn-y-Pwll staff claim that children prefer to know the boundaries of workers' tolerance in relation to their behaviour.

Leaving the Project

Many intermediate treatment groups have been set up to run for a fixed period of six to nine months. This is a long enough period of time for adolescents to become dependent on a group with which they have identified and which meets some of their emotional and social requirements. Several of the case studies considered the problem created by ending a group. Those with an ongoing programme of work have found it possible to fix the time for ending a child's involvement according to his needs or wishes, rather than the constraints imposed by the organisation.

At one extreme, Eastern Ravens works with children for a very long time, and departure from the project often coincides with starting work, or other reasons of the young person's choosing. Although the average length of attendance of the original participants in the Dundee activity centres was 12 months, it varied from six to 38 months, and there were opportunities for members to move away gradually from the project, and to return on a casual basis or as volunteer helpers. While Knowles Tooth and Chapelfield both aimed to involve participants for 12 months, the former had room for flexibility as an ongoing programme, and the latter aimed to integrate its members into local youth facilities. Tyn-y-Pwll offered the shortest period of involvement, but the staff encouraged children to maintain contact through letters and occasional visits. The distance of the project from the children's home area placed a major responsibility on the referring social workers to undertake follow up work in the community.

CONCLUSION

A flexible policy in relation to length of membership is only possible in a continuing project with a changing membership. This seems to have the best chance of resolving problems of overdependence and of preparing children for transfer to other community facilities. However effective intermediate treatment may be, while it lasts, in maintaining a young person in the community and preventing the need for committal into an institution, its value is likely to be judged, along with other measures available to the court, by its capacity to sustain any behavioural changes for a period beyond the young person's direct involvement in the project. For this reason, at least, the attention given to preparing a young person to leave the project is of crucial importance.

References

1 Paley J. and Thorpe D. (1974), *Children—handle with care: A critical analysis of the development of intermediate treament,* Leicester: National Youth Bureau.
2 Home Office (1976), *Children and Young Persons Act, 1969: Observations on the eleventh report from the expenditure committee,* Government White Paper, Cmnd. 6494, London: HMSO.
3 Personal Social Services Council (1977), *A future for intermediate treatment: Report of the Intermediate Treatment Study Group,* London: PSSC, pp.55-56.
4 For an account of different theoretical classifications of group development, see Douglas T. (1971), *A decade of small group theory, 1960-1970,* Bristol: Bookstall Publications.
5 DHSS (1972), *Intermediate Treatment: a guide to the planning of new forms of treatment for children.*

CHAPTER 13

EVALUATION

INTRODUCTION

Nothing so universally applauded as 'evaluation' can be entirely virtuous. Its skirts cover such a variety of activities that the strangest creatures pop out in its name. But at a minimum they involve the systematic collection of information to find out what is going on and some framework for judging the meaning or worth of what is found. This chapter draws on the case studies to consider some of the reasons for evaluating projects and the various types or methods of evaluation that can be used. It concludes more hazardously with some reflections on these case studies as evaluation.

PURPOSES OF EVALUATION

For programmes of social intervention like intermediate treatment, the purposes of evaluation that get stated explicitly fall broadly into three categories, though the boundaries between them may be blurred. One broad purpose is to improve the day to day practice—the ongoing work with clients or targets of intervention; a second, standing back a step, is to improve the overall functioning of the project as an organisation; and the third is to promote the project and ensure its viability, or to promote the ideas it stands for. Each of these is well represented in the case studies. There is also a fourth function, or personal motive at least, which needs to be explored, and this is to help those engaged in the work to cope with its inherent uncertainties or to understand for themselves what is going on. A slightly different way of regarding these four purposes is to consider the first two as 'evaluation', at the level of practice or of organisation, and the second two as 'validation', for others or for oneself.

Improving Practice

The first of these four is the intention to obtain feedback that will improve the practice of the agency in relation to its targets of intervention. Its purpose is to help the project staff to answer questions about how they can work more effectively with the people they are trying to change. These will certainly include the children, but could also include families, community groups, teachers or other social workers, depending on the aims of the project. Moreover, in the case of the children at least, the evaluation may be at the level of the individual or of the group. The former is a well established part of casework, with its cycle of diagnosis, formulation of treatment plan, implementation, evaluation and revision of plan. The use of individual treatment plans or contracts with youngsters is described in most of the case studies, and examples of treatment plans are given in the account of the Monday Group at the Dundee Ferry Road Centre: their function as a baseline for evaluating change or progress is clear. At Knowles Tooth, the planning meeting before each residential weekend considers any developments for the child since the previous visit and any special needs that have to be considered; then, at six monthly intervals, there is a major review to see whether the child should remain in the programme for a further six months.

However, most intermediate treatment projects work with young people in groups, and improvements in practice therefore require feedback at the level of the group. Typically, workers monitor and record what has just happened in one meeting as an aid to planning the next one better, and an example of this is the post mortem described after one Knowles Tooth weekend group. At Chapelfield the weekly evaluation of the group was seen as the hallmark of purposeful intervention. The practice of group work and of individual casework or counselling are not, of course, separate operations, and indeed may sometimes be in conflict. Projects will differ in their balance between the two levels: Dundee and Chapelfield both evaluated progress as an aid to practice, but in the case study accounts — though not necessarily in the actual practice — the Dundee Monday Group evaluation focuses more on individual children within the group and Chapelfield more on the group as a whole.

The basic approach considered here is that the staff evaluate their work with various young people so that they themselves can work more effectively with these same young people. There are three variations on this worth considering. To take the simplest variation, Tyn-y-Pwll staff evaluate the children at the end of the short course, when they are on the point of leaving: this cannot help staff with the present group, but may help them in planning and running future short courses with other young people.

Another function is to provide a report to the referring social worker who sent the child on the course and who may be making recommendations to the court. Knowles Tooth mentions its assessment role on behalf of referring agencies. This assessment role is discussed in the previous chapter; the point here is that in this second variation, the child is being evaluated in the hope that other workers, elsewhere, can provide a better quality of practice with that child. By extension, this applies to the decisions of the court or children's hearing, and to the evaluation and recommendations made by project staff to try and influence the court decision. In this case, however, the project staff may feel a conflict between an advocacy role on behalf of the youngster and a social enquiry approach on behalf of the court. An honest evaluation may suggest that the child is getting little out of the project and is still getting into trouble; but staff may still think it is in the child's interest that they struggle on, rather than recommending care or some custodial outcome. It is interesting that the Pontefract reports for the court emphasised the 'positive' side of the youngsters' experience at the centre, combined with *'optimistic recommendations on how further involvement would be a justifiable alternative to some kind of residential or custodial court order'* (p.222), yet the courts almost invariably followed the project's recommendation. Staff attributed this partly to the fact that some tangible plan for specific activities was included, and it may well be that an intermediate treatment project's credibility in the eyes of a court lies less in golden guarantees to keep a youngster out of trouble than in realistic plans to work seriously with him.

In the third variation, it is the young people rather than the staff who do the evaluating, and here almost a different purpose emerges — not evaluation to improve practice so much as evaluation as a method of practice. If the aim of a project is to help young people better to understand themselves, or others, or their relationships with others, then what better way than to get the group to reflect on and record their individual and group progress. At Dundee, *'group records are always available for members to read. This is in fact encouraged, since it enhances the feedback effect of group membership.'* (p.148). At Chapelfield, group recording around a tape-recorder was at first chaotic, but later was *'taken seriously, and reckoned to be worthwhile, if challenging, by staff and members alike.'* (p.201). The Tyn-y-Pwll final assessments were made by the staff, but discussed in the whole group, where the child and other children could register disagreement. These were explicitly evaluative: *'a means of checking how successful each member of the group has been in achieving those goals set at the very first group meeting.'* (p.75). Implicit here may be the view that to have a justified sense of accomplishment the children needed to receive an open and honest assessment.

The aim of getting a youngster to look to the future and take responsibility for his or her own life was tackled, indirectly at least, at Dundee and Pontefract by involving them in preparing reports for court hearings; the further step at Dundee of encouraging them to write their own reports may be a subtle step towards de-clienting, or at least towards reducing the status gap between staff and young people. The latter is illustrated in a different way at Tyn-y-Pwll, where in the final group assessment the children used the same form on which they had been assessed to comment on the performance of staff.

Improving the Project Overall

The practice-oriented aims discussed above tend to be focused on 'them', the youngsters—either individually or at the level of group functioning. By contrast, a second type of purpose is aimed directly at improving the operation of the project overall.

Usually this is a special, 'one-off' exercise. It may become a necessity because a crisis is brewing, as when Eastern Ravens Trust called in its founder in 1974 to diagnose the Trust's problems. Or it may be on a planned basis, such as Knowles Tooth's invitation to the National Children's Bureau to undertake a one-year research exercise to help them with their review of the progress of the project. But continuous monitoring of operations is a feature of most projects, even if this is at a very simple level. Robert Adams describes how he came in as project leader at Pontefract with ideas about changing the orientation of the project but no cut and dried plan for how to do so. The diary which is used in the case study can be seen as the continuous monitoring of and reflection on organisational shifts: some dead reckoning and some new fixes on the stars before correcting course. For the Knowles Tooth evaluation an action-research perspective was adopted, so that during the year, *'Dave Evans' intention was to act as a sounding board for the ideas of the staff, and, through this ongoing dialogue, the monitoring of the programme became a cumulative evaluation of the social work processes involved.'* (p.116).

Where the aim is to strengthen the organisation, the evaluation is usually concerned, not with whether the project is attaining its objectives, but rather, how it is tackling them. The questions typically ask how efficiently resources are being used, how appropriate are the methods or programme elements, and how closely the project is adhering to its tenets or principles of good practice. The evaluator may well be asked to interpret the findings in the form of recommendations to management. The Knowles Tooth case study provides an example: an issue that emerged was the relation between the centre and the neighbourhoods it served and it was found that the concentration of staff resources on the residential weekends detracted from other aspects of the programme like home visiting. The author concludes by recommending that the project should bear more relationship to the local communities, while pointing to the 'costs' involved: the more closely staff worked in one locality, the less they could work as a team at the centre.

Some projects have fairly precise and measurable principles about how they should operate. One purpose of the Eastern Ravens evaluation was 'to check out the assumptions about the basic precepts of the work.' (p.103). At one level this was an empirical question of whether in fact children attended regularly, whether group membership and leadership remained stable, whether groups were indeed 'long-term'. But at the other level it asked whether it was desirable for groups to be kept small or for children to join when they were seven or eight years old. This highlights the distinction between evaluation aimed at better attainment of accepted objectives, and evaluation of the objectives themselves. Usually the distinction is less clear cut, since organisations have hierarchies of objectives, so that a goal at one level is simply a means at a higher level; usually, too, this hierarchy is not explicit, so that an evaluation of means slides imperceptibly into a re-evaluation of goals.

Promoting the Project

It is pointless trying to improve the functioning of a project if its very existence is threatened by outside forces. It would be mistaken, clearly, to imply that the viability of an organisation is unrelated to the efficiency and effectiveness with which it carries out its mandate. But at times it may well be buffeted by forces outside its control, and it is perfectly rational for an organisation to devote some resources to such 'maintenance' functions as the public relations and political footwork necessary to ensure continuing resources. So one of the purposes of evaluation may be to demonstrate that the project is worthy of support by those who can determine its fate. Norman Alm is quite explicit about the purpose of the Dundee follow-up study: it was undertaken 'in order to provide the Social Work Department with a basis for weighing up the success or otherwise of the project. This was particularly germane since it would in time have to decide if it wanted to take on the full financial load of running the centres after the five year urban aid grant had ended.' (p.167). 'The primary objective was to "sell" the scheme.' (p.168).

It is in fact open to question whether, or in what circumstances, political decisions about funding are based on evidence about how the project is working. Ammunition from evaluation does not by itself win battles. There is then the more specific issue about the kind of evidence that is likely to carry weight with the suppliers of funds or referrals. It seems to be generally assumed that a project must show it is effective in achieving its objectives, and that, in the case of intermediate treatment, this inevitably includes the reduction of delinquency. For example, David Ward quotes the view that reducing delinquency is a welcome consequence rather than an overriding aim of such projects, but goes on to say, 'Nevertheless, it has to be accepted that this is the criterion by which the value of the project is likely to be judged by the public, the courts, and *indeed by some within professional social work.'* (p.203). He, like nearly all the case study contributors, then adduces evidence on the level of offending among project participants.

Project promotion may face a dilemma if the criteria for public consumption are different from the criteria used internally. This can arise quite innocently if the project has an overall, general aim of delinquency control, whereas its more specific objectives, to which the programme inputs are addressed, concern adolescent care and development. The criteria used in planning the Dundee follow-up survey included *'helping the social growth and development of the youngsters'* and *'diverting them from further delinquency.'* The author notes, *'Of these the first is the most significant to us in our day to day assessment of how members are getting on. Obviously the hope is that the second will often follow from the first.'* (p.167). It remains a matter more of faith than of research evidence that the better adjusted and more socially skilful youngster is thereby less delinquent.

Around these issues, two further points can be made. First David Ward's assumption that the criterion expected is delinquency reduction at least needs questioning. The growing use of detention centre and Borstal sentences, in spite of the known high recidivism rates of these institutions, suggests that the courts, at least, have other considerations in mind as well as rehabilitative effects. It may well be that in the case of intermediate treatment, if the measures taken are seen as enjoyable for the participants, then there is a much stronger pressure to prove that they are also effective. Nevertheless, it is quite possible that external critics judge a project, not by its success in reaching stated objectives, but by evidence of, for instance, good management, hard working staff, imaginative programme, good attendance or careful supervision of the children. The other point is that proving effectiveness in reducing delinquency takes a long time and is technically very difficult if not impossible. The same is true of other criteria, such as improving self esteem or social skills. For workers to ask that judgement of their project in particular — or of intermediate treatment in general — should be postponed until they have gathered convincing evidence is probably not the best way to promote or defend either.

The Eastern Ravens case study illustrates that the purpose of an evaluation directed to a wider audience need not be defensive or apologetic; it may be intended positively to promote the project and the ideas it stands for. The staff undertook the evaluation, not only to check out for themselves their basic assumptions, but *'to check the effectiveness of the work and establish some authority with which to recommend our method to other organisations.'* (p.103). The Knowles Tooth case study, which in effect represents the findings of the year long evaluation, concludes that *'the Knowles Tooth programme is an effective way of providing intermediate treatment services'* (p.135) and emphasises that *'it is vital that the experience of the Knowles Tooth staff is used to the full'* (p.135) by agencies considering or developing a similar type of project. At Chapelfield the workers *'believed that their planned approach . . . would offer a useful model for other practitioners in the field, and new procedures for their own agencies.'* (p.180).

287

Coping with Uncertainty

The desire of Eastern Ravens to have some firm evidence with which to back their recommendations to other agencies touches on a further purpose of evaluation — one which is often implicit and which does not in any obvious way meet an organisational need, either to ensure viability or improve project operations. Face to face work involves a large measure of faith, which may sometimes need buttressing with an external, seemingly objective, validation of one's commitment and methods, as much to reassure oneself as to convince others. Intermediate treatment shares with many of the social services an undercurrent of pessimism about the relevance of sticking plaster solutions to what are seen as structural problems. In addition it carries a tension between protecting society from its problem young people and protecting the young from society. The desire for validation of one's work may therefore be especially strong among those engaged in this field.

The case studies provide few signs that the evaluations were prompted by a need to cope with uncertainties about the worth of the project, but there are hints of this at Chapelfield, the least permanent of the six projects and the one most beset by lack of external support. Here the weekly monitoring was important, not only in what it revealed about the work, but in the fact that it took place at all. The sessions for planning, recording and evaluation became *'symbolic of the continuance of the project'* (p.200); they were an assertion not only of survival vis-à-vis the parent agencies, but also of purpose and control over what happened within the project.

Finally, a further motivation can be detected in some of the evaluation described. This is still a very personal one, but concerned less with validating one's work than with understanding it — the desire to find some order in the flux of events and relate this coherently to a more general understanding of society, and to the theories and findings of other writers. The Chapelfield case study suggests that from the outset of the project the author had an interest in research and some explicit theoretical framework to guide it. A similar tone echoes through the Pontefract case study, especially the author's reflections at the end, which evince an interest not just in understanding the meaning of the project and its various changes, but what he calls an 'appreciative' stance towards the situation of working class youth.

TYPES AND METHODS OF EVALUATION

This section considers the main approaches to evaluation and their relevance to the more general purposes just discussed. It touches on some of the methodological issues raised in the case studies, but makes no attempt at a systematic overview of methods.

Structure and Process

The little world of an intermediate treatment project is a social reality of some complexity, especially if one considers how it is embedded in a wider social network. It therefore requires a conscious effort and some formal procedures to try and stand outside the immediate and partial perspective of any one participant and gain a clearer insight into what is taking place. The case studies do provide some account of their internal structure and external linkages on various dimensions, but usually only the formal structure is described, and the reader is sometimes left wondering how it operated in practice. David Ward has clearly been influenced by a 'systems' approach in his examination of the relationship between the Chapelfield project and its parent agencies, and the interest of this account may owe something to this approach for raising issues that might otherwise be overlooked.

A number of the case studies, including Pontefract and Chapelfield, refer to diaries about the project overall, and at Knowles Tooth, Dave Evans' monitoring provided many opportunities for collecting data on the processes at work in different aspects of the project. Such process records are essential for an understanding of how a project is developing, but they are rather rare in projects of this kind. Three reasons can be suggested for this. First is the lack of theoretical or operational framework for asking questions and collecting information; secondly, there may be doubts about its value, and whether the regular effort and time commitment pays off in useful feedback about how to improve the project, which is the purpose of this kind of evaluation. Thirdly, there is an understandable tendency in social work for staff and management to focus on how the clients respond, rather than on what they themselves are doing.

This reluctance is illustrated by turning to the level of a particular intermediate treatment group rather than the project overall. Here, by contrast, an analysis of structure and process is widely accepted as desirable, and indeed necessary for better day to day practice. Among the case studies we have analyses of changing group structure from Chapelfield and the Ferry Road Monday Group, and nearly all provide extracts from process accounts of a particular group, or base their analysis of group development on detailed extant sources. In comparison with organisational analysis, the pay off in improved practice is more apparent and immediate, and group work practitioners are more likely to be familiar with appropriate explanations of group development and with ways of recording group processes.

The time commitment can, however, be very great, as is indicated by the range of records to be covered in the Chapelfield weekly evaluation meeting: a factual record of the group meeting, a description and evaluation of group process, a critical account of staff roles, and an individual account and evaluation of performance, not counting records of other work outside the group meeting. No wonder the evaluation became the lightning rod for agency displeasure about the staff time consumed by the project. One of the insistent demands of practitioners in this field is for guidance and instruments that will help them to monitor their groups productively within the time available.

Service Delivery

The relevance of evaluation is most apparent when it entails testing findings against some criterion. One such approach regards intermediate treatment as a 'service' to be delivered to certain customers. The question here is whether the service is indeed being delivered. A simple starting point is whether the project attracts and holds the children it is intended for. Some of the case study projects, including Knowles Tooth and Tyn-y-Pwll, are concerned about the type of referrals they are receiving, and a problem here is to define selection criteria that are clear and useful—a precondition for testing whether they are being met, quite apart from communicating them to referring agencies. Holding the youngsters in the project and getting regular attendance is presumably a requirement of effective work. Tyn-y-Pwll, working at the 'heavier' end with often difficult girls, reports that there were only two girls it was unable to hold. Dundee analyses 'length of time in programme'; Chapelfield and Eastern Ravens report attendance rates. The Pontefract study discusses the problem of introducing and maintaining newcomers in pre-existing natural groups.

Going a step further, and analysing the quality of the experiences and opportunities offered to the young people is much more difficult, and is not attempted here in any systematic way, though the programme outlines give a glimmer of what was on offer. What *is* provided, at least in the Eastern Ravens case study, is a test of whether the project was delivering the service in accordance with its basic tenets. Some of the 'boundary' principles, such as stable group membership and stable leadership, are quantified and laid open to examination. Other kinds of principle, for example, about style of leadership or opportunities for participation, would present a much greater challenge to the evaluator.

A further step beyond that is the evaluation of the efficiency with which the service is being provided. This may be tackled at the mundane level of cost per child or of staff time commitment, or at the more fundamental level of whether the resources are being used appropriately to attain objectives. The Knowles Tooth research, rather like the earlier Eastern Ravens review, is of this kind. It involves clarifying the basic purposes of the project and the underlying assumptions; and then identifying problem issues or obstacles to implementation. From this may come recommendations for substantial change such as that made by Dave Evans to integrate the residential work more fully with work in the home community. This type of evaluation, and indeed most facets of the service delivery approach, are most useful for serious attempts to improve overall project functioning, though they may have implications for improving existing day to day practice, and for project promotion.

Outcome Evaluation

For projects like intermediate treatment, it is usually not enough to show that a service has been provided. The attainment of aims must be tested by the project's impact on those it was intended for, and the project is expected to bring about *change.* There may be exceptions to a change orientation, and hints of this are expressed in the Tyn-y-Pwll and Dundee case studies. Insofar as Tyn-y-Pwll was a *'short-term refuge for deprived children'* (p.61) one could be satisfied if the experience of the participants was intrinsically good and enjoyable, and Edward Donohue in his overall assessment includes the comments that *'The vast majority . . . enjoyed their stay, . . . all were valued members of a caring group.'* (p.78). Norman Alm also raises the question whether the experience is not itself the objective, and both case studies, quite appropriately, draw on evidence of how fondly the children recall their participation and how much they keep in touch.

Generally, however, for these and the other projects, the focus is on planned change. Nearly always in intermediate treatment, it is the children—and perhaps their families—which are expected to change, but this need not be the case. The

Chapelfield project explicitly draws on the systems theory of social work to identify a range of change targets, including the community and the project's own parent agencies, and the evaluation assesses how effectively the project achieved its aims in these areas. Pontefract was concerned with the way in which its participants were treated and labelled by others, and therefore one test of its success, however achieved, would be changes in the actions and attitudes of other agencies and people in the local communities.

At the level of individual children, an important issue arises from the search for evidence of change in meeting aims which the project may be uncertain how to accomplish. The oft cited example is reduction in delinquency or prevention of reoffending. Evaluation of this kind needs to be seen in terms of the purposes discussed at the outset. As Robert Adams says of Pontefract, *'The way the Club publicised statistics of outcomes for individuals seemed to be associated with the politics of justifying the project to those outside it, including funding bodies, and reassuring workers that they were doing a good job.'* (p.236). Outcome evaluations are generally not useful for improving the project in its overall development or its day to day practice, for they give no guidance in themselves about what needs to be done. Dave Evans makes this point clearly: *'In the evaluation of any social work programme, the difficulty often lies, not in determining whether it has been successful or not, but rather which aspects have contributed most to the outcome.'* (p.133). There is, however, one crucial way in which an outcome evaluation can be directly helpful to a project: the effort to measure outcomes and goal attainment provides a great incentive to clear thinking about what the aims are and exactly what changes are sought.

One final point about outcome evaluation concerns the inferences that can be drawn from evidence of change or the lack of it. First, any change can be due to influences quite other than the intervention of the project. At Pontefract the workers felt that the problem behaviour of the young people had been reduced, but in seeking the causes of this, they came to think that the policy of the local authority in rehousing the residents of the Redpath 'ghetto' *'dwarfed the effect of the Club's work with the boys from the area.'* (p.232). Secondly, any programme of intervention can have unanticipated effects, even counter to the stated aims. The dysfunctional effect of the Chapelfield project on the working of the two parent agencies is one example. At Pontefract, it was recognised that working with one of the groups might for a period have actually contributed to the level of group offending. Any outcome evaluation must therefore not only be cautious about attributing to the project any changes for the good, but must also be open to any unintended and perhaps harmful changes.

Consumer Surveys

Consumer research is not so much a different type from outcome evaluation or service delivery, but rather a possible method for achieving these. However, since it is described or referred to in four of the case studies, it merits some comment. At Knowles Tooth this aspect was apparently more exploratory and unstructured, while at Dundee and Eastern Ravens a survey was designed for quantitative analysis. In the latter cases one is struck by the near absence of any negative response to the projects, although some care was taken with methodology, and it is not as if the surveys had asked crudely for an endorsement of the project. A key factor is the perceived relationship of the interviewer to the project, and these were, variously: social work students on placement, temporary staff, and outside evaluators attached to the project and called in by the project for a brief period or for up to a year. But no matter who does the interviewing, a survey that calls for or implies an evaluation of the project itself faces great difficulty in eliciting 'full and frank' responses. The findings may be useful for presenting the project in a good light and for boosting staff morale, but may be of limited use in assessing how valuable the project really is to its consumers.

The most helpful type of consumer survey for the project itself, and one which Eastern Ravens undertook, asks which aspects of the project are most valued and what changes are wanted. A difficulty here is that different groups of consumers — children, parents, social workers, people in other agencies — may have perceptions of the project's aims that differ from each other and from those of the project staff. Eastern Ravens found that parents thought it kept their children out of trouble, the children valued the new experiences, while the project itself was concerned about emotional deprivation. It should perhaps be a matter of concern that such disparate views are held, but if a project is to take any action on this, it must be clear which is its primary consumer group and whose opinions it should value most. It must also be clear how far it it prepared to ignore consumer views that clash with the project's own principles of work, as Eastern Ravens did over the issue of mixed sex groups, and Pontefract over girls' attendance at the Club.

So while consumer surveys can be useful for eliciting views about the project's areas of strength and appeal, there will always be problems about methodology, and the project should have some idea in advance why it wants the survey and how responsive it is prepared to be to consumer wishes.

THE CASE STUDIES AS EVALUATION

So far the case studies have been used to illustrate some general issues about the purposes of evaluation, about approaches and methods. But there are other issues in the politics and practice of evaluation, which will be briefly taken up here, by considering each case study as itself an overall evaluation of the project. These issues concern the resources and constraints that help determine the kind of account that emerges; they concern the identity of the people doing the evaluation, the kind of data available, and the way in which the data is used.

A key factor is the relationship of the evaluator to the project. Of the six case studies, two were written by project staff still deeply involved in the project; for three others, the authors had been central to the project's development, and only one — Knowles Tooth — was written by an outside researcher. This relationship is likely to influence the reasons for undertaking the case study in the first place, the way it is tackled, and the skills, time and knowledge available.

The author's relationship to the project needs to be borne in mind in considering why the case study was ever written, in terms, for instance, of the various purposes of evaluation discussed at the beginning of this chapter. The reasons that the contributors might give may not be fully apparent from the case studies themselves, but they must be very compelling, given all the labour involved. It is conceivable that in a couple of cases there was already the desire to review the project, and the opportunity to publish provided the spur and the framework; Eastern Ravens, in fact, undertook its consumer survey as part of its case study contribution. Publications may also serve to promote the project —

not in any crude or immediate hope of protecting next year's funding, but in spreading abroad the reputation of the project, and from a deep seated belief that it does have something to offer the wider world: the principles on which it is based, the achievements in practice, the lessons from its trials and errors. There may also be more personal motives that need to be acknowledged, for example the authors' desire to communicate their own ideas and experience or to publish their research.

A further consideration is the time and resources available to the writer, who may be undertaking the task in addition to other, regular duties. Useful evaluation is likely to be expensive: it needs above all many hours of skilled and careful labour, extending over months or even years rather than weeks. This is illustrated by Knowles Tooth, a project which, after two years development and four full time staff, was able to get the services of a full time researcher for nearly a year. This ratio of resources between direct provision of services and its evaluation would not seem extravagant to those who propose that ten per cent of the budget for any experimental project should be earmarked for evaluation, but might surprise those who call for more evaluation as a way of saving public expenditure. The project that does not have funding for evaluation may be able to arrange collaboration with someone pursuing his or her own research interests, and this is exemplified in a couple of the case studies, but the mutual expectations need to be very clear in advance. Alternatively, project staff may themselves do the work, perhaps with the advice of a consultant on the design, methods and analysis of the evaluation. The case studies rely nearly entirely on data collected and records kept by project staff, and, as noted above, have been written in addition to the author's other duties, whether or not still involved with the project.

The research specialist is assumed to have the advantages, not only of particular skills, but of a scientific detachment that makes him more willing and more able to make a sound evaluation of a project, in comparison with project staff generally, and the founder or leader in particular. This is too simplistic a view. The project leader is privy to certain information on the purposes and hopes, the conflicts and the problems of the project; the 'neutral' outsider must first gain access to this kind of information, and will need the co-operation of the staff. It is not uncommon for evaluation research to be sabotaged by staff, even when — or especially when — set up by project managers, and one of the attractions, therefore, of 'action research' that provides staff with a flow of feed-back, is that staff are more likely to see the value of the research and less likely to be suspicious of what the researcher will finally say. The outsider has a different, but no less partial perspective than the insider, and though not as vested in the project's success as its key staff, is probably not immune to protective feelings about the project's reputation. Indeed, project leaders who choose to write in some depth about their project may well be willing to admit its shortcomings, for they see these in the context of wider successes or aspirations. The constraint on candid evaluation is, rather, one of loyalty to colleagues, protection of their clients and the neighbourhoods from which they come, and a reluctance to anger those, such as funding sources, that have power to hurt the project.

The Data and its Use

A different kind of constraint is the data available: the case studies, after all, are retrospective, and most of what is reported was past history. While project records are described and sometimes cited in the case studies, the reader will have drawn his own impression about the author's reliance on contemporary records or on memory. Two points stand out. First, some of the case studies were evidently based on quite a wealth of contemporary material, and the lack of research staff or archivist did not prevent these small organisations from documenting their development. Secondly, there were much fuller records on the clients, individually and in groups, than on other 'systems' in the organisation; the reason, suggested earlier, is that staff can much more easily see the relevance to good practice and project development of monitoring, for instance, the young people's group rather than the staff meetings. Furthermore, to the extent that the case studies make a careful analysis of the 'historical evidence' they help dispel the myth that normal project development is a march of progress — clear-sighted, purposeful, steadfast — towards achieving the project's goals.

As important as the raw data are the questions it is used to answer, and the case studies have been shaped, in varying degrees, by the outline which the editors prepared and asked the contributors to follow. This outline is set out in Appendix II, with a short account of the process by which the case studies emerged in final form and some comments on both. In summary, the outline was found to have a number of shortcomings in practice, and the contributors differed in how useful they found it. Moreover, the case studies would have been extremely long if they had covered every point in the outline, and in the editing process we tried to ensure that a particular issue was dealt with more fully in the case study where it was most relevant, at the expense of other aspects of that project.

These factors are important in assessing the case studies overall. There nevertheless remain substantial differences between them which reflect the very approaches taken by the contributors in communicating about their respective projects. On the value of quantitative measures for evaluation, for example, there is a contrast between the attention given by Dave Ward to the re-offending rates of the Chapelfield children and the view expressed by Edward Donohue that *'The courses have never existed to provide data for eager statisticians.'* (p.76). *'In the last analysis there is nothing more concrete than the subjective evaluations of the staff, the social workers and the children themselves, to determine whether Tyn-y-Pwll is successful or not.'* (p.77). Another dimension on which they vary is the degree to which they seek to distance themselves from their own involvement with the project. In some of the case studies there is more emphasis on communicating the reality of the life of the project as experienced by an insider; in others, an effort to stand further back to make a cool appraisal. In short, the contributors responded in very different ways — formal, evocative, reflective, declaratory, and the question remains, to what extent the task of communicating about this kind of work is a scientific one, and to what extent a literary one.

CONCLUSION

This chapter began by considering some of the purposes of project evaluation. It concludes by asking what purposes are served by the case studies, themselves viewed as evaluations. Clearly, they are not the long awaited tablets from heaven proving that intermediate treatment works. Each case study, in its own way, evaluates the operation of the project and its effectiveness in achieving its aims. The task of preparing a case study required the writer to collect and organise in a fairly systematic way evidence on which the evaluation was made. It is outside the scope of the case studies themselves to assess whether their preparation or their findings have led to change in any of the projects, designed to improve the quality and effectiveness of the service provided, but a few examples quoted of changes following evaluation suggest such a potential for the case studies.

In the context of this book, they would need to be viewed in the light of the purposes stated in its introduction — to stimulate, to teach and to share experience. The reader who is concerned to establish, maintain or improve intermediate treatment provision must judge what guidance the case studies offer in the transmission of learnings from one project to another. Clearly, this would not simply take the form of replicating a particular model, since this would fail to take account of the history, setting and personalities in the original project. But at very least, the case studies can be seen as an organised expression of belief in the potential of young people, and in the possibilities for imaginative and caring ways of working with them in the community.

CONCLUSIONS

CHAPTER 14
DIRECTIONS FOR
INTERMEDIATE TREATMENT

INTRODUCTION

The purpose of this chapter is to highlight certain key issues which have been raised directly or indirectly by the case studies, and which are relevant to both the future of intermediate treatment and the form it will take. On some of these issues, we, as a group of editors, have arrived at an agreed stance, while on others we have had to be content with stating the dilemma as clearly and objectively as possible. One of the most worrying aspects of intermediate treatment, which largely accounts for its comparatively slow development, is that, more than ten years after the passing of the 1969 Act, there is still plenty of scope for argument about the fundamental questions. Consequently we propose to limit ourselves to the basic issues of policy and practice, and to comment on these in relation to four questions:

- What is the purpose of intermediate treatment?
- For whom is it intended?
- Who should provide it?
- What form should it take?

These are deceptively simple questions, and one of the main reasons for their continuing capacity to excite controversy is that it is very difficult to take them separately because they all interact and the answer to one influences the answer to all the others.

THE PURPOSE

Endless time can be spent in circular arguments which suggest that the nature of intermediate treatment cannot be defined, until the group of children for whom it is designed has been clarified; and that it is impossible to establish appropriate criteria for selection until the purpose of intermediate treatment, and the methods to be employed, have been clearly set out. As far as the legislation is concerned, intermediate treatment was conceived as part of society's response to juvenile delinquency and other forms of problem behaviour among the young. Indeed, in the tariff system of the court, it is fairly high up the ladder, the last step before a care order or a custodial period within the penal system. However there were many, particularly in the social work profession, who were convinced that delinquency was very largely a symptom of deprivation, and were determined to use the 1969 Act as a launching pad for the preventive service to which they had long aspired. While this should not be interpreted as a deliberate attempt to thwart the intentions of the legislators, it was the main source of the arguments about the primary objective, often couched simply in terms of treatment versus prevention.

Managers and practitioners both recognised the need to satisfy a number of purposes if they were to cater for the very wide spectrum of children with whom they were concerned. On the one hand it was necessary to have a delinquency control programme available to the courts for dealing with young offenders and, in particular, providing a last chance for serious or persistent offenders to remain within the community. On the other hand, a much broader based social education service also seemed justified, aimed at preventing children from getting into trouble and specifically from entering the juvenile justice system. Although there has been much argument, few intermediate treatment practitioners have been asked to choose between these desirable objectives, and theoretically at least, intermediate treatment has been thought to be capable of serving all of them, quite often within the same programme. Before falling into the trap of thinking that this is the natural way of ordering things, it is worth remembering that in the United States a fairly clear distinction is drawn between diversion programmes which are intended to allow the early offender to bypass the juvenile court, and community based delinquency intervention programmes which can be used by the courts as an alternative to residential care. However, in establishing intermediate treatment in this country, policy makers, administrators and practitioners have not been content with embracing these two rather different populations, but have also tried to cater for a whole army of other, socially deprived children and young people.

Regardless of whether intermediate treatment is capable of fulfilling all the roles that have been assigned to it, the fact unfortunately remains that it has signally failed to provide an alternative to institutional care, and its period of development has coincided with a dramatic increase in the number of children receiving custodial sentences. It is this one depressing fact which persuades us that intermediate treatment should not attempt to be all things to all children, and that particularly in a time of financial cutbacks, resources should be directed towards reducing the number of children in residential care, and maintaining in the community those at risk of committal to institutions of any kind.

In urging a greater, rather than an exclusive or rigid focus on the heavier end of the delinquent spectrum, we recognise the danger of stigmatising children unnecessarily by placing them in projects associated with delinquency control. Although we would want to avoid putting young offenders in community-based programmes where they are segregated from their contemporaries, even this is almost always preferable to confinement within a residential institution. Furthermore while intermediate treatment is predominantly undertaken by social workers and probation officers, and while these professional workers continue to provide a residual rather than a universal service, their intervention, no matter how benign, is almost certain to be stigmatising even when great efforts are made to include non-identified delinquents in the programme. It is acknowledged that intermediate treatment can be relevant, beneficial and enjoyable for very large numbers of young people. In addition it goes against the grain to limit participation, particularly when much juvenile delinquency is a passing phase which can be expected during the adolescent period, and does not warrant the attention it receives. Nonetheless the current practice of including all children who might benefit from an intermediate treatment programme has almost certainly had the effect of identifying and probably stigmatising a new client group, rather than of providing a more creative, imaginative and effective way of dealing with those who would otherwise be placed in institutional care of some kind.

Even if tackling delinquency is accepted as the primary task, the fundamental issue still remains whether efforts should be directed at altering the individual's behaviour, modifying the juvenile justice system by which children are processed, or bringing about change in the social environment. Traditionally delinquency intervention programmes have been concerned with the first of these three options. This is not surprising, as they are usually initiated by agencies such as the probation or prison service which necessarily concentrate on individuals and their delinquency simply because their mandate is derived almost exclusively from the courts. Although most of these programmes have been singularly unsuccessful in achieving their appointed aim, the general assumption, shared by politicians, judges and the public is that the individual must be changed.

It is widely accepted by professional workers, theoretically at least, that the way the juvenile justice system is currently operated is counter productive, in that court appearances and custodial measures probably reinforce delinquent patterns of behaviour. Certainly it is our view that the police, magistrates and social workers should be expected to justify bringing children to court and removing them from their homes. In other words, unless it can be proved that diverting children from the courts and treating them in the community is positively harmful, it does not have be more effective than court appearances and custodial measures to represent a better policy. Finally it is left to radical criminologists and a handful of pressure groups to argue the case for social change. While most of the projects recorded in this book have a primary concern with changing individual behaviour, they all recognise the deficiencies of the social environment in which most of their members live. A few have tried to address themselves to these deficiencies by creating opportunities for achieving some social change, however marginal, and for alleviating some of the effects of the firmly entrenched structural forces in the environment. We welcome this aim, not only because of any changes achieved but also because it opens up opportunities for young people to influence decisions affecting them.

One of the factors inhibiting this development is that intermediate treatment has emerged from a child care philosophy which regards the needs of the child as paramount. Owing to its origin within the social work profession, strongly influenced by psychodynamic theories, these needs have too frequently been perceived in a pathological sense. The individual treatment approach tends to create its own stigma because of the association with the medical model and psychiatry. While we have identified many aspects of practice based on a treatment approach, we have also been struck by the shift in several projects to a broader based strategy, incorporating elements of both a social education and a social change philosophy. We approve, for instance, of attempts to provide opportunities for participation in decision making and for learning relevant social skills, and we accept the importance of raising the consciousness of young people to issues of local and national significance to them. At the same time we recognise the potential conflicts involved in adopting more than one philosophical approach in the same project and the confusion which can arise when the expectations of the referring agent are different from those of the project staff.

For this reason, it would be better if there was a much clearer expression by many project staff of their underlying philosophy and the practical effect of this on their method of operation. There is definitely a need to make explicit some of the more unpalatable objectives. One of the most striking omissions from the aims listed by the case studies is that of preventing worse things happening to young offenders. It is true that this would entail acknowledging the direct relationship between the project and delinquency control, and many practitioners fear that such an unequivocal stance would create barriers between the young people and themselves. The experience from other fields of work suggests that this fear is unfounded and that, on the contrary, a clear recognition of the nature of the problem and the reason for the project's existence is essential to a successful outcome. This helps to explain why it is that when expectations have been made clear, the same peer group pressures to which delinquency is often attributed can be harnessed to work in the opposite direction.

THE CONSUMERS

Intermediate treatment has attempted to cater for the needs of a wide range of children. Although they cannot be divided into watertight compartments, and there are many children who fall into more than one category, it is possible to identify at least five categories. The first group consists of those children who have established a delinquent career and are in serious danger of being taken away from their own homes and placed in a community home or penal establishment. The second group are sometimes called status offenders because it is their status as children which is used to justify intervention on account of behaviour such as truancy. To the extent that this group is in real danger of being unnecessarily removed from home, intermediate treatment is justified. The third category comprises a much smaller group of deeply troubled and disturbed children. For some people such a category is contentious, since they feel that attaching an undeserved pathological label smacks of attributing the blame to the child rather than the tragic family situation which is usually responsible for the problem. It is true that the term 'disturbed' has been used far too readily in the past; but a comparatively small number of these children do exist and quite appropriately demand social work resources, which may often be best provided in the form of intermediate treatment. It would certainly seem a tragic injustice to exclude them merely on the grounds that they had omitted to break society's laws.

The fourth group is made up of those who have either been detected offending and could be diverted from court or are on the fringe of delinquent activity and likely to become more heavily involved unless something is done. The objective of including them is usually to prevent or reduce their delinquency, and rests on two assumptions. The first is that accurate predictions can be made about delinquent careers and the second is that intermediate treatment is effective in terms of changing delinquent behaviour. The fifth group is a large one consisting of many thousands of deprived children who have been failed by their families and the educational system. They are deprived in the sense that their personal growth and development have been stunted by lack of stimulation and opportunities for learning, exploration and the acquisition of coping skills. This involves a great waste of human potential, and few would deny that intermediate treatment is capable of providing the compensatory education and enrichment programmes required. However the protagonists of prevention rarely use this argument, mainly because they are well aware that they would be submerged by the demand, and because the responsibility for this task so obviously rests with the education and youth services.

Apart from the pressure to do something for the whole range of deprived, seriously troubled and delinquent children, there is the related but different issue of whether it is best to meet their needs separately or together. There are three main arguments in favour of the policy of mixing. The first is that in many places, numbers and resource considerations make it almost inevitable. The second is that it reduces the stigma that would otherwise be attached to delinquent children participating in an exclusively delinquency programme. Thirdly the advantage for the workers, and only by implication for the children, is that the practitioners find it much easier to make a significant impact when the group is mixed as opposed to consisting entirely of seriously delinquent, alienated children.

The notion that it does not make sense to restrict intermediate treatment, designed to reduce delinquency and encourage personal growth, to those who have already been adjudicated as delinquents, is an attractive one. There are two reasons why it is being increasingly questioned, with pressures to use intermediate treatment in a much more focused and restricted way. The first and more important is that, against all hopes and expectations, the 1969 Act has ushered in a period characterised by an increase in custodial orders and a decrease in supervision orders. Generally speaking, intermediate treatment has failed to provide an alternative to residential care. Instead it has identified a new client group, which would previously have been spared the mixed blessing of social work intervention; and so the second concern is with the way in which intermediate treatment has been used by the state to extend its control into communities where the disadvantaged and poor working classes live. Most social workers are blithely unconscious of this danger, because they do not accept this sinister role and point to the way in which their programmes both attract and hold virtually all children on a voluntary basis. Nonetheless the point remains that, however enjoyable, intermediate treatment does represent intervention where non-intervention might be more appropriate, given the nature of adolescence, and the fact that most children come through it with nothing more than a short and mild flirtation with crime.

Given the current situation, in which intermediate treatment is predominantly undertaken by social workers and probation officers, we have been driven somewhat reluctantly to the view that the target group must become very much less multi-dimensional. Nonetheless the issue of focus remains a complex one. It is not that we are opposed to non-delinquents enjoying the kind of experience presently being offered through much intermediate treatment. It is not even that we are impervious to the argument that the mixing of delinquents and non-delinquents is less stigmatising and actually helps to create the climate in which it is easier for workers to be effective. The problem is that while social workers have the option about whom they will work with, they are likely to choose the less rather than the more difficult. If the priority is to develop intermediate treatment as an alternative to residential and custodial provision, options have to be closed, so that resources, energy, imagination and skill can be channelled in that direction. However, the fact that we favour a residual role for the social and probation services does not mean either that we want them to have a monopoly of providing it or that we wish to deny large numbers of children the opportunities for enrichment that intermediate treatment programmes can afford. It means rather that we want other more appropriate agencies, including education, to incorporate the insights gained into the professional thinking and practice of their workers, and to direct more of their attention and resources towards the comparatively large group of socially deprived children.

THE AGENCIES AND WORKERS

The case studies provide many illustrations of the heavy and varied demands placed on the intermediate treatment practitioner. Where projects are aiming to maintain more difficult children in the community, staff are often stretched to the limits of their resources and skills. The high rate of turnover among specialist staff and the alarming speed with which generic workers undertaking intermediate treatment burn themselves out, can largely be attributed to these pressures. Staff are drawn from a variety of different disciplines, notably social work, youth work and teaching. Each of these disciplines has its own values and practice skills, which are transmitted through quite different training courses, and through professional acculturation. Intermediate treatment at present is primarily the responsibility of social services departments, which have to perform a wide range of tasks and which, since their inception, have encouraged the practice of generic social work with a range of clients rather than specialist concentration on a particular client group or method of intervention.

These factors pose a number of dilemmas related to the staffing of inter-mediate treatment. The first issue is whether the responsibility should be discharged by one agency or shared by all those organisations with a legitimate interest in young people. The received wisdom, supported to some extent by the legal and administrative framework, is that social services departments should assume the primary, but not the sole, responsibility, and that there is much to be gained by co-operation between the various professions working with young people, and the co-ordination of their efforts. Notwithstanding the encourage-ment of politicians and policy makers, and the apparent agreement of all the agencies involved, the reality is that differences in values, training and organisational structures usually create obstacles to effective joint working at the operational level. It seems that the best examples of joint practice emerge when staff, who are not rigidly set in the traditions of their own discipline, and who are removed from the organisational structures which reinforce these traditions, are able to accept the insecurity of a less clearly defined role, which stems from joining together with others from different disciplines to develop a method of working appropriate to the objectives of the project.

This kind of creative co-operation is more commonly achieved under the umbrella of a voluntary organisation. It is not the only significant contribution made by voluntary bodies. It can hardly be an accident that they should be so well represented among the case studies chosen for this book. In turn this inevitably prompts the question of whether it would not be better for the whole task of intermediate treatment to be delegated to the voluntary sector. It is our view that, although the voluntary field should be given an enlarged role, it should not be an exclusive one, since this would almost certainly have the effect of reducing the importance of intermediate treatment in the eyes of all those working in the large statutory organisations. Equally, although the local authority should have overall responsibility for intermediate treatment, this does not mean that it is either necessary or desirable for the social services department to assume a monopoly of its practice. With regard to co-operation between different pro-fessions and agencies, it remains our experience that, for all general purposes, this is most easily achieved when they have clearly understood, distinctive and complementary rather than competing roles. So, although we agree that each major professional group involved—social workers, both field and residential, youth workers, teachers and community workers—has a contribution to make, and encourage the practice of joint working, the way forward almost certainly lies in encouraging the educational and youth services to concentrate on prevention and after care, while we urge the social and probation services to focus by far the greatest part of their attention on those young people who are at serious risk of being removed from their own homes and communities.

Having tacked, if not nailed, our colours to the mast in terms of suggesting that the main thrust of intermediate treatment should be directed at the heavier end of the delinquent spectrum and undertaken primarily, if not exclusively, by a combination of the social and probation services and a variety of voluntary organisations, the next important question is whether intermediate treatment should become a part of mainstream social work or be a specialist activity undertaken by relatively few in the profession. The arguments in favour of specialisation are related to the development of particular skills, the consistent maintenance of a programme, and the importance of liaison with other professional groups involved with young people. On the other hand, specialist staff operating in a generic agency tend to operate outside the general line management structure of the organisation. Consequently their activities are often perceived as being peripheral and therefore an easy target for cutback in periods of financial restraint. In addition specialist staff are often penalised in the promotion stakes because their experience is seen as being too narrowly focused to enable them to manage a generic team successfully.

One of the strongest arguments for specialisation is that there is currently no qualifying course, whether for social work, teaching or youth work, that equips the worker adequately for intermediate treatment practice. Certainly the overloading of the curriculum of social work courses means that few of them focus much attention on direct practice skills in work with adolescents. Youth and community work courses seem to offer a more relevant curriculum in this respect, but turn out students whose opportunities for intensive group and individual work will be limited by their responsibilities for staff and plant management. In the short term, the quickest way of developing new skills is through specialisation, and the real objection is not to the concept but to the ill considered way it has been introduced. The long term future of intermediate treatment depends upon it being recognised as an essential, if not the main strategy for responding to young offenders. While it is to be hoped that some of the knowledge gained and methods developed through the practice of intermediate treatment will be absorbed by all the professions working with young people, the reality is that if it does not become part of mainstream social work, it is most unlikely to become an integrated part of any other profession's work. The main problem with specialisation within a largely generic organisation is that it inevitably becomes associated with peripheral activities. The solution lies in intermediate treatment or work with young people and their families becoming one of a number of complementary specialities, which can only be entered when generic competence has been achieved and further training undertaken. Whatever strategy is eventually adopted, whether it be a specialist or generic approach, the most important thing is for senior and middle management to make it clear that intermediate treatment is not an optional extra but an essential, and probably central, part of the agency's work.

THE WORK

The values held by workers dominate the development of projects, whether they lead to a treatment, a social change or some other approach. The staff as a group need to be clear about their respective values, and as a team, should state these as clearly as possible to children, parents and managers. Hidden agendas are, in the long term, just as shortsighted when applied to the administrator as to the client. It is also vital that workers should be able to distinguish between the values which inform their rhetoric and the values which determine their actions. Participatory decision making, for instance, is limited within constraints imposed by the staff and their agency. Children will soon expose spurious forms of democracy regardless of the apparent ideological beliefs and statements of the workers.

It is possible to identify from the case studies certain principles which help to create an environment in which effective practice can be carried out. Firstly, there is a need to create a caring environment in which the new member feels accepted. The residential situation presents opportunities for this through the offer of physical care. The young person is also offered a choice of adults who are more likely to recognise his positive qualities than other authority figures, who often emphasise the negative, deviant aspects of his personality and behaviour. Unlike the supervision order, which imposes an adult figure on the child, the participant in intermediate treatment has some choice about the adult to who he will relate. The sharing of similar conditions during residential periods by both staff and children is emphasised in several of the case studies. This reduces the distance between children and staff and gives them a greater chance of coming to grips with each other as people rather than as stereotyped players of allotted roles. This is a further advantage of the residential element in intermediate treatment, which should always be distinguished from the institutional experience which some of them will have had.

Another principle which we would want to emphasise is that of participation and self-help. While the pathological approach tends to create dependence and passivity in the 'sick' role, intermediate treatment can actually offer the young member several opportunities for a stronger role in relation to his peers, the staff and the community. One aspect of participation is satisfied by group meetings and decision making. Although many practitioners find that the holding of regular periods of group discussion with bored or over active children a difficult and thankless task, perseverance does bring its own rewards. Few children are accustomed to the medium, but, skilfully run, they can be used to help children participate in the decision taking process, handle conflict with other members and adults, discuss individual and group progress, and initiate group action within the community. At its best, the group discussion provides young people with a chance to play a more active role in contributing to their own development and to that of their peers. It goes hand in hand with allowing young people to make, and learn from, their own mistakes, and enabling them to stand on their own feet.

However, if intermediate treatment is to become the major component of community based intervention with young offenders, the notion of community involvement must be explored thoroughly and transformed into hard reality, as opposed to merely being part of the current rhetoric. The case studies offer some guidelines; but these need further testing out in practice. Firstly the programme and activities must be directed towards the community rather than taking the children away from it. Secondly, involvement implies a two way movement, that of the community towards its problem youth, and vice versa. It also ultimately implies a sharing of responsibility rather than an alienation of one party from the other. In practical terms, this means that community service should be seen as directly contributing to the benefit of the immediate community, to which the children belong.

This raises a related issue. It is virtually impossible for the community involvement to be local unless the whole project is neighourhood based, drawing its members from a comparatively small catchment area. However, it needs to be appreciated that the more involvement and interaction a project has with its own community, the more visible its policies become, such as the exclusion of less troublesome young people. Although centres serving a whole town or city are not usually faced with this problem, they frequently face conflict when they ask different groups from different areas to share the same facilities. By the same token, they also provide opportunities for resolving these difficulties and helping young people to become more tolerant of each other.

Moving from community involvement in particular to activities in general, the key factor should be to ensure that these are both enjoyable and relevant to the stated objectives of the project. Practitioners have no need to be ashamed of the fact that children usually enjoy their intermediate treatment programmes, since this attribute almost certainly contributes to their effectiveness. Nonetheless activities should also be relevant since they are not seen by the children merely as a means to an end and it is unfortunate that so many workers should fall into this trap. This means-end view can be understood as a swing away from the kind of programme which placed so much emphasis on achievement that young people could be forgiven for thinking that getting to the top of the mountain was the main objective. However it remains true that the child's perception of why he is there, and his understanding of the aims of the project, are more likely to be enhanced if the activities bear a relation to the objectives, and if this link is made explicit where necessary.

A more contentious issue is the question of responsibility for work with families of children involved in intermediate treatment. Statutory agencies who are accountable to the courts for supervision orders find it difficult to delegate this, even within their own departments, let alone to a voluntary organisation. Indeed the case studies reveal only one case where the statutory agency involved generally delegated the work with families. The evidence of several case studies, and our own experience, points to the advantages which those workers involved intensively with children have in work with their families. The advantages of combining both kinds of work, in terms of the quality of practice, outweigh the problems of accountability and should become a more widespread feature of intermediate treatment practice.

Finally a fundamental dilemma which faces all practitioners is whether the children's interests are best served by closed or open groups. Closed groups, with a definite membership and fixed time span, have been very popular for two main reasons. In the first place, they are based on current social work theories of time-limited, contract work, which does actually help to concentrate the mind of both workers and clients. Secondly many generic workers are not prepared to make an open ended commitment to a group of colleagues and children, simply because they recognise the limits to their own physical and emotional stamina. However there is little doubt in our minds that those projects which allow open ended membership, reviewed at intervals by adults and children together, provide a greater degree of flexibility, can be tailored more accurately to the individual needs of members, and, on the evidence of one case study at least, are more successful in linking children with community resources. Although the open group tends to lack the focus created by the structure of the closed group, it does help to reduce the inequality of the relationship, insofar as the child has much more chance of negotiating the length of his participation and working through any dependency he may have acquired. Consequently it lends itself particularly well to a social change or social education approach.

CONCLUSION

It is probably clear that we have not found it easy to reach these conclusions. Frequently we have been forced to weigh conflicting ideas in the balance as we have edged our way forward from analysis to actual decisions on policy and practice. The crucial problem is that, although we want to reduce the unhealthy and artificially heightened attention directed towards young people, we are all too aware that a policy of increased non-intervention might create a vacuum which could easily be filled by less humane strategies than are currently being deployed. Furthermore we are conscious that intermediate treatment is a two edged sword, capable of either enriching or stigmatising both the children and the communities in which they live.

Consequently there is a part of us which feels that its potential is enormous and that it should be made much more widely available; and there is another part of us which sees it, however benign the motives of the practitioners, as the tentacles of state control stretching ever deeper into the private lives of dis-advantaged children and their neighbourhoods. Our solution to that dilemma is to urge that the stigmatising effect is reduced by shifting the balance of power towards children and the communities in which they live, by encouraging universal agencies to provide it as a right to be claimed rather than a treatment to be imposed, and by proposing that social workers and probation officers should assume an increasingly residual role, concentrating on those for whom custodial measures genuinely appear to be the only alternative.

CHAPTER 15
SOCIAL JUSTICE AND PROBLEM YOUTH

INTRODUCTION

The purpose of this chapter is to consider the idea that community provision for problem youth needs a more radical reshaping than is possible within the legal, social and administrative frameworks which bound the case study projects. It is not our intention to belittle the work of the practitioners who have developed intermediate treatment as we have seen it above, but there is a place for referring to possible future directions that youth policy might take, which do not arise directly from the experience recorded in the case studies. However, we emphasise that in this brief postscript there is room only for an indication of some areas for further consideration and possible experimentation rather than a comprehensive prescription for policy and practice.

The chapter falls into two parts. In the first, we consider ways in which the dominant view of youth needs re-ordering, as a means of attacking the inequality and injustice to which working class youth, in particular, is subject. From this perspective, it then assesses certain radical stances that have been espoused as ways of responding to problem youth: the abolition of existing control measures; non-intervention; and the natural justice approach. Finding these unrealistic or inadequate, we go on to suggest in the second part that radical changes of a different kind are necessary, and to consider how what is now known as intermediate treatment could develop so as to involve young people themselves in the reshaping of society's view of youthful problems and its approach to them. Here, two lines of development are explored. One concerns principles of practice with young people; the other, principles for restoring to local communities the means to deal with the conflicts and the issues raised by problem youth.

We started the book with a general account of the social and political climate in which intermediate treatment has developed. It seemed important at that point to locate case studies of practice in a discussion of the climate of ideological conflict which surrounds provision for problem youth. It seems important now to suggest that changes in the future nature and scope of intermediate treatment will not come about through mere technical prescriptions alone. The question of what form future provision will take will not be determined by requests for increased resources. Neither will questions about its usefulness, particularly to young people on the receiving end of the experience, be answered by pointing to the increase in intermediate treatment budgets which might be occurring in some local authorities, as residential care prices itself out of some pockets.

The argument which underpins this chapter is that throughout all the conflicts and confusions concerning provision for problem youth, there exists a dominant view of youth, which finds its reflection in a persistent class-based relation between the providers and the consumers of services for problem youth. It follows that any attempt to change this relation raises questions of a moral and political rather than a technical order. We begin, therefore, with a summary of our views on the place of problem youth in the structure of British society today.

CHANGING THE PLACE OF YOUTH IN SOCIETY

The basis for this discussion is the argument that the target group of those seen to be in need of social services—whether to treat them, compensate for their deprivation or inadequacy, or punish them for offences or truancy—includes a disproportionately large number of young people in the lowest socio-economic groups, and that this reflects class based inequalities and injustices in our society. For example, Robert Holman points out that poverty and deprivation are prime factors associated with reception into care. [1] The implication of this is that something should be done to redress the imbalance of poverty and inequality. Yet in fact, the whole trend in social policy has been based on assumptions about the personal inadequacies and psychological shortcomings of the families and children concerned. [2] Overall, the maintenance of the unequal distribution of wealth, the persistence of social inequalities of educational and job opportunities, the survival of class stratification—all undiminished in post war Britain [3]— provide overwhelming evidence of the discriminatory social context in which young people in social classes four and five are singled out disproportionately for punishment or treatment for their behaviour.

Moreover, whilst certain classes of people generally are subject to social and economic inequalities, various cultural and historical factors, touched on in Chapter 1, have contributed to the additional oppression of children and young people in particular, leading to a kind of response to the activities of young people that is often unsympathetic and lacking in understanding. We have suggested that this is a feature of post war British society, although it needs to be seen in the context of a much longer history of childhood and adolescence as an exploited and constantly misrepresented stage in human development.

A further factor is the post war changes in the forms of local government, within which work with problem youth takes place. The increasing size and decreasing numbers of local authorities visible in the local government re-organisation of the early 1970s reflect an emphasis on more centralised, bureaucratic control over local affairs. This exacerbates the powerlessness of problem youth as an over-segregated minority, within the much larger oppressed group of children and families on the receiving end of many local services, over whose shape they have little or no control. As Paul Corrigan puts it: *'All of these changes have involved in some way the movement of power away from localities and into more centralised bodies that can, at one and the same time, be more easily run from Whitehall and can be more easily insulated from local demo-cratic pressure.'* [4]

The future of community based work with problem youth can be associated with struggles against these features of social inequality, injustice and anti-democratic trends in contemporary Britain. At the outset, this general analysis suggests three quite unambiguous prescriptions which are easier to make than to fulfil. We shall record them at this early stage and then go on to cover less certain ground.

1   Redressing the inequalities of a class society

There clearly needs to be 'something effective' done to compensate adequately for poverty, inequality and its social accompaniments in the context of righting economic imbalances in class relations.

2   Changing the focus on delinquency

Two things pervade the over-concern with the activities and behaviour of young people which is a feature of post war Britain. First, there is a tendency to exaggerate the youth question by drawing attention to hooliganism, vandalism and reports of increasing delinquency. These aspects of youthful behaviour seem particularly prone to amplification by agencies like the police and by the media. [5] Second, the current preoccupation with law and order has accompanied an increased tendency during much of the 1970s to use institutional measures, especially Borstals and detention centres, to control or treat young offenders. This has happened in the decade following the 1969 Children and Young Persons Act, with its largely unrealised potential for encouraging the decarceration and decriminalisation of young people. Even in the present climate of cutbacks, there is a worrying dependence, on the part of government, the courts and the public, on the availability of deterrent custody. Both these trends need to be reversed. It involves a massive redirection of public and professional resources and attention. It implies more responsible media activity. It requires that all those involved in the youth business should unite in giving voice to the research evidence about the ineffectiveness of custody, and to the justification of such changes in terms of reasonableness and fairness to young people themselves.

3   Changing the focus on 'growing up'

It seems unlikely that society's focus on delinquency will change much without a major shift in the way people view children in general and 'problem' children in particular. The contemporary moral architecture of punishment, welfare and treatment of children in trouble rests on a dominant societal view of childhood, which tends to deny young people access to rights and responsibilities which might otherwise be considered appropriate to those growing up in Britain today. There is a strong case for adults and young people themselves to initiate campaigns which reduce a fixation on youth by the public and the child care profession that regard it as dependent, immature, not responsible sexually and not able to think politically, and certainly not able to contribute seriously to what are generally seen as the adult activities of work and creative cultural pursuits, at least until after 16 years of age.

Of course, the difficulty with the kind of general prescriptions offered above is that the greater their generality the easier it is to nod in their direction, without any serious consideration of their practicality. And in fact any proposals radical enough to make a significant difference to the present way in which problem youth is dealt with are likely to appear as impracticable ideas, whilst any proposals mild enough to fit existing constraints are likely to be weak and ineffectual.

RADICAL STANCES ON PROBLEM YOUTH

In Chapter 1, we referred to some radical stances that have developed in relation to the 1969 Children and Young Persons Act. Of these, the move towards less intervention and the move towards a rights rather than a needs approach to juvenile justice, have implications which we refer to now. We go on, in the second part of this chapter, to advocate other approaches, which are associated more directly with moves to reduce social injustice and inequality; but first, ideas about abolitionism, radical non-intervention and natural justice are discussed.

Abolitionism

Reflecting on society's need to have some people locked away, Nils Christie suggests that, given the generality of offending in society, the amount of social intervention undertaken bears more relation to the amount of existing resources and plant available than to any notion of the deterrent effect of locking up an arbitrary number of people involved in crime. Perhaps, given the lack of feedback from the agencies of social intervention generally to the public at large about what they are doing, the numbers subjected to official processing of various kinds could be cut drastically and nobody would notice. Christie notes: *'On grounds of pure logic it is rather difficult to see that it would* **matter** *to society at large if the prison population went down to half, or doubled or tripled . . . And most people would not know. The newspapers would continue their campaigns for law and order. There is no efficient feedback system with regard to information . . . There are no logical upper limits to the number. There are no logical lower limits either.'* [6]

The practical implications for the custody of young people involve three elements:

- preventing the building of any more institutions;
- decarcerating as many young people from institutions as possible;
- excarceration, or avoiding putting them in institutions in the first place, through measures which restrict sentencing options.

A more radical approach argues for thorough-going abolitionism. Thomas Mathiesen's analysis of the Norwegian prisoners' organisation KROM suggests that genuine alternatives to present coercive institutional measures can only be developed by outflanking the tendency of authorities to manipulate reformers. He argues that alternatives can only develop in circumstances in which all existing measures are abolished first. Four strategies on the part of reformers are necessary. [7]

1 **An open policy,** which insists upon the abolition of all present measures of control of deviants as an essential prerequisite for the generation of genuine alternatives. Mathiesen suggests that the experience of prisoners' rights groups is that if the authorities are allowed any leeway, like keeping existing measures going whilst new schemes are thought out, or exempting from the scheme a number of 'essential' secure units or other controls for the 'hard core', then genuine alternatives will not be born. All that will happen is 'more of the same', dressed up as something different. [8]

2 **A defensive policy,** which works to prevent any measures being created of the kind being opposed in the open policy.

3 **An exposing policy,** which involves setting out to unmask the ideologies, and even the myths, upon which existing measures rely.

4 **A voluntary policy.** The alternative measures are seen as created in the first place as voluntary. That is, the question of any fresh compulsory measures for

deviants will be only be considered after all possible alternative voluntary measures have been worked through and developed.

In relation to problem youth in Britain, abolitionist thinking might be applied to the closing of all custodial institutions and the generation of a variety of real alternatives. The implications of radical decarceration strategies have been discussed in the Jay Report [9], and it is common for reference to be made to the experiment in Massachusetts, with all its difficulties and weaknesses, as a way of closing off further debate in this area. [10] All that can be said at present is that abolitionist thinking is difficult enough to countenance in Scandinavia or Holland, where the climate of thinking about the control of juvenile delinquency is much more liberal than in Britain. In this country its implications await more full-bodied consideration.

Non-Intervention

It might seem that what is implied by the discussion of abolitionist thinking above is a laissez faire, 'hands off the delinquent' stance adopted by reformers riding the bandwagon of labelling theory. The most artful and articulate exposition of the case for non-intervention, by Edwin Schur [11], recommends decriminalisation, voluntary treatment, a narrowing of the scope of the jurisdiction of the juvenile court, and less use of social control measures masked by rhetoric about therapy or rehabilitation. But at its core it implies *a policy to increase societal accommodation to youthful diversity, with the basic injunction: leave the kids alone wherever possible.* [12] And it is this inactivity which may be most romantically appealing yet most practically deficient. The weakest point of the exhortation to society to become more accepting of youthful deviance is the silence of non-interventionists about how this is to happen. Stanley Cohen caps the critique: *'Moreover, although some aspects of* (the) *delinquency problem — and indeed many other social problems as defined by the powerful for social workers to deal with — can wither away, the structural features of society which both create real problems for certain members and then exacerbate these problems by dealing with them unfairly, will not. Non-intervention can become a euphemism for benign neglect, for simply doing nothing.'* [13]

Natural Justice

Increasingly vocal pressure in the juvenile justice field has come from those concerned with protecting the rights of young people. Whilst in part this movement has reflected a widespread disillusionment with the range of treatments and other disposals offered to date, fuelled by research pointing to the almost equal ineffectiveness of all measures, it has drawn on other influences as well. In particular, it has gathered steam from the development of adult prisoners' rights organisations in Western Europe and the USA. The radical cutting edge of rights movements amongst inmate, client and other oppressed groups needs to be appraised cautiously in terms of its potential drawbacks. In reasserting the classical view that the nature of the offence should be the criterion guiding sentencers, the justice advocates represent a shift towards the notion of 'just deserts'. This notion could easily become the instrument for the development of more punitive sentencing policies by conservative judiciaries.

This danger aside, recent arguments in favour of a return to justice [14] suffer from the weakness that they may do nothing to lessen the individualisation which dominates juvenile justice in particular and welfare provision in general.

The powerlessness of the child is thus envisaged as being reduced only through the use of professional advocates, hired from the middle class to negotiate the mystifying territory of the court procedures. Further, the children's rights movement says more about where the boundaries of social intervention should be drawn than about what should be done within them. Finally, and more fundamentally, it does nothing to attack the social origins of the problems of young people. Stanley.Cohen reminds us that it fosters *'the illusion that justice can be achieved by a penal system which in fact helps maintain an unjust, unfair social order.'* (15)

The non-intervention and justice approaches seem to have merits which fail at the point where some meaningful link needs making between the prescription offered and the general analysis locating the origins of the problems of young people firmly in the structural economic and social conditions of Britain. It is extremely difficult to devise any practicable way of linking up directly the way we work with problem youth so as to engage with the social nature of such structural factors. Some community workers have worked haltingly towards this, and there are signs of efforts in this direction in the thinking of the workers in the Pontefract and Chapelfield case studies, although awareness was by no means successfully translated into practice. In the rest of this chapter, we explore how this task could be tackled. We argue that it requires a re-ordering of the dominant view of intermediate treatment, so that it is founded on certain radical principles of practice, and embedded in a totally different approach to the resolution of young people's problems at local level.

PRINCIPLES OF PRACTICE
More Orthodox Practice

We present first a summary description of more orthodox practice of intermediate treatment and then advocate a more radical version, which is generally in the form of an antithesis to this. Orthodox approaches exhibit a number of distinguishing features to a greater or lesser degree. (16)

- They may involve **compulsory participation.** That is, they tend to operate at the behest of the juvenile justice system, or otherwise through the influence of social workers, to offer children the Hobson's choice of taking part or else . . .

- They may display **individualisation,** through introducing children to the programmes and activity essentially as individuals. Even where intermediate treatment is provided for an existing group, there is a tendency to individualise the arrangements of treatment for each child.

- The management of intermediate treatment schemes tends to be **non-participatory.** That is, they are set up and run for children rather than by them. Rather than involving children genuinely in their running, workers may assume they know best about the shape of intermediate treatment. As a result, whilst making token gestures towards consulting children, they in fact manipulates events towards tacitly prescribed ends, or within implicit boundaries.

- The schemes tend to be **marginal,** in two ways. Firstly, they may look varied, imaginative and innovative on the surface, but may not deliver the goods in terms of any effectiveness in offering opportunities to youth for improving their position in relation to structural and other disadvantages facing them. Secondly, schemes may retain only lightweight status in relation to the massive deployment of resources on residential provision.

More Radical Practice

The principles of a more radical approach represent the polar opposite of orthodox practice, and we shall identify its main elements as the converse of the ones outlined above.

We begin with the notion of **voluntariness**, which contrasts with compulsory participation. Reference was made above to the efforts of activists in Norway to reduce the scope of compulsory arrangements for processing offenders. Obviously, cultural and social differences between Britain and Scandinavia preclude a crude transplantation of ideas, but a contradictory position arises in relation to voluntariness even without considering these. Firstly, any attempts to make intermediate treatment less marginal in relation to juvenile justice procedures would seem to necessitate hanging on to its position as a compulsory measure available to juvenile court magistrates. But whilst this seems to rule out voluntariness at a decisive point in the judicial process, there is plenty of scope for it to be considered at the next stage in judicial decision making: where a young person has been judged by a court as requiring official intervention for whatever reason, he or she should at that point be given a choice between the range of measures available. At present this seems to be precluded by a number of factors which are of doubtful status: a feeling that the medicine needs to be unpleasant and therefore unchosen in order to be effective; a presumption that youth is incapable of making a responsible choice; and a lack of a genuine range of choices.

In contrast with the way much current practice individualises young people, there are a few encouraging signs of community based work developing along lines which enhance the power of youth over the process of intermediate treatment. We have indicated above that some of the case studies seemed to be exploring this territory. **Collectivisation** is a term which, although clumsy, tries to capture the possibility of viewing the way in which children become involved in social intervention as something to which they can relate collectively, rather than being subjected to it individually. The case for collectivisation rests on the way in which the 1969 Act legitimates and perpetuates a focus on the individual child as a client, and is part of a wider pattern of the individualisation of the consumers of education, health and welfare services in our society. This tends to keep people 'cliented' and powerless, and unable to do much to shape the services they receive. This powerlessness leaves young people in an extremely weak position when it comes to struggling collectively against any impositions placed on them by others in society. Apart from the 'Who Cares?' groups developing from the initiatives of the National Children's Bureau [17] and the 'Ad-Lib' group of children in care in Leeds [18], there are few indications of widespread moves towards the growth of self-help groups amongst children deemed in need or in trouble. There is a wider vacuum. There is no nationwide confederation of formal organisations to represent the voice of children and young people at all ages and in all settings, and isolated efforts like the National Union of School Students and the development of local youth councils have had uneven histories.

Thus, the challenge for workers involved in intermediate treatment is two-fold: first to raise the consciousness of young people and encourage the development of such organisations, in their own right but ensuring they do not categorise and segregate youth in intermediate treatment from organisations with a broader youth constituency; secondly, to promote patterns of intervention in neighbour-hoods which try to connect youth, in a variety of formal and informal existing groups and organisations, with the initiation and running of community pro-grammes of which intermediate treatment schemes are a part. Of course, this kind of approach might seem as strange to some children as to some workers, since both have been accustomed to working within more traditional parameters of a worker-client caste system. Further, among unorganised youth, workers may have to undertake the precarious, slow and exhausting job of penetrating youth cultures and subcultures so as to build bridges for negotiation, without artificially smoothing out any conflicts of perception or interest which may exist between youth and adults.

Participatory management of schemes of intermediate treatment should flow naturally from the points made above. In the terms of more radical practice, efforts to maximise the choices young people have over what happens to them and to improve their power relationship with adults through collectivising them can be linked with efforts to share executive management with them. But efforts to develop bridges across the power divide between workers and young people and reduce its distance should be pushed further, towards their de-clienting. This is easier to advocate than to monitor or achieve in practice, since workers can readily create a smokescreen of participation to cloak the essential relations of social control underlying many seemingly democratic activities and situations.

In more radical practice, the balance between intermediate treatment and other use of resources, such as residential provision or youth policing, would be changed to make intermediate treatment less marginal and to increase its centrality. There are powerful arguments for measures which progressively decarcerate more children and young people from institutions. But tipping them out of institutions into community based programmes with little or no connection with neighbourhood groups or access to power to change youth crime condi-tions is of limited use. Making intermediate treatment more central involves bringing it more into the foreground of relevant experiences in the lives of young people, and associating it with the kind of broad-based measures to change the status and staging of youthful problems discussed elsewhere in this chapter. Thus, the challenge is not just to increase the emphasis on intermediate treat-ment by capturing more resources in line with a real decrease in youth policing and residential provision, but is about increasing its meaningfulness to young people as a resource they can develop collectively to reduce the inequalities, injustices and oppression they suffer.

NEIGHBOURHOOD JUSTICE

We have suggested that any community intervention with problem youth should form part of a broader based community programme aimed at building up the consciousness, capacity and power of local people, including its young people, to engage actively in the struggle against social injustice and inequality. However, the present arrangements for processing young people through the juvenile justice system are not consistent with this. The limitations of radical change lie not just in the restrictions on the development of voluntary participation, but arise from the way in which judicial processing seems to *distance* the measures adopted from the community where problems arise and to reflect an over-attention to the child as the problem and a neglect of social problems in the world of the child. Nils Christie draws attention to some of the features of our society which contribute to the alienation of communities from the procedures by which their youthful problems get examined and processed, and observes that such mechanisms may even amount to official theft by authorities of the rights of local people to find local ways of dealing with problems. He suggests that at one extreme some problems, such as wife-beating or child abuse, may actually be over-privatised in a society where some relatively oppressed individuals or groups are socially isolated and have no network to appeal for public support. At the other extreme, crimes may be committed by large organisations against the people who are too weak or ignorant to realise they have been victimised. *'In both cases the goal for crime prevention might be to re-create social conditions which make the conflict visible and therefore manageable.'* [19]

It is arguable that in many places there is hardly any sense in which a notion of neighbourhood or community survives, at least in a way which would support a local informal means of processing youthful problems. However, we feel it is still worth considering the extent to which the number of young people presently processed through the juvenile court might be drastically reduced by the use of local informal mechanisms. This would involve problems of less serious law breaking [20], although measures to protect the rights of children who proceeded to, or preferred to be dealt with by, a juvenile court, would be strengthened.

In any informal local procedure for dealing with youthful problems, just as in the juvenile court itself, the process by which a finding of guilt is reached should be distinguished from the stage at which decisions may be made to meet certain needs of the child. Further, just as it might be argued that in pursuance of a finding of guilt the local community has a right to exact punishment or other disposals, so it can be argued that a child has a right either to be punished, or to select a disposal from among a range on offer. This means that, in circumstances where others decide that the need for punishment is satisfied or does not arise, a child should be able to select what happens to him or her from a range of measures, including educational, social and other programmes, many of which might now be considered as intermediate treatment.

It is conceivable that restructured mechanisms by which youthful problems are processed locally could include enhancing children's power to the point where they might negotiate as participants in a quasi-civil litigation where a

317

settlement needed to be reached. An example might be a case of pilfering from a shop that reflected bad relations between a shopkeeper and some local young people. The process would bring the parties together face to face to negotiate what should be done, in the presence of other residents who could help the process and set the incident in its wider context.

Restitution by Agencies

To see the practical implications of re-ordering local juvenile justice procedures, a well established and even punitive measure like restitution can be instanced. Traditionally, restitution has meant merely that the offender pays back the victim or society, but Eglash has described 'creative restitution' as a means by which offenders may be required to make recompense whilst being able to choose the form in which they do this[21]. He believes this has the advantage of giving both victim and offender an active and constructive role. The victim contributes to achieving justice and developing subsequent rehabilitative programmes; the offender is enabled to remain in contact with the victim as a helper rather than being removed from the situation and labelled as harmful.

The attempt to develop restitution as a constructive way for offenders to make recompense may still run the risk of being experienced by them as simply punitive, and it is really the other side of this coin which interests us here: the notion of restitution to children by agencies and by authorities. This should be considered as part of a wider strategy aiming to bring about enhanced community control over the processing of local problems, and involves a widening of the definition of collective responsibility for action on social problems, beyond that of the traditionally 'clientted' child or 'problem family.' Thus, during a series of proceedings about the problems young people are felt to present in a locality, evidence may accumulate also about social factors contributing to those problems. It should then be possible over a period to articulate some notion of collective agency responsibility for taking remedial action, rather than the present situation, where social issues of importance repeatedly get transformed into imperatives for the treatment and control of individuals and their families. For example, if a number of young people are getting into trouble while truanting from a particular school, it should be possible for the local community to hold the school accountable for a regime that results in high truancy and to exact redress, as well as responding to the behaviour of individual young people.

The result of developing more local, informal approaches to juvenile justice would be not just a lessening of the alienation of people from the means by which problems are processed, but also a decrease in the dominance of bureaucratic and undemocratic features of the state over their lives. Given our earlier analysis, it follows that the mechanisms of neighbourhood justice should be linked to wider strategies of consciousness raising and local community action. It feels a decade too late to be talking about the need for local community action, now that most of the Community Development Projects have undeservedly bitten the dust. But in keeping alight the hopes and ideals that were vested in the CDPs, we need also to examine specifically the contribution of young people, as partners with adults, in that endeavour. There does seem to be a vacuum in our thinking about the positive role young people could play as a pressure group for social change, or more modestly, as a defender of rights or an advocate on behalf of the weak or less articulate. Because of the cultural traps in which children, and 'problem' children especially, are contained, and kind of move towards giving them a collective voice is likely to be an uphill struggle. The clue to the distance we have still to move lies in the phrasing used above: 'giving' children a voice is difficult enough to envisage, let alone the notion of them finding a voice for themselves.

De-professionalisation

In enabling local community action, and reducing the dominance of bureaucratic and undemocratic features of the state in people's lives, the task of the professional has come to be defined most clearly in the role of the community development worker. Here we want to focus on those aspects that concern the development of neighbourhood justice and activating children and young people as critics of the services they consume. This implies great changes for workers with traditional policing and youth social work roles. As professionals they will need to work through the paradox of de-professionalising as many services as possible, whilst improving their effectiveness in the professional ways described below.

Their tasks will include working to establish local problem solving, not simply as professionals in a segregated, mystifying juvenile justice process, but in the interests of local community members. They will need to improve the collective awareness and power of children and young people, within the neighbourhood and as part of the wider organisation of youth. They will need to develop relations with networks of organisations relevant not just to some narrow professional area, but to all aspects of local people's lives, and this means working with social and community groups, trades unions, working men's clubs and the like. The implication is not that there are no tasks for professionals, and we are certainly not advocating a less professional approach, but rather that a limit should be set on the present shape of official intervention, which professionalises the processing and segregating of young people in trouble. De-professionalising is essential, if the responsibility of people for each other and for themselves is to be encouraged.

Two present groups of workers particularly affected would be police and social workers. Relevant to our thinking are some of the ideas of Russell Ackoff on the subject of the preventive policeman: *'He would work with schools, clubs, and other organisations in the community to make it as self-policing an area as possible.'* Further, *'the preventive officer would testify . . . on the crime-producing conditions operating on anyone from his area who is being tried for a crime. He would serve as a witness against the state, not as a witness for it.'* [22] For the police there might be particular problems of role conflict and other issues in their relationship with social workers. But rather than pursue these here, we consider less fleetingly the changes implied for social workers. In Nils Christie's view: *'Social workers are oil in the machinery, a sort of security counsel. Can we function without them, would the victim and the offender be worse off? . . . I have no clear answer, only strong feelings behind a vague conclusion: let us have as few behaviour experts as we dare to. And if we have any, let us for God's sake not have any that specialise in crime . . . let us try to get them to perceive them- selves as resource-persons, answering when asked, but not domineering, not in the centre. They might help to stage conflicts, not take them over.'* [23]

In practice this might mean that a social worker had responsibilities towards the particular young person in trouble, towards both young people and others in the community at the point where they were in conflict, and towards the community as a whole in enabling wider changes. In relation to the individual young person, the worker would be much less the supervisor, and much more the advocate, the catalyst, the broker of resources, with a view to minimising the impact of official intervention on a child, and deferring or even eliminating the need to subject a child to full exposure to the juvenile justice system. At the point of conflict, the worker would have a number of crucial jobs to do in opening up situations to direct community negotiations by the parties concerned, in understanding and interpreting the transactions between deviants and their neighbours, and employing existing networks or opening up new ones which would enable problem aspects to be reduced. Beyond this, the worker would be engaged in raising the level of awareness of the underlying issues and actually bringing people, including young people, closer to opportunities for ameliorating conditions which may be identified as relating to their definition of themselves as problems.

Thus, if the processing of deviants can be brought closer to both the causes and the outcomes of deviance, neighbourhoods may be able increasingly to exert influence over the social conditions which produced youthful problems. The larger aim is that by this process they may lay the basis for collective action on the wider structural causes of social injustice and inequality.

References

1 Holman R. (1976), *Inequality in child care* (Poverty Pamphlet No. 26), London: Child Poverty Action Group.
2 Taylor L., Lacey R. and Bracken D. (1980), *In whose best interests? The unjust treatment of children in courts and institutions,* London: The Cobden Trust and MIND.
3 George V. and Wilding P. (1976), *Ideology and social welfare,* London: Routledge and Kegan Paul. Goldthorpe J.H. *et al.* (1979), *Social mobility and class structure in modern Britain,* Oxford: Clarendon Press.
4 Corrigan P. (1979), 'The local state: The struggle for democracy', *Marxism Today,* Vol. 23, No. 7, p. 204.
5 See, for instance, Cohen S. (1972), *Folk devils and moral panics: The creation of mods and rockers,* London: MacGibbon and Kee.
6 Christie N. (1978), 'Prisons in society, or society as a prison', in Freeman J. (ed.), *Prisons past and future* (Cambridge Studies in Criminology), London: Heinemann Educational, p.187.
7 Mathiesen T. (1974),*Politics of abolition,* Oxford: Martin Robertson.
8 As happened in California. See Lerman P. (1975), *Community treatment and social control: A critical analysis of juvenile correctional policy,* Chicago and London: University of Chicago Press.
9 *Children and young persons in custody: Report of a NACRO Working Party* (Chairman: Peter Jay) (1977), Chichester: Barry Rose.
10 Bakal Y. (ed.) (1973), *Closing correctional institutions: New strategies in youth services,* Lexington, Mass.: Lexington Books, D.C. Heath.
11 Schur E.M. (1973), *Radical non-intervention: Rethinking the delinquency problem,* Englewood Cliffs, N.J.: Prentice-Hall.
12 Cohen S. (1975), 'It's all right for you to talk: Political and sociological manifestos for social action', in Bailey R. and Brake M. (eds.), *Radical social work,* London: Arnold, p.82.
13 Cohen S. (1975), *op. cit.,* p. 84.
14 See, for instance, Taylor L. *et al.*, *op. cit.*
15 Cohen S. (1979), 'How can we balance justice, guilt and tolerance?', *New Society,* March 1 1979, Vol. 47, No. 856, p. 477.
16 Use is made here of some ideas developed by Paul Corrigan, in the context of adult education, at a recent workshop at Leeds University.
17 Page R. and Clark G.A. (eds.) (1977), *Who Cares? Young people in care speak out,* London: National Children's Bureau.
18 Stein M. (1979), 'Children of the State , *Social Work Today,* March 13 1979, Vol. 10, No. 28, pp. 26-29.
19 Christie N. (1977), 'Conflicts as property', *British Journal of Criminology,* Vol. 17, No. 1, p.7.

20   Fox S.J. (1970), 'Juvenile reform: An historical perspective', *Stanford Law Review,* Vol. 22, June 1970, pp. 1187-1239.
21   Eglash A. (1977), 'Beyond restitution: Creative restitution', in Hudson J. and Galaway B. (eds.), *Restitution in criminal justice: A critical assessment of sanctions,* Lexington, Mass.: Lexington Books, D.C. Heath, pp. 91-99.
22   Ackoff R.L. (1974),*Redesigning the future: Systems approach to societal problems,* New York and Chichester: Wiley, p. 152. See also Alderson J.C. (1980), *Community policing,*   Exeter: Devon and Cornwall Constabulary.
23   Christie N. (1977), *op. cit., p. 12.*

[faded, illegible reference text]

APPENDICES

APPENDICES

APPENDIX I
LEGAL AND
ADMINISTRATIVE
FRAMEWORK

This appendix summarises the main legislation in Britain relating to children and young people in trouble, and describes the roles of the major agencies that deal with them. In the main, this account applies only to England and Wales, while the final section outlines the position in Scotland.

Developments in the Juvenile Justice System

The first separate court for juveniles was introduced by the Children Act of 1908, one year after the implementation of the Probation of Offenders Act, which allowed courts to appoint probation officers. These two Acts followed a period of some 60 years of growth of residential institutions for children who would previously have been sent to prison. The first juvenile court in Britain was a court of summary jurisdiction, and in personnel and procedure was little different from the adult magistrates' court. Children were to be kept separate from adults, and the proceedings of juvenile courts were to be held in private. The imprisonment of children under 14 was abolished, and restricted for those aged 14 to 16. Parental responsibility for a child's behaviour was to be emphasised. However, the courts maintained the procedures of adult courts, and were less 'welfare' oriented than either their American or Scandinavian counterparts.

Concern about the operation of juvenile courts led to the 1933 Children and Young Persons Act, which introduced specially constituted juvenile courts, with magistrates selected to sit on the juvenile panels. (In Scotland, apart from four areas, the sheriff's court continued to handle juvenile as well as adult cases.) The 1933 Act also removed the distinction between reformatory and industrial schools and merged them into the approved school system, whereby each school had to be 'approved' by the Home Office. The length of detention in the schools was reduced, but the period of supervision on licence was increased.

Post war developments

The post war period was marked by two very different trends. One was an increase in the availability of custodial sentences for juveniles: the 1948 Criminal Justice Act established detention centres for boys of 14 and over, and the 1961 Criminal Justice Act lowered the minimum age for Borstal training from 16 to 15. The other was the development and increasing influence of local authority children's departments, from their introduction by the 1948 Children Act and the recognition of the importance of preventive family work in the 1963 Children and Young Persons Act. The role of the children's department had been primarily to care for children removed from their natural parents, but increasingly in the late 1950s and 1960s the emphasis turned more to preventive work with families. The Probation Service, however, retained the major responsibility for work with young offenders in the community. The 1963 Children and Young Persons Act raised the age of criminal responsibility to ten but is better remembered for the introduction, in Section 1, of power to enable local authorities to spend money on maintaining family units and to prevent children having to be removed into care. This section can be invoked to authorise local authority expenditure on 'preventive' intermediate treatment.

The basic legislation remained the 1933 Act, and doubts about its relevance to the problems of rising juvenile delinquency in the 1960s led to a series of steps to introduce reform, which eventually produced the 1969 Act. The Government introduced a White Paper, *Children in Trouble* [1], in 1968, and this formed the basis of the 1969 Children and Young Persons Act for England and Wales. The White Paper intended that the age of criminal responsibility would be raised from ten to 14, but included an offence as one of the conditions which could lead to care proceedings being taken. It was also intended to restrict the grounds on which young persons, aged 14 to 16 inclusive, could be brought before the court for an offence. As many children as possible would be dealt with outside the court through informal liaison between police, social workers, and parents.

The 1969 Act transferred major responsibility for decisions about the most appropriate form of treatment from the court to the social services department, which could determine the placement of a child in residential care, and in effect, the length of time a child remained away from home. Under care proceedings the court was to be left primarily with a choice between a care order and a supervision order, which could include a condition of intermediate treatment. Apart from the transfer of responsibility for approved schools into the new community home network operated largely by the social services departments, the courts were to be deprived of their powers to commit juveniles to attendance centres, to detention centres, or through the higher courts, to Borstals.

Although the 1969 Act includes all these proposals, many of them have not been implemented. The age of criminal responsibility has stayed at ten; the police may take a child or young person to court for an offence without consulting social services or probation departments first; juveniles can still be committed to detention centres, and, through crown courts, to Borstal. The major changes brought about by the Act have been in the operation of care orders within the community home system and in the development of intermediate treatment facilities; in addition, police cautioning of juveniles has greatly increased in the period since the Act was passed.

Developments since the 1969 Act

Because of the controversy surrounding the 1969 Act, discussed in Chapter One, the Government and other official bodies have kept the operation of the Act under close scrutiny. As the Act itself gave no details of the forms of intermediate treatment to be introduced, the Department of Health and Social Security published a guide for children's regional planning committees in 1972, in which it defined intermediate treatment as *'forms of treatment which allow the child to remain in his home but bring him into contact with a different environment, interests and experiences which may be beneficial to him.'* [2]

The House of Commons Expenditure Sub-committee, which reported in 1975 [3], recognised the value of intermediate treatment and other forms of community care. It recommended the development of a wider range of facilities than had developed up to that time. The Committee also urged that the power to commit children to residential care be restored to magistrates. The Government's response, in the form of a White Paper in 1976 [4], held the line of the 1969 Act in maintaining the responsibility of the social services department to decide where children placed in their care should live. However, it did recognise the increasing demand for secure places in residential care and indicated the Government's intention to assist local authorities with capital grants for these. At the same time, the White Paper encouraged local authorities to develop non-residential forms of care, and a 1977 DHSS Circular [5] called for a modest shift of resources from residential care into intermediate treatment. The White Paper also indicated that the Government was sympathetic to the idea of granting the courts powers to deal with breaches of supervision orders. Such powers were introduced by the 1977 Criminal Law Act.

Proceedings and Powers of the Juvenile Court
Criminal proceedings

A child or young person may appear before the juvenile court in England and Wales under either criminal proceedings or care proceedings. Criminal proceedings are used to prosecute for an offence, but the child must be at least ten years old. At the time of writing, in 1980, the powers of the court in relation to a finding of guilt are as follows:

1　**To make a care order,** committing the child to the care of the local authority in which he lives. This gives the authority the right to restrict the custody of the child to such extent as the authority considers appropriate. Under a care order, the local authority may place the child in a foster home, a community home, in some other appropriate residence, or may place him in the care of his parents, while the order remains in force. Thus the local authority rather than the court determines which disposal is made. The order is not reviewed by the court at regular intervals, but may be revoked by the court on the application of parents, child or the local authority. The order ceases to have effect at the age of 18, except that where the young person is already 16 when the order is made, it expires at the age of 19.

2　**To make a supervision order,** which places the child under the supervision of the local authority or probation service for a maximum of three years. The order may include certain conditions, for example:
   a　that he should reside with a named individual;
   b　that he should submit to appropriate psychiatric treatment;
   c　that he should comply with directions given by the supervisor to participate in schemes of intermediate treatment, some of which may involve periods of residence away from home.

Section 37 of the 1977 Criminal Law Act gave the courts power to deal with a breach of a supervision order, made in respect of a child or young person found guilty of an offence. This provision covers requirements of intermediate treatment under Section 12(2) of the 1969 Act. Section 37(2) introduces sanctions of a fine up to £50 or an attendance centre order for non-compliance with a requirement included in a supervision order.

Although the 1969 Act does not use the term 'intermediate treatment', Section 12(2) states that a supervision order may require the supervised person to comply with the directions of the supervisor. These could include directions to do one or all of the following:
   a　live in a place specified for a period or periods so specified;
   b　present himself to a person specified at a given time and place;
   c　participate in activities specified.
This section also emphasises the discretion of the supervisor in deciding the form of these directions.

327

The length, as originally set out in Section 12 (subsection 3) was either for 90 or 30 days. Schedule 12 of the 1977 Act modified the length of the requirement and replaced subsection 3 by: *'the aggregate of the periods specified in directions given by virtue of the preceding sub-section (12[2]) shall not exceed ninety days or such shorter period, if any, as the order may specify for the purposes of this paragraph.'* The supervisor has discretion whether to impose the requirement at all, and if so, decides the number of days up to the maximum specified by the court order. The superviser also has discretion whether to impose these in one consecutive period or to spread them out through the period of the supervision order.

The court has a number of other disposals it can make, and in fact the first two in the following list account for about two thirds of all disposals in criminal proceedings.

3   Absolute or conditional discharge

4   Fine

5   Binding over the child to be of good behaviour, or the parents to exercise proper care and control over him

6   Attendance centre order, where such a facility is available to the court

7   Detention centre order, for boys only, aged 14 and over.

8   Borstal training, if the offender is 15 and over, and where he or she is convicted by or committed to a crown court for sentence.

9   For serious crimes, which carry a sentence of 14 years or more if committed by an adult, detention under Section 53 of the 1933 Children and Young Persons Act, in a place approved by the Secretary of State.

10   Hospital order, under the Mental Health Act, 1959

11   Guardianship order, under the Mental Health Act, 1959

12   Payment of restitution or compensation to the victim of the crime, which may be imposed in addition to one of the above disposals.

Care proceedings

A child or young person under 17 may appear before the court in care proceedings, but under Section 1 of the 1969 Act any action by the court depends on two requirements. The first is that one of a number of conditions, including the commission of an offence, is proved to the satisfaction of the court. In practice, contrary to the intentions of the Act, care proceedings are used only infrequently as a means of dealing with offences. The conditions are:

'(a) his proper development is being avoidably prevented or neglected or his health is being avoidably impaired or neglected or he is being ill-treated; or

(b) it is probable that the condition set out in the preceding paragraph will be satisfied in his case, having regard to the fact that the court or another court has found that that condition is or was satisfied in the case of another child or young person who is or was a member of the household to which he belongs; or

(c) he is exposed to moral danger; or

(d) he is beyond the control of his parent or guardian; or
(e) he is of compulsory school age within the meaning of the Education Act 1944 and is not receiving efficient full-time education suitable to his age, ability and aptitude; or
(f) he is guilty of an offence.'

Secondly, the court must then be satisfied that the child is *'in need of care or control which he is unlikely to receive unless the court makes an order.'* Only if both requirements are met can the court take action. The main disposals available are the care order and the supervision order, as described above, including the option of the intermediate treatment requirement.

Administrative Responsibility

Central government responsibility for work with young people in trouble rests largely with two departments. The Department of Health and Social Security is responsible for oversight of Government policy and advice to local authority social services departments, on all matters relating to the personal social services, including the supervision of juvenile offenders by local authority social workers and the community home system. The DHSS has major central government responsibility for the development of intermediate treatment, and has given considerable attention, through national and regional seminars and through the reports of study groups, to this interest in the mid and late 1970s. It has also provided funding for some voluntary agency intermediate treatment projects. The Home Office is responsible for all Prison Service establishments, including detention centres, Borstals and remand centres, which all receive juvenile offenders. It also has central government responsibility and provides the major source of finance for the Probation and After-Care Service. A further central government department, Education and Science, also has an interest in this field through its involvement with the Youth Service and through the requirements of full time education for any offenders in residential care or day care.

In order to provide regional co-ordination and a sharing of resources between local authorities, the 1969 Act created 12 children's regional planning committees in England and Wales. These committees, consisting of representatives of each local authority in the region, were given the responsibility for co-ordinating local authority plans for both the community home system and intermediate treatment and for submitting regional plans for approval to the Secretary of State. It was also intended that they should plan and jointly finance certain regional provisions, which would not be cost effective for a single local authority.

At local level, the social services department is responsible for all children placed in care, for the provision of community homes and of suitable foster homes. The department shares with the Probation Service the task of preparing social enquiry reports, and of supervising juvenile offenders on court orders. Although the pattern varies considerably, social services departments generally provide this service for younger children and the Probation Service for older juveniles. Apart from these functions, the Probation Service normally supervises all juveniles discharged from detention centres and Borstals, unless they are already subject to a care order.

The statutory responsibility for intermediate treatment at local level lies with the social services department, who have the duty to provide and fund it.

However, the Probation Service has traditionally undertaken work of this nature, and has continued to play a substantial role in the actual provision of intermediate treatment, either through separate programmes or jointly with social services departments. Funding for intermediate treatment has been made available to the Probation Service at local level by allocation from the social services department budget.

The Youth Service, which in most authorities is part of the education department, was seen to have an important role in providing resources, which would enable the young offender to develop new interests and experiences beneficial to him within his own environment. The skills and experience of youth workers were seen as very relevant to the development of intermediate treatment. Although the Youth Service has no specific statutory responsibility for young people in trouble, some workers in the Youth Service see this as a priority.

The contribution of the voluntary sector has been significant in pioneering new methods of work with young offenders. Four of the six case studies in this volume operate from the voluntary sector, though in most cases with substantial financial support from statutory bodies. The relationships between the voluntary service provider and the statutory agencies responsible for referral of children and financial support vary considerably and no national pattern is descernible. Nevertheless the contribution of the voluntary sector is recognised at both national and local levels, especially in developing new approaches, even if its share of the total provision of intermediate treatment is relatively small.

The Position in Scotland

Following the report of the Kilbrandon Committee [6], the Social Work (Scotland) Act of 1968 introduced children's panels to deal with the majority of young offenders, and also merged the Probation Service and relevant local authority agencies into new social work departments. The children's panels are staffed by lay people with considerable knowledge or experience of children's problems. They have no power to deal with issues of fact, where these are disputed, and the proceedings are based on the acceptance by the child and parents of the grounds for referral. If the child denies an offence, the matter is dealt with in the sheriff's court, presided over by a professional judge. Only when the offence is proved is the child referred back to the children's panel for disposition.

The central figure in this system is the reporter, who convenes the children's hearings, and also decides on the basis of reports received whether a child should be brought before the panel, or dealt with informally by the social work department, the police or the education service. Alternatively, the reporter may deal with the case himself, and for instance may interview or write to the parents indicating the possible consequences of any further offences.

The panel, comprising three lay members, meets in an informal setting to discuss with the parents and child and any representative they choose to accompany them the best disposition in the interests of the child; normally, a social worker prepares a report for the hearings and attends. The powers of the children's hearing are to discharge the child or to make a supervision order to the social work department, which may include a condition of residence in a place specified or of attendance at some approved facility. The panel therefore has powers to require children to participate in programmes which, following the

English development, have come to be known as intermediate treatment. However, there is no specific statutory basis to intermediate treatment, and referral nearly always depends on agreement between the various parties, including the child. The panel reviews a supervision order on request and must do so annually until its completion. If the family cannot agree to the action taken by the panel, they have the right of appeal to the sheriff's court.

At central government level, the main agency concerned is the Social Work Services Group of the Scottish Education Department. It has oversight responsibilities for child care, the children's hearings, intermediate treatment and social work provision for young offenders; it also funds and has oversight of the 'list D', or former approved schools.

POSTSCRIPT

In October 1980 (after the manuscript of this book was completed), the Government published a White Paper, *Young Offenders* [7], which proposed significant changes in the sentencing of juveniles. The main proposals were as follows:

1   Detention centres would remain available for boys aged 14-16, but for them, as for young adults, the length of sentence would be between three weeks and four months (carrying one third remission), instead of three to six months. The section of the CYP Act 1969, never implemented, to end DC and attendance centre orders for juveniles, would be repealed.

2   For custodial sentences of over four months, a youth custody order was proposed. This would be a determinate sentence, fixed by the court, but also carrying one third remission, and would replace the existing indeterminate sentence of Borstal training. It would be available for 15 to 16 year old boys and girls, as for young adults, with a maximum sentence of one year for juveniles.

3   A residential care order was proposed, empowering the court to require the child's removal from home for a specified period up to a maximum of six months. This would be in addition to the existing care order. It would be available for a juvenile who was already the subject of a care order as a consequence of offending, through the 'offence condition' of care proceedings or through criminal proceedings, and who was subsequently found guilty of an imprisonable offence. On expiry of the RCO, the child would continue to be subject to the ordinary care order, which is indeterminate.

4   The community service order, currently an adult sentence only, would be available for 16 year olds who had been found guilty of an imprisonable offence and might otherwise receive custodial sentences.

5   As regards intermediate treatment, *'the Government proposes to give the courts a specific power to order a juvenile offender under supervision to undertake a programme of specified activities'* [8], which the supervisor and court agreed was suitable for the child and which the child had agreed to undertake. This might be known as a supervised activities order or an intermediate treatment order. (Under Section 12 of the CYP Act 1969, the court merely authorises the supervisor, at his discretion, to require participation in intermediate treatment.) Moreover, *'the courts should be able themselves to consider the most appropriate programme'*; they would have *'the power to determine broadly a suitable programme of activities'*, in the

331

light of professional advice from the supervisor. [9] The White Paper argued that this would give magistrates greater confidence in intermediate treatment, so that they would use it more, particularly as an alternative to care or custody for serious or difficult offenders; it *'should also encourage local co-operation and stimulate the development of intermediate treatment facilities'* [10].

Following continued debate about the role of the probation service with regard to juveniles, and especially to intermediate treatment, the Government said it would *'enable probation and after care committees to provide facilities of this kind in a way which is consistent with proper co-ordination of local arrangements'*. [11]

References

1   Home Office (1968), *Children in Trouble,* Government White Paper, Cmnd. 3601, London: HMSO.
2   Department of Health and Social Security (1972), *Intermediate treatment: A guide for the regional planning of new forms of treatment for children in trouble,* London: HMSO, p. 6.
3   *Eleventh report from the Expenditure Committee: Children and Young Persons Act, 1969* (Social Services Sub-Committee), (1975), HC 534-I, London: HMSO.
4   Home Office (1976), *Children and Young Persons Act 1969: Observations on the Eleventh Report from the Expenditure Committee,* Government White Paper, Cmnd. 6494, London: HMSO.
5   Department of Health and Social Security (1977), *Children and Young Persons Act, 1969: Intermediate treatment* (Local authority circular [77] 1), London: DHSS.
6   *Children and young persons: Scotland* (Kilbrandon Report), (1964), Cmnd. 2306, Edinburgh: HMSO.
7   Home Office (1980), *Young Offenders,* Government White Paper, Cmnd. 8045, London: HMSO.
8   Home Office (1980), *op. cit.,* para. 50.
9   *Ibid.*
10 *Ibid.*
11 *Ibid.,* para. 51.

APPENDIX II

THE CASE STUDY APPROACH

Theoretical Considerations

Case studies have been used fairly widely in the social sciences. They are defended by those who draw attention to their capacity for telling a rich and colourful story, for their qualitative depth. They are attacked on the grounds that they lack rigour, quantification and generalisability. Those who criticise them tend to emphasise the difficulty of proceeding from the account of particular situations to any kind of theory building. Even to make any generalisations that transcend the individual case there are two basic requirements: first, that a number of cases could be selected which are in some way representative; and secondly the case studies must employ a common approach or framework that provides sufficient structure for comparing them.

It is one thing to criticise the way case studies have often been undertaken, and another to assert that they can never do more than describe or illustrate a situation. Phoebe Hall and colleagues [1] consider that the latter view is pessimistic. At one extreme it is argued that social phenomena cannot be studied scientifically and that consequently the best that can be hoped for is some impressionistic conclusions. At the other extreme is the view that methods from the natural sciences not only can but must be applied, since these methods alone are genuinely scientific and capable of unearthing the truth. At this point attitudes towards research commonly become polarised between quantitative methodology, emphasising variables that can be measured or amounts that can be counted, and qualitative methodology that seeks in other ways to capture the essential nature of what is being studied.

This is not the case for discussion of these issues, but it should be noted in passing that we do not subscribe to the view that qualitative research of the case study variety necessarily lacks rigour, nor to the implication that its anecdotal tendency must reflect the values of the writer to a greater extent than do those approaches — sometimes thought more value free and scientific — which draw their methodology from the natural sciences, or from empiricist or positivist roots. Given the limited purposes of this book, case studies seemed the most appropriate way of communicating about intermediate treatment projects, since they enable contributors to assemble a variety of material, much of which may be gathered retrospectively and informally, and they allow that material to express the uniqueness of its own setting.

Method Employed

When planning this publication, the editors approached some project leaders directly and also advertised in the social work press, in order to attract the interest of potential contributors. Those responding were told that the intention was to publish a collection of 10-15,000 word case studies of 'well established and well documented' projects, providing 'a fairly comprehensive description, analysis and evaluation.' They were asked to provide preliminary material, including existing articles or reports, basic details about the project's aims, programme and resources, and a short statement about the way they intended to tackle the evaluative aspect of the case study. At this point most of the potential contributors dropped out because they found that the task was more than they could undertake.

In selecting among the dozen remaining, the editors chose those projects which individually were 'well established and well documented', and collectively represented the greatest variety of provision and sponsorship. However, it has to be conceded that, as a consequence of this selection process, the sample is not fully representative of the different kinds of intermediate treatment provision currently available. In terms of the four broad categories described in Chapter 3, none relies on individual placement of children in community programmes, since there are few such projects anywhere. Only one describes the kind of evening group project that constitutes the most common form of provision at the moment, and this single example is in many ways atypical of the category. Such projects, by their time-limited nature, are unlikely to be well established, and it is rare to find examples that are well documented or where its workers have the time or energy to write a substantive case study afterwards. On the other hand, five case studies do between them cover most of the main varieties of centre based projects and have encountered most of the issues that are likely to arise in such settings.

Once the projects were selected, the relationship between contributors and editors was agreed at a meeting of all participants. Each contributor would write a 10-15,000 word paper providing an all round description, analysis and evaluation, in accordance with a framework provided by the editors. The editors could require revisions and the final version would have to be acceptable to both editors and contributor, under whose name it would be published. In addition, the editors would write the introductory chapters and some further chapters involving comparative analysis and comment on the case studies. Contributors would have the opportunity to comment on these chapters and the editors would take these comments into consideration.

In addition to trying to fill a gap in the literature, the editors from the outset had a secondary, methodological, purpose in mind: to develop and test out a framework for communicating about social intervention programmes such as intermediate treatment. This framework, to be used by each of the case study contributors, was intended to:

- encompass all relevant dimensions of a project;
- require description, analysis and evaluation;
- apply equally to the variety of projects to be found in the intermediate treatment spectrum;
- facilitate comparison between projects;
- leave scope for individual styles of writing, peculiarities of individual projects, and for the kind of material that best captures the flavour of the face-to-face work.

The framework that emerged, influenced by one developed by the Gulbenkian Community Work Group [2], is reproduced in full at the end of this appendix. It falls into six sections, of which the third, fourth and fifth were seen as central.

1 Introduction (overview, writer's relationship to the project);

2 Background (community and organisational context, origins and earlier development);
3 Project description (aim, resources, structure, participants);
4 Project in action (project development, practice in working with young people, in running the project, in work with community);
5 Evaluation (procedures, general project evaluation, outcomes for young people);
6 Conclusions.

When the first drafts of the six case studies were received, they were found to vary enormously in the way they had been tackled and in their adherence to the framework. (It should be mentioned in passing that the names of children, and sometimes of staff and places as well, have been disguised to preserve anonymity.)

There followed a process where, with the help of comments from outside readers, the editors worked with the contributors to suggest additions, cuts and changes. During this stage the editors came to put less stress on the framework, but instead called for more emphasis on the project in action and on sections describing unique features of the project, to illustrate issues not well covered elsewhere. The complementarity of the case studies became more important, at the expense of comparability. The resulting drafts in some cases much exceeded the space available, and the editors then undertook the responsibility for editing them into a final form that was acceptable to the contributors.

Comment

The editors' original hopes of contributing to the methodology of project case studies were scaled down as the preparation of the book progressed. We can, however, offer a few comments on the framework we adopted, with the hindsight of its application.

First, it does point to some organisational issues and some approaches to evaluation which tend to be overlooked and which we continue to regard as relevant. If they are poorly covered in some of the case studies, it is because their authors did not have material on them or were not persuaded of their importance.

Secondly, we hoped it would be possible, for expository and critical purposes, to set out analytically and to interrelate the general value orientation, aims and objectives of a project, and the methods and programme used to implement these aims. It was also hoped that a distinction could be drawn between what was originally planned and what eventually took place, to throw light on the reasons why projects depart from their planned course. The framework was designed with these hopes in mind, but they were realised only partially and may have been unrealistic. It would be rare for a social intervention project to be established with stated values and aims so clear and detailed that all else followed from them. Moreover, projects do not develop by rigid adherence to their original model nor by neatly planned shifts in their operations; instead, they are characterised by a process of continual and sometimes imperceptible change. Only at times of special need, such as writing a case study, does the practitioner actually sit down and try to formulate explicitly what he has come to believe about the needs of children and the rationale for his way of working with them. To that extent, some of the analytic distinctions in the framework were hard to make in practice.

Thirdly, in communicating about a project, this continual change or dynamic aspect is in conflict with the static approach. The latter takes a snapshot at a given moment in time, with the action frozen to permit a clearer picture of the whole and its various parts. The dynamic approach recognises that the processes of change are crucial to understanding how the project functions. The framework attempted to separate these two aspects by asking for both a description of the project and an account of the project in action, and this distinction proved hard to sustain.

Our fourth comment is that systematic coverage of all the points in the framework could — and did — result in very long case studies, and it would be misleading to offer the framework in its present form as an outline for short reports.

The case study writers themselves differed greatly in how useful they found the framework. For some it was helpful, for others it was difficult to follow closely, or in trying they found it sometimes clumsy, repetitive or restrictive. The resulting differences in structure between the case studies became if anything more pronounced in the editing process, particularly given the editors' desire to see that at least one case study developed those issues not covered in the others. Consequently, the case studies are less directly comparable with each other than originally intended. This, together with the fact that the sample is small and scarcely representative, makes regularities harder to spot and generalisations more speculative.

We are left, nevertheless, with the more modest belief that this framework can be adapted and used by others wanting to preserve or present a record of their work. If nothing else, our approach to case studies has enabled six projects to work together towards that aim, alongside each other.

References

1 Hall P. *et al.* (1975), *Change, choice and conflict in social policy,* London: Heinemann.
2 Community Work Group (1973), *Current issues in community work* (Calouste Gulbenkian Foundation report), London: Routledge & Kegan Paul.

CASE STUDY FRAMEWORK PROVIDED TO CONTRIBUTORS

A INTRODUCTION
a) Summary overview of project, to orient readers — general purpose, type, sponsorship, duration, period covered in this analysis.

b) Writer's perspective — relationship to project, purpose in writing this.

B BACKGROUND
1 Setting
a) Community served by project/where located — characteristics — geographical, social, needs; size of catchment area.

b) Neighbourhood service network — other agencies serving young people in area; gaps in service.

c) Organisational context — independent or part of larger agency; vol./stat.; sponsorship; funding.

2 Origins and Earlier Development
— more or less brief, according to time between start and period under review.

a) How and why project was established — at whose initiative, to meet what needs; planning stages.

b) Planned aims, objectives, methods — emphasis on what originally *planned* (cf. planning reports?)

c) Developments prior to period under review — significant events, and changes up to period discussed, in aims, resources, methods, etc.

C PROJECT DESCRIPTION
— more static or enduring features described; if not constant then as at *beginning* of period discussed.

1 Aims and Objectives
— explicate and clarify *relationship* between: theory/aims/objectives/planned means of intervention.

b) Objectives for clients
— which young people — target group, selection criteria.
— what impact or client changes
— by what means — structured programme, techniques of intervention, time period.

c) Any other objectives
— families, community, project itself, parent agency — implict and explicit objectives; conflict between objectives.

2 Resources
a) Funds — source(s).

b) Manpower — skills, training etc. — management, staff, volunteers, outside consultants, advisory board.

c) Buildings, facilities, equipment — own or have access to.

d) Support or back up services
— parent agency (if any) — credibility in various quarters; input from community.
— community

C PROJECT DESCRIPTION
3 Structures — systems, networks.
a) Internal organisation
— management and staff structures — formal and informal roles; also volunteers and young people; different structures for different purposes (decision/support/treatment).

— project divisions — different project units or groups.
— programme — timetabling, programme elements.

b) External linkages
— with parent agency (if any)
— referral system — out as well as in.
— other agencies, as resources
— community — families, community groups.
— descriptive stats., case history/ies.

4 Young People
a) Characteristics
— background — demographic, social, needs, other characteristics.
— how joined project — experiences prior to referral, how referred,
expectations and attitudes.

b) Involvement — intensive, e.g. hours per week
extensive, e.g. how long; drop outs.

D PROJECT IN ACTION
— dynamic aspect: change over time during
period described (1—narrative); analysis of
process (2-4).

1 Developments
— recount changes over time period under discussion.

a) 'Treatment cycle' — for individual or group, within project framework e.g. group diary.

b) Project developments — shifts in project as a whole, planned and un-
planned.
— significant events
— changes in project — in objectives, resources, methods, structures
etc.

2 Practice: Work with Young People
a) Providing for individuals — individual assessment, treatment planning,
review, 'after-care'.

b) Methods and techniques of intervention — groupwork, individual counselling, family
casework, activities, residential etc.

c) Planning/implementing (group) programme — creating and using situations for growth/
treatment.

d) Role of young people — in planning, review, etc.

3 Practice: Running the Project
a) Decision-making — who makes, how, on what issues and policies.

b) Worker support, training, development — including volunteers.

4 Practice: Work with Community
a) Work with other agencies re. individuals
— referrals to project
— linking young person with community
resources — advocating; 'after-care'.

b) Work with families — and others important to participants, e.g.
friends not in project.

c) Work with community
— use of community resources by project
— project contribution to community

E EVALUATION
1 Provision
a) Re. individual young people — what provision for records, assessment, evaluation, feedback? By whom, for what purpose,
b) Re. project as a whole how?

338

2 Project Evaluation

— How successful has the project been in providing and maintaining a 'treatment programme'?

a) Young People
— target group
— engaging participants in project

— Has the project reached the target group intended and are the young people staying in the project as planned?

b) Translating objectives into planned intervention
— bringing together necessary resources
— implementing appropriate programme and methods

— Has the project provided the intended 'treatment' experience, as required by objectives and
— individual needs? Factors include e.g. facilities, worker skills, time with young people.

c) Project viability

— Has project ensured continuing survival and development; if time-limited, what success in communicating learnings?

3 Outcomes

— Distinguish outcomes/changes that can reasonably be attributed to project from those that cannot; distinguish intended and unintended outcomes; short-term and longer-term (follow up?).

a) Young people

— How successfully has project achieved stated objectives for clients?

— assessments by workers and others
— assessments by young people
— measured changes in attitudes, skills, behaviour

— e.g. supervisors, workers in other agencies, agencies, parents.

b) Other outcomes

— Parent agency, other agencies, families, community.

F ISSUES, RECOMMENDATIONS OR CONCLUSIONS

— Author's free range.

AUTHOR INDEX

SUBJECT INDEX